Russian Research Center Studies, 3
Revised Edition, Enlarged

JUSTICE
in the
U.S.S.R.

An Interpretation of
Soviet Law

HAROLD J. BERMAN

REVISED EDITION, ENLARGED

Shambaugh Library

Cambridge, Massachusetts, and London, England
HARVARD UNIVERSITY PRESS

340.0947
B456j

REVISED EDITION, ENLARGED
(First published, 1950, under the title JUSTICE IN RUSSIA)

Fifth Printing 1978

Manufactured in the United States of America

Library of Congress Catalogue Card Number: 64—4942
ISBN 0—674—49151—3

Foreword

Substantial changes have taken place in the Soviet legal system since 1950, when this work was first published. These have not affected the basic interpretation of the earlier edition—indeed, the changes have confirmed the author's principal theories concerning the nature and functions of Soviet law. However, with Stalin's death Soviet law entered upon a whole new stage of development, and it has been necessary to add a considerable amount of new material. The author has taken the opportunity also to revise some of his earlier formulations and to correct minor errors. As a result, the book is more than a "second edition." It is approximately one-third longer than the original version.

The title has been changed from *Justice in Russia* to *Justice in the U.S.S.R.*, although the author's emphasis upon the influence of Russian history and of prerevolutionary Russian law on Soviet legal development has not been lessened.

The author has also been able to draw on the experience of five visits to the U.S.S.R. since 1955, including a year of study at the Institute of State and Law of the U.S.S.R. Academy of Sciences in 1961-1962. Access to Soviet courts and conversations with Soviet judges, procurators, Ministry of Justice officials, lawyers, and legal scholars have added vividness to the picture of Soviet law which in 1950 was perforce derived chiefly from books. In addition the striking improvement in the quality and quantity of Soviet legal literature since 1955, as well as the appearance of many books and articles on Soviet law written by American and other non-Soviet scholars, have made possible a somewhat more detailed analysis than that which was presented in the earlier edition.

Nevertheless, the reader should be warned that this book does not attempt to give a complete and systematic presentation of the various branches of Soviet law. It is rather an "interpretation"—an exploration of the theory and practice of Soviet law in the light of the social and economic conditions which underlie it, the historical factors which help to shape it, and the conception of man which it embodies.

I am deeply grateful for the help of Peter Maggs, Research Associate in Law of Harvard University, who has worked closely with me in preparing this new edition. His suggestions have been invaluable, and his careful research has helped to save me from many pitfalls.

Acknowledgment of permission to reprint passages from other publications will be found in the Bibliographical Note on p. 385.

Harold J. Berman

Cambridge, Massachusetts
May 1963

Contents

III. PARENTAL LAW

Corrigenda

The latest RSFSR Criminal Code and Code of Criminal Procedure should be referred to throughout as the 1960 (instead of 1961) RSFSR Criminal Code and 1960 RSFSR Code of Criminal Procedure. These codes were enacted in October 1960, and took effect January 1, 1961, but are commonly identified as of the date when they were enacted.

Nariady, translated throughout as "procurement permits," are at the same time "allocation orders." (Cf. pp. 104, 107, 118, 122, 123, 137, 138, 139, 147.)

INTRODUCTION

Introduction

WE WOULD like not to have to think so much about the Soviet Union. If it were not for the Soviet Union perhaps we would not have to think so much at all. We might settle back more or less complacently and cultivate our own garden.

We are forced to think about the Soviet Union because of the power struggle going on in the world today. She appears to us primarily as a problem of foreign policy. Yet it is impossible to develop a sound foreign policy toward the Soviet Union on the basis of international politics alone; we cannot estimate what its leaders want in the world merely from our contacts with them in Germany, Yugoslavia, Cuba, China, and other places outside Soviet borders. To understand Soviet aims and methods abroad we are compelled also to concern ourselves with Soviet aims and methods at home. We must be in a position to evaluate the strength and weakness of the Soviet system, and the beliefs and values on which it is founded.

Here law occupies a position of crucial significance, for a legal system expresses in a most vivid and real way what a society stands for. It represents both what is preached and what is practised. It tells what is officially and publicly considered to be right, and what is officially and publicly done when things go wrong. Of course, what is officially and publicly considered and done may conflict with what is unofficially and secretly considered and done. It is surprising, however, how much we can learn from Soviet codes and statutes and reports of cases, as well as from the extensive commentaries and criticisms in Soviet legal periodicals and treatises, about how the system actually works.

From a purely political viewpoint, then, the study of Soviet law has become a matter of urgent practical importance. Certainly we cannot make an enduring peace with the U.S.S.R., or even a temporary settlement, without some understanding of her legal system—her concepts of law and justice as well as her actual legal practices. If, however, the avenues of peace are cut off by a new world war then we shall surely have to know Soviet law, since if we win we shall presumably have the task of governing the Soviet survivors who have been brought up on it; on the other hand, if the Soviets should win we might possibly have to face the not so very pleasant prospect of being brought up on it ourselves.

Behind these considerations of international politics lie issues more profound and more subtle. The power struggle between Uncle Sam and Mother Russia conceals within it a struggle of social systems. "Behind the new equilibrium of force," writes John Condliffe, "stalk the ghostly figures of Karl Marx and John Calvin." Calvin, Locke, Rousseau, Paine, Jefferson—the line runs from the English Revolution of 1640-1689 to the French Revolution of 1789 with the American Revolution coming as a sort of compromise between the two. It was against these "bourgeois" revolutions that Marxism reacted. Lenin and the Russian revolutionaries of 1917 thought of themselves as missionaries of a new social order of world-wide dimensions, in which there would be an end to the economic and political individualism of the eighteenth and nineteenth centuries, based on private property and class domination. "The contest of two systems," of which the Soviet leaders now speak, was conceived originally as a contest within each country. For some in America today it continues to have that aspect. The external threat posed by Soviet power in Europe and Asia still serves to dramatize, in a few minds, the internal threat posed by powerful labor unions, government control of business, socialized medicine, anticlericalism, Negro equality, or anything else which can with imagination be identified as "Communism."

In investigating the extent to which Soviet law embodies a new social order, we cannot evade the questions posed by the changes which are taking place in our own legal system. It is not true that if the Soviet Union did not exist we would have no serious problems. Indeed, the tensions latent in our social order might flare up with far greater intensity if we could not externalize and objectify them as issues of foreign policy. Soviet law, because it is Marxist and socialist, challenges us to rethink the crucial social and economic questions which confront our own legal system.

Yet Soviet law is not a product of Marxian socialism alone, and the conflict between socialism and free enterprise is by no means the only issue that is posed by the present international struggle. Soviet law is also a product of Russian history. It is Russian law—just as our law is not "capitalist" law, or "democratic" law, but American law. Each system is a mixture not only of socialist and capitalist features, but also of precapitalist elements, stemming from many different periods of past history. Law cannot be neatly classified in terms of social-economic forces. A legal system is built up slowly over the centuries, and it is in many respects remarkably impervious to social upheavals. This is as true of Soviet law, which is built on the foundations of the Russian past, as it is of American law, with its roots in English and Western European history. Some of the basic differences between Soviet law and American law stem from the polarity which has existed between Russian history and Western history for almost a thousand years. Not only Marx and Calvin, but Protestant kings and Russian tsars, Catholic popes and Orthodox saints, have left their impress on the "contest of two systems."

Because Soviet law is Russian law, grounded in Russian history, it challenges us to rediscover the historical bases of our own law, and to seek a clear understanding of the differences and similarities between the Russian and the Western heritages.

There is a third aspect of Soviet law which deserves a separate identification. Implicit in the Soviet legal system is a new conception of the role of law in society and of the nature of the person who is the subject of law. The Soviet legislator, administrator, or judge plays the part of a parent or guardian or teacher; the individual before the law, "legal man," is treated as a child or youth to be guided and trained and made to behave. I have called this the "parental" aspect of Soviet law, though it should be understood at the outset that the concept of parentalism does not necessarily imply benevolence. The parent may be a cruel stepmother; the teacher may be a Wackford Squeers. We shall see that Soviet law contains, in its parental aspect, both good features and bad, oppressive as well as benign elements.

"Parental law" is not confined to Marxian socialism or to Russia. Its development has accompanied the increasing centralization of power in all industrial countries during the past fifty years, and the increasing helplessness of the individual and the weakening of the ties of family and of local community. The Soviet Union has probably gone further than any other country, however, in focusing on the role of law as a teacher and parent. Soviet law thus challenges us to examine the potentialities and dangers inherent in parental law.

We might view the whole Soviet legal system analytically, in terms of the needs and interests of a socialist state. We might study the whole system historically, in terms of the characteristic features of Russian society over the past thousand years of its development. We might approach the whole system philosophically, in terms of the parental concept of law and of man implicit in it. It has seemed more fruitful to use these three methods—the analytical, the historical, and the philosophical—as three screens to be placed successively over Soviet law. Under each screen different legal institutions come to prominence. None of the three screens gives a complete picture in itself. Together they may suggest the main outlines of the Soviet legal system as a whole, and its main implications not only for an understanding of the Soviet Union but also for an understanding of law.

LAW AND FORCE

There are two words for law in Russian, as there are in all the major European languages except English. One is *zakon,* which means a particular law or statute. The other is *pravo,* which means Law in the large sense, with a capital *L,* connoting embodied Right or Justice. In Russian the word Law, *pravo,* is also related to the word truth, *pravda.* This may derive from an older conception that Law is revelation, that it is ordained by nature itself. The first written collection of laws in Russian history was entitled *Russkaia Pravda,* Russian Truth.

This book is primarily about Soviet Law with a capital *L*—the Soviet system of justice. In a sense it is about Soviet truth, since it is an attempt to view the Soviet legal system in terms of the nature of Soviet life, the underlying assumptions of the social order. Of course there is a good deal here about particular laws as well, for there is no such thing as Law without laws, though there may be laws without Law.

The term Soviet Law will at first seem to many people to be a self-contradiction. It is widely believed that the Soviet system is run solely by terror, the only principle of order being that of hierarchical subordination backed up by the secret police. From the proposition that the Soviet regime places heavy reliance on the use of force, it is often deduced that the Soviet legal system is merely window-dressing.

These are dangerous delusions, which in the long run only weaken us. They conceal the inner resources of the

Soviet social order. The Soviets do have a working legal system, founded on rather definite principles of law and justice.

A system of law and a system of force exist side by side in the Soviet Union. There are certain areas into which law penetrates only slightly. For example, until 1953 a person who was suspected of antagonism to the regime could be picked up by the secret police, held incommunicado for a long period of time, tried secretly by an administrative board, and sentenced to hard labor—without benefit of defense counsel and without any possibility of appeal. On the other hand, there are other areas which even under Stalin were on the whole governed by well-defined legal standards. For example, crimes such as theft or assault or murder, suits between state business enterprises for breach of contract, disputes over rights of inheritance, workers' grievances against wrongful treatment by management, and many other types of conflict within the social order, were and are generally dealt with publicly by regular procedures and established norms.

One would suppose that political and ideological repression would undermine the legal system. How can there be respect for law when the most important political decisions are made secretly behind the scenes and when the rulers themselves have no qualms about resorting to force when they feel that the stability of the regime is threatened? The evidence tends to show a surprising degree of official compartmentalization of the legal and the extralegal.

In this connection we might recall the experience of the Roman Empire. The absolutism of the Imperial rule, and its brutality, did not prevent the coexistence of a legal system. A modern illustration may be found in the United States, where the fact that in some areas Negroes are often deprived of a fair trial and are sometimes victims of violence does not mean that law is nonexistent in those areas. In each of the examples cited, the acceptance of force and violence in certain types of situations undoubtedly has a deleterious influence on the legal system as a whole. But that influence may be a subtle one.

This book attempts to shed some light on the relationship between law and force in the Soviet system. It seeks explanations which will fit both the Soviet "police state" and the Soviet "welfare state." It does not, however, attempt to describe the Soviet system of force in any detail. As a result, the data here presented may give a total impression far more favorable to Soviet Russia than the one which many people now have. It should be encouraging to them to learn that there is another side to the story. However, they should be warned that it is not the author's purpose to give a complete picture of "life in the Soviet Union," but rather to portray the development of the Soviet legal system, to show its relationship to the Soviet social order as a whole, and to seek its significance for the Soviet people and for us.

-I-
SOCIALIST
LAW

Chapter One

MARXISM—LENINISM—STALINISM

AN AMERICAN GENERAL who served in the Soviet Union during World War II said: "If you want to know what the Russians are going to do next, read Karl Marx." Fortunately or unfortunately, the relation between theory and practice is not so simple. Certainly one could not deduce from the most careful study of Marx's writings the actual provisions of the Soviet legal system, any more than one could deduce from a study of the New Testament the nature of the present-day canon law of the Christian churches. The analogy may be fruitful. The writings of Marx and his collaborator Engels are in effect the New Testament of Communism. Lenin is the Pauline apostle to the gentiles who adapted the gospel to a new generation and a new people. Stalin is the Soviet Emperor Constantine, who made of the new religion a State Orthodoxy.

Marx and Engels claimed to provide a scientific basis for understanding and shaping society and history. There were indeed moral and ethical overtones in their denunciation of "bourgeois" law as "justice for the rich and not for the poor"; but the moral and ethical qualities of their prophecy were to them secondary. They wished above all to be social scientists, seeking the causes of social (and therewith legal) development, attempting to uncover the basic assumptions upon which social systems rest and the forces which make them operate as they do. Their political activities were, in their own view, simply the practical application of their scientific theories.

It was on the foundation of the Marxian analysis of the origin, growth, and decline of societies that the Russian revolutionaries set out to construct a new social order. Led by Lenin, these men were thoroughly grounded in Marxism and were fanatical believers in its doctrines. Lenin, however, had given the original Marxist theory a new twist and had developed it in new directions. In the years which have followed the events of 1917, there have been other new twists and directions. Soviet Marxism has moved from Marxism-Leninism to Marxism-Leninism-Stalinism and on to Marxism-Leninism as interpreted by Khrushchev.

The official Soviet modifications of Marxist theory have been the source of much confusion both inside and outside the Soviet Union, both among Communists and non-Communists. On the one hand, Marx and Engels had themselves conceived of their theory as dynamic and subject to development; all knowledge, they said, must be treated not as dogma or as a set of principles but rather as a "guide to further study and empirical investigation" and as a "guide to action." Marxism, according to its founders, is "no doctrine, but a movement." In reinterpreting Marxism and adapting it to the Russian Revolution and the Soviet state, Lenin, Stalin and Khrushchev have continually emphasized "creative" as against "dogmatic" Marxism. On the other hand, a philosophy which is susceptible of perpetual revision tends to lose its value as a basis either of criticism or of understanding.

Yet even if our conclusion were to be that the Soviet rulers today only pay lip-service to Marxism and that there is nothing left of the original teachings of Marx and Engels, it would still be true that we cannot understand Stalinist and post-Stalinist law without first understanding Marxist theory. In the first place, the vocabulary and doctrine of classical Marxism have provided the conceptual framework for Soviet law; Soviet law is *clothed* in Marxism. In the second place, classical Marxism served the Soviet leaders in the first years of the Revolution as one of the chief sources of guidance for their politics and law; the program of the *Communist Manifesto* was in effect enacted as statutory law by the new Bolshevik regime. In the third place, with all the changes that have taken place in Russia since 1917, and especially since the mid-1930's, Marxism continues to serve the Soviet rulers as a means of justification and rationalization of Soviet law, to whatever extent they may have ceased to accept it in fact as the basis for an applied science of society.

Marxism does not "explain" Soviet law. It does, however, provide us with a first clue to the explanation. In particular, it helps us to understand what Soviet jurists mean when they speak of their legal system as "socialist" in character; and it helps us to isolate and identify the socialist elements which actually exist in it.

CLASSICAL MARXISM

The method of Marxism was called a century ago, by Marx and Engels, historical materialism. A "materialist" in the Marxist sense is one who views matter, or nature, as the ultimate reality, upon which the ideal and the spiritual depend. Man is a product of nature and is bound by its laws; his thoughts are therefore a reflection of the natural, or material, conditions of his existence. But man must not be viewed in the abstract; he is a social being, living in society, and society, too, is bound by the laws of the natural or material conditions which surround it—its geography and climate, its population factors, but above all its mode of producing food, clothing, shelter, and the other necessities of life. In Marx's words, "The mode of production in material life determines the general character of the social, political, and spiritual processes of life." Man in society has to make a living; he has to produce. Production and the exchange of products are basic. As these change, men's thoughts change, men's politics change, men's laws change. Economic activity precedes and determines social beliefs and values, and also the institutions which manifest those beliefs and values.

Thus law for Marx and Engels is "superstructure," an unconscious or semiconscious ideological reflection of economic relations. "The economic structure of society," wrote Engels, "always forms the real basis from which, in the last analysis, is to be explained the whole superstructure of legal and political institutions, as well as of the religious, philosophical, and other conceptions of each historical period." And again, "The jurist imagines that he is operating with *a priori* principles whereas they are really only economic reflexes."

Plekhanov, who was the leading Russian Marxist until Lenin robbed him of that crown, summarizes the progression from "foundation" to "superstructure" as follows:

1. The state of the forces of production.
2. Economic relations conditioned by those forces.
3. The socio-political regime erected upon a given foundation.
4. The psychology of man in society, determined in part directly by economic conditions, and in part by the whole socio-political regime erected upon the economic foundation.
5. Various ideologies reflecting this psychology.[1]

Neither Marx nor Engels (nor Plekhanov after them) denied that the legal superstructure "reacts in its turn upon the economic basis and may, within certain limits, modify it." They emphasized that "ultimately," "in the last analysis," economic conditions are decisive. At the same time they rejected, in Plekhanov's words, "the eclecticism which cannot get beyond the idea of a reciprocal action between the various social forces and does not realize that such reciprocal action between forces cannot solve the problem of their origin." They clung to a monistic formula just because such a formula did provide an explanation of the origin of political-legal institutions and therewith a basis for radical attack upon them. In terms of Plekhanov's progression, it is futile to try to alter "the socio-political regime erected upon a given foundation" while leaving unchanged "the state of the forces of production" and "the economic relations conditioned by these forces." Since law originates in economics, it is necessary to change the whole economy before any fundamental reform of law can be achieved.

It was the Marxist contention, however, that "the state of the forces of production"—that is, the nineteenth-century industrial system—was already in contradiction with the socio-political order, since the factory represented a "social-ist" mode of production, with the workers forming a col-lective labor force instead of each individually producing for himself, while the socio-political order was based, still, on private property and private enterprise. What really had to be changed, therefore, were the "economic relations," that is, the relations between economic classes.

Economic classes are the medium, in the Marxian scheme, through which economic necessities are transmuted into socio-political institutions such as law. The mode of pro-duction (pastoral, manorial, industrial) gives rise to rela-tions of production—relations between those who have appropriated to themselves the means of production (cattle, land, factories) and those who do the actual producing (slaves, serfs, workers). Class—that group which gets its character from its relationship with other classes in the process of production and distribution—determines ideol-ogy. Ideology is thus the reflection of class relations; it is class consciousness. On the personal level it is not the individual himself who thinks and acts but the class to which he belongs: he thinks and acts primarily as a noble-man, a merchant, a petit bourgeois, a proletarian. On the social level it is not particular individuals who govern society but rather that group which owns the means of production: the state is simply an executive committee of the ruling class.

A *historical* materialist adds to this sociological per-spective the dialectical element of the struggle of opposites. "The world," said Engels, "is not to be comprehended as a complex of ready-made *things*, but as a complex of *proc-*

esses, in which things apparently stable . . . go through an uninterrupted change of coming into and passing out of being." As matter is always in motion, following certain laws of action and reaction, combination and dissociation of atoms, attraction and repulsion of negative charges, so society is dominated by the historical strife, interpenetration, and synthesis of opposing economic classes. The class that controls the means of production depends on the labor of an opposite servant class. As the mode of production changes and the servant class grows in numbers and strength, the tension between the two main opposing classes increases; finally, out of the cumulation of quantitative changes in the social-economic order (increased concentration of capital, increased impoverishment of the proletariat), there is reached a "nodal" point (depression) when the old order is burst and, with a violent wrench (revolution), a qualitative change (the new socialist society) is produced. "At a certain stage of their development," Marx wrote, "the material forces of production in society come in conflict with the existing relations of production, or— what is but a legal expression for the same thing—with the property relations within which they had been at work before. From forms of development of the forces of production these relations turn into their fetters. Then comes the period of social revolution." [2] So it was with the transition from a pastoral economy to manorial feudalism; so it was, later, when bourgeois capitalism rose to supersede the feudal order; so it is now proceeding with the emergence and development of the industrial proletariat. Thus society moves like a sailboat (to borrow a simile from former President Lowell of Harvard), tacking first in one direction and then in another in order to reach its appointed objective. But the rulers of a given social order resist change; as it becomes more imminent and more crucial, they increase the coercion and oppressiveness of their law, thereby only accelerating the dialectical process which results in their ultimate downfall.

Historical (or dialectical) materialism offers a critique of law rather than a science of law. Marx sought to expose the illusions of social consciousness, as Freud sought to expose the illusions of personal consciousness, in order to free the rational from its bondage to the non-rational. Rights, according to the Marxist, are reflexes of subconscious economic interests. But Marxism, like Freudianism, offers no solution "within the system." Marxism cannot tell a judge whether to characterize a certain act as a breach of contract or as a personal injury. It cannot explain why in nineteenth-century capitalist England the doctrine of unjust enrichment was viewed with disapproval by the courts while in nineteenth-century capitalist America it was accepted. Historical materialism might interpret, for example, the extension of the powers of the federal government during the past forty-five years of American history as a device whereby the ruling class has consolidated its power and brought its national political position in line with its national economic position; but it cannot explain why, in particular, the interstate commerce clause of the Constitution should be the legal instrument used for the justification of this extension of federal control, and, more important, it can provide no basis for decision as to how far the interstate commerce clause may be stretched for this purpose without upsetting the constitutional system of a working federalism. Plekhanov admitted this when he wrote (relying on and expanding some statements of Engels) that economic conditions determine the "content" of law though not its "form." But in law, "form" is of the essence.

Engels hinted at the complexity of the process by which law develops in a letter, written in 1890 to the German socialist Conrad Schmidt, in which he said:

> In a modern state, law must not only correspond to the general economic position and be its expression, but must also be an expression which is *consistent in itself* . . . And in order to achieve this, the faithful reflection of economic conditions is more and more infringed upon. All the more so the more rarely it happens that a code of law is the blunt, unmitigated, unaltered expression of the domination of a class—this in itself would already offend the

"conception of justice" . . . Thus to a great extent
the course of the "development of law" only consists:
first in the attempt to do away with the contradictions arising from the direct translation of economic
relations into legal principles, and to establish a har-
monious system of law, and then in the repeated
breaches made in this system by the influence and
pressure of further economic development, which
involves it in further contradictions.

Thus consistency of law, conceptions of justice, and principles of legal development are understood as defying, to
some extent, the "direct translation of economic relations
into legal principles." In fact, Engels could not make sense
out of the internal developmental structure of a legal system, and at one time he wrote, referring to English law,
that there was no point in "wasting one's time on this
juridical confusion, this chaos of contradictions."

Classical Marxism thus contents itself with exposing
what it conceives to be the ultimate sources of law. In
broad terms it states that law is politics, that justice is a
cloak for class interests, and that "bourgeois" justice is
permeated with conceptions of private property and private contract which exclude the interests of the propertyless masses. Under capitalism, the "formal" equality of individuals is only a mask for the "real" inequality of social
classes. Marxist writers cite with relish Anatole France's
scornful reference to the "majestic equality of the law"
which forbids rich and poor alike to beg in the streets and
to sleep under the bridges.

Throughout history man has been imprisoned by the
struggle of classes, wherein ideology and law have served
only to conceal harsh economic reality. But that is only
half of Marxism. The other half is its vision of the future—
of the proletariat in the messianic role of standard-bearer
of a new classless society, in which mankind will finally
have cast off its chains. The proletariat is the last class;
with its triumph over the bourgeoisie, and with its extermi-
nation of the last vestiges of capitalism, a new society

without class antagonisms will emerge. The coercive institutions with which ruling classes of the present and past
have held class antagonisms in check and thereby preserved
their own dominant position will no longer have any reason
for being. There will be no need for state and law, since
these are merely instruments for maintaining property relations that will have vanished.

The future classless society was for Marx and Engels
not something to be predicted or predescribed, but was
rather a logical conclusion from their premises. It derived
from their conception of the nature of history as a story
of the struggle of classes. Just as theorists of the French
Revolution of 1789 had postulated an original state of
nature to which democracy, by eliminating prejudice and
privilege, would restore mankind; just as Cromwell and the
Puritans of the seventeenth-century English Revolution had
looked back to ancient rights and liberties of Anglo-Saxon
and medieval times as the foundation of their attack on
royal prerogative and their vision for the future; just as
Luther and the Protestant Reformers of the sixteenth century had found their inspiration in an early uncorrupted
Christianity existing before popes and emperors had come
on the stage of history, and had sought to rebuild the future
in the image of that remote past—so Marx and Engels
found in the original condition of society a primitive communism which served as a foundation and precursor of the
classless society to come. In his *Origin of the Family, Private Property and the State,* Engels built on the theories of
the American anthropologist Henry Lewis Morgan in describing the earliest tribal societies as communist in character, with sharing of wives and children, with common
ownership of goods, with no special organs of government.
Only when a new type of economy developed, according
to Engels, did there emerge a division of labor and a class
structure. The patriarchal minority appropriated the means
of production—cattle and sheep—in the new pastoral economy and created a slave class to do the work. Only then
did the family as we know it emerge; only then did property

become a legal institution; only then did the state as a special form become necessary as a means of protecting the dominant position of the ruling class.

"The state," declared Engels, "has not existed from all eternity. There have been societies which have managed without it, which had no notion of the state or state power. At a definite stage of economic development, which necessarily involved the cleavage of society into classes, the state became a necessity because of this cleavage." But history repeats itself on newer and higher levels. It is an ascending spiral in which we can find our direction only by looking down at the shadows cast by the curves below us. "We are now rapidly approaching a stage in the development of production at which the existence of these classes has not only ceased to be a necessity, but becomes a positive hindrance to production. They will fall as inevitably as they once arose. The state inevitably falls with them. The society which organizes production anew on the basis of free and equal association of the producers will put the whole state machinery where it will then belong—into the museum of antiquities, next to the spinning wheel and the bronze axe."

With no class of society to be held in subjection, the state will gradually become superfluous; in Engels' controversial phrase, it will "die out" or "wither away." [3] The "government of persons" will be replaced by the "administration of things" and the "direction of the processes of production." In the words of the *Communist Manifesto* (1848), "when in the course of development, class distinctions have disappeared, and all production has been concentrated in the hands of a vast association of the whole nation, the public power will lose its political character . . . In place of the old bourgeois society, with its classes and class antagonism, we shall have an association, in which the free development of each is the condition for the free development of all."

It is easy to dismiss this as utopian nonsense. The twentieth century is less optimistic about man than the nineteenth. Certain English liberals, contemporaries of Marx, developed ideas curiously parallel to his. They, too, conceived of law and government as an evil to be surpassed; but they visualized that it would be surpassed by the extension of the free expression of the individual will. As time and enlightenment went on, they believed, social relations would be more and more determined by free contract. In 1937 Roscoe Pound, in discussing this trend in earlier English jurisprudence, noted "the contrast between the idea of a gradual superseding of law by a regime of free self-determination through contract and the idea urged increasingly today of superseding law by a regime of free administrative activity." [4]

Marx and Engels were pessimistic about the past, optimistic about the future. They foresaw a time in which coercion, compulsion, would gradually become unnecessary; when consciousness would at last be freed from economic determinism; when a collectivist society of enlightened materialists would solve all problems rationally and freely. Yet they vigorously denounced utopias and utopianism. Their vision of the future rested, so they thought, not on wishful thinking but on scientific analysis. Since mankind is in bondage to the "capitalist mode of appropriation"— that is, to private ownership of the means of production —and since that and all other modes of appropriation are destined to be dissolved in a classless society, the days of our bondage are numbered. It is property, ownership, which tempted man at the dawn of history and led to his expulsion from the garden of tribal communism. The future communist society will abolish the exclusiveness of ownership; or, more accurately, the abolition of exclusive ownership and the introduction of social ownership will lead to the future communist society. Private ownership is a legal institution, depending on the sanction of the state; social ownership will be an administrative institution, depending only on public consent.

Classical Marxism is therefore a critique of law and a science of the overthrow of law, a science of revolution. In seeking to explain law, it explains it away. The only solution to bourgeois injustice is to overthrow the ruling class, smash its system of state and law altogether, and introduce a new social order based not on law but on administration. Indeed, this is not only desirable but inevitable. The future will spell out its own details.

However unsatisfactory such a theory may appear to statesmen and lawyers, it found increasing favor among those who identified themselves with the dispossessed, the propertyless masses, to whom it offered both a reason for being and the predestination of greatness. It is, indeed, an eschatology—based on faith in history rather than faith in God—which, like the New Testament foolishness of which St. Paul spoke, makes no sense to those who don't believe in it but a great deal of sense to those who do. It is a kind of foolishness which when once believed, though subsequently modified, rationalized, or even abandoned, nevertheless leaves great consequences in its wake.

LENINISM

Prerevolutionary Marxism went in two directions. In the West, chiefly in Germany, it became a reformist program for waiting out the collapse of capitalism. Engels himself, in his last written work, seems to endorse a program of legal, democratic reform, and the statement is attributed to him that "the time of surprise attacks, of revolutions carried on by small conscious minorities at the head of unconscious masses is past." [5] Although the German Social Democrats had their counterparts in Russia, too, in the Mensheviks and the "legal Marxists," it was ultimately a quite different Marxism which, under Lenin's leadership, won the day. Lenin seized on the second half of Marxism —not its economic determinism but its messianism, its eschatology, its faith in the impending triumph of "consciousness," of Reason, over the material conditions of existence. In fact the Communist Party, which was Lenin's creation, was formed as a disciplined conspiratorial elite of superconscious revolutionaries who would lead the "unconscious masses" to power and then, in time, would transform the proletarian dictatorship into a classless socialist society. The proletariat is unconscious, Lenin said, and of itself cannot go beyond trade unionism; it must therefore be pushed from outside by the Party. "The Party," he wrote in 1917 in *State and Revolution*, "must be teacher, guide and leader."

In *State and Revolution*, Lenin formulated for the first time a theory of the transitional period of proletarian dictatorship, or, in effect, party dictatorship in the name of the proletariat. A lawyer himself by training (he had received a "first" in the state law examination of 1891 and had practiced law for a year before turning professional revolutionary), Lenin accepted the classical Marxist conception of state and law as instruments of coercion, but called for the use of a new proletarian state apparatus to crush the bourgeoisie. He thus rejected the appeal of the anarcho-syndicalists for immediate abolition of all state apparatus. At the same time, the theory of the "withering away" of the state, once the classless society had emerged, was made central to Lenin's doctrine of socialism.

During the six years in which he ruled after the revolution, Lenin worked to develop a powerful central state apparatus. Extreme centralization of power was needed, he argued, because of the shortage of trained and reliable Communists. In his postrevolutionary writings he emphasized constantly the importance of checking up on activities of lower level authorities, and of keeping accounts and statistics for the Party vanguard in directing the masses. He transformed the former private banking system into an instrument of state financial control. He restored the Procuracy and strengthened its supervisory powers.

Lenin's thinking about the legal structure of the new Soviet state was influenced by the sharp dichotomy between public and private law which had been developed by European scholars since the sixteenth century partly on the basis of a revived Roman law. His thinking was also in the tradition of European legal positivism which considers all laws as "commands of the sovereign." Thus he conceived that the proletarian government would give public law commands in the interest of the proletariat, but at first he saw no place for institutions of private law, such as property and contract, in the new socialist society which he was building. In 1921, however, when he directed a strategic retreat to a mixed socialist-capitalist economy— the New Economic Policy (NEP)—he realized the need for a temporary reintroduction of these private law institutions, which he considered to be bourgeois in character. At the same time he insisted that they be made to serve the immediate interests of the State and that they be subject to a wide variety of government controls, both direct and indirect. Thus, for Lenin private law was to play a temporary and limited role in the transition period of the NEP, and even then it was to have a public-law character.[6] Public law itself was to give way, ultimately, to other forms of social control once the need for coercion was eliminated.

Lenin and the Bolsheviks despised the legalism of the West—the legalism of both the capitalists and the socialists. Under War Communism (1917-1921), the New Economic Policy (1921-1928), and the First and Second Five-Year Plans (1928-1937), Soviet jurists, building on Lenin's themes, elaborated the thesis that law is in its very essence a bourgeois fetish. "The feudal state was a state by divine grace, a *religious* state. The bourgeoisie called its state a legal state. Religion and law are the ideologies of oppressing classes, one gradually replacing the other. And if we ought now at the present time to contend with the religious ideology, then we ought to a far greater degree to contend with the legal ideology." So wrote A. G. Goikhbarg, one of the leading Soviet jurists, in 1924.[7] P. I. Stuchka, first President of the U.S.S.R. Supreme Court, wrote in 1927 that "Communism means not the victory of socialist law, but the victory of socialism over any law, since with the abolition of classes with their antagonistic interests, law will die out altogether." [8]

Most Soviet legal philosophy of the first two decades after 1917 rang with such high-sounding but essentially barren phrases. It was left to one Soviet writer, E. B. Pashukanis, to develop these notions into a theory of law which had substantial intellectual content. Pashukanis be-

came the leading figure in Soviet legal development and
acquired a high reputation in Western Europe as well.

Pashukanis sought to explain not merely the origin of
law in class domination but also its particular unique features, which distinguish it from other means of class domination. These he saw as a reflection of the market. The
economic traders who exchange commodities in the market
require a legal system for the enforcement of their transactions; they therefore identify themselves as juristic persons,
"right-and-duty-bearing units," who, primarily through the
medium of contracts, create reciprocal legal relations which
express their reciprocal economic relations. The cornerstone
of law is John Doe, the abstract individual, who by entering into transactions with other individuals creates mutual
rights and duties. This John Doe is nothing but the legal
version of economic man. Just as a commodity is viewed
as an abstraction expressing the commensurability of all
things in the market, so a right is an abstraction expressing
the commensurability—or reciprocity—of relations in the
law court. Law therefore rests ultimately on the intentional voluntary conduct of individuals dealing with each
other on a reciprocal basis.

According to Pashukanis, the agreement of the intention
of the parties, which is the foundation of contract law, is
at the same time the foundation of all other branches of
the legal tree. It enters into labor law, where the relationship
between labor force and management is viewed as a series
of individual employer-employee contracts; it enters into
family law, where marriage is treated as a contract and
even the parent-child relationship is considered in terms
of mutual rights and duties; it extends to criminal law,
which originally was based on retribution (an eye for an
eye), then passed through a stage of money composition,
and now rests on a sort of bargain between the state and
the individual whereby a particular act is given an equivalent punishment, regardless of the social-economic implications involved; even in constitutional law Pashukanis saw
the idea of government by consent, "social contract," as

underlying a political order based on an alleged harmony of individual expressions of will. Thus all law is, in essence, commercial in character; all law presupposes the reasonable prudent individual who engages in arm's-length transactions with other equally abstract legal entities.

Of course Pashukanis saw in this a cloak for bourgeois class interests. But he claimed to go deeper into the nature of law than any Marxist hitherto. He was concerned with law "not so much as an ideological process (*i.e.*, one that belongs entirely in the history of ideas, outlooks, *etc.*) but much more as a real process of the legalization of human relations, which accompanies the development of a goods-and-money economy (in Europe a capitalist economy) and brings with itself thoroughgoing all-round changes of an objective nature. Thereto belong the origin and fortification of private property, its universal extension both to subjects and to all possible objects, the emancipation of land from relations of lordship and vassalage, the transformation of all property into movable property, the development and dominion of relationships of obligation, and finally the separation of political power as a special force—standing next to the purely economic force of money—and, following from that, the more or less sharp separation of spheres of public and private relations, public and private law." [9]

Thus law is in its very essence a capitalist, or bourgeois, institution. It may exist in embryonic form in feudal or slave societies, but essentially those societies are religious or military in character. "Law reaches its highest point of development under capitalism," wrote Pashukanis in 1930. To speak of "proletarian law" is therefore incorrect. The proletarian state may use bourgeois law, and must use it insofar as vestiges of the capitalist economy remain; but it cannot develop proletarian law, since law is by its nature based on individualism and contractualism. In saying that the legal system to be used by the interim proletarian state is at bottom a "bourgeois" system, Pashukanis could rely on the authority of both Marx and Lenin. The latter had stated, just before the revolution, in discussing the law to be applied during the transition to full communism, "There are no other [legal] norms besides those of bourgeois law." [10]

With the abolition of the market and of economic individualism there will come, in Pashukanis' words, "the withering away of law in general, that is, the gradual disappearance of the juridical element from human relations." Here, too, Pashukanis could rely on the works of Marx and Lenin, though he extended their general theory of politics to the field of law, with which they had concerned themselves only slightly.

The men who preached this conception of law were not only the theoreticians of the new Soviet regime but also the compilers of its codes, the chief judges of its courts, the heads of its legal profession, the commissars of justice. At first, in accordance with their theories, law tended to die out. Later, with the partial restoration of capitalism under the New Economic Policy, there was a restoration of what was frankly conceived as "bourgeois" law. When the period of the Five-Year Plans was introduced in 1928, the revolutionary offensive against law as such was resumed. Not until 1936 did Pashukanis definitely renounce his early theories—too late to save himself from destruction;[11] with their renunciation came the revision of practically every branch of the Soviet legal system.

To understand the significance of the renunciation of the theories of Pashukanis, Stuchka, Goikhbarg, and the other jurists of the first two decades of Soviet history, it is necessary to examine the actual development of the Soviet legal system during that "first stage of development of the Soviet state" (as it came to be called after 1936).

SOVIET LAW UNDER WAR COMMUNISM, 1917-1921

In the first years of the Revolution, the Soviet leaders, believing in the imminence of world-wide socialism, strove to rid their country of every vestige of capitalism. Much of what they did was the product of emergency: war raged against counterrevolution from within and intervention from without. However, they attributed to their responses a more lasting significance.

Nationalization and socialization proceeded at a rapid rate. Private ownership of land and the means of production was abolished. A Supreme Economic Council was established for the public management of business, and its agencies not only supervised but actually operated the confiscated industries. Private trade in consumers' goods was prohibited. Inheritance was declared to be abolished. The distribution of commodities by ration cards, the payment of wages partially in kind, and the carrying on of moneyless transactions between state business enterprises seemed to herald the dawn of pure communism. Particularly, the establishment of a system of general compulsory labor and of appropriation of farm surpluses in the villages led to the belief, expressed by Lenin in May 1918, that "our Revolution has succeeded in coming to immediate grips with the practical realization of Socialism." "We are fighting for the principle of communist distribution," he announced in 1918 in regard to the decree establishing the People's Commissariat of Food Supplies. "We are approaching the complete abolition of money," Zinoviev claimed in 1920. According to Trotsky, "the Soviet government hoped and strove to develop these [early] methods of regimentation directly into a system of planned economy in distribution as well as production. In other words, from 'war communism' it hoped gradually, but without destroying the system, to arrive at genuine communism." Trotsky explains this by "the fact that all calculations at that time were based on the hope of an early victory of the revolution in the West."

The first Constitution of the Russian Republic, enacted in 1918, explicitly declared: "The basic task of the Constitution . . . at the present transitional moment is the establishment of the dictatorship of the city and village proletariat and the poorest peasantry in the form of a powerful All-Russian state authority for the purpose of complete suppression of the bourgeoisie, the destruction of exploitation of man by man, and the installation of *socialism, under which there will be neither division into classes nor state authority"* (italics supplied).

As for the traditional apparatus of political and legal institutions, the first efforts of the Soviet regime were directed chiefly toward their destruction, and toward their replacement, as Lenin had prophesied in *State and Revolution,* by a proletarian state operating through a system of "accounting and control." A Council of People's Commissars, seventeen in number, was established to manage the affairs of the new republic; it had almost absolute governmental power in fact, though according to the 1918 Constitution it was responsible to a Central Executive Committee of not more than two hundred members, which in turn was responsible to a Congress of Soviets, composed of representatives of local soviets. The previously existing system of courts was dissolved and new People's Courts instituted, with the instruction that they were to be guided by "revolutionary legal consciousness" wherever there was a gap in the decrees of the workers' and peasants' government. The practice of law was at first opened to "all who enjoy civil rights"; but this attempt to abolish the legal profession as such was soon rejected in favor of the establishment of a body of legal representatives appointed by the local government organs on a salary basis, with clients' fees to be collected by the state treasury. In fact, during this period civil litigation consisted largely of minor matters and criminal law was to a great extent in the hands of the notorious Cheka (abbreviation for Extraordinary Commission for the Struggle against Counterrevolution, Sabotage and Official Crimes) and of special revolutionary tribunals set up to deal with such crimes as organized insurrections, sabotage against the government, and willful destruction of necessities. These revolutionary tribunals enforced what was officially called the Red Terror. They were instructed to be guided "exclusively by the circumstances of the case and by revolutionary conscience."

At the same time a whole series of experiments was undertaken in dealing with those civil and criminal cases which continued to come before the regular courts.[11a]

The People's Commissariat of Justice enacted in 1919 certain "Leading Principles of Criminal Law," which stated:

> In the interests of economizing forces and harmonizing and centralizing diverse acts, the proletariat ought to work out rules of repressing its class enemies, ought to create a method of struggle with its enemies and to learn to dominate them. And first of all this ought to relate to criminal law, which has as its task the struggle against the breakers of the new conditions of commonlife in the transitional period of the dictatorship of the proletariat. Only with the final smashing of the opposing overthrown bourgeois and intermediate classes and with the realization of the communist social order will the proletariat annihilate both the state as an organization of coercion, and law as a function of the state.[12]

Apart from the "Leading Principles of Criminal Law," the new regime produced a Labor Code, to signalize the victory of the workers over the capitalists, and a Family Code, to free marriage, divorce, and other domestic relations from the control of the churches. This, it was thought, was a sufficient basis for the myriad of individual decrees issued by various organs of the new state.

The dominant spirit of Soviet law in these first years was thus a spirit of nihilism and of apocalypticism—of ruthless destruction of prerevolutionary law and of glorious transition to a new order of equality and freedom *without* law. It was the spirit of Cheka and the spirit of anarchism in its literal significance. In spite of Lenin's warnings against "the sickness of leftism," the new Soviet law was afflicted with that congenital revolutionary disease.

With the end of intervention and civil war, and with the failure of the revolution in the West to materialize, the hope of transforming "war communism" into "genuine communism" proved illusory. The "heroic period" was completely bankrupt. Production and distribution both were at a standstill. "We went too far on the path of nationalization of commerce and industry, and in the suppression of local trade," Lenin stated in April 1921; "was it a blunder? Yes, without question." The whole program of War Communism, he now said, "was but a temporary measure." And so the New Economic Policy, or NEP—a "strategic retreat," a "bourgeois" restoration.

SOVIET LAW UNDER THE NEP, 1921-1928

The NEP was a mixed system, neither capitalism nor socialism. On the one hand there was the reappearance of money, of private trade, of well-to-do peasants (kulaks), of private business managers operating under state licenses (nepmen). The system of surplus appropriation of farm produce was replaced by taxes in kind. Foreign firms were invited to do business in Russia on the basis of "concessions." In 1925 the hiring of labor and the renting of land was legalized for agriculture. On the other hand there was strict supervision of these capitalist elements in the interests of the proletarian dictatorship. Kulaks and nepmen were restricted, disfranchised, heavily taxed. A large "socialist sector" of industry—the "commanding heights" of banking, insurance, large-scale transport, production of raw materials, foreign trade—remained in the hands of the state. The state continued to own the land and to distribute it according to use; it continued also to own the means of production and to fix prices. As early as 1923 wholesale private trade was again prohibited, leaving only retail trade in the private sector. This was a new strategy but toward the same end: it was visualized that from the commanding heights the whole economy would gradually be socialized.

Since the market was restored, however, it followed with ruthless logic that there would have to be a restoration of bourgeois law—there being no other kind. Lenin therefore sent his jurists to the prerevolutionary Russian codes, as well as to the German, Swiss and French codes, to copy their provisions and to adapt them to the new Soviet conditions. It is said that he demanded that they produce a new Civil Code in three weeks. Actually, it was written in the record time of four months.

In 1922 and 1923 there appeared a Judiciary Act, a Civil Code, Code of Civil Procedure, Criminal Code, Code of Criminal Procedure, Land Code, and a new Labor Code. The Family Code of 1918 remained in force until it was replaced by a new Family Code in 1926. A new Criminal Code was also enacted in 1926. These codes gave Soviet Russia a legal system which on paper and in its main outlines is similar to that of the countries of continental Europe, including prerevolutionary Russia, differing from that of England and the United States in technique but alike in many of its basic principles.[13]

The Judiciary Act established a hierarchy of courts and a system of trials and appeals familiar, with variations, to all Western countries. Its most unusual feature (possibly borrowed in part from the German practice in commercial cases) was the provision for trial by a three-judge court, with two of the judges, called people's assessors, chosen from the general population for ten-day periods. The Civil Code dealt in traditional terms with such matters as legal capacity, persons, corporations, legal transactions, statute of limitations, property, mortgages, landlord and tenant, contracts and torts, unjust enrichment, inheritance. Ownership was defined in Napoleonic terms as "the right to possess, to use, and to dispose of" one's property. Contracts were required to include agreement on the subject matter of the contract, the price, the time for performance. No American lawyer would be shocked by the provision that "by the contract of sale one party (the seller) undertakes to transfer property to the ownership of another party (the buyer), while the buyer undertakes to accept the property and to pay the price agreed upon." In criminal law there were established the usual general provisions concerning complicity, attempts, juvenile delinquency, insanity, self-defense, and so forth; in addition, the so-called "Special Part" of the code listed minimum and maximum penalties for various crimes grouped according to their common objects, such as crimes against the state, crimes against the administrative order, crimes by officials, crimes against property, crimes against the person, and so forth. In family law the civil registration of marriage and divorce was introduced into Russia for the first time in the 1918 Family Code, and the legal status of women was made equal in every respect to that of men. The new Labor Code restored the voluntary character of employment on a contractual basis.

With the formation of the various republics into a federal union in 1923, a new all-union constitution was enacted, establishing on paper a system of representative government which had certain important features in common with democratic systems generally.

On the other hand, to safeguard the interests of the proletarian dictatorship and in anticipation of the transition to classless socialism, the NEP codes contained certain provisions which reflected the revolutionary purposes of the new Soviet social system. In civil law it was provided that any legal transaction "directed to the obvious prejudice of the state" shall be invalid and that any profits which have accrued from such a transaction shall be forfeited to the state as "unjust enrichment." In criminal law the doctrine of analogy was formulated: abandoning the French Revolutionary principle of "no crime, no punishment without a [previous] law," the code permitted sentence for an act not directly prohibited but analogous to an act so prohibited. More than that, the General Part of the Criminal Code made the entire criminal law hinge on "social danger" and "measures of social defense," rather than on crime and punishment as such. Throughout all branches of law, the underlying principle for the decision of doubtful cases continued to be "revolutionary legal consciousness"—a phrase which gained meaning from the conscious policy of discrimination against nonproletarians and persons of nonproletarian origin in both private and public law, as well as from the actual domination of the Communist Party behind the façade of a democratic structure.

Perhaps the most striking provision of NEP law is the

famous Article 1 of the Civil Code: "Civil rights shall be protected by law except in instances when they are exercised in contradiction with their social-economic purpose." By this overriding principle (subsequently copied, as was the doctrine of analogy, by the Nazis) an attempt was made to counteract the absolutist and conceptual character of the private rights granted in other sections of the code. A man could own his house, but if he had an extra room in it he could be required to take in a tenant; a mill could be leased to a private individual, but if he failed to operate it for a certain period in order to avoid taxes, it could be taken away from him; an owner of a boat had full rights of possession, use, and disposition over it, but if another man seized it in order to rush his wife to the hospital the owner might be given no relief against the trespasser, on grounds of "social-economic purpose." Thus Article 1 brought back in through the window what had been shown out through the door. Yet Article 1 itself involved a concession: it provided an article of the code on which to rely, and it accepted the dualism of private rights and public policy.

"We look at the court as a class institution, as an organ of government power, and we erect it as an organ completely under the control of the vanguard of the working class," wrote N. V. Krylenko, later People's Commissar of Justice, in 1923. "Our judge is above all a politician, a worker in the political field." If so, why erect this elaborate structure of rights and procedures? Because, in the words of the same author, "a club is a primitive weapon, a rifle is a more efficient one, the most efficient is the court." The proletarian dictatorship needed this most efficient weapon to protect its position in the transition period of a mixed economy. But the transition period moves forward toward socialism, and the proletarian dictatorship adapts bourgeois law to serve not only its immediate interests but also its ultimate goal. Thus the NEP codes contain many provisions which are "revolutionary" not merely in the sense that they are useful to the revolutionary state, but also in the sense that they implement the revolutionary vision of a classless socialist order. In family law, the era of the postcard divorce was inaugurated,[14] and in many cases the courts accepted *de facto* cohabitation and separation as the ultimate criterion of marriage and divorce. In regard to liability for personal injury, the element of fault was minimized if not entirely eliminated: "Our code does not view the fault of the person causing the injury as essential for the imposition of liability," stated Goikhbarg, the principal author of the Civil Code. This followed from the assumption that "compensation for injury is, generally speaking, an institution beneficial to the workers" and that therefore "it is necessary to give extensive interpretation to the liability of the person causing the injury (except where the liability of the state is involved), and a narrow construction to rules permitting the defendant to escape liability." A similar social policy underlay the code provision (familiar to some other legal systems as well) that "where a person, under the pressure of distress, concludes a transaction clearly unprofitable to him, the court, on the petition of the damaged party, or on the petition of a proper government agency or social organization, may either declare the transaction invalid or preclude its operation in the future." [15]

The character of these and other "revolutionary" provisions introduced in the Soviet codes remained obscure to outsiders (and to many insiders as well) who failed to appreciate the centrality of the "withering away" theory. Léon Duguit in France, the exponent of the theory that "social solidarity" is paramount to all law, and that the protection of "social functions" should fix the scope and limits of individual rights, hailed the new features of Soviet law as steps toward "liberalizing" and "socializing" law. As a matter of fact they were conceived by their authors as steps toward the elimination of law.

SOVIET LAW UNDER THE FIRST AND SECOND FIVE-YEAR PLANS, 1928-1937

In 1928 the NEP compromise was abandoned; total planning was inaugurated as a means of rapid industrialization, collectivization, and militarization. Gradualness was replaced by a gigantic leap. The basic decision which the Soviet leaders made at that time was not only economic, but also political and social. The NEP could not meet the need for large-scale mechanized agriculture except by increasing the landholdings of the kulaks and this, it was felt, would threaten the entire socialist character of the Revolution, and perhaps the political position of the regime. Large-scale mechanized agriculture was necessary for a program of rapid industrialization, which in turn was essential if the Soviet Union was to "overtake and surpass" the West. "Those who fall behind get beaten," said Stalin in 1931. Indeed, with a remarkable sense of timing, he gave Russia just ten years from that time to match the industrial might of the most advanced Western countries, "or we shall be defeated." And so the Five-Year Plan was launched, replete with military phraseology, with "assaults on fortresses," "communiques," the "labor front," the "collective farm front," "shock brigades," and so on.

This was War Communism revisited, but now independent of world revolution. Politically and socially, the speedy transformation of the Soviet Union into a classless society was again envisioned. At the Communist Party Conference which approved the draft of the Second Five-Year Plan in 1932, Premier Molotov stated: "The leading idea of the Second Five-Year Plan is that all classes and their causes are to disappear by 1937 in the U.S.S.R." The Party Conference declared: "The chief political task of the Second Five-Year Plan is to do away with the capitalist elements and with classes in general; to destroy fully the causes giving rise to class distinctions and exploitation; to abolish the survivals of capitalism in the economy and the consciousness of the people; to transform the whole working population of the country into conscious and active builders of a classless society." This explicitly included the aim of "destroying the difference between the worker and the peasant," who were now to become a single body of urban-and-rural proletariat, not a class in the Marxist sense because of the absence of exploitation, because of the social ownership of the means of production, and the social character of the Plan.[16]

Now for the first time positive content was given to the Marxist idea of the disappearance of state and law under socialism. It was thought that Law, an instrument of the class-dominated state, would be replaced by Plan, the manifestation of the will of a classless society. Through the Plan all the characteristics of the original Marxist dream would be realized. Planning would eliminate exploitation; money would be transformed into a mere unit of account; private property and private rights generally would be swallowed up in collectivism; the family would disappear as a legal entity, with husbands and wives bound only by ties of affection and children owing their allegiance and their upbringing to the whole society; crime would be exceptional and would be treated as mental illness; the coercive machinery of the state would become superfluous.[17] The Plan would give unity and harmony to all relations. The Plan itself would differ from Law, since it would be an instrument neither of compulsion nor of formality but simply an expression of rational foresight on the part of the planners, with the whole people participating and assenting spontaneously. Society would be regulated, administered—much as traffic at an intersection is regulated by traffic-lights and by rules of the road; but in a society without class conflict there would be few collisions and to deal with them it would be unnecessary to have a "system" of "justice." Social-economic expediency would be the ultimate criterion; disputes would be resolved on the spot.

The legal developments which accompanied the so-called Second Revolution of the early 1930's may be better understood if viewed in the light of two controversies which shook Soviet theory and practice at the time of the introduction of the First Five-Year Plan. One of these controversies was in the field of economics; the other was in the field of philosophy. They were closely interrelated, and their outcome was fateful for the progress of Soviet law.

The economic controversy arose over the crucial question of the rate of industrialization. One group of economists, called the "geneticists," argued that the basic problem in working out a rational plan for the whole economy was that of determining "the conditions of economic equilibrium," and that unless equilibrium relations were respected the Plan would fail. Concerned with the harmful effects upon the peasantry of too fast a pace of industrialization, the geneticists stressed the existence of certain factors which could not be altered by planning. They urged that economic laws not be disregarded, and said that the Plan should be used as a means of projecting or extrapolating trends. Their opponents, called "teleologists," argued an approach in terms of purpose, rather than origin. They said: "The primacy of teleology was determined for us as far back as the days of the October Revolution when we acted contrary to the 'eternal laws' of capitalist development." The Revolution had "abolished economic laws." "Our task is not to study economics but to change it," wrote one of their leaders. "We are bound by no laws. There are no fortresses which Bolsheviks cannot storm. The question of tempos is subject to decision by human beings." Needless to say, the teleological doctrine became official; the geneticists were damned as "Right Opportunists," and were associated with Bukharin and the opponents of the Plan.[18]

A parallel controversy raged in the field of philosophy between the "mechanists" and the "dialecticians." Here again the name of N. I. Bukharin, the leading theoretician of the NEP, was prominent. Building on Bukharin's conception of a social order as a balance or system of forces which is only changed by the application of some outside force, the mechanists viewed the main task of society as that of adapting or adjusting to its environment. They argued for a determinism which excluded both chance and self-movement. They derived their social ideas from a conception of nature or matter as fundamentally mechanical in character, consisting of rigid or fixed elements which are in equilibrium until moved by some external cause. Against this philosophy the proponents of the dialectical approach started not with fixity but with motion. They viewed society as capable of moving itself and of thereby transforming its external environment. Thus like their brothers the teleologists, they stressed the power of human will and activity. In effect the mechanists were saying that man must accept the inevitable, while the dialectical view was that man can anticipate and shape the inevitable. The difference was as crucial as that which separates the Mohammedan view of Fate from the Calvinist belief in Predestination.

Both the economic and the philosophical controversy involved the use of a concept of law. The geneticists and the mechanists, in emphasizing the determinist elements of Marxism, warned against the dangers of violating economic and social laws: the teleologists and the dialecticians said that the Five-Year Plan had already introduced "a different order of lawfulness," in which man was at last master of his own destiny. The concept of economic or social law, as an observed regularity, is, of course, different from the concept of law in the "legal" sense, as a rule or norm which is mandatory in character and to which the idea of rightness attaches. Nevertheless there is a connection between these two concepts. A law of either sort is something upon which one can depend; it connotes stability, that which is "laid."

The victory of the teleologists and dialecticians therefore had great relevance to the problem confronted by the legal theorists when the Five-Year Plan began to render a great deal of NEP law obsolete. The acceptance of the idea that "plan" should gradually replace "law" was a renunciation of stability for dynamism. Pashukanis, in restating and adapting his earlier views to the new situation, declared in 1930: "Unquestionably the fundamental fact from which our work should now start is that we are entering upon the period of socialism." It would be foolish, he said, to try to substitute for the "bourgeois" law of the NEP a new "proletarian" law, since the new period of direct transition to socialism was not a social-economic stage in itself; it was rather a time of rapid changes which could not be crystallized in the form of a legal system but must be shaped by ever-shifting social-economic policy. "That which we need more than anything else," he continued, "is political elasticity." By elevating the transition period into a "final system," the proponents of a new legal order only "hold development back."

Pashukanis wrote:

> The relationship of law to politics and to economics is utterly different among us from what it is in bourgeois society . . . In bourgeois-capitalist society, the legal superstructure should have maximum immobility—maximum stability—because it represents a firm framework of the movement of the economic forces whose bearers are capitalist entrepreneurs . . . Among us it is different. We require that our legislation possess maximum elasticity. We cannot fetter ourselves by any sort of system. . . Accordingly, at a time when bourgeois political scientists are striving to depict politics itself as law—to dissolve politics in law—law occupies among us, on the contrary, a subordinate position with reference to politics. We have a system of proletarian politics, but we have no need for any sort of juridical system of proletarian law . . .
>
> We have a system of proletarian politics and upon it law should be oriented. Once we even wished to arrange the curriculum so that, for example, the course in land law would be replaced by a course in land *policy* and law, because among us law can play no independent and final part: this was the design when War Communism was going out. During the years of the New Economic Policy and of the rehabilitation period, the system of codes was introduced and began again to develop, and at the same time attemps to pack and to tie all law into a system were renewed. Now, when we have passed to the reconstruction period, the utmost dynamic force is essential . . . Revolutionary legality is for us a problem which is ninety-nine per cent political.[19]

The other leading Soviet jurists echoed these views. Vyshinsky, then Procurator (Attorney General) of the USSR, wrote in 1935: "The formal law is subordinate to the law of the revolution. There might be collisions and discrepancies between the formal commands of laws and those of the proletarian revolution. . . . This collision must be solved only by the subordination of the formal commands of law to those of party policy." [20]

How should the policy of the transition period be determined and to what would it lead? Pashukanis' answer is simplicity itself. "The social-economic conception for whose sake the proletarian dictatorship exists and actively manifests itself is socialism and communism." "Of course when this dominant (socialist) sector shall have absorbed everything, the disappearance of law will begin forthwith. How can you wish to build a final legal system when you start from social relationships which already involve the necessity that law of every sort wither away?"

Of course Pashukanis did not advocate that during the transition period the coercive machinery of the state should be weakened. He accepted the statement made by Stalin in 1930: "We are in favor of the state withering away and at the same time we stand for the strengthening of the dictatorship of the proletariat, which represents the most powerful and mighty authority of all forms of the state which have existed up to the present day. The highest possible development of the government power with the object of preparing conditions for the withering away of government power, this is the Marxist formula. Isn't it 'contradictory'? Yes, it is, but this contradiction is a living thing, and completely reflects the Marxian dialectic."

But the strengthening of the power of the state does not necessarily involve the concomitant strengthening of the legal system. This, in fact, was Pashukanis' point. Law, for him and for Soviet jurisprudence generally, is only one of the possible means of social control. Social control in itself is not synonymous with law. "The idea of absolute obedience to some external authority establishing rules (a norm-creating authority) has nothing to do with law," according to Pashukanis. Indeed, as Vyshinsky said, a law may conflict with the interests of the state. It is not illogical, therefore, given their premises, that during the period of "direct transition" to socialism in the early 1930's Soviet lawyers and judges and prosecutors, though advocating absolute obedience to a strong state, nevertheless actively anticipated and fostered the withering away of law, that is, "the gradual disappearance of the juridical element from human relations."

The First and Second Five-Year Plans were chiefly directed toward the replacement of private commerce and individual farming by a totally planned economy. This policy took precedence over all the provisions of the codes and all the previously admitted principles of legal order. The collectivization of agriculture, for example, was carried out with an unabashed disregard for legality. There were, of course, statutes authorizing collectivization, but they gave very broad powers to local administrative authorities to confiscate the entire property of kulaks, including personal belongings, and to deport them. "Provisional extraordinary measures are permissible," said Stalin. When the ruthlessness of collectivization had gone too far, Stalin, whose only official position was that of Secretary of the Communist Party, published an article entitled "Dizzy with Success," warning party members that the program was being pushed too fast; as a result of this article alone, the pace of collectivization slowed down. Here was an example of pure policy-making, without benefit even of legislation.

In the domain of industrial production and distribution, relations between economic units were governed during this period to a large extent by *ad hoc* rules and decisions of administrative organs, with strict subordination of lower to higher links. The Plan was the foundation upon which these rules and decisions rested. In 1931 the so-called State Board of Arbitration (Gosarbitrazh), established to resolve conflicts arising between state economic enterprises, was reorganized. Gosarbitrazh looked primarily to the Plan for guidance and was not bound by the Civil Code. The "local contracts" which were the subject of dispute before the arbiters were for the most part merely a detailization of "general contracts" made between the chief administrations of the various commissariats. They were interpreted in the light of economic expediency, as administrative acts, rather than according to the intent of the parties.

Many parts of the Civil Code became obsolete and the whole of it was treated with considerable disdain. In the law schools courses in civil law were dropped; instead "economic-administrative law" was taught, emphasizing the problems of public regulation of economic relations. John Hazard, who studied Soviet law at the Moscow Juridical Institute during this period, reported that "law concerning the rights of individuals was relegated to a few hours at the end of the course in economic-administrative law and given apologetically, as an unwelcome necessity for a few years due to the fact that capitalist relationships and bourgeois psychology had not yet been wholly eliminated." [21]

Drafts of new criminal codes which appeared annually from 1930 to 1935 minimized the element of personal guilt and modified the "bourgeois" system of a fixed scale of punishments corresponding to the gravity of the acts committed. Indeed, the Special Part of the Criminal Code, defining particular crimes and the sanctions attached to them, was to be eliminated entirely; the law enforcement agencies were to be guided only by the broad principles declared in the General Part. These draft codes, though not officially adopted, actually guided the courts in their decisions; behind them was the authority not only of Pashukanis, who was at that time Director of the Institute of Soviet Construction and Law and editor of the leading Soviet political-legal journal, but also of People's Commissar of Justice Krylenko and many others. A Soviet legal treatise of 1935 considered liability for injuries as "in the nature of a supplement to the system of social insurance [which] is regulated by adapting the principles of the latter . . . where the injury is not covered by it."

Of course many cases continued to come before the courts and to be decided on the basis of conventional principles of law. Also the supreme courts, through decisions and directives, attempted to raise the judicial standards of the lower courts. But the general deterioration of the legal system was strikingly evident. Law schools decreased in number and law students even passed resolutions questioning the necessity of continuing their studies. There was no future in it! High officials of the People's Commissariat of Justice said in 1930 that in six or seven years at the most all litigation, civil or criminal, would disappear. It is said that some judges actually closed their courts in anticipation of this occurrence.

With the decline in the role of law went an increase in the role of other means of social control. It was in this period that the basic system of party, police, and administrative controls was elaborated. The Communist Party during the early thirties underwent a process of complete centralization; Stalin consolidated his own power position and that of the Politburo over the Central Committee of the Party and over the Party Conference and the Party Congress. He did this in part through the People's Commissariat of Internal Affairs—the NKVD—which at this time achieved its full development as an effective instrument of police repression and terror.[22] Finally, this was the period in which a new managerial-administrative class was created to direct and operate the planned economic order. The Party, the secret police, and the administrators had of course existed at the start; with the drive for rapid industrialization and total planning, their role was enhanced and their structure established.

STALINISM

In 1936 the original Marxist vision of a classless socialist society in which "the public power will lose its political character" was officially recognized as impossible of achievement in the foreseeable future. It was not officially denied that for the world as a whole such a social order is desirable and that ultimately it will come. As far as the Soviet Union was concerned, however, it was proclaimed in 1936 that a socialist society had indeed finally been achieved, that the transition period to socialism was at last over, that such classes as now existed (the workers and the peasants, to which was added a third group, the so-called intelligentsia, which was officially defined not as a class but as a "stratum") were "friendly" classes, not "hostile" or "antagonistic" economic classes in the Marxian sense; but instead of the withering away of state and law, of money and property, of the family, of criminal sanctions, and the rest, there was to be a wholesale restoration of these institutions on a new "socialist" basis. Nor would they disappear, it was later said, when the Soviet Union has moved from socialism, the first stage of the classless society, where each "receives according to his work," to communism, the final stage, in which each will "receive according to his need."

The formal reason given for this radical departure from earlier Marxist and Leninist doctrine was the existence of socialism (and eventually communism) in one country; surrounded by capitalist powers, Soviet socialism requires the protection of a state, and the state in turn requires law. But such a reason is theoretically inadequate to explain the fact that the new classless (or class-conflictless) socialist state, supported by classless socialist law, now came to be treated not as a necessary evil but as a positive good. Although every turn of Stalin's new policy was supported by ample quotations from Lenin's works, as well as from Stalin's earlier writings, the sense of these quotations was entirely shifted by the new periodization of Soviet history into the "first stage of development of the Soviet State" up to 1936, and the second "socialist" stage from 1936 on. In this new period, political and legal structures hitherto accepted as temporary concessions to capitalist survivals were given new "socialist" dignity.

Beginning in the mid-1930's, the Soviet regime restored the traditional institutions of social stability, one after the other. The full extent of this restoration has not generally been appreciated. It has been obscured in the first place by the violent mass purges which accompanied it, though these must be understood in part as the liquidation of those groups which were identified with the prerestoration conceptions of socialism. It has been obscured, secondly, by the war and prewar preparations, which some have interpreted as giving a temporary emergency character to Soviet internal developments in the mid-1930's; yet the direction of these developments did not fundamentally change in the postwar period. The restoration has been obscured, finally, by the Soviet fiction of continuity, which represents Russian history since 1917 as a single advance "according to Marx" and which dismisses past inconsistencies as due to the "Trotskyite" aberrations of wreckers and saboteurs or, after 1956, to the megalomania of Stalin.

To whatever aspect of the Soviet social order one turns, however, one finds a fundamental shift of emphasis since the years 1934, 1935, and 1936.

1. *In its cultural aspect,* Soviet society returned then to a sense of tradition, to Russian history, to patriotism—not simply as a matter of wartime propaganda, but primarily because of the need for a sense of continuity with the past which made itself felt independently well before the outbreak of hostilities. In 1934 the teaching of Russian history was re-introduced in the schools. Stalin began to compare himself to Peter the Great; the leading role of the Great Russian people both before and after the Revolution was reëmphasized; a trend away from internationalism was inaugurated which culminated in the postwar period in bitter attacks upon "cosmopolitanism." During the War the "International" was dropped as the national anthem and replaced by a new "hymn" beginning with the words: "Unbreakable union of free republics welded together by the great Rus"—Rus being the historic name for old Russia. Shortly after the War the names that "smacked of Revolution" vanished: people's commissars became ministers, the Red Army became the Soviet Army.

In part, this "ideological" change was undoubtedly a response to the apparent failure of the earlier Marxist-Leninist internationalism to command the support of the people, either at home or abroad, after twenty years of the most intense propaganda efforts. In part it was a realistic acceptance of the fact that the Russian past had actually survived into the present and was necessary to the future.

Similarly, strong bonds of family life, legal and economic as well as spiritual, were restored—again, not simply to increase the birth rate, but primarily because the disintegration of the family which was threatening under the original conception, especially in the cities, was endangering the stability of Soviet social relations. By 1935, for example, juvenile delinquency had increased to an alarming extent, and harsh legal measures were taken to deal with it; in Moscow and other cities the rate of abortions was higher than the rate of births, and in 1936 it was prohibited to perform abortions except in unusual cases (as when the mother had a serious disease which could be passed on to the child); the number of registered and *de facto* divorces had become extraordinarily high, and in 1936 graduated fees were imposed for the registration of successive divorces. Ultimately, in 1944, a judicial process of divorce was established for the first time since the Revolution. As with the restoration of Russian tradition, so with the restoration of the family, the change was both a response to a crisis and a realistic reappraisal of older doctrine.

The same may be said of the new policy toward the Church which began in the mid-1930's. The failure of the so-called "Five-Year Plan for the elimination of religion" was by then obvious and admitted. Yaroslavsky, head of the League of the Militant Godless, reported in 1937 that two-thirds of the adults in the villages and one-third in the cities still believed in God, and he asked for more funds for the work of his organization. Not only were his requests not granted, but the League declined rapidly in importance and was ultimately abolished. The 1936 Constitution enfranchised the clergy. In 1937 wage penalization for attendance at religious festivals was discontinued. In 1940 the seven-day week was restored, with Sunday as a common day of rest. During the War the role of the Church as having a legitimate part to play in the life of the people (but not of the Communist Party) was finally recognized, antireligious publications were discontinued, some theological academies and seminaries were opened, many thousands of new churches were licensed, monasteries were exempted from taxation, a religious periodical was published—not to satisfy American public opinion, but primarily to satisfy Soviet public opinion; not because the Russian Church was weak but because it was strong. That Stalin and the Party remained ardently atheist in principle only bears witness to the fact that the new policy was based on practical social needs.[23]

2. *In respect to the Soviet economy,* there was likewise a fundamental revision of theory and practice beginning in the mid-1930's, based upon a breakdown of the older theory and practice. The First and Second Five-Year Plans had succeeded in industrializing Russia to a remarkable extent; by 1936, however, it was apparent that production in itself is no solution to the basic economic problems. The problem of the quality of the products had become very serious. The problem of disproportions in production (factories built but no raw materials to supply them, raw materials produced but no factories to process them) had become even more serious. Behind such problems as these lay the breakdown of personal responsibility, personal initiative, personal ability. It was in response to such problems, and because of the apparent inadequacy of earlier doctrine, that the emphasis since the mid-1930's has been on competition ("socialist emulation"), on reward for incentive, on profits, on prices that reflect more adequately market conditions, on "economic accountability," on "economic laws." This was a return to the economic and legal institutions of the NEP, but within the framework of a planned economy.

After its introduction in 1935 the Stakhanovite movement became increasingly important, with its rewards for workers on the basis of the fulfillment and overfulfillment of norms. From 1934 on, managers of state economic enterprises were given greater control of their organizations, with considerable freedom from the influence of both the trade union and the party organ within the plant. Since 1936 (except for the war years) a certain percentage of the profits of a plant has gone into a Director's Fund, from which bonuses and workers' benefits are distributed. Finan-

cial stability was encouraged as a check on the overexu-
berance of production drives. The role of contracts between
state economic enterprises became greatly enhanced, with
far greater freedom for real bargaining. Not only a trend
toward decentralization of operations, but even some tendency toward decentralization of planning was evident after
1936. In 1941, a law was passed transferring the planning
of production and distribution of products of local industry for local consumption from the central planning commission in Moscow to local administrative and executive
bodies.

As far as the economic rights of the individual are concerned, there was a new stress on personal ownership of
one's house, of one's personal belongings, of one's savings
account and government bonds (on both of which there
are interest rates up to 3 per cent). Inheritance was freed
from crushing taxation and a greater freedom of testation
was introduced; a Russian could now not only become rich,
but he could pass on his riches to his heirs with a maximum
inheritance tax of 10 per cent. On the collective farm, the
property rights of the individual peasant household were
restored and extended. While almost all Soviet farmers are
members of collective farms, they do a very considerable
part of their work on the small plots belonging to their
individual households and not to the collective. The free
market to which they may bring the produce of their household plots, as well as that portion of the produce of the
collective which is distributed to them as wages, became
increasingly important.[24] Here again Stalin's repeated denunciation of "equality-mongering," and his accent on individual initiative, on personal rewards and punishments,
were a concession to the "logic of facts," which, he said,
"is stronger than any other logic." "Having emerged from a
period of dearth in technique," Stalin declared in May
1935, "we have entered a new period, a period, I would
say, of dearth in people, in cadres . . . The old slogan,
'Technique decides everything' . . . must now be replaced
by a new slogan, the slogan 'Cadres decide everything.' "

3. *Politically and legally,* also, there was, from the mid-

1930's on, what Sir John Maynard has called a "new respectability," at the same time that important Party officials and intellectuals generally were being mercilessly eliminated. The full story of the political crisis of the mid-1930's has not yet been told. Yet we know that the assassination of Kirov in 1934 paved the way for a series of ruthless mass purges in which hundreds of thousands, at the least, were disposed of either through death or sentence to labor camps or exile to remote places. We know, secondly, that in these purges almost all the original revolutionaries of 1917 disappeared, those of the Right who were identified with Bukharin and those of the Left who were identified with Trotsky. We know, finally, that the Stalinist political science which emerged from this holocaust put very great emphasis on stability, orthodoxy, legality, as a means of consolidating the strength of the regime.

Soviet propaganda has stressed the changes wrought in constitutional law after 1936. From the viewpoint of civil liberties and political democracy these changes were insignificant. They were overshadowed by the absolute supremacy of the Communist Party and particularly its Politburo, for whom terror continued to be an important instrument of policy. The 1936 Constitution was important only as a symbol of the stability and legality which the regime ardently sought but for which it was unwilling to sacrifice its faith in force. One might say that the Constitution regularized the external system of government, without much affecting the actual process of political decision. It substituted direct for indirect elections, but retained the one-party system. It removed the earlier political and civil restrictions from nonproletarians. The dictatorship of the proletariat, strictly speaking, was over, so far as internal class relations were concerned.[25] Lines, avowedly wavy, were drawn between the legislative, administrative, and judicial branches of government—not a "separation of powers," according to the Soviet writers, but a "distribution of functions." After the enactment of the Constitution administrative discretion was restricted somewhat; for example the power of taxation was subjected to judicial review, insofar as the treasury could be compelled to prove in court that the assessment was authorized. In regard to legislation, a postwar law gave dissenting minorities on legislative bills committees the right to present their own reports to the supreme legislature and to defend their proposals in open debate—a right which was politically meaningless so long as speeches in the Supreme Soviet continued to be choruses of praises and complaints and not real debates, with all decisions taken unanimously. Other changes whose political importance was at best prospective included the implementation, by new procedural rules, of the responsibility of representatives to their constituents and of the right of recall by electors.

Soviet politics, for all its new-found outward respectability, continued in fact to remain the monopoly of the Party. In its application to civil life generally, however, Soviet law underwent profound changes not only in form and in theory but also in substance and in practice. Here the emphasis on strict legality, the independence of the judiciary, and due process, reflected the effort of the regime to bring about a stabilization in those areas of social relations in which political power could not be directly affected.

"We need stability of laws now more than ever," said Stalin in his Report on the Draft Constitution in 1936. With "stability of laws" as their slogan, Soviet jurists and lawmakers denounced the radical ideas of the first phase of the Revolution, and in one field of law after another restored conservative and even conventional doctrines and practices, proclaiming them to be truly "socialist."

The new party line concerning law was authoritatively laid down in 1938 in a series of articles by Procurator-General Vyshinsky, who replaced Pashukanis as dean of the Soviet legal profession, and by his book of the same year on Soviet public law. In comparison with the intricate and scholarly theory of Pashukanis, Vyshinsky's doctrine seems on the one hand extremely simple and even naïve, and on the other highly emotional and vituperative. His invective goes in two directions: first, against the law of other states, with their "inhuman, bestial relationship to the exploited masses of the people," and second, against the doctrines of the leading jurists of the first twenty years of the Revolution, particularly against "the rotten theory of the wrecker Pashukanis," with its "putrid vapor, whereby our enemies sought to sully the pure source of great and truly scientific thought." On the other hand, no words are exalted enough to do justice to "the genius Stalin," to the great Stalin Constitution, "that genuine charter of the rights of emancipated humanity," and to the greatness of the Soviet legal system.[26]

It must be remembered, however, that Vyshinsky's task was far more difficult than the task which had confronted Pashukanis, Krylenko, and their confrères (of whom Vyshinsky had, of course, been one).[27] Vyshinsky faced the necessity of developing a theory which, in the interests of stability, would put socialist law on its own feet, give it a life of its own, apart from economics and politics in the narrow sense of those words, and which at the same time, in the interests of the fiction of the continuity of the Revolution, would *appear* Marxist-Leninist. Vyshinsky in 1938 was thus exploring new territory; he was pioneering. A good deal of the invective and distortion was to cover his tracks against the wolves who stood ready to fall upon and devour all who dared to deviate. There could be no apparent deviation; everything had to look like mere exegesis on the holy writ of Marx, Lenin, and Stalin. The distaste engendered by his method should not obscure the fact that behind the revision of the catechism lay very real issues. This was not just an ideological pillow fight.

Vyshinsky attacked Pashukanis' thesis that law reaches its highest stage of development under capitalism. In fact, he wrote, "the development of capitalist society goes in the direction of the decay of law and of legality"; in its imperialist and fascist stages, capitalism leads "not to the strengthening of legality and of the rule of law but to the final destruction of the rule of law." "History demonstrates that under socialism, on the contrary, law is raised to the highest level of development."

"Reducing law to economics, as Stuchka did, asserting

that law coincides with the relations of production, these gentlemen slid into the bog of economic materialism." "Stuchka and his followers liquidated law as a special, specific social category, drowned law in economics, deprived it of its active, creative role."

On the other hand, "reducing law to politics, these gentlemen depersonalized law as the totality of legal rules, undermining their stability and their authoritativeness, introducing the false concept that in a socialist state the application of a statute is determined not by the force and authority of Soviet law but by political considerations."

Law is, of course, "a political category," Vyshinsky said. "At the basis of Soviet law lie the political and economic interests of the workers and peasants." "But nevertheless it is impossible to reduce law to politics, as it is impossible to identify cause and effect. If law is a form of politics, then how is one to explain Article 112 of the Stalin Constitution which says that our judges are independent and subject only to the law?" "The reduction of law to politics would signify the ignoring of those tasks standing before law such as the tasks of legal protection of personal, property, family, testamentary and other rights and interests."

Yet when it came to the elaboration of a positive theory of law, and not merely to a renunciation of the negative and nihilistic theories of the past, Vyshinsky could scarcely get beyond platitudes. "Our law is the embodiment in statutes of the will of the people," he wrote. "In capitalist society reference to the will of the people serves as a screen which covers the exploitational character of the bourgeois state. In our conditions the matter is in principle otherwise." "Our laws are the expression of the will of our people as it directs and creates history under the leadership of the working class. The will of the working class with us is fused with the will of the whole people." [28]

Such generalities hardly constitute a theory of law. Yet they do offer *some* theoretical foundation on which to elaborate a workable legal system. By declaring Soviet law to be socialist in character, Vyshinsky provided Soviet lawyers and judges with a basis for utilizing and interpreting the hitherto "bourgeois" NEP codes, whose dignity was now restored. By defending the independence of law from economics, he laid a foundation in theory for court decisions requiring contracts between state economic enterprises to be fulfilled in certain types of cases even when the terms of the contracts were in violation of authorized plans. By attacking the reduction of law to politics, he paved the way, for example, for the 1947 directive excluding from court proceedings documents submitted by public organizations which have no direct connection with the case at hand. These practical implications of Vyshinsky's argument are not mentioned in his writings. They are to be read where Soviet eyes are trained to read—between the lines.

The actual developments in Soviet law after the mid-1930's were not meager. The 1936 Constitution provided for the promulgation of All-Union codes to replace the various codes of the separate constituent republics. The new codes would eliminate the old dichotomy of bourgeois law and socialist no-law. Pending the drafting of the All-Union codes, there was a return to stricter adherence to the existing law. "Revolutionary legality" was redefined as the strict observance of those laws which the Revolution has established: from a symbol of flexibility the phrase was converted into a symbol of stability. Article 1 of the Civil Code, requiring that rights be enforced only when exercised "according to their social-economic purpose," was rarely used and was attacked by some as tautological. In criminal law, the principle of "no crime, no punishment without a [previous] law" was reasserted as a socialist principle, and the doctrine of analogy was severely limited, so that it became in effect (despite Soviet claims to the contrary) merely a method of amplification of a statute by interpretation. The words "crime" and "punishment" were restored: the "formal-juridical" element was now emphasized as having an importance equal to that of the "material" element of social danger and social defense. Personal guilt was considered an essential element of a crime. In family law, not only was divorce now a matter for the courts to decide, but certain formalities were required for marriage, without which it would not be recognized as valid. In the field of commercial contracts between state economic enterprises, Gosarbitrazh was transformed from an arbitration tribunal into an economic court, and was declared to be bound by the Civil Code. In contract law generally, Soviet law was said to start from the principle of *pacta sunt servanda*. In the law of personal injury, fault was restored as the chief criterion of liability. A new Judiciary Act was promulgated in 1938 to lay the foundation for more orthodox trial procedure. The need for "judicial culture" (that is, proper court procedure) and "judicial authority" was emphasized. "Judicial activity requires the deepest trust in the court," Vyshinsky stated in 1938. "The judge must fight for that trust." Law schools were expanded, and legal education returned to more orthodox paths.

The nihilistic theory of law which had previously dominated was now denounced; yet the practice of force and violence survived. Is not this practice evidence that the denunciation of a "negative" attitude toward Soviet law was purely verbal? How can law and force exist side by side? It was the Soviet thesis that they can. Vyshinsky in 1938 wrote with utter frankness that alongside "suppression and the use of force," which are "still essential" so long as world-wide communism does not exist, it is necessary to have "also" due process of law. Behind such a thesis is the assumption that politics is beyond law, and that law only extends to those areas of society in which the political factor has been stabilized. Where the stability of the regime is threatened, law goes out the window. No fundamental legal opposition is tolerated. Where real opposition is even suspected, it is dealt with by "suppression and the use of force." The Soviets had the delicacy at least not to call this law. Yet the line was not always easy to draw, and the inherent conflict between law and force resulted in some strange paradoxes. The law punished discrimination on the basis of nationality, yet the Ministry of Internal Affairs removed and dispersed whole national groups which were considered insufficiently loyal—the Volga Germans, the

Crimean Tartars, the Karachai, the Kalmyks, the Chechen and Ingush, and the Balkars. Anti-Semitism was a crime in law, but Jewish "cosmopolitans" were sent to labor camps as counterrevolutionaries. Legal guilt was purely personal but political guilt could be avenged against relatives and friends.

In illustrating this duality of law and terror the case of Dmitri Buligin—a former Soviet citizen who emigrated to the United States—may be instructive.[29] As consultant for an engineering office, Buligin, a professor at the Leningrad Engineering Institute, was asked in 1940 to draw up blueprints for an important construction project in Kazan. Progress had to be reported directly to Moscow, to what was then called the Technical Council of the People's Commissariat (later Ministry) of Heavy Industry. After the layout was finished, a hearing was called in Moscow, which Buligin attended as supervising engineer. Over his protest, the Council altered the plans, for the sake of economy and speed. Buligin was accordingly compelled to direct his team of engineers to carry out the revised plans. After construction got under way, the director of the engineering office received the following telegram: "Foundation sagged under machine Number Five when tested. Investigation started. Send your representative."

The director sent Buligin to Kazan, where he was greeted by an investigator of the Ministry of Internal Affairs, who told him that he was suspected of a "deliberate act of sabotage," designed "to prevent the new plant from getting into the production needed to strengthen our country's war potential." The investigator questioned him about his relations with his uncle abroad, and about his relations with all the people who had worked with him on the project, and then asked him to prepare a written report on the basis of his observations at the scene of the construction. Buligin concluded, in his report, that the sagging was due to weak layers of soil which should have been detected by the engineers in charge of boring.

On his return to Leningrad, he "received a summons to visit the Big House" (NKVD headquarters), where a new investigation began all over again. "Why haven't you told us anything about Alutin?" he was asked. Alutin was his chief assistant. "We've had to arrest him. He's a rather suspicious character, you know. His father was a priest. And he has relatives abroad. In the Engineering Institute he did not have a good record, either. He didn't participate in any of the social work. Did you know him well?" Buligin defended Alutin, who by this time had been arrested and was under detention.

After two more months in which he was called several more times for severe questioning, Buligin was formally shown an indictment that had been drawn up on the basis of the preliminary investigation. Four persons were indicted—Alutin, the engineer in charge of the borings, a foreman, and Buligin. "I was pleasantly surprised," Buligin reports, "that none of us were accused of counterrevolutionary sabotage, as had constantly been taken for granted by the agents in talking to me. Instead we were accused of criminal negligence, under Article 114, which carries a maximum penalty of ten years in prison, whereas Article 58, on counterrevolutionary crimes, could have meant capital punishment.

"I inquired about court procedure, about the sort of defense I might be allowed, about what rights would be accorded us in the trial. The investigators avoided my questions, suggesting merely that I find a lawyer to give me the information I sought."

The next day Buligin, who alone of the four accused was not detained, owing to the fact that the Institute considered him indispensable, went to see a lawyer. Buligin writes:

> I had met him somewhere before, and I remembered his name. I wanted to hear his opinion of the case in general, and to know whom to approach first. I told him my whole story, with all the details. His first reaction was to congratulate me on my luck in not being indicted under Article 58. "Such cases are usually decided without any trial, by the NKVD itself," he explained, "and no defense attorneys are allowed in at all."

The day came for the trial. I felt awkward, standing alongside my three co-defendants. I was at liberty, and they had been in jail. They sat on a bench between two guards, but I was given a chair next to my attorney's table.

I was happy to see two engineering experts taking part in the trial. They were well-known professors. I was acquainted with one of them, and knew the other by reputation.

The trial took place in the Leningrad City Court, and lasted four days. There were three judges on the bench—the main judge and two lay associates. One associate judge was a carpenter, and the other was a janitor. This was a municipal court—higher than a people's court. The next highest court was the Supreme Court [of the RSFSR] itself. The chief judge, a professional jurist, bent over his two associates from time to time, seemingly just for the look of the thing, and they always bowed their heads in solemn agreement to whatever he was saying. During the whole trial, only one inconsequential question was asked by either of these two associate judges.

The lawyer assigned to the other two defendants was quite an old man, who constantly yawned, and even took little catnaps.

My attorney was very alert. He constantly took notes, and insisted that I consult him each time before he spoke or asked questions. He frequently stopped me from speaking. Even so my voice, in my own defense, was heard more frequently than that of the others. During recess, I heard people refer to "the trial of Buligin and three others." My co-defendants spoke so little, and stared about with such scared looks, that it was evident they had been bulldozed by their detention and jail environment, and had undoubtedly undergone severe grilling. I tried to defend Alutin as much as I could. The two professors were there only to answer technical questions. Their answers were clear and to the point, and it was very evident that they were well acquainted with the case.

The prosecutor's questions were about the same as had been hurled at me during my interrogation. He seemed interested only in people, not in technical details. Damage had been done, people must have done it, and they must pay the penalty. This was his simple logic, which he hammered upon again and again. He spoke with emphasis, staring pointedly at me several times when he said: Most probably the accident came about not only because of negligence, but for some other reasons. This was an obvious hint at sabotage.

All but two of the ten or so witnesses were on our side. The two exceptions were motivated by dislike of Alutin. One was a young engineer, from the same graduating class as Alutin, and a Party member. The other was the director of the engineering office. The former criticized poor Alutin to the right and to the left. I had the impression that beside the personal animosity for him, he also resented the fact that Alutin had been placed above him, while he had to remain as his assistant.

The director was afraid the blame might be laid to him, and he tried to put the whole responsibility on Alutin and me. He told the court that he wasn't a specialist, only an organizer, and that the responsibility was mine. Why hadn't I gone to Kazan myself? he asked, although he knew perfectly well why I couldn't have. Why hadn't I demanded a more detailed analysis of the borings? Why had I selected such an assistant as Alutin, who he said didn't have a serious attitude toward his work. These were his only arguments.

A very interesting point came up which the two engineering experts and the defense lawyer grabbed. During the questioning of the foreman, it came out that a representative of the People's Commissar had gone to Kazan for an inspection, when the ground for the foundation had already been dug up. He had noticed water seeping from underground, and had seen the laborers standing in the water. This Moscow official, the testimony revealed, gave orders to pump out the water, and to keep the drainage work going all during construction. His orders were instantly obeyed. The foreman let this information slip out while trying to impress the court how faithfully he had always obeyed the orders of his superiors.

The constant flow of water might easily have washed away some of the clay layers of soil, which could have caused the uneven sagging of the foundation. In their conclusions, both experts pointed out that this could have caused the accident.

But the court didn't consider this point at all. A representative of the People's Commissar cannot be blamed for anything—unless he first has fallen into disfavor in the Party! But engineers and technicians, well, those were the people who could be blamed!

The sentences handed down were six years of imprisonment for me, four years for Alutin, and three years for the technicians and the foreman.

Buligin had reckoned on the possibility of a conviction, but the harshness of the sentence was a shock to him. However, he writes, "I took the verdict calmly, for I believed it was so absurd that it certainly would be overruled by the Supreme Court."

After several weeks of extreme discomfort at "The Crosses," the old Leningrad prison constructed for political prisoners before the Revolution, Buligin was sent to a labor camp. Meanwhile his lawyer brought an appeal in the Supreme Court of the RSFSR, which reversed the conviction and remanded the case for a new trial on the ground that the lower court had ignored statements by the two experts, and also that it had erroneously refused to call witnesses requested by the defense. His sentence having been revoked, Buligin was told by the head of the labor camp that he could not be kept prisoner for more than seventy-two hours afterward. Also, according to law, he had to be reinstated in his old job.

The new trial was in the hands of new investigators, not of the NKVD but of the regular investigating and prosecuting arm of the government, the Procuracy. The new investigators examined the witnesses upon whom the defense had wished to rely in the earlier trial, including some of the people who had taken part in the meeting of the Technical Council and who had therefore heard Buligin's protest against the revision of the plans.

The second trial proceeded much more calmly than the

first. All four accused were now at liberty. One of the two lay judges was an engineer, Buligin having been advised of a little-known right—apparently a local Leningrad custom —to request that in a case involving technical matters there be one specialist on the bench. The engineer-judge asked pointed technical questions of the expert witnesses. After a trial of three days, the judges deliberated for about six hours and then brought in a verdict of acquittal for all four.

The prosecutor appealed the acquittal, but Buligin's attorney explained that that was only a matter of form, for the record. Buligin went to Moscow to represent himself in the R.S.F.S.R. Supreme Court. After a perfunctory hearing lasting ten minutes, the acquittal was affirmed.

The Buligin case sheds light on the difficulties which attended the efforts to maintain separate systems of law and terror in the Stalin era. Buligin had confidence that once his case was out of the hands of the NKVD and in the courts, justice would be done. His optimism ultimately proved justified, but overtones of political considerations were present in the trial and almost defeated him. Many of his less fortunate countrymen were disposed of by the Special Board of the Ministry of Internal Affairs.

Nevertheless, the "Restoration of Law" after 1936, though a movement rather than an accomplished fact, was one of the most significant internal developments in Soviet Russia since 1917. From 1917 to the mid-1930's, Soviet policy followed from the fundamental principles of Leninist philosophy. As Leninism was a transformation of classical Marxism, exalting the second half of Marx's teachings, not his economic determinism but his apocalyptic vision of a future society of conscious social scientists—so Stalinism was a transformation of Leninism. Stalinism is the name appropriate to the new theory and practice of socialism introduced by Stalin in the mid-1930's after he finally consolidated his power within and over the Party; it represents what Soviet writers called "the second phase of development of the Soviet State," beginning in 1936. Stalinism retained the Leninist emphasis on the power of human and social consciousness to overcome and transform the material conditions of existence; but a different conception of consciousness was involved. Consciousness to Lenin and to his disciples meant enlightenment, science in its application to human activities, reason; it was the accurate and enlightened reflection of social-economic needs—true (class) interest rightly understood.[30] Lenin tolerated the oppressive features of the proletarian dictatorship because he believed that that was the only path toward a free society in which reason would replace coercion, in which all non-rational factors—all tradition, all emotion, all passion, all morality as such—would be subordinated to and transcended by reason. State and Law were only temporary instruments toward that end. In Stalinism, however, consciousness meant the exaltation of nonrational elements. Stalin deintellectualized the Party; he purged it of the men who were in love with revolutionary ideas. The revolutionary ideas themselves became liturgical rather than rational in Soviet Russia. Marxism was chanted. Not reason as such but loyalty, patriotism, discipline, responsibility, were now stressed. It was in this context that law was restored, not only as legality but also as a system of justice. Without a legal system and a legal order—without Law with a capital L—the Stalinist regime could neither control the social relations of the people nor keep the economy going nor command the political forces in the country as a whole. It was rediscovered that law is not a luxury but a necessity, that at the very least it satisfies a basic need for some outlet for the feelings of justice, of rightness, of reward and punishment, of reciprocity, which exist in all people. Stalin did not want the Russian people merely to obey; he wanted them also to believe in the rightness of the order which had been established. This fact breathed in every word of Soviet legal literature from the statutes and cases to the treatises and law reviews.

Stalinism rehabilitated the superstructure. Having solved the basic economic problem by the elimination of antagonistic classes—so went the theoretical justification—it was possible to concentrate on the moral and legal aspects of social relations. There was no longer an economic excuse for moral or legal deviations. But whatever the justification and whatever the reason, the Soviet state was struggling to legalize its position; it was seeking in law a justification of authority which the original apocalyptic vision no longer provided. The Soviets turned away from the original Marxist question: how can the coercive, formal institutions of politics and law be superseded by a wholly rational social order in which "the free development of each is the condition for the free development of all"? They now asked the questions: how can economic, political, and sociocultural institutions be integrated through law? How can law change to meet changing conditions and yet provide stability in a society which badly needs stability? What is the relation of personal claims and interests, of litigation, to the broad purposes for which society exists? These are the age-old questions, the "accursed" questions, which have troubled statesmen and legal philosophers throughout history.

Chapter Two

SOVIET LAW REFORM
AFTER STALIN, 1953-1962

STALIN'S SYSTEM from the mid-1930's on was based on a coexistence of law and terror. Law was for those areas of Soviet life where the political factor was stabilized. Terror, whether naked or (as in the purge trials of the late 1930's) in the guise of law, was applied when the regime felt itself threatened. But these two spheres were not easy to keep separate either in theory or in practice. It was not a peaceful coexistence. In the first place, the borderline shifted: the crime of theft of state property, for example, which was supposed to be dealt with by due process of law, could easily merge with counterrevolutionary crimes and thereby become subject to repression by the secret police. In the second place, even though terror diminished after 1938, it continued to have a deleterious effect on the legal system itself. Urgently needed law reforms were delayed and sidetracked because of people's fear of being labeled "deviationist."

With Stalin's death in March 1953, his successors began to attack the "violations of socialist legality" which had taken place under his auspices. At first the attack was relatively cautious. Reforms of criminal law and procedure were promised, with apparent reference to political cases. Then in April 1953, fifteen doctors (most of them Jewish) who in the last months of Stalin's life had been charged with a Zionist espionage plot to murder, by medical means, a whole series of top Soviet leaders, were exonerated, and leading security officials were charged with "impermissible procedures" in extorting confessions from them. The exposure of the "Doctors' Plot," which some have supposed Stalin had trumped up as a signal for a new wave of purges, was accompanied by articles in the press proclaiming the "inviolability" of Soviet law. After the arrest of Beria in July 1953, some of the excesses of Stalinist terror were attributed not to the dictator, but to his chief of secret police. This deception gradually wore thin, however, and in February 1956 N. S. Khrushchev, who a year earlier had succeeded in bringing about the resignation of G. M. Malenkov as head of the Soviet state, attacked Stalin by name at the 20th Congress of the Communist Party, denouncing him for the "cult of [his own] personality" and for persecution of loyal party members in violation of their legal rights. In October and November 1961, at the 22nd Party Congress, the attacks on Stalin were renewed with even greater vigor. Vyshinsky's name was added to Stalin's as co-author of a legal system which permitted falsification and distortion of legality for the persecution of people innocent of any crime.[1]

The attack upon Stalinist terror facilitated the introduction of wholesale reforms in almost every branch of Soviet law. Indeed, the law reform movement which started in 1953 and gathered increasing momentum throughout the following years may prove to have been the most significant aspect of Soviet social, economic and political development in the decade after Stalin's death.

In interpreting this reform movement, however, one must start with Stalin—however much his successors would have liked to expunge his name from the memory of their people. For despite the very substantial changes which they introduced, the Soviet legal system remained Stalinist in its basic structure and its basic purposes. The organization and functions of the lawmaking, law-enforcing, and law-practicing agencies—of the legislature, the Procuracy, the courts, the administrative organs, the bar—were not essentially different ten years later from what they were when Stalin died. The main outlines of Soviet criminal law and procedure, civil law and procedure, labor law, agrarian law, family law, administrative law, constitutional law, and other branches of the Soviet legal tree—remained basically the same as before.

Also, if one looks behind the structure to the purposes of Soviet law, it remained a totalitarian law, in the sense that it sought to regulate all aspects of economic and social life, including the circulation of thought, while leaving the critical questions of political power to be decided by informal, secret procedures beyond the scrutiny or control either of legislative or judicial bodies. It remained the law of a one-party state. It remained the law of a planned economy. It remained a law whose primary function is to discipline, guide, train, and educate Soviet citizens to be dedicated members of a collectivized and mobilized social order.

If this is so, it may be asked, what is the significance of the post-Stalin reforms? Indeed, many Western observers treated each successive development in Soviet law after Stalin's death as mere smoke without fire—or even as a smokescreen designed to conceal the absence of any fire. Others viewed the reforms as half-hearted concessions designed to appease the appetite of the Soviet people without really satisfying their hunger. These grudging responses are reminiscent of Soviet interpretations of American law reforms: the New Deal, we are told by Soviet writers, did not really alter the fundamental nature of the American capitalist system; the Supreme Court decision in the School Segregation cases did not end discrimination against Negroes; American law remains "bourgeois."

Viewed from a sufficiently lofty height, the scene never changes. This may only mean, however, that the viewer does not see what is really going on. To give an example: in December 1958, the Supreme Soviet enacted new Fundamental Principles of Criminal Law which, among other things, reduced the maximum period of detention of criminals from 25 to 15 years.[2] This was part of a general movement toward greater leniency in penal policy. In 1961 and 1962, however, the death penalty (which previously had been restricted in peacetime to certain crimes against the state and to first-degree murder) was extended to a wide variety of other crimes, including certain non-violent crimes such as counterfeiting and bribery.[3] One of the main reasons for the excessive harshness of 1961-1962 was the disappointment of the Soviet leaders in the results of the excessive softness of 1958, for in fact the rate of serious crimes increased in 1959, 1960 and 1961.[4] The point is that those Western observers who did not take seriously the earlier policy of leniency are in a poor position to evaluate the later policy of repression.

Of course, if the observer abandons all elevation and descends into the midst of the events, he loses all perspective and sees only flux. The foreign journalist in Moscow—and the readers of his articles at home—tend to see a whirling, eddying stream. The only solution is to seek a composite picture, from various perspectives.

Such a composite picture would reveal at least seven major tendencies in Soviet law reform in the decade after March 1953.

First, there was a tendency toward the elimination of political terror.

Second, there was a tendency toward the liberalization both of procedures and of substantive norms.

Third, there was a tendency toward the systematization and rationalization of the legal system.

Fourth, there was a tendency toward decentralization and democratization of decision-making.

Fifth, there was a tendency to introduce popular participation in the administration of justice.

Sixth, there was a tendency in 1961 and 1962 to threaten those who will not co-operate in building communism with harsh criminal and administrative penalties.

Seventh, there was developed a new Soviet theory of

state and law which rejected some of the Stalinist innovations in Leninist doctrine.

THE TENDENCY TOWARD
THE ELIMINATION OF TERROR

Important steps were taken after March 1953 to eliminate those features of the previous Soviet law which permitted the disguise of terror in legal form.

First, the Special Board of the Ministry of Internal Affairs was abolished.[5] It was this Special Board which had been the chief instrument of terror. It was a three-man administrative committee—the Russians called it a troika—which was empowered by a 1934 statute to send people to labor camps without a hearing, in a secret administrative procedure, without right of counsel and without right of appeal.

Second, the security police were deprived of the power to conduct investigations of crimes under their own special rules without supervision by the Procuracy.[6]

Third, the special procedures for court cases involving the most serious anti-state crimes were abolished. The laws of 1934 and 1937 permitting persons charged with certain such crimes to be tried secretly, in absentia, and without counsel, were repealed.[7]

Fourth, the military courts, which had previously had a wide jurisdiction over civilians, particularly in the case of political crimes, were deprived of all jurisdiction over civilians except for espionage.[8]

Fifth, the law permitting punishment of relatives of one who deserts to a foreign country from the armed forces—though they knew nothing of the desertion—was abolished.[9]

Sixth, Vyshinsky's doctrine that confessions have special evidentiary force in cases of counterrevolutionary crimes —based on the transparently false notion that people will not confess to such crimes unless they are actually guilty —was repudiated; confessions were now treated as having no evidentiary force in themselves, and the matters contained in a confession must be corroborated by other evidence.[10]

Seventh, Vyshinsky's doctrine that the burden of proof shifts to the accused in cases of counterrevolutionary crimes was also repudiated. The new Soviet codes place the burden of proving the guilt of the accused squarely on the prosecutor. Although the phrase "presumption of innocence" is avoided in the codes, all that American jurists generally mean by that phrase is spelled out in Soviet law.[11]

Eighth, Vyshinsky's broad definition of complicity, borrowed from the Anglo-American doctrine of conspiracy, was repudiated. Persons may no longer be held liable for acts of their associates unless they intended those acts to take place.[12]

Ninth, the law on so-called "counterrevolutionary crimes" was slightly narrowed and made a little less vague. The term "counterrevolutionary" was eliminated and the term "state" (*i.e.,* anti-state) substituted. The crime of "terrorist acts," which hitherto had been interpreted to include any violent act against a state or Party official, or, indeed, his close relatives, whatever the motive, was restricted to murder or serious bodily injury of the official himself committed for the purpose of overthrowing or weakening the Soviet authority.[13] The law on State secrets was substantially relaxed—though it is still far wider in its scope than most Americans would consider tolerable—and a new list of information constituting a state secret was enacted which is less broad and more precise than the earlier list.[14]

Finally, there took place from 1955 to 1957 a systematic re-examination of all cases of persons previously convicted of counterrevolutionary crimes and the release from labor camps of the overwhelming majority of such persons, with full rehabilitation.[15]

The restoration of procedural due process of law in political cases is a signal achievement of the post-Stalin regime. The Soviet citizen is now protected against police terror, false charges and faked trials to a far greater extent than ever before in Soviet history. No longer need he fear the midnight knock on the door as a prelude to transportation to a Siberian labor camp without a fair hearing.

Yet one cannot speak of the total elimination of political terror so long as open opposition to Communist Party policy—the "Party line"—can lead to criminal sanctions, however "objectively" and "correctly" imposed. The 1958 Statute on State Crimes carries over from the earlier law on counterrevolutionary crimes the provision against "agitation or propaganda" directed against the Soviet system. To defame the Soviet political and social system, or even to possess written materials of such defamatory nature, if for the purpose of weakening Soviet authority, is punishable by deprivation of freedom of up to seven years.[16]

The law of anti-Soviet agitation and propaganda is only one of many features which keep alive the fear of Soviet citizens that the terror may return. This fear, and the conditions which give rise to it, will be discussed more fully below. But it is important to stress at this point that the fear of a return to terror is itself a form of terror. Therefore, one must view the developments of the ten years after Stalin's death as reflecting only a tendency—though an extremely important tendency—toward the elimination of terror.

THE LIBERALIZATION OF SOVIET LAW

Even apart from political crimes, Soviet law underwent substantial liberalization after Stalin's death. It would be impossible to list the hundreds, indeed thousands, of needed reforms which were introduced. A brief account of some of the most important may suffice, however, to indicate the direction and scope of the tendency toward liberalization.

In criminal law and procedure, the "tightening up" of the rules with respect to burden of proof, the evaluation of confessions, and the doctrine of complicity, which have already been mentioned in the discussion of political crimes, gave increased protection to persons accused of

other crimes as well. In addition, the right to counsel prior
to trial, though still limited, was significantly extended;[17]
time for supervisory review of an acquittal in a criminal
case, formerly unlimited, was reduced to one year;[18] powers of search and seizure were somewhat restricted;[19] the
doctrine of analogy, whereby a person who committed a
socially dangerous act not specifically made punishable by
law could be sentenced under a law proscribing an analogous act, was finally eliminated;[20] penalties were substantially lightened for many crimes—for example, new laws
imposing lighter sentences for petty rowdyism ("hooliganism") and petty theft of state or public property removed
the necessity of many long years in labor camps for such
trivial offenses;[21] some crimes were eliminated altogether—
for example, abortion[22] and also absenteeism from work
and quitting one's job without permission.[23] Large-scale
amnesties of 1953 and 1957 released all except those sentenced for, or charged with, the most serious offenses.[24]

With respect to the system of detention, a 1957 law
eliminated the term "labor camp," substituting "labor
colony" for all places of confinement (except prisons,
which are used only for temporary detention or, very
rarely, for the most serious crimes) and introduced a
new regime for prisoners which permits far more leniency
in their treatment.[25] Those convicted of less serious crimes
are permitted to have their wives (or husbands) visit and
stay with them from time to time; they are paid substantial wages for their work and are required to send home
allotments to their dependents.[26] Also liberal parole provisions were introduced.[27]

Liberalization was not confined to criminal policy. After
1953, and especially after 1955, there was a re-examination
of every branch of law and a weeding out of many of the
harshest features. For example, a new civil right was
created to obtain a court order for public retraction of a
newspaper libel.[28] In labor law, the rights of trade unions
were enhanced and the procedures for settlement of workers' grievances were improved.[29] Similar examples could be
multiplied from many other fields of law.[30]

In 1961 and 1962 there was a contrary trend, away from liberalization, in certain areas. These backward steps, however, did not stop the liberal momentum of the post-Stalin reforms.

SYSTEMATIZATION AND RATIONALIZATION

The tendency toward liberalization of law generally is, of course, an important supporting buttress of the tendency toward elimination of political terror. For such tendencies to have permanence, however, deeper foundations are required in the legal system as a whole. From that standpoint, the efforts of the post-Stalin regime to systematize and rationalize the Soviet legal system are of great significance.

The Stalin Constitution of December 1936, and the Vyshinsky jurisprudence which surrounded it, rehabilitated the various republican criminal, civil, labor and family codes of the NEP period of the 'twenties which had largely fallen into disrepute in the period from 1928 to 1936. Of course the NEP codes, designed for a transition period of mixed capitalism-socialism, were inadequate for the new period of full socialism with its planned economy. The Stalin Constitution therefore called for the creation of all-union codes to replace the earlier republican codes.[31] But until such new all-union codes were adopted, the earlier ones were to prevail, together with the thousands of statutory and administrative changes introduced into them.

During the remaining sixteen years of Stalin's reign, however, new all-union codes were not adopted, although many drafts were produced. Only with the removal of the political and ideological pressure of Stalinist autocracy did it become possible to introduce new codes, and, together with them, a reorganization of the entire system of legal administration.

The first major event in this development was the adoption in August 1955 of a new Statute on Procuracy Supervision. The Procuracy is the cornerstone of the Soviet legal system. It combines functions of our Department of

Justice, Congressional investigating committees, and grand juries. It not only investigates and prosecutes crimes, but it supervises the entire system of administration of justice, and has power to investigate and protest to higher authorities (whether administrative or judicial) any abuse of law which comes to its attention. Until 1955 it operated on the basis of a 1922 statute upon which were encrusted many legislative and administrative modifications. The 1955 statute clarified and consolidated its supervisory powers over judicial and administrative acts.[32] Incidentally, the new statute also added sanctions against officials of the Procuracy for negligence in failing to expose illegal practices in places of detention of criminals.

The second major event was the removal of certain aspects of Ministry of Justice control over the courts and the reorganization of the Supreme Court of the U.S.S.R. and of the republican and regional courts. This took place in 1956 and 1957. The result was a streamlining of the court system and an increase in its independence.[33]

In December 1958 the Supreme Soviet of the U.S.S.R. adopted a series of Fundamental Principles of various branches of law—Fundamental Principles of Criminal Law, Fundamental Principles of Criminal Procedure, and Fundamental Principles of Court Organization—together with new comprehensive Statutes on State Crimes, Military Crimes, and Military Tribunals. Subsequently, in December 1961, the Supreme Soviet adopted Fundamental Principles of Civil Law and of Civil Procedure. As of 1962, Fundamental Principles of Family Law and of Labor Law were in preparation; indeed, a Statute on the Procedure for the Hearing of Labor Disputes adopted in 1957 was itself a systematization of many aspects of labor law.

On the basis of the various Fundamental Principles, the republics adopted their own new codes of criminal law and criminal procedure and in 1962 were in the last stages of work on new codes of civil law and civil procedure.

Of the many other important pieces of legislation of the first post-Stalin decade, mention should also be made of the 1961 statute on administrative commissions of local municipal councils, which restricted the powers of administrative bodies to impose fines and established a procedure for appealing from such fines;[34] the 1960 Statute on State Arbitrazh, which reorganized the procedures for hearing the hundreds of thousands of contract disputes which arise each year between state economic enterprises;[35] and the new statutes on the organization of the legal profession in the various republics, which strengthen the independence of the advocate and his responsibility to his client.[36]

Two other items deserve mention in connection with the systematization of Soviet law. The Juridical Commission of the Council of Ministers of the U.S.S.R. was given the function of determining which laws have lost their force in the light of the new legislation. In the twenty years between 1937 and 1958, the U.S.S.R. Supreme Soviet enacted over 7,000 statutes, edicts and decrees, and the U.S.S.R. Council of Ministers issued about 390,000 decrees and regulations. Few of these were formally declared to have lost their force. Yet in 1960 only about 15,000 of these approximately 397,000 normative acts actually remained in force. The Juridical Commission has attempted to cleanse the Augean stables of Soviet legislation by systematically listing, little by little, those laws and other normative acts which are no longer valid.[37]

In connection with this, it is important to note a 1958 law on the publication of laws.[38] Of the more than 7,000 laws of the Supreme Soviet enacted between 1937 and 1958, only some hundreds were published. Of the 390,000 decrees and regulations of the Council of Ministers, only some thousands were published. The rest were merely distributed to the appropriate officials concerned with their enforcement and to other authorized persons. The 1958 law attempted to increase the publicity of laws by requiring that all laws and acts of the U.S.S.R. Supreme Soviet and all edicts and decrees of its Presidium which have "general significance" or are of a "normative character" be published in the Journal of the Supreme Soviet.

Also decrees of the Council of Ministers which are of general significance or have a normative character are required to be published in the Collected Decrees of the Government of the U.S.S.R.[39]

The systematization and rationalization of Soviet law is not something which can be accomplished in a few years. Indeed, it is something which must go on continually. The recognition of its importance, and the very great efforts devoted to it, are an encouraging sign of the determination of the post-Stalin regime to establish a far higher degree of legal security than that which existed in the past.

THE TENDENCY TOWARD DECENTRALIZATION AND DEMOCRATIZATION

Implicit in the tendencies toward an all-embracing, liberalized and systematic legality is the belief in the possibility of a wide decentralization of decision-making and a still wider participation of the public in the formulation of issues for decision.

Two qualifications must be made at the outset, however, in discussing the tendency of the post-Stalin period of Soviet history toward greater decentralization and democratization. The first is that there has been no sign that the present Soviet leadership has any intention of allowing this tendency to go beyond its power to control it. The limits of decentralized decision-making and democratization are set by the central authorities. The second qualification is that this theory of "democratic centralism"—centralization of authority combined with decentralization of operations—was also Stalin's theory. The difference since his death is a difference in degree.

The tendency toward decentralization and democratization was greatly accelerated after Stalin's death, however, by the very nature of the tendencies toward elimination of political terror, toward liberalization, and toward systematization and rationalization of the law. Apart from all other considerations, these tendencies have imposed an absolute requirement of help from hundreds of thousands of people at various levels of the official hierarchy and in various parts of the Soviet Union. In addition, the main purpose of these tendencies—to overcome the rigidities of the system inherited from Stalin, to stimulate local and individual initiative and enthusiasm—has necessitated the enlistment of maximum co-operation from the maximum number of people.

When one thinks of America one thinks of one hundred and eighty million people of diverse outlooks, diverse traditions, and diverse interests, scattered across a great continent which includes not only New York City and Washington, D.C., but also Texas and California and Mississippi and Vermont and a host of other very different kinds of communities. But too many, when they think of the Soviet Union, stop with the Kremlin. It should not need demonstration that even if one imagined the entire Soviet population to be a disciplined army, the Commander-in-Chief would be greatly in need of subordinate units of command with considerable autonomy of action. He could not run the lives of 220 million people, including thirty or forty major nationalities, spread across one-sixth of the earth's surface —by pushbutton from Moscow. When an American scholar presented the "pushbutton" theory to a leading Soviet jurist some years ago, he merely replied: "It would take too many pushbuttons!"

This is not to say that centralization is not the major fact of the Soviet political and economic system. "Bolsheviks are centralists by conviction," said John Maynard in 1948. Under Stalin this Bolshevik conviction was strengthened by fear of "the leader" (*vozhd'*), who often urged decentralization but did not hesitate to crack down when it tended toward deviation.

The decision in 1957 to abandon the rule of the 1936 Constitution calling for all-union codes and to substitute a rule calling for separate codes in each of the fifteen Soviet republics, based, however, on All-Union Fundamental Principles; the earlier decision to dissolve the All-Union Ministry of Justice into separate republican ministries of justice, and the later decision to do the same with the Ministry of Internal Affairs;[40] and, most important of all, the decision in 1957 to split the economy of the country into about 100 economic regions, each with its own Council of National Economy, and to divide among these regional councils some of the functions of the former economic ministries with their central offices in Moscow— these decisions in the direction of decentralization were called for by the enormous bureaucratization of Soviet social and economic life, which had become almost too stifling to endure.

Yet decentralization in itself is not democratization; it may be, and to a certain extent it has been, simply a moving of the center to the localities, a stretching of the chain of command. It has also been more than that, however. The lower links in the chain have unquestionably been given more initiative. And even where ultimate decisions have been reserved for Moscow, a far greater hearing has been given to the voices of the localities.

This is illustrated by the process of law reform itself. Khrushchev and his immediate associates could give the word that the time had come for substantial law reforms and could indicate the lines along which the reforms should run. But the word could not become a reality without an enormous effort on the part of the people who would be directly affected by these reforms. These include not only the professional lawyers who would have to draft them and the officials who would have to administer them, but also the various people who would have to live under them.

The comprehensive legislation enacted in the late 1950's and early 1960's were worked on by representatives of hundreds, indeed thousands, of organizations. All the major governmental agencies expressed detailed views on their various provisions. There was endless discussion of them in the universities, in research institutes, in economic organizations of various kinds, in scholarly journals, and in the daily press.

In addition, popular participation in lawmaking has

been stimulated by the expansion of the committee system of the Supreme Soviet of the U.S.S.R. and of the Supreme Soviets of the fifteen republics. Tens of thousands of expert consultants have reported to these committees. And apart from major all-union and republican legislation, there has been a substantial increase in the powers of the local municipal councils and a vast amount of activity of local governmental organizations, involving the participation of literally hundreds of thousands of Soviet citizens.

Of course it would be a mistake to suppose that Soviet federalism and Soviet democracy involve—as ours do— a struggle between opposing political units and groups, a competition for political leadership. In the Soviet Union all power resides in the Communist Party, which remains, as stated in the Constitution, the "central core" of all organizations, whether they be state organizations or social organizations. Despite the development of greater intra-Party democracy after 1953, the Party remains a disciplined elite, subservient to its leadership. Decentralization and democratization of decision-making in the spheres of government, law, and economic administration is not a threat to Party supremacy; indeed, it is required by the Party as a means of maintaining its supremacy.

Yet Party control is, in a much deeper sense, challenged by the development of autonomous centers of discussion and initiative, even though it remains the "central core" of such centers. The cohesion of Soviet jurists, for example, is striking. Whether they are judges, procurators, Ministry of Justice officials, law professors, research workers, legal advisers of state institutions and enterprises, advocates, or notaries, the seventy to eighty thousand jurists in the Soviet Union are bound together by the closest professional ties. They meet together in many different kinds of activity; they discuss and debate common problems; they work together; and they are bound not only by their common legal education but also by their common vested interest in the preservation of legality. As a class, they have grown greatly in importance during the years after Stalin's death.

POPULAR PARTICIPATION IN
THE ADMINISTRATION OF JUSTICE

In describing the movement away from political terror, harshness of punishment, chaos and irrationality of legislation, and overcentralization of decision-making, one runs the risk of leaving the false impression that the Soviet legal system is becoming just like ours. It is true that Stalin's successors have sought to eliminate the dualism of law and terror which formerly characterized the Soviet system, and in so doing they have taken important steps in the direction of a more humane, more rational and more democratic legal system. Yet they have sought to do this without abandoning the dynamic revolutionary development of the Soviet state and of Soviet society; indeed, their purpose has been to instill new vitality into that revolutionary development by softening the motive force of fear and strengthening the motive force of common effort, common struggle, common enthusiasm. The Soviet people are now being asked voluntarily to make sacrifices which formerly were evoked from them in part by threat of force. No doubt both the leaders and the people are greatly relieved at the decrease in emphasis upon terror and coercion and the increase in emphasis upon the liberal, rational and democratic elements in their legal system. But these elements are not—for the leaders, at least—ends in themselves, but rather a means toward lifting their society to new heights of economic progress, political power and social solidarity.

Law is conceived as a major instrument for achieving these goals. Law is conceived, above all, as a means of educating Soviet people to be the type of socially conscious, dedicated members of society which are required if socialism is to be maintained and if communism is to be achieved.

This concept of the dynamic function of law in molding not merely the conduct of men but also their morality and their very characters—a concept to be discussed more fully in Part III of this book—is perhaps the greatest challenge which Soviet law presents to the West. One aspect of this concept is the greatly increased participation of ordinary Soviet citizens—of society, the public, *obshchestvennost'*, as Soviet terminology has it—in the administration of justice.

It is Soviet theory that under communism the functions of state organizations (which operate in part by coercion) will be turned over entirely to social organizations (which operate only by persuasion). In anticipation of this glorious day, the role of social organizations was greatly increased from about 1959 on. Neighborhood and factory meetings were convened for a variety of purposes and were given certain semi-judicial functions. Also a voluntary auxiliary police force was organized—the so-called *druzhiny,* or bands—to help keep order; they direct traffic, take drunks into custody, and 'in general attempt to enforce law and order among the people on the streets. In addition many special volunteer commissions have been formed and given semi-official status—to observe conditions in the labor colonies and to make recommendations, to report to municipal councils on housing questions, to report on local observance of "socialist legality," and for a host of similar purposes. Trade unions and the Young Communist League (Komsomol) are also considered to be social organizations, and their functions have been extended.

Many of the functions of Soviet social organizations are also performed in the United States by volunteer workers and social organizations. Indeed, probably no country in the world can match the United States in the amount of public-spirited activity of volunteer social organizations. Yet there is a difference in kind between Soviet social organizations and their American counterparts—a difference which is striking. In part it is a difference in the scope of the activities of Soviet social organizations and especially their powers over the lives of their members; in part it is a difference in the amount of official pressure that can be brought upon them, due especially to their links with the state through the Communist Party.

For example, the Komsomol organizations in the universities call for student volunteers to work during the
summer holidays in the so-called "virgin lands" of the
East. The volunteers are recruited, however, by lists posted
on bulletin boards, and refusal to go courts expulsion
from the Komsomol and probably—at least it is so
assumed by the students—from the university.

A second example may be found in the activities of the
"Comrades' Courts," now operating under a 1960 statute,
which meet in apartment houses or in factories to consider minor offenses committed by neighbors or fellow-
workers. Their punitive powers are limited to a ten-
ruble fine.* Mostly they issue reprimands and warnings.
However, they may also recommend eviction from the
apartment or disciplinary action (including demotion but
not discharge) by the factory management. Such eviction or disciplinary action may be resisted through regular
court proceedings, but nevertheless the recommendation
of the Comrades' Court is a serious matter.[41]

One other example: Soviet courts sometimes go "on
circuit," so to speak, to apartments or factories, to hear
criminal cases involving persons in those places. The purpose is to demonstrate to the entire "collective" and to
the public the social danger of the offenses charged and
to educate people in the requirements of the law. But the
tendency to convict and to mete out harsh punishment is
very strong when such an educational purpose is in the
forefront of the procedure itself.

Some Western students of the Soviet scene have exaggerated the evils of this kind of new "social justice." To
evaluate them properly, one must put oneself in the Soviet
situation, where true social co-operation in informal volun-

---

* A ruble is now officially valued at $1.11. On January 1,
1961, a currency reform resulted in the substitution of one new
ruble for ten old rubles, with corresponding ten-fold reductions
in prices, wages, and all other accounts. References in this book
to "old" rubles and "new" rubles refer to the pre-1961 and post-
1961 ruble respectively.

tary groups, entirely independent of the state, hardly exists. The Comrades' Courts in action have impressed outside observers by the good spirit with which they are received. Especially important is the fact that their powers are very limited and that these limits are enforced by the courts and by the legal system.

The great danger, of course, is the potentiality of abuse of these social organizations by the Communist Party and the state. The still greater danger is the dream of a far-off time when there will be no legal system and no state but only one vast social organization, one vast Communist Party. It is, no doubt, a dream which can never be realized; but so long as it is held it inhibits the achievement of true legal security.

THE RETURN TO HARSH CRIMINAL AND ADMINISTRATIVE PENALTIES

A sixth major tendency in Soviet law in the post-Stalin period was the return in 1961 and 1962 to harsh criminal and administrative penalties against those who refuse to co-operate in building communism.

In May and June 1961, the three largest republics, comprising three-fourths of the Soviet population, finally enacted the notorious anti-parasite law which had been first proposed for public discussion in 1957 and later adopted in the smaller republics during 1957 to 1960. This law, in its final form, provides for "re-settlement" (*vyselenie*) in "specially designated localities," for two to five years, of persons who "are avoiding socially useful work and are leading an anti-social parasitic way of life." Money or property acquired by such persons "by non-labor means" is subject to confiscation. Persons may be sentenced under this law by the judges of the regular courts in a summary procedure and without the usual guarantees of the criminal law and without right of appeal, or else by general meetings in the factories or collective farms with review by the local municipal council.[42]

To a Western lawyer, and—judging from private conversations—to many Soviet lawyers as well, the antiparasite laws contradict the provision of the 1958 Fundamental Principles of Criminal Procedure that no person may be punished for a crime except by sentence of a court. Official Soviet doctrine, however, has reconciled these laws with the Fundamental Principles on the more-than-tenuous theory that the offender is not being punished for a crime, nor is he being confined; he is simply "resettled" in another place where he must take a socially useful job! This is considered an "administrative," not a "penal," measure.

In the first year of the operation of this law in the R.S.F.S.R., according to a statement made by the Minister of Justice at a public lecture in Moscow in May 1961, 10,000 people in Moscow were charged under the antiparasite law; 8,000, he said, received only warnings; 2,000 were sent out of Moscow; of these, only a small number were subjected to confiscation of property. It may be inferred from the relatively few instances of confiscation that the law is principally a device for getting rid of vagrants and putting them to work.

Also, the extension of the death penalty in 1961 and 1962 to a wide variety of crimes, many of them economic crimes not involving violence, reflected the regime's determination to take extreme measures against those who most flagrantly violate the tenets of communist morality. In May 1961, the death penalty (which had been abolished altogether in 1947, and restored in 1950 for treason, espionage, wrecking, terrorist acts and acts of banditry, and in 1954 for murder committed under aggravating circumstances) was extended to theft ("plunder") of state or social property in especially large amounts, counterfeiting money or securities for profit, and the commission of violent attacks in places of detention by especially dangerous recidivists or persons convicted of serious crimes. In July 1961, the death penalty was extended to speculation in foreign currency. In February 1962, it was extended to attempts upon the life of a policeman or volunteer auxiliary policeman (*druzhinnik*) on duty, to rape committed by a group or by an especially dangerous recidivist or entailing especially grave consequences or committed on a minor, and to the taking of bribes under aggravating circumstances by an official who holds a responsible position or who has been previously tried for bribery or has taken bribes repeatedly.

In a case tried in July 1961, the statute imposing the death penalty for foreign currency speculation was applied retroactively by a special decree of the Presidium of the Supreme Soviet authorizing the retroactive application "as an exception" in the specific case. (The decree was never published as it was not considered to be "of general significance." [43]) There is reason to believe that there were other such cases of retroactive application of the death sentence, specially authorized by similar edicts. The 1961 law was the first example of a Soviet criminal law expressly made retroactive, so far as the author has been able to discover, since 1929.

Judging from Soviet press accounts of individual trials, probably over 250 Soviet citizens were executed for economic and other crimes in the year from May 1961 to May 1962, and probably an equal or greater number were executed from June to December 1962. One can only say "probably" because Soviet crime statistics are a state secret! (In 1961, 43 persons were executed in the United States.)

This harsh policy was also reflected in increased penalties for lesser crimes. Soviet jurists have publicly criticized the tendency of some procurators and courts to treat the imposition of the death penalty for serious crimes as a signal for reversing the entire trend toward liberalization.

What significance should we attach to these developments? As is so often the case with violations of basic principles of judicial procedure, the particular individual victims do not command our affection. They were, presumably, scoundrels. It is rather the abuse of the integrity of the legal process that concerns us, for one abuse suggests another.

During the years after Stalin's death much was heard of "the thaw"—to use the title of Ilya Ehrenburg's 1954 novel —that is, the unfreezing of Soviet life, the reduction of terror, the increased freedom to criticize, the greater encouragement of individual initiative, the relaxation of tensions. But the *long-range* problem of government in the Soviet Union is whether the Soviet leaders are willing and able to establish not merely a season, or a climate, or a policy, of freedom and initiative, but also a legal and institutional foundation which will make freedom and initiative secure from their own intervention. Until that problem is solved, the fear of a return to Stalinist terror will haunt the Soviet people, and especially the intellectuals. In research institutes and universities, as well as among educated people generally, debates rage over the "liquidation of the consequences of the cult of personality," which is Party jargon for preventing a recurrence not only of violence but also of all the rigidities that went with it. Nobody—presumably from Khrushchev on down—wants such a recurrence. But nobody can guarantee that it won't happen.

In 1957, Deputy Procurator General P. I. Kudriavtsev, responding to a series of questions on guarantees against a return to Stalinist terror, said to the author: "Do not forget that we have in the Soviet Union the dictatorship of the proletariat, and that law must serve the state authority." To the question: "Suppose the law conflicts with the interests of the state, which prevails?"—he replied, "The interests of the state." He amplified: "Compulsion may be necessary. The Special Board of the MVD was necessary in its time, in the late 'thirties. Only it was later abused. The Cheka, which Lenin introduced, was entirely justified. No revolution is bloodless—ours is the most bloodless revolution in history, far more bloodless than the French or English revolutions." I asked: "When will your revolution be over?" He replied: "We live in an age of war and revolution. The revolution goes on." And then, to make crystal clear the connection between this basic historical perspective and the law reforms we had been discussing, he said: "If it becomes necessary we will restore the old methods. But I think it will not be necessary." [44]

In addition to preserving the possibility of a return to physical terror "if it becomes necessary," Khrushchev replaced the Stalinist dualism of law and terror by a new dualism of law and social pressure: one is free from arbitrary arrest by the secret police, but one is not free from the social pressure of the "collective"—whether it be the more innocuous pressure of the collective of the neighbors in the crowded apartment houses or the less innocuous pressure of the factory, one's co-workers, or the local Party organization. The new dualism still stands in the shadow of the old.

Yet it would be a great mistake to assume that the "thaw" ended with the harsher methods adopted in 1961 and 1962. Such an assumption underestimates the importance of the legal and institutional changes which had in fact taken place. The law reforms had already counted. They had acquired a momentum which was hard to stop. A vast structure of procedures and rights had been built, and though its foundations needed to be greatly strengthened, it was not something which could easily be toppled.

THE REFORM OF SOVIET THEORY OF STATE AND LAW

Stalin's successors have denounced their former leader for the terror which he unleashed, and have declared many of the policies which he sponsored, as well as many of his theories, to be a betrayal of Leninism. They have created a new political, economic and social climate in the Soviet Union, which is far more tolerant of experimentation and of dissent. The strengthening of the legal system has played an important part in effectuating this change in the atmosphere of Soviet society. It is true that the legal system, and the political-economic-social system of which it is a part, remains Stalinist in its basic structure and outlines; but here the old French proverb is applicable in reverse—the more it stays the same, the more it changes.

In many respects the post-Stalin regime is less conservative than its predecessor. It places somewhat less theoretical emphasis upon historic continuity with the pre-revolutionary Russian tradition, upon the stability of the family, upon toleration of religion; it has sought to reduce inequalities of income and possibilities for acquiring personal wealth, and to subordinate even further (as we shall see in detail in the next chapter) the economic autonomy of producing units to the central planning authorities; it has re-emphasized the supremacy of the Party over the state and has sought to revive the "popular" and "revolutionary" aspects of Soviet law. There is something of the dynamic spirit of the early 'thirties in this—in law, something of the spirit of Pashukanis rather than of Vyshinsky, although officially Páshukanis' theories still remain in limbo.

As leader of both Party and state, Khrushchev has sought to establish his own legitimacy as well as the legitimacy of his policies by tracing their derivation to Lenin rather than to Stalin.[45] He continually attacks the dead dictator for his betrayal of truly Leninist principles. The effect of this, however, is often a return to the more volatile ideas and policies which Stalin supported in the first phase of the development of the Soviet state, prior to 1936, but which he later denounced.

Yet basically Khrushchev has introduced a third phase of development, which is different from both the first and the second phases though it builds on both. This third phase was officially termed in 1959, at the twenty-first Party Congress, "the period of expanded construction of communism" (*period razvernutogo stroitel'stva kommunizma*). Although this phrase is often translated "transition to communism," it is meant to add something to the Stalinist doctrine that socialism (achieved in 1936) is itself a stage of gradual transition to communism. (Lenin, following Marx, had said socialism *is* the first stage of communism.) Now Khrushchev says that the "full and final victory of socialism" has been achieved, and a new period of "expanded" construction will lead to the eventual attainment of communism. However, communism itself is now divided into stages. The 1961 Party Program calls for the achievement of the first stage of communism in twenty years.

From the point of view of political and legal theory, the principal difference between the present phase as defined by Khrushchev and the earlier socialist phase as defined by Stalin is that Stalin taught that before the state begins to wither away it must get stronger and stronger. Only the strongest possible state, in Stalin's view, could pave the way for ushering in the stateless society. In connection with this, Stalin also said that the class struggle becomes sharper and sharper as communism draws nearer and nearer—chiefly because of the existence of a hostile capitalist-imperialist world which will do all in its power to prevent communism from arriving. The dictatorship of the proletariat therefore always had to stand guard over the progress of the Soviet Union toward communism, although, except for Soviet people who had fallen under the evil influence of the capitalist world-outlook, there were supposedly no antagonistic classes left even under socialism.

After Stalin's death, Khrushchev denounced the doctrine of the increasing intensification of the class struggle under socialism, which he rightly called merely an excuse for repressions against those whom Stalin considered potential enemies. The 1961 Party Program states that in the Soviet Union "the dictatorship of the proletariat has ceased to be a necessity." And the state must begin now—not in the distant future—to be replaced by voluntary social co-operation; coercion must begin more and more to give way to persuasion as the proletarian dictatorship has been replaced by an "all-people's state" and as this state itself begins to turn over its functions to "social organizations."

To American ears, these doctrines sound more pleasant than the older ones, but equally difficult to take at face value. Of course it is possible theoretically to imagine a society in which there would be no need for coercion; the Christian Church has always preached such a kingdom. But to suppose that any existing political community, and especially the Soviet, is ready for such a transformation strains credulity. One is drawn inescapably to the conclusion that the doctrines, though perhaps believed in a very general sense, are primarily designed to symbolize a policy. That policy is, first, to extend the influence of the Communist Party, which is *the* "social organization" par excellence in the Soviet Union, defined as a social organization in the Constitution and also described therein as the "central core" of all other social organizations; [46] and, second, to draw into public administration more and more people, in order to strengthen the society and eliminate the shortcomings of a rigid bureaucratism.

The theoretical question of the nature and functions of law during and after the period of transition to communism is one that has exercised the ingenuity of Soviet jurists. The definition of law given by Vyshinsky in 1938,[47] which of necessity was accepted in all published legal writings thereafter, stressed three elements: the source of law in the will of the state (ruling class), the sanction for law in the coercive power of the state, and the nature of law as a body of rules. Except for its reference to class interests, this definition does not differ essentially from positivist definitions familiar to Western legal thought, although in the gloss on Vyshinsky's definition it was possible to detect strong elements of a natural-law philosophy, since in Soviet society it was assumed that law corresponded to the needs and interests of the whole people (there being no class antagonism).

Until the 22nd Party Congress it was possible for Soviet jurists to continue to repeat Vyshinsky's definition. Stalin's crimes, they said, consisted partly in his disregard of the very rules which he had been responsible for enacting, and partly in his insistence upon the enactment of some bad rules. With the end of his tyrannny, the bad rules could be replaced by good ones. And with the development of the new "people's state" and the gradual replacement of coercive sanctions by persuasion, law would become (in many of its aspects, at least) more lenient and more permissive and would help to pave the way for its own very gradual disappearance once the first stage of communism was achieved.

At the 22nd Party Congress in 1961, however, Vyshinsky was singled out for special attack and Soviet jurists were charged with being still under the influence of the cult of his (and not merely Stalin's) personality. Specifically, they were attacked for not having found a new and better definition of law to replace Vyshinsky's, which was linked with Stalin's terror.[48] After that time a series of discussions took place in which Soviet jurists debated what exactly was wrong with the definition and what should be substituted for it.[49]

Much of this debate was in terms very familiar to a Western lawyer. It was said by some that certain Stalinist laws (*zakony*) lacked the essential qualities of "legality" (*zakonnost'*) and therefore could not be called "law" (*pravo*). Examples are the laws of 1934 and 1937 establishing a special summary secret procedure for the trial of certain counterrevolutionary crimes. Others countered that "a law is a law," and the trouble with those laws was simply that they were bad laws, not that they were not law. If we deny the quality of "law" to bad laws, it was argued, a person may simply refuse to obey a law of which he does not approve.

In supporting a new definition of law which would stress "legality" as an essential element, some Soviet jurists have contended that a sharp distinction between the "is" and the "ought" is foreign to Marxism. Legal rules, they say, must be understood not merely as factual descriptions of commands or standards laid down by the state, but also as statements of goals, to be interpreted in the light of these goals. It has also been contended by some that law includes much more than commands; it may consist of administrative recommendations, for example, or of procedures for voluntary settlement of disputes by negotiation or arbitration.

The question of the nature of law bears directly, of course, upon the role it is to play in a society conceived of as moving away from institutions of coercion toward institutions of persuasion and cooperation. If those who tend toward the narrower concept of law reflected in Vyshinsky's definition win the day, it would appear that law will continue to be under the theoretical cloud of the "withering away" doctrine. If the broader concept gains the favor of the Communist Party leadership, the sharp distinction between the coercive functions of law and the cooperative nature of the ideal society will be blunted and law will be considered to have not merely a temporary but a permanent value for communist society.

The Party Program of 1961, and statements of Party leaders supporting the Program, leave this question open. The Program is warm enough in its support of law and legality during the transition period. It states:

"The further *strengthening of the socialist legal order* and the perfecting of norms of law which regulate economic-organizational and cultural-educational work and which contribute to the accomplishment of the tasks of communist construction and to the all-round flourishing of personality are very important.

"The transition to communism means the fullest extension of personal freedom and the rights of Soviet citizens. Socialism has given and has guaranteed to the working people the broadest rights and freedoms. Communism will bring the working people great new rights and opportunities.

"The Party sets the objective of enforcing strict observance of socialist legality, of eradicating all violations of the legal order, of abolishing crime and removing all its causes.

"Justice in the U.S.S.R. is exercised in full conformity to law. It is built on truly democratic foundations: election and accountability of the judges and people's assessors, the right to recall them before expiry of their term, publicity of court proceedings, and participation of social prosecutors and defenders in the work of the courts, with the courts and investigating and prosecuting bodies strictly observing legality and all procedural norms. The democratic foundations of justice will be developed and improved."

Yet even this endorsement of law and legality contains an inherent ambiguity. For the development of the "democratic foundations" of justice—by which is meant principally the increase in the role of social organizations (*e.g.,* through members who are deputized to appear in criminal cases alongside the regular prosecutor and defense counsel as "social" prosecutors and "social" defenders)—is a threat to the independence of the courts.

Moreover, in proclaiming the doctrine of the gradual transformation of "socialist statehood" into "communist self-administration," the Party Program leaves open the question of the role of law once communism is achieved. Khrushchev, in reporting on the Party Program at the 22nd Party Congress, stated that "the fact that the dictatorship of the proletariat has ceased to be necessary in no way means any weakening of the social order and legality. . . . Law, freedom, honor and the dignity of Soviet man will be strictly protected by society and the state." But neither he nor the Party Program indicates what will happen to law when the state disappears. However academic such a question may appear, it has a strong bearing on the attitudes of Soviet people—both leaders and led—toward the absolute value of law. If law is defined as norms enacted by the state and enforced by the coercive sanctions of the state, it is destined, like the state, to find its way ultimately into the "museum of antiquities" (to use Engels' phrase). If, however, law is defined as an institutional process of resolution of conflicts, based on general standards objectively applied—a definition which many Americans would endorse and toward which some Soviets are groping— then it is not inconsistent with the "unified, generally recognized rules of communist social life," observance of which will become the "inner need and habit of all people" under communism, according to the Party Program.

If one compares the controversy of the early 1960's over the role of law in Soviet society with that which

raged in the mid-1930's, one is struck by certain similarities and some very sharp differences. In both cases,
there was a search for a single orthodox theory of law, a
single orthodox definition of its origin and destiny, its
nature and functions. In both cases there was an effort to
found such a theory on Marxism-Leninism, and by the
same token to make it an instrument for the building of a
certain type of political-economic-social system as well as
for justifying the existing regime. Although the participants
in the debates were for the most part law professors and
legal scholars, they were acting—in the 1960's as in the
mid-1930's—under general instructions of the leaders of
the Communist Party and were highly conscious of the immediate political implications of every word which they
uttered. The clash of ideas was not conceived primarily as
a means of discovering truth; it was rather like a legislative
debate over the enactment of a statute, with the parties
grouped in various blocs, than like an academic debate
about the nature of social reality.

However, the spirit of the later debate was one of far
greater moderation than that of the earlier one. There was
no Vyshinsky to dominate it, and no Stalin in the background. Those who were publicly attacked for heresy did
not, as before, expect to disappear to Siberia, or worse.
Even Vyshinsky, though denounced, was not made the subject of ridiculous accusations of being a traitor, "wrecker,"
and capitalist agent—as Pashukanis, Krylenko and others
were in the 1930's.

Moreover, the style of the debate in the 1960's was more
rational. There was much less reliance on phrases and texts
taken from Marx, Lenin and their political successors. The
chanting of the Marxist liturgy could still be heard, but it
did not dominate as it had earlier. Indeed, one could read
whole articles on legal theory which hardly referred to
Marxist-Leninist texts, although it was still unthinkable that
anyone would propose an explicitly anti-Marxist or anti-
Leninist—or, indeed, an explicitly *non*-Marxist, or *non*-
Leninist concept.

Soviet jurists, like the Soviet leaders themselves, are

striving to create the impression that they have eliminated the Stalinist distortions of Leninist theory and have returned to the true teachings of their master. No doubt many of them think of themselves as true Leninists. Yet their legal theory is at best a distant reflection of Leninism, since Lenin had no developed legal theory. For Lenin, as we have seen, law was accepted as a necessary evil during the temporary period of proletarian dictatorship which preceded, in his view, the imminent advent of classless socialism. If one seeks a historical analogy, one may point to the eschatological world-view (or end-of-the-world-view) of St. Paul; the Roman Catholic Church did ultimately build on Pauline passages reflecting a natural-law theory, and the Protestant Reformation subsequently sought to eliminate what the Reformers thought to be Roman Catholic distortions of Pauline thought. There was both a continuity and a discontinuity between the doctrines of St. Paul, St. Thomas Aquinas and Martin Luther. In a sense, Khrushchev appears as a Soviet Reformer, going back to the original Leninist texts to reinterpret them against his predecessor. But the Leninist texts will not support the actual developments in Soviet law, which are a response to political, economic and social needs that Lenin could not possibly visualize. If we may carry the historical analogy one step further, we may compare the relationship between Soviet law and Khrushchev's Leninism to the relationship between German law in the 16th century and Luther's Paulinism. There is, of course, a relationship; but it is a relationship in terms of outlook and approach and attitude, not a relationship in terms of theory.

We must seek the operative theory of Soviet law, therefore, not in the Leninist texts which Soviet jurists cite, but in the evolution of the law itself. In the first two chapters we have taken a general view of that evolution over the first four-and-a-half decades. In the next chapter we shall focus particularly on the manner in which Soviet legal development has responded to the problems posed by the establishment of a planned economy.

Chapter Three

SOVIET ECONOMIC LAW

THE SOCIALIST MOVEMENT of the nineteenth century reacted against the individualistic conceptions of law and
economics which had dominated the thinking of the late
eighteenth century and which had found concrete expression in the French Revolution of 1789. Basic to the French
Revolution was the idea that the individual is at the center
of things, that it is he who should determine what is in
his own best interest, and that government is essentially a
means of minimizing frictions between conflicting individual interests and thereby of providing an opportunity for
the free development by each of his own capacities. In law
and economics this was reflected in the exaltation of rights
of private property and private contract. Not only Marx
and Engels, but other socialist thinkers of the nineteenth
century as well, started out by rejecting the thesis that the
pursuit of individual self-interest leads to social harmony.
Thinking in the same terms as the exponents of nineteenth-
century liberalism, they reached the opposite conclusions.
The individual, they said, is a product of society; it is
society which should determine what is in the interests of
its members; social life should be so organized as to prevent the oppression of the poor by the rich. The socialists

therefore minimized rights of private property and contract. They proposed the abolition of the profits of the middleman or entrepreneur, and exalted public ownership of the means of production. The economy, in their view, was not something to be left to the will of private individuals; it was rather something to be consciously regulated and controlled by the public authority.

With all the changes in the Soviet social system since 1917, the fundamental socialist principle of public ownership and control of the basic factors of production has been preserved intact. Economic life is essentially public, not private, in character. As Lenin instructed the compilers of the Civil Code in 1922, "Everything pertaining to the economy is a matter of public and not private law." On the other hand, Soviet experience since 1917 has demonstrated the total inadequacy, in itself, of the principle of public ownership. Public ownership is a negative formula; it means the absence of private ownership—and no more. What the state owns, nobody owns. Everybody's business is nobody's business. The fundamental economic and legal questions still remain. How is the economy to be mobilized? Who is to have the possession, use, and disposition of the property now declared to be in the exclusive ownership of the people as a whole (that is, of nobody)?

As Leon Trotsky later wrote in *The Revolution Betrayed:* "A revolution in the forms of ownership does not solve the problem of socialism but only raises it!"

To the "problem of socialism" in this sense, Soviet experience has given an answer quite different from that anticipated by the nineteenth-century socialists, including Marx and Engels. That answer, in a word, is Planning. As the distinguished English economist Alfred Pigou pointed out in 1937, Soviet developments since 1917 have caused European economists to give a new definition of socialism, adding to the older criteria of public ownership and no profits for middlemen the new criterion of a national economic plan for the community as a whole.

By planning, in this context, is meant not merely the projection of future economic growth but the establishment of a governmental machinery for detailed allocation of the entire nation's resources according to a unified, centrally determined program. Today it is often taken for granted that state ownership of the means of production presupposes the establishment of such a machinery. The earlier socialists, however, made no such assumption.

The concept of national economic planning is not to be found in the works of Marx and Engels. The nearest they came to it was in Engels' idea that the "government of persons" would be replaced by the "administration of things" and the "direction of the processes of production." This was more a political than an economic concept, however, since it had reference primarily to the absence of coercion. Nor is administration and direction the same thing as planning, for planning in the Soviet sense involves not the mere establishment of limits and controls by administrative boards, or the licensing of nationalized enterprises to individuals or boards, but state management and operation of economic units under an all-embracing centralized program of production and distribution. In a few scattered sentences in *Das Kapital* Marx refers to a time when there will be "conscious and prearranged control of production by society," and to the necessity for "keeping accounts" of economic factors after the abolition of the capitalist mode of production; and the *Communist Manifesto* mentions as one of the first steps which a proletarian government would undertake "the improvement of the soil generally in accordance with a common plan." It was left to actual Soviet experience, however, to develop the modern theory and practice of a planned economy. Undoubtedly the Marxist emphasis on economic collectivism contributed to this development; also, as we shall see later, Russian history provided an important background for it; in addition, the military experience of World War I, and particularly the lesson in efficiency offered by the German General Staff, gave a practical example of military planning which was consciously carried over by the Bolsheviks to the economic sphere, the State Planning Commission being referred to at its inception in 1921 as an Economic General Staff.

With the introduction in 1928 of a system of national economic planning in the Soviet Union, the nineteenth-century antithesis of socialism and capitalism (or socialism and individualism) was given a new intensity. Planning seemed to be not merely a third criterion of socialism, supplementary to public ownership of the means of production and abolition of the entrepreneurial functions, but rather the only criterion. Planning, it was thought, meant ultimately the end of *all* ownership, including state ownership, and the introduction of a new social order in which the very categories state, ownership, law, would disappear. "The word property has no passport to cross the frontiers of the collectivist state," wrote Walton Hamilton in 1934.[1]

In 1936, however, property was again admitted to full citizenship. Not only "state ownership" but also "personal ownership" and "social ownership" (that is, ownership by collective farms and coöperative organizations) were restored to dignity. Moreover, the property and contract rights of state economic enterprises were greatly enlarged, though they were still more restricted than under the NEP. Economic life remained essentially public in character, but the public interest itself required a considerable decentralization of operations and a considerable extension of personal initiative and reward. A fusion of public and private law took place. These developments of the period 1937 to 1953 became even more accentuated after Stalin's death.

This means that the dualism of socialism and capitalism (or socialism and individualism) has become greatly complicated in the Soviet economic and legal system. Both in practice and in theory there has been, over the past twenty-five years, an attempt to create an equilibrium between the integration of the whole and the autonomy of the parts, between the interests of society and the interests of personality, between the dynamics of change and the stability of continuity.

PLAN AND LAW

One may speak of this equilibrium, as Soviet economists and jurists have spoken of it, in terms of the interdependence of Plan and Law. Planning is the integrating, social, dynamic element; legality is the decentralizing, personal, stabilizing element. Of course the concepts "plan" and "law" overlap. Nevertheless the distinction between them makes sense. Plan is that aspect of the social process which is concerned with the maximum utilization of institutions and resources from the point of view of economic development; law is that aspect of the social process which is concerned with the structuring and enforcing of social policy (plan) in terms of the rights and duties arising therefrom.

The reconciliation of these interdependent but conflicting functions of Plan and Law—that is, the establishment of an institutional and legal framework which will enable planning to work—has been one of the major problems confronting the Soviet leadership. The difficulties encountered in solving this problem are well illustrated by a comparison of the structure of the Soviet system of industrial planning prior to Stalin's death with that which has emerged from the Khrushchev reforms beginning in 1957.

From the late 1930's to 1957, Soviet industry was divided principally along "branch" as contrasted with "territorial" lines. Separate industrial ministries were responsible for particular branches of the economy throughout the entire country. These ministries were represented in the U.S.S.R. Council of Ministers, which had final responsibility for making and executing the national economic plan. The State Planning Commission (Gosplan), which drafted the five-year, annual and quarterly plans for the economy as a whole, was a body of technical experts responsible to the economic ministries of the Council of Ministers. Thus the procedure for promulgating and implementing the national economic plan was ultimately in the hands not of the technical experts but of responsible state officials who acted within the limitations of a definite administrative order.

Of the forty-eight members of the Council of Ministers in 1950, thirty-eight were heads of particular industries (oil, iron and steel, chemicals, aircraft, shipbuilding, munitions, machine building, and so forth), or of systems of communications (railways, maritime fleet, post, telegraph and telephone), or of spheres of economic activity such as foreign trade, internal trade, and finance. Other (noneconomic) ministries included those of Internal Affairs, State Security, Armed Forces, Higher Education, Public Health, Foreign Affairs, Justice. Each of the then sixteen constituent republics of the U.S.S.R. also had a council of ministers, constituted similarly to the All-Union Council and subordinate to it.

An economic ministry was divided into chief administrations (*glavki*) for subindustries or for areas or for both, and certain glavki were further subdivided into trusts.[2] A typical ministry, *glavk*, or trust contained departments of planning, finance, procurement and sale, construction, manpower, and accounting. The general directives and plans of the Council of Ministers and its administrative organs were implemented by more specific directives and plans of ministries, glavki, and trusts, allocating production or consumption to individual enterprises, regulating interrelationships among enterprises jointly producing certain products, and issuing general plans of operations.

The individual factory, plant, or economic enterprise was owned by the state and calculated as part of the assets of the ministry to which it belonged. Its director was directly subordinate to the minister, in the case of the largest enterprises, or to the head of the glavk or trust (who in turn was subordinate to the minister). Thus the Soviet manager or director was—and is—a state official, a member of the all-embracing political-economic hierarchy. His task is to operate a given portion of state property in accordance with the directives and plans issued by superior state economic organs.

However, even in Stalin's day these directives and plans did not spring full-blown from the dictator's brow, nor were they self-executing once they were declared. Plans generally involved the presentation of applications by economic enterprises and other operative organizations concerning their requirements for the coming year, together with statements of their own plans of operations. These applications and statements, which were based on the individual plans drawn up by the planning sections of the individual enterprises and organizations, were presented to superior organs (trusts, glavki, ministries), which corrected and coördinated them and then submitted them to Gosplan. In this way applications and statements moved up step by step from the immediate operative organizations, the producing and consuming plants, to the highest regulating and planning organs. The plans drawn up by Gosplan were then returned to the particular ministry or administrative organ concerned, and thence transmitted, in the form of "planned tasks," down through the glavki and trusts to the operative units. On the basis of the draft plan of Gosplan, a ministry could make its own plan, the two different plans being submitted to the Council of Ministers for examination, coördination, and ratification. It was the Council of Ministers (or an economic committee thereof) and the individual ministries, not Gosplan, which issued the plans.

The plans could be very general, leaving the particular decisions to be made by the lower economic links, or they could be very detailed. In any case, planning involves a great deal more than drawing up blueprints. The Plan, in Stalin's words, is not merely a program but is rather a "creative process," embracing all aspects of production and distribution; it is "a living reality." Planning is not finished until the plans are executed, and increasingly the executors of the plan have been given responsibility and discretion in making the operational decisions.

The period prior to 1952 witnessed an extraordinary multiplication of industrial ministries. In 1930 there were three. In 1935 there were six. From 1936 they increased rapidly from year to year until 1948 when about ten were abolished, leaving 38 economic ministries represented in the U.S.S.R. Council of Ministers. In 1952 there were 40. In addition there were approximately 100 republican economic ministries. At the same time the number of glavki within the individual ministries increased. This process of multiplication went hand in hand with the abandonment of the earlier idea of total economic control by Gosplan in Moscow—an idea which was never actually put into practice, but which nevertheless had a strong influence on practice during the First and Second Five-Year Plans.

Four years after Stalin's death his successors substantially altered the system of planned economy which had developed in the last fifteen years of his rule. In 1957 most of the industrial ministries were abolished. Their planning and coordinating functions were turned over to Gosplan; their operational functions were divided among approximately 100 regional economic councils, each of which administered the various industries within its territorial jurisdiction. Although many Western observers spoke of this reorganization as a decentralization of industry, it had in fact both decentralizing and centralizing effects. The operational production unit, the enterprise, was made subordinate to a regional authority controlling many branches of industry, instead of to a ministry with headquarters in Moscow which controlled a single industry throughout the country. The individual enterprise was thus given more leeway in its local operations; it did not have to go to Moscow for permission to procure raw materials produced by a plant which might be across the street but which formerly was subordinate to a different ministry. But the planning decisions, and power to allocate permits to procure goods and materials, which previously had been conducted by the various organizations which had executive responsibility for their implementation, namely, the ministries and their subordinate chief administrations (glavki), were now transferred to the jurisdiction of Gosplan. Although the republican organizations of Gosplan were also given increased powers, in fact it was the U.S.S.R. Gosplan in Moscow which, under the 1957 reorganization, made the important decisions both as to production and as to distribution.

The "territorial" principle of industrial administration

was, however, not fully carried out. The regional economic councils were divided into "branch administrations" and "functional administrations." The branch administrations are the former ministerial glavki, each charged with the supervision of enterprises of a particular industry within the region. The functional administrations are charged with carrying out tasks which cut across industrial lines. Thus in the City of Moscow regional economic council there were in 1960 about twenty-five members of the council itself, who governed fourteen branch administrations and ten functional administrations. Branch administrations existed for the automotive, machine-building, furniture-making, metallurgical, shoe and leather, textile, chemical, electrical and other industries. The functional administrations included: economic, production, technical, material and technical supply, internal relations, capital construction, personnel and educational institutions, and others. The branch administration runs its subordinate enterprises in much the same way that the former ministerial glavk ran its enterprises. It issues plans to them, appoints their officers, and has the right to redistribute raw materials, equipment, profits and superfluous working capital among them. Though subordinate to the regional economic council, the branch administration tends to protect the interests of its own industry and to look to its corresponding industrial committee in Gosplan for support in so doing.

The change from the ministerial-branch principle of economic administration to the Gosplan-territorial principle (except for a few industries which were left under ministerial control) illustrates some of the basic dilemmas of the Soviet planned economy. Under the ministerial system, not only each enterprise but each industrial ministry had a direct interest in its own success and a direct responsibility for its own plans and operations. However, the country was too big to endure a division into only 40 or 50 basic industrial units, embracing (as was the case in 1957) 200,000 enterprises and 100,000 construction projects. Local resources could not be used rationally when local organizations wishing to use them had to apply to their administrative superiors in Moscow to do so. In the first place, as one Soviet commentary stated in 1957, "the remoteness and isolation of the ministries from their enterprises led to . . . paper-bureaucratic methods of management." In other words, the enterprises often had to wade through masses of red tape to get permission from their ministries to do the simplest things. In the second place, ministries (and their subordinate enterprises) tended to protect their own interests at the expense of the economy as a whole. They hoarded goods that were in short supply and engaged in vertical integration in order to overcome bottlenecks of distribution. To take a typical example, the Odessa Bread Trust produced its own bakers' uniforms and constructed its own workshops.[2a] To take an extreme example, the Ministry of Machine Tool Production controlled only 55 out of a total of 171 plants primarily making machine tools; the rest were scattered among eighteen other ministries. Finally, such duplication led to enormously inflated staffs of administrators.

The 1957 reorganization of industry succeeded to a considerable extent in overcoming many of the defects of the ministerial system of administration. The individual enterprises were brought much closer geographically to their superior organizations. Within a single region trade among the various enterprises was freed from many of the earlier "departmental" obstacles. And perhaps as important as any other achievement of the reorganization was the reduction in staff which it permitted. A 1960 Soviet statistical handbook reports that the number of administrative personnel in the national economy was reduced from 14 per cent of the total number of workers and employees on January 1, 1954, to 9.7 per cent on September 1, 1959—a reduction of over 30 per cent!

Yet a heavy price was paid for these improvements, in that the planning and allocating of production and distribution was taken away from the heads of industries, the ministers and their subordinates, and given over to Gosplan. Gosplan's numerous committees for the various branches of industry, though consisting generally of the same people who previously had worked in the planning departments of the ministries, were now even more remote from the operating units, the enterprises; although they had administrative functions—namely, the granting of permits to enterprises for procurement of goods—they were now immediately responsible to Gosplan itself, not to administrative heads of industries. The three-link system of economic administration which formerly predominated—ministry-glavk-enterprise—gave way (in fact though not in theory) to a four-link system—Gosplan-regional economic council-branch administration-enterprise. Together with the difficulties attendant upon the increased centralization of allocation of procurement permits, the 1957 reorganization produced opposite difficulties connected with the establishment of autonomous economic regions. "Localism"—that is, the tendency of a region to pursue, so far as it could, an autarchic policy, satisfying its own needs before supplying other regions—became a critical problem, to which the Soviet leaders responded by creating new super-regions and republican economic councils to co-ordinate the regional councils created in 1957 and by merging, at the end of 1962, the 100-odd regional councils into approximately 40. The difficulties both of centralism and localism will become more apparent in our subsequent discussion of corporation, property and contract law.

What has been said so far, however, should suffice to dispel the popular image of the Soviet planned economy as an economy run by pushbutton from Moscow. This image is bolstered by Soviet scholarship and by Soviet propaganda, both of which stress that it is the state which manages the economy, through the national economic plan, in the interests of the whole people (as those interests are conceived by the Communist Party and declared through its top leadership). The image is also bolstered by much Western scholarship, which speaks of the Soviet economy as a "command economy." The picture presented is analogous to that of a military organization in which the General Staff plans the overall operations, giving orders to commanders who pass them on down the line, with ever fuller detail, until they reach the platoon commander who shouts to his men, "Ready, Aim, Fire!"

This image disregards the elementary requirements of the administrative and legal structure which is necessary to make a planned economy work. Indeed, too often an economic system is thought of as existing apart from its institutional and legal structure. A market economy such as ours could not exist without a law of corporations which limits the liability of investors, a law of credit which facilitates expansion on the basis of present estimates of future potentialities, a law of contracts which gives economic value to bargained promises. Similarly, a planned economy cannot operate without a body of administrative law which assigns control over various economic functions to various state organizations; a body of planning law which establishes procedures not only for promulgating but also for implementing plans; a law of state enterprises which gives producing units the power to administer their capital and labor and to procure and dispose of goods and materials; a financial law which maintains the stability of the monetary unit so that the value of performance can be measured and appropriate rewards granted for efficiency; and a law of property and contract which enables the operators of the economy to respond rationally and responsibly to the intentions of the planners. It is these and related aspects of Soviet law which are embraced in the expression "Soviet economic law."

From 1959 to 1961 many leading Soviet jurists proposed that economic law—in the above sense—be codified as a special branch of the Soviet legal system. Others opposed this proposal, and a sharp debate was carried on concerning it. The proponents argued that there should be, in addition to the Civil Code, which would deal with the personal rights of citizens (including their personal rights of property and contract), a Code of Economic Law, which would deal with the legal relations of state economic organizations with each other. It was said, for example, that the contract of delivery (*dogovor postavki*) between two state enterprises, being governed by plan (as well as by the intention of the parties), is essentially different from "civil-law" contracts such as the contract of rent of an apartment or the contract between an author and a state publishing enterprise or the contract of sale of a house by one citizen to another. Their opponents, on the other hand, said that the planning and administrative-law aspects of the procurement and supply of goods by state enterprises could be separated analytically from the contract-law elements, and that the administrative-law elements must be governed by general principles of administrative law and the contract-law elements by general principles of contract law.[3] The proponents of a separate body of economic law lost the argument in December, 1961, when the new Fundamental Principles of Civil Law were adopted; these included a special chapter on the contract of delivery, with a few principles related specially to that type of contract, but the general principles of civil law were made applicable to it as to other types.

The debate contained overtones of the theory of the early 1930's that civil law would be swallowed up in economic law. The proponents of a Code of Economic Law did not go so far as to revive this theory. Nevertheless, their defeat was a reaffirmation of the idea that legal regulation of the economy, and particularly of industry, cannot be divorced from the legal regulation of society as a whole. Plan is not the same thing as Law, nor is the law which is associated with planning the same thing as the law which is associated with personal relations among Soviet citizens; but Plan and Law are interdependent, and economic law—the law of the planned economy—must be integrated into the general body of Soviet law. So, at least, it was decided in the mid-1930's and so it was decided once again in 1961.

Thus it is impossible to discuss Soviet economic law without discussing the rights and duties of enterprises as juridical persons, property law, contract law, and other traditional branches of what in some Western countries is called "private law." The granting of juridical personality and of property and contract rights to Soviet state economic enterprises is a clear concession to non-socialist realities. At the same time, the interdependence of Law and Plan has given a new socialist cast to these traditional institutions.

THE JURIDICAL PERSONALITY
OF THE STATE ECONOMIC ENTERPRISE

Basic to the relationship between Plan and Law is the recognition that planning itself requires what the Soviets call "economic accountability" (*khozraschet*), by which they mean the principle that each enterprise should pay its own way and should respond for its liabilities with its assets. "The essential feature of the Soviet *khozraschet* system," wrote M. I. Bogolepov, a leading Soviet expert on finance, in the late 'thirties, "is the combination of the method of the balance sheet and the method of the plan." The method of the balance sheet has in fact become the foundation of the method of the plan. "Accounting figures form the point of departure for every kind of plan." [4] And the plan not only starts from the balance sheet; it also ends with it. It is recognized that effective planning of an integrated national economy is not possible unless the integrity and responsibility of the individual links in the economy are maintained.

The balance sheet of the Soviet state economic enterprise is expressive of the attempted synthesis of public control and individual initiative. "Logically," conceded the same author, writing in 1945, "[capital accumulation] could be entirely contributed to the Exchequer, for the State is the owner of industry. In actual fact, however, the process is much more complicated. This is necessitated by the following considerations: the State seeks to create among the managers and workers of its establishments a direct interest in the results of their efforts. State-owned establishments are run as juridically independent economic units. Each establishment, having received from the State for its exclusive use both equipment and capital, proceeds to operate on its own, with its own financial accounting, bank account, credit facilities, and, finally, with the right to make a profit. In the distribution of this profit the establishment considers its own requirements, contributes a definite sum to the workers' welfare, and provides bonuses for good workers." [5]

Although economic accountability (*khozraschet*) is a concept which dates from the NEP period, when state enterprises were competing with private business, it lost its reality in the period of the First and Second Five-Year Plans, when the drive was for production almost regardless of cost. At that time virtually all state enterprises were financed by the state treasury out of the national budget; if they fulfilled their plan for gross output they did not have to worry about excessive financial expenditures since (as they said) "the budget will refund." The critical change here, as in so many other aspects of Soviet institutional development, was in 1936, when it was ordered that an end be put to state subsidies of enterprises.[6] Although there were numerous exceptions to this rule, the principle it established has prevailed: first, that each economic enterprise should be profitable in the sense that the monetary value of its operations should exceed that of its expenditures, and second, that each enterprise must be financially responsible for its obligations. The term "accountability" (which is often misleadingly translated "accounting") has not only an economic but also a legal dimension. Bogolepov brings this out in the passages quoted above. Operating on a business basis means being "juridically independent."

The Soviet state economic enterprise has been considered a juridical person since the mid-1930's and is so characterized in the 1961 Fundamental Principles of Civil Law. Although the term "corporation" is eschewed, it is in many respects like government corporations in some Western European countries and like those government corporations in the United States which carry on economic activities with relative financial autonomy.[7] Operating without a joint stock and as an agency of the state, it obtains, through its legal form, unity in its internal structure and autonomy in its dealings with others. It is peculiarly adapted to managerial control and to commercial methods. It has greater scope for flexibility than would be possible if it were a regular government department.

The Soviet state economic enterprise has a charter which declares the nature and amount of its basic capital (buildings, machinery, tools and productive equipment) and of its working capital (stocks of raw materials, fuel, goods, cash, bank credit). It leases land from the local municipal authorities under an Act of Perpetual Use. The director of the enterprise has broad powers to make management decisions concerning the use of basic and working capital as well as concerning the regulation of labor within the enterprise. Although "Production Conferences" of union officials, leading workers and technicians have been given certain powers with respect to management since 1955, and especially since 1958, the principle of "one man control" (*edinonachalie*) by the director has not been substantially modified.

While the planned tasks for the enterprise are set by higher planning organizations in the annual plan, the director has considerable influence on the making and interpretation of this plan. Under the principle of "planning from below," the enterprise initially presents its own draft plan to its superior agencies; thus the final plan which it receives is a corrected version of its own draft. Within the final plan, the director has a large measure of control over the internal organization of the plan. He may alter production methods; provided there is no interference with plan fulfillment, he may contract to manufacture parts or other items for other state enterprises; he may set the prices for certain categories of items, though not for his basic products.

Investment decisions by enterprise directors are severely limited by approved plans. However, even in this respect there is some leeway, in that twenty per cent of the Enterprise Fund must be spent on plant modernization. The Enterprise Fund (formerly called the Director's Fund) consists of a percentage of planned profits ranging from one to six per cent and of profit beyond plan ranging from 30 to 60 per cent. Out of this fund also come individual bonuses to workers and employees (including the director himself) and investment in workers' housing and recreational facilities. Consent of the union must be obtained for all expenditures from the Enterprise Fund (see Chapter 15).

The director also has the initiative in hiring, firing, promoting, demoting and assigning workers, although his powers in these respects are limited by labor laws. While wage scales and the amount available for payrolls are set by higher planning authorities, the director may adjust the piece-rates according to the special conditions in the plant (quality of the machinery, *etc.*). This right gives him a large freedom to maneuver. He may also use extra working capital derived from profits to hire extra workers. Indeed, the enterprise may employ its working capital within a given year (in the words of a Soviet writer) "in any way it deems fit for the fulfillment of its plan; it may sell it, pledge it, or acquire other working capital; no special sanction from higher authorities is required for such transactions."

The enterprise's unity in its internal structure is subject to heavy controls from its superior organizations. The director is appointed by the chief of the appropriate branch administration of the regional economic council, and these organizations are in turn subordinate to higher authorities. The system is strictly hierarchical, with Communist Party organs exercising supervision at various points. Moreover, indicators of success of enterprise operations are determined by all-union decrees, and on the basis of these indicators bonuses (which form a substantial part of the income of the director and other managerial personnel) are awarded. The large number of indicators of plan fulfillment (a 1954 decree listed nine, including output in quantitative and in monetary terms, economy in use of raw materials and equipment, labor productivity, reduction of cost of production, balance of income and expenses, and others)—imposes a substantial weight upon the director and the enterprise as a whole.

Yet the very multiplicity of indicators permits a good deal of juggling by the director in adapting enterprise activities to the desire for bonuses. The "cult of gross output," which some Western economists have attributed to the Soviet system, is tempered by the profit motive ("balance of income and expenses"). Whatever the relative importance of profits among the success indicators, there is no doubt that they are taken seriously by Soviet enterprise directors. A 1959 decree makes reduction of costs (*sebestoimost'*)—which under the Soviet system is the equivalent of profits—the chief basis for the awarding of bonuses to managerial personnel.[8]

The corporate form of the Soviet state economic enterprise has given it a different character from that of an administrative agency. The director of the enterprise is in one sense like a Western civil servant, but in another sense he is like a Western business executive. He measures his success not by the welfare of the economy or the polity as a whole, but by the economic achievement of his enterprise. He often earns more than the administrative officials who control many aspects of his operations. He often has much more freedom of maneuver within his enterprise than even a high official of a ministry.

In addition to internal unity, the juridical personality of the Soviet state economic enterprise gives it autonomy in its relations with other enterprises. By definition, juridical personality includes the capacity to have property and contract rights and to sue and be sued. The property and contract rights of economic enterprises have proved to be as essential to the Soviet planned economy as they are to traditional market economies.

PROPERTY AND CONTRACT

Article 6 of the Soviet Constitution states: "The land, its natural deposits, waters, forests, mills, factories, mines, rail, water and air transport, banks, post, telegraph and telephones, large state-organized agricultural enterprises (state farms, machine and tractor stations, and the like) as well as municipal enterprises and the bulk of the dwelling houses in the cities and industrial localities comprise state ownership, that is, belong to the whole people."

The effect of Article 6 is to remove from private commerce that property in which the "whole people" has a vital interest. Only by collective action, through the organs of the state, may such property be possessed, utilized, and disposed of, and only its administration, not its ownership, may be thereby affected. For ownership is in the state alone, and not in any of its organs.

Ownership is defined in Soviet law, as in European law generally, as including the right of possession, use, and disposition of the thing which is owned. What the state owns it has the right to possess, use, and dispose of. But what a state economic enterprise possesses, uses, and disposes of —it does not own! May one speak, then, of a "right" of possession, use, and disposition in the state economic enterprise? Or does not the enterprise merely exercise certain economic-administrative functions delegated to it by the state?

How are we to test the difference between a right and a function? According to Duguit and other sociologically minded jurists, a right is defined by its social function. The theory of Soviet jurisprudence under Pashukanis was somewhat similar: rights were considered to be fictions reflecting a market economy, and under planning they were replaced by economic-administrative functions. The predominant Soviet theory since 1936, however, has been that rights really do exist, and, in particular, that Soviet economic organs have not merely the functions but also the rights of possession, use, and disposition of the property assigned to them. Yet they do not own that property. Their property rights are derived not from ownership but from "operative administration"; they are derived, that is, from economic-administrative functions. They are nevertheless rights.[9]

The 1961 Fundamental Principles of Civil Law carefully avoid the word "ownership" in describing the rights of state organizations in property which is "secured" to them. Yet their rights of possession, use and disposition of such property, and their cperative administration over it, are expressly reaffirmed. It cannot be said that enterprises exercising such rights are doing so as agents of the owner, for the state is expressly declared to be not legally responsible for their acts, nor can a regional economic council (or ministry) be sued for the debts of a subordinate enterprise. The absence of enterprise ownership is perhaps to be understood as a symbol of the fact that its "administrative" rights in land, buildings, equipment, goods, and money are strongly conditioned by plans and directives of its superior organs. Moreover its rights are shared by those organs: a superior regional economic council (or ministry) may order an enterprise to dispose of its working capital in a particular way, and it may even wind up the enterprise, in which case the basic capital of the enterprise reverts to the regional economic council (or ministry) and the working capital is used to pay the enterprise's debts. Thus rights of possession, use, and disposition are only a part of a total process of production and distribution carried on under plan.

It is the fact that the property rights of a state economic enterprise are conditioned by plan that gives them their socialist character. In adopting the Roman law categories of *jus possidendi, jus utendi,* and *jus disponendi,* and divorcing them from the Roman *dominium,* Soviet lawmakers have made it clear that these property rights (in socialist property, at least) exist not to protect ownership but rather to protect and direct the *administration* of the property in behalf of the socialist economy. Thus the contract of delivery between two state economic enterprises is explained in property law as the transfer of state property from the administration of one state organ to the administration of another state organ.

Administration in the Soviet sense is not merely direction or supervision, but involves all aspects of control, including the realization of that control. It is thus something less than ownership, but something more than giving orders. The Russian word for it, *upravlenie,* has the connotation of government; the root *prav* is the same as that in *pravo,* meaning law. A regional economic council or ministry actively supervises the industrial establishments subordinate to it. The economic units to which it delegates "immediate operative administration" derive their property rights from that administration.

In an important sense the property administered by a Soviet state enterprise is not "owned" at all. The term "ownership" does not adequately describe the legal rights either of the state or of the enterprise in the plant, equipment, goods and money which the state has turned over to the enterprise to administer. Various state agencies retain the power to remove such property from the administration of the enterprise. Yet while it is in the enterprise's administration, the enterprise has the right of exclusive disposal of it. The enterprise may, for example, use its working capital as it wishes; but at the end of the annual planning period, the higher authorities may take it away. The enterprise's property rights are temporary; yet while they exist they are complete.

The contract of delivery (*dogovor postavki*).[10]—The fact that administration, and not ownership, is involved in the property relations between a state economic enterprise and its superior economic and administrative organs, as well as in the contract relations between one enterprise and another, makes those relations no less serious from the point of view of the rights of the parties. The proof of this is in the vast amount of litigation of claims against each other by state economic enterprises—to which we shall turn in the next section. On the other hand, the absence of the concept of enterprise ownership as such, and more particularly the system of national economic planning which has been developed to give content to the abstract concept of state ownership, have given a different meaning to the property and contract rights of Soviet state enterprises from that which the same terms have in other systems of law and economy. This becomes clear from an analysis of the role of the Soviet contract for the delivery of goods within the system of planning of distribution.

Here it is necessary once again to compare the system which prevailed prior to the industrial reorganization of 1957 with the developments from 1957 to 1962.

Prior to 1957, the economic ministries of the U.S.S.R. Council of Ministers, on the basis of the annual national economic plan worked out by Gosplan, issued to each other allocations (called *fondy,* or "funds") of goods and materials. If, for example, the Ministry of Coal was supposed to produce 150 million tons of coal in a given year, it would issue to the Ministry of Ferrous Metals, the Ministry of Light Industry, and all the other ministries which had need thereof, "funds" of coal in varying amounts, depending on their planned requirements and within the total planned output of 150 million tons. The recipient of a fund, which in essence constituted a right to a certain amount of the product, would then distribute it to its subordinate chief administrations (glavki), which in turn would distribute procurement permits (*nariady*) to the subordinate enterprises within their respective jurisdictions. On the basis of a *nariad,* the enterprise requiring goods or materials would approach a producing enterprise with a proposal to enter into a contract for delivery of the particular amount of the particular goods (in our example, coal) over a particular period of time (usually a year).

Not all goods, however, were "funded" goods. Those less critical for the economy, or less easily distributed by central authorities, were either "centrally planned" goods, whose distribution was determined by the producer ministries (rather than by the Council of Ministers through Gosplan), or else "decentrally planned" goods, whose distribution was determined by contract between the producer and consumer glavki or enterprises. Funded goods in the early 1950's included about 1,600 products (such as coal, oil, chemicals, metals, and the like, and also meat, milk, grain, bread sold by bakeries to wholesalers and retailers, and many other types of goods); centrally planned goods included over 5,000 less important items (such as steel tape for packing, certain types of bolts and rivets, etc.); decentrally planned goods consisted chiefly of products of local industry locally consumed (such as certain types of building materials, various household items, and the like).

Before 1936 contracts of delivery of funded and planned

goods tended to be assimilated almost entirely to plans of distribution issued by higher authorities. The higher economic organs entered into so-called general contracts, in execution of which the lower links concluded so-called local contracts. The general contract determined which of the subordinate enterprises should conclude local contracts with each other and fixed the most important terms of those contracts. Before receiving a copy of the general contract, the parties could not conclude a local contract.

In regard to the distribution of industrial goods, at least, it was felt by 1936 that "the excessive regimentation by the general contract of the terms of local contracts limited the initiative of the middle and low links." General contracts proved particularly ineffectual as a basis for short-term contracts, single (spot) agreements, or commercial orders—transactions which were becoming increasingly important. To correct the evils of general contracts, the Council of Ministers declared that henceforth so-called direct contracts, concluded by the producing and consuming (or trading) enterprises themselves, were to comprise the basic form of contractual relationships.[11] Thus a definite line was drawn between plan and contract. The principle was established that, while higher organizations do the planning, nevertheless (in the words of one Soviet writer) "contractual relations should be established between the economic enterprises which immediately execute the contract."

With the decline of general contracts, control over the economic transactions of the enterprises and glavki (for in 1936 the glavki procurement and supply offices were put on a *khozraschet* basis and became increasingly active) came to be exercised through annual agreements, called Basic Conditions of Supply, which were drawn up jointly by supplier and consumer ministries. The Basic Conditions generally stated what standards were to govern the quality of the goods to be supplied in the coming year, what methods of payment were permissible, under what conditions contractual penalties could be applied and what their limits must be, under what circumstances a purchaser could refuse to accept a demand for payment, and similar matters. They were, in effect, rather detailed trade regulations agreed upon by representatives of the producers and purchasers of a given type of product, binding upon such producers and purchasers, but leaving considerable scope for initiative and independence in the direct contracts concluded in conformity therewith.

Stricter control over direct contracts was exercised by the glavki in many instances through specific orders for procurement and supply of goods. Contracts between subordinate enterprises drawn up in accordance with specific orders—so-called planned contracts—were largely, though not entirely, *pro forma* acknowledgments by the enterprises of obligations which already existed by virtue of the specific orders of the glavki. For more abundant commodities, for local products locally consumed, for particular objects (such as an individual machine or "beyond-plan" goods produced specially), contracts were considerably freer.

By 1949, the system of direct contracts had hit serious snags. During the war contract relationships had been replaced almost entirely by plans and allocation orders, and with the end of the war many industries failed to return to the practice of signing contracts, direct or otherwise. Apparently the enterprises were evading the planned tasks and orders issued to them by their superior glavki and were entering into informal deals with each other. In this way they were succeeding in fulfilling and overfulfilling their plans in money terms, while evading the requirements of the plans of distribution. At the same time the glavki, too, were apparently more concerned with their balance sheets than with the actual plans of distribution, for the charge was leveled at them that they were lax in issuing orders for procurement and supply by the lower links. The only legal sanctions available in such cases of evasion of plan were administrative and criminal: someone might be punished. Apparently these sanctions were not strong enough.

On April 21, 1949, the Council of Ministers issued a

decree requiring that glavki and other central organs of producers and consumers should (if their superior ministers so decide) once again enter annually into general contracts, and that the subordinate enterprises should conclude local contracts on the basis of the general contracts. The system of direct contracts continued to exist alongside the system of general and local contracts, at the discretion of each ministry. The Basic Conditions of Supply continued as the framework for both the general contracts and the direct contracts.[12]

The 1949 decree explicitly gave one glavk a contractual remedy against another glavk for failure to present specifications and orders to a subordinate enterprise, as well as for failure by a subordinate enterprise to conclude a local contract. Its main purpose thus seems to have been to increase the financial responsibility of the glavki for the acts of their subordinate enterprises and thus to give added incentive for strict supervision of the planned tasks. On the other hand, the local contracts were supposed to leave a fairly large field for maneuvering. As stated in the decree, "In local and direct contracts there shall be provided the concrete obligations of the supplier and the consumer: the exact quantity of the product to be supplied; the terms of delivery; the quality of the product and, in appropriate instances, its composition and assortment; the price of the product and the general cost of delivery; the method of payment, the property liability for nonfulfillment of the contract." This provision gave the new local contract a character very similar to that of the direct contract and quite different from that of the pre-1936 local contract.

Nevertheless, the reinstatement of the general contract, even though not in the rigid form of the pre-1936 period, often resulted in a stifling of local initiative, according to Soviet writers. This was due in part to the fact that the glavki were required to issue "distribution lists" stating which enterprises should enter into delivery contracts with each other. Although these distribution lists were often either not issued or else ignored, and were finally abolished in 1955, they substantially reduced the power of the enterprises to exercise whatever freedom to bargain over terms which the general contracts permitted.

With the elimination of most of the glavki in the 1957 reforms, and the transfer of their functions to branch administrations of the regional economic councils, came also the elimination of the system of general contracts that had bound them together. The direct contract became once again the sole link between purchaser and supplier. At the same time, however, the issuance of *nariady*—as has already been indicated—was put in the hands of Gosplan; and, in addition, Gosplan was charged with the issuance of *nariady* for both "funded" and "centrally planned" goods, the distinction between the two types henceforth being eliminated.

The content of direct contracts between the enterprises is now regulated in the first instance by two 1959 Statutes on Deliveries, one for producer goods and one for consumer goods.[13] The two statutes govern "problems common to all suppliers and consumers," leaving special problems of contracts for delivery of particular types of goods to be regulated by Special Conditions of Delivery issued by State Arbitrazh. The Basic Conditions of Supply formerly worked out by the ministries and glavki have been eliminated except in the case of military supplies. Also supplies for export and import continue to be regulated by special regulations.

Under the Statute on Deliveries of Producer Goods, the supplier, on receipt of a *nariad,* is required within ten days to present to the purchaser named in the *nariad* a signed draft contract. The contract must identify the type, quantity and, in appropriate instances, the assortment of products subject to delivery in the course of a year, with a breakdown by quarters; the contemplated times of delivery; quality, technical standards, samples, and the like; prices for the goods and total amount of the contract; terms of payment; credit and shipping documents; and similar matters. The Statute lays down rules—sometimes fairly detailed

—concerning these terms, as well as rules concerning property liability for breach of contract.

The Special Conditions of Delivery issued by State Arbitrazh for particular kinds of goods supplement the Statutes on Deliveries; in many respects they resemble the standard contract terms which trade associations in Western countries sometimes require their member firms to use.

If the purchaser named in the *nariad* disagrees with any of the terms of the draft contract presented by the supplier, he may file a "protocol of disagreements" in Arbitrazh.

It is apparent that the contract of delivery under Soviet law has two quite different functions: it is both a means of controlling distribution by higher authorities and a means of giving enterprises initiative in the procurement and supply of goods. The vacillation in the policy concerning general and direct contacts, as well as the shift from industrial (ministerial) to central control over the issuance of *nariady* and over the content of contracts, illuminates the fundamental dilemma of a planned economy. "Excessive regimentation" freezes the flow of commodities; yet excessive contractual freedom frustrates the plans of distribution. The dilemma lies at the very heart of the system of "democratic centralism"—centralized planning and decentralized operations. It affects most immediately and directly the middle links in the chain of authority, the branch administrations (the former glavki), which gravitate back and forth from planning to operative functions and from concern for the national economic plan to concern for the success of their subordinate enterprises.

Yet despite the enormous weight of the annual plans of distribution of goods, of the *nariady* issued by Gosplan, and of statutory regulation of contract terms, the initiative and responsibility of the operative units remains a factor of fundamental importance. Soviet legislation and legal literature emphasize "contract discipline," and say nothing of "freedom of contract"; yet the duty to contract, so essential to the planning function (for without contracts the plans remain up in the air), gives rise to contract rights.

That these are rights, and not only economic-administrative functions, is apparent from the cases in Arbitrazh, to which we now turn. For a right is a claim enforceable by a lawsuit before a competent tribunal, which adjudicates on the basis of established norms, after a fair hearing, and not solely on the basis of economic-administrative expediency.

ARBITRAZH

Property and contract disputes between economic enterprises belonging to different regional economic councils or different ministries are adjudicated in a special system of tribunals called State Arbitrazh (*Gosarbitrazh*). Disputes arising within a single regional economic council or ministry are decided by Departmental Arbitrazh (*Vedomstvennyi Arbitrazh*), which is under the general supervision of State Arbitrazh. Since 1960, legislation has also provided for decision of disputes by one or more arbitrators (*treteiskii sud*) selected by the parties, with appeal to the appropriate Arbitrazh on questions of law.[14] The *treteiskii sud* (which thus far has been used relatively infrequently) is a genuine arbitration tribunal; Arbitrazh, despite its name, has nothing to do with arbitration, for its jurisdiction is compulsory and it decides disputes according to law. Arbitrazh is really a system of economic courts with powers of both a judicial and administrative character.

Arbitrazh is completely separate from the regular courts and closely linked to the administrative branch of the state. The organs of State Arbitrazh are immediately subordinate to the supreme administrative bodies of the territories in which they operate, that is, the Council of Ministers of the U.S.S.R., the councils of ministers of the various constituent and autonomous republics, the executive committees of territories and regions. Similarly, departmental Arbitrazh is subordinate to the economic council of the region in which it is located or to the head of the ministry. The administrative body appoints the members of the Arbitrazh subordinate to it, supervises its activities, and has power to reverse or modify its decisions or remand for retrial. The chief arbiter may also review the decisions of other arbiters. Although the arbiter is not a professional judge, he is often a lawyer by training, and is in any event assisted by lawyers. Uniformity is maintained by the State Arbitrazh of the Council of Ministers of the U.S.S.R., which may on its own motion remove cases from the lower organs (whether of State or of Departmental Arbitrazh) to its own jurisdiction. In addition, the chief arbiter of the All-Union State Arbitrazh convokes periodical consultations of all organs of State Arbitrazh for joint discussion of questions confronting them and for the establishment of uniformity.[15] State Arbitrazh periodically publishes *Collections of Instructions* containing reports of cases, instructions of the chief arbiter, and relevant new statutes.[16]

When reestablished in 1931, after the introduction of planning had rendered its predecessor obsolete, Arbitrazh was intended to be first and foremost an arbitration board, whose primary efforts were to be directed toward reconciling the parties to a dispute (that is, the managers of the respective enterprises); failing reconciliation, Arbitrazh was to decide the dispute in the light of the governing plans and regulations, with particular emphasis on economic policy and expediency. It was clearly understood that Arbitrazh was not governed by the provisions of the Civil Code. It was not a judicial but an arbitrational and administrative body. At one time lawyers were excluded from its proceedings.

In the mid-1930's Arbitrazh was converted in effect into an economic court. It was declared to be bound by the Civil Code and by the norms of Soviet law in general. The emphasis on reconciliation diminished, and directors were no longer required to appear personally but could send their lawyers instead. The earlier "procedural nihilism," as it was now called, was denounced, and the rules of the Code of Civil Procedure were held to govern where appropriate. Emphasis was placed on an accurate record of the proceedings and on the written opinion of the arbiter.

The 1931 decree establishing State Arbitrazh stated: "In deciding disputes, State Arbitrazh shall be guided by the laws and regulations of the central and local organs of state power and also by the general principles of the economic policy of the U.S.S.R." Earlier interpreted as authorizing a disregard for both law and contract, this provision is now understood differently. The leading authorities on the practice of Arbitrazh wrote in 1938:

> It is proper to reject the clearly untrue arguments of the opponents of State Arbitrazh that only the courts should be guided by law, but State Arbitrazh is freed from it. It is proper definitely to condemn and to punish those arbiters who imagine that an arbitrational decision may go contrary to law because a decision not corresponding to law is "economically convenient." State Arbitrazh does not have the right to depart from law even by one step . . . Since not all questions arising out of economic relations are regulated by law or by decree of the government, the statute [on State Arbitrazh] indicates that in such cases the general principles of the economic policy of the U.S.S.R. are applicable. Accordingly, the arbiter must be politically and economically literate, must see that his decisions correspond to the general directives of the government. [But] may State Arbitrazh in deciding a dispute depart from the terms of a legally concluded contract? No . . . Of course the arbiter is not bound by the literal sense of the contract in those cases where it appears that the economic relations were in fact not such as the contract stated.

The importance of planning is in no way minimized; on the contrary, it is stated unequivocally that every dispute between state business enterprises must be decided in the general interests of the state, that is, in the direction of realizing the planned tasks set by the state. But the subordination of Arbitrazh to civil law, the necessity for procedural correctness, and the protection of the legal rights and interests of the parties are now acclaimed as essential to the life of the Plan itself. "The defense of the interests of the state, of socialist ownership," write the same authors, "is achieved by means of the defense of individual enterprises and organizations representing that ownership." The protection of their operative independence and property rights—that is, the thorough carrying out of business accountability—"creates the most suitable conditions for fulfillment of the plans issued for their activity . . . Conversely, disdain for the operative independence of the individual organizations, for their rights to property, depersonalizes the responsibility for maintaining that property, creates fissures and breaches in the legal position of the economic organizations." [17] In other words, whereas economic expediency was previously hailed as the ultimate criterion for the decision of disputes, it is now stated that the judicial protection of property and contract rights as such is itself the highest expediency. In this way the judicial process complements the planning process, giving it a measure of stability which it otherwise lacks.

The combination of Plan and Law, the merger of administrative and judicial functions in Arbitrazh, and the concept of the consistency of property and contract rights with the planning-administrative system, are exemplified in the 1960 Statute on State Arbitrazh of the Council of Ministers of the U.S.S.R.,[18] which replaced the 1931 decree. The new statute systematizes the rules under which State Arbitrazh operates and also widens the scope of its administrative activity. It lists the following "chief functions" of State Arbitrazh:

"(a) to ensure protection of the property rights and lawful interests of enterprises, organizations and institutions in the settling of economic disputes;

"(b) to strengthen and develop cooperation between enterprises, organizations and institutions in the matter of fulfilling the national economic plan; to combat manifestations of localism and narrow departmental tendencies;

"(c) in settling economic disputes, to bring active influence to bear on enterprises, organizations and institutions in the matter of their execution of laws as well as of resolutions and directives of the U.S.S.R. government on questions of economic work, applying property sanctions for failure to fulfill plans and assignments for deliveries of products, for delivery of poor-quality or incomplete products and for other violations of state discipline and contract obligations;

"(d) to assist in the fulfillment of plans and tasks for deliveries of products and other obligations and also in the elimination of shortcomings in the economic activity of enterprises, organizations and institutions uncovered by the Arbitrazh tribunal in the course of hearing economic disputes."

In addition, the 1960 Statute on State Arbitrazh gives that body considerable control over the types of contracts to be entered into by the enterprises, providing that it shall issue standard terms for the delivery of particular types of producers' and consumers' goods as well as instructions on the procedure for inspection of goods prior to acceptance; that it shall interpret to enterprises the Statutes on Deliveries of Producer and Consumer Goods, the Statute on Terms of Deliveries of Goods for Export, and the terms of fulfillment by import combines of orders of Soviet organizations; that it shall declare invalid contracts that conflict with laws or state plans; that it shall study the work of the Arbitrazh tribunals of regional economic councils, ministries and departments and shall instruct them on the application of the statutes on deliveries and other all-union normative acts; and that it "shall report to the U.S.S.R. Council of Ministers on the most serious violations of state discipline and of legislation on the quality and completeness of goods for delivery as well as on manifestations of localism and on other violations of socialist legality in the activity of enterprises, organizations and institutions."

The 1960 statute also sets forth the procedure by which State Arbitrazh shall operate in the decision of cases. It has power to summon parties and witnesses, to require the submission of documents and information, to appoint experts and to verify circumstances of a case directly at enterprises. The defendant is required to be notified of the suit and to be given an opportunity to reply in writing as well as to appear. The parties may appear either through their directors or their attorneys. "Decisions shall be taken on the basis of a discussion of all circumstances of the dispute at the session of Arbitrazh." Although there is no appeal from a decision, the parties may apply for a reexamination of the decision by the Chief Arbiter.

Individual regional economic councils have adopted decrees regulating their Arbitrazh tribunals similarly to the way in which the State Arbitrazh is regulated.

Thus the "property rights and lawful interests of enterprises," which Arbitrazh is commissioned to protect, are seen as essential to "the fulfillment of plans and tasks," which Arbitrazh is commissioned to assist. "In settling economic disputes," the 1960 statute states, "State Arbitrazh of the Council of Ministers of the U.S.S.R. shall be guided by the laws of the U.S.S.R. and of union and autonomous republics, by the decrees and regulations of the U.S.S.R. Council of Ministers and of councils of ministers of union republics and of autonomous republics, as well as by decrees and regulations of regional economic councils and orders and instructions of ministries and departments and decisions of local organs of state authority, issued within the limits of their competence." These laws, decrees, regulations, orders, instructions and decisions establish both the planning system, with its complex administrative apparatus, and the property-contract system, which enables the individual enterprises to carry on their economic operations with some degree of initiative and responsibility.

THE LAW IN ACTION

The decisions of Arbitrazh test the character of the property and contract rights of Soviet state economic organizations. It is in these decisions that Plan and Law interact most vividly. It is here that we may find evidence of the importance of the restoration of law since the mid-1930's for the actual operation of the Soviet planned economy.

The number of lawsuits between state economic enterprises is very large. In 1938, for example, over 330,000 cases were litigated in State Arbitrazh. No over-all statistics are available for the postwar years, and even in the pre-war period none were published concerning the number of cases in the Departmental Arbitrazh of the individual ministries. Judging by reports of the numbers of cases in individual regional economic councils (*e.g.*, in 1958 2,135 suits were decided by the Arbitrazh of the Sverdlovsk Regional Council, which governed 1200 enterprises), it is safe to assume that the amount of enterprise litigation has not decreased and has probably substantially increased in the postwar years.

Most of the cases in Arbitrazh (whether State or Departmental) involve disputes over breaches of contract for the supply of goods. In many such cases the purchaser claims that the goods delivered by the supplier were of lower-than-contract quality or were incomplete or were not delivered on time or were not delivered at all. In others the supplier and purchaser dispute over terms of payment and price, for although prices are, in general, fixed, there are often permitted deviations from fixed prices and there are also many ways of evading the official prices. Still other cases in Arbitrazh involve the liability of carriers for damage to goods or for failure to deliver them on time.

Apart from suits involving breach of contract, Arbitrazh also has jurisdiction over so-called "pre-contract disputes," in which enterprises that are required by the state plan to enter into contracts with each other cannot agree on the terms of such contracts. Either party may bring suit in Arbitrazh to have the disagreement resolved, or the superior planning organs may institute such suit, or Arbitrazh itself may initiate the action. Usually it is one of the parties that initiates the suit.

Arbitrazh also hears tort claims of one state enterprise against another, as, for example, where a defective machine supplied by one enterprise causes property damage to another enterprise.

The above list of types of cases tried in Arbitrazh, though far from exhaustive, indicates some of the principal causes of controversy between Soviet state enterprises requiring adjudication. The following discussion will focus on two

aspects of the work of Arbitrazh—the settlement of pre-
contract disputes and the determination of rights and duties
under the contract of delivery.

Pre-contract disputes.—Decrees of the Central Committee of the Communist Party and of the Council of Ministers make obligatory the conclusion of contracts both for
the delivery of goods and for the rendering of services.
Each year a campaign is carried on for the timely conclusion of such contracts on an annual basis. In the case
of the scarcest and most important goods, the annual contracts concluded by enterprises may have little to add to
the plans of distribution issued by the planning authorities;
in many cases, however, there is considerable leeway for
"detailization." In any event, the goods are not supposed
to move without a contract. And without a contract neither
the purchaser nor the supplier will feel secure: the purchaser will not be sure that the supplier will deliver the
goods to it and not to another enterprise, and the supplier
will not be sure that the purchaser will accept the goods
and pay for them.

Suppose, however, that the parties are unable to agree
on the terms of a contract, although plans of distribution
impose on them the obligation to enter into one. Since
1934 it has been possible, under such circumstances, for
either party to bring suit in Arbitrazh to have the disagreement resolved, or (as stated above) for suit to be initiated
by Arbitrazh or by the agency which issued the distribution
plan. Usually the supplier brings suit, the purchaser having
rejected the proffered terms.

Pre-contract disputes are often concerned with the attempt
of one or both of the parties to avoid liability for nonperformance. For example, Arbitrazh in pre-contract cases
has ruled against the inclusion of a term in the contract
giving the supplier the right unilaterally to decrease the
quantity of goods to be supplied if the supplier received
orders for the same product from the other enterprises. It
has ruled against a clause which would release the supplier from the obligation to deliver if certain materials
were not received from a third party—in one case, for

example, if the railroad failed to furnish empty cars for shipment of the goods. (In such a situation the supplier would have recourse against the railroad on the basis of a separate contract with it, but would be liable to the buyer nonetheless.)

Other pre-contract disputes have involved the question of the penalty clause which is required to be inserted in all contracts between Soviet state business enterprises. Penalties for nonperformance, to be paid to the injured party, apart from losses proved to have been suffered from such nonperformance, may be measured at a percentage of the cost of the goods or of their price, or they may be fixed at a definite sum. Generally it is required that penalties be proportionate to the significance of the sale, the character of the obligation, and the degree to which performance has been rendered. The percentages of penalty for various breaches are often fixed by the statutes on deliveries.

A typical example of the role of Arbitrazh in the settlement of pre-contract disputes is furnished by a 1960 case between a Delivery Section of the Tadzhik Economic Council and a State Plant of the Leningrad Economic Council.[19] The former was required by plan to conclude a contract with the latter for delivery to it of a given quantity of cottonseed oil. The supplier sent to the purchaser a proposed contract containing a clause that equal amounts should be shipped once a month. The purchaser would not agree to this term and proposed that shipments should be in equal amounts every ten days, arguing that it had no facilities for storing larger shipments. The supplier brought the case to State Arbitrazh of the Council of Ministers of the Turkmen S.S.R., which decided in favor of the supplier on the grounds that the railroad provided the suppliers with tank cars only once a month and that it was under an obligation to use them as soon as they were furnished. On appeal by the purchaser to the Chief Arbiter of State Arbitrazh of the Council of Ministers of the U.S.S.R., the decision of the Turkmen State Arbitrazh was reversed. The Chief Arbiter relied on a provision in the Statute on Deliveries of Producer Goods stating that the parties may agree on times of delivery shorter than a month in the interest of uninterrupted rhythm of work of the consumer enterprise, and also on a provision of the Charter of Railroads stating that the railroads should arrange for shipment of goods at times which assure the equality and rhythm of shipments during the month and during the day. The Chief Arbiter ordered that the parties agree to shipment in equal amounts twice a month, and at the same time he requested the Director of the Tashkent Railroad to order that necessary steps be taken to provide the supplier with tank-cars at proper times.

In assessing the significance of this case (and of many others of a similar nature), one is struck by the fact that neither party really suffered a defeat—provided that in fact the Director of the Tashkent Railroad would be able to respond to the request of the Chief Arbiter to provide tank-cars more frequently. (In any event, the cottonseed supplier could resort to Arbitrazh once again, by way of pre-contract dispute, to compel him to do so.) The Chief Arbiter has actually helped the parties to arrange their affairs more rationally from the point of view of both. Drawing on his broad powers over the carrier, he has helped the supplier and purchaser to draw a better contract. Yet he has done so not as an arbitrator attempting to reconcile them, but rather as a judge with broad administrative powers, basing his decision on broad provisions of the Statute on Deliveries and of the Charter of Railroads.

By no means are all pre-contract disputes resolved painlessly for both parties, however. In May 1961 the author attended a trial of a pre-contract case in State Arbitrazh of the U.S.S.R. involving the question whether a supplier of lumber must supply equal amounts in each quarter or whether the amounts could be varied by seasons in view of the fact that at certain times the rivers dried up and the logs could not be floated on them. The representatives of the purchasing organization argued that it would be too great a burden on it to have to receive large amounts at particular times. Argument on both sides was very heated.

Legally, it centered on the interpretation of the Special Conditions for Delivery of Lumber. Economically, it centered on which organization could best bear the risks of storing the lumber during periods when there was an oversupply, and which should carry the cost of the capital tied up in the lumber during such periods. The arbiter asked many questions and entered into discussion with the representatives of the parties (each had two representatives). After about an hour-and-a-half of argument, the arbiter announced his decision in favor of the purchaser and said that he would present a written opinion within a few days. When the author asked him on what he had based his decision, he replied that the Special Conditions of Delivery of Lumber, which he himself had drafted, contemplated the delivery of equal amounts in each quarter as a general rule, and that nothing in the factual situation of the present case compelled a departure from that rule. He viewed his decision as one based on law.

Yet this judicial power is subject to abuse by virtue of the breadth of its scope. Managers often resort to Arbitrazh solely to clear themselves of responsibility for executing contracts on terms of which their superior administrative authorities may not approve. Fearing an unpleasant reaction, they seek to transfer the responsibility to Arbitrazh. In addition, if they are unable to fulfill their production plans because of difficulties in procurement of materials, they may point to the fact that they had urged those difficulties upon Arbitrazh in pre-contract cases.[20]

Rights and Duties under the Contract of Delivery.—The contract of delivery for funded goods is, in one aspect, a completion of the planning process; that is, the contracting enterprises add to the plans which they have received from superior agencies details concerning time and place of delivery, quality, quantity, assortment, packing, and other matters which cannot efficiently be regulated except by the parties themselves. Contracts of delivery of goods not subject to comprehensive planning give more leeway for exercise of initiative by the enterprises themselves. Especially in regard to consumer goods, there is often a considerable amount of bargaining not only over the matters listed above, but also over the nature of the goods to be delivered. With respect to many consumer goods there has been a tendency in recent years to establish trade fairs where representatives of producers and distributors examine samples and place orders; at such fairs enterprises may be induced to adapt their production to consumer tastes. But even with respect to contracts for delivery of funded goods, the agreement of the parties with respect to their contractual rights and duties is not merely a detailization of plans; it has another dimension which is equally important, namely, an acceptance of the responsibility to perform the contract. Without a contract, the rights and duties of the enterprises are essentially administrative in nature; with a contract, they are also contractual. Being contractual, they are subject to litigation in Arbitrazh under the rules of contract law.

The Fundamental Principles of Civil Law adopted by the U.S.S.R. Supreme Soviet in December 1961 and effective May 1, 1962, lay down basic rules which govern all contracts, whether between state enterprises or between private citizens. Many of these general principles are not essentially different from those which may be found in the legal systems of non-socialist countries. Thus it is provided that a contract is deemed to be concluded when the parties have reached agreement on all its essential points; that in the event of breach of contract, the obligor is obliged to compensate the obligee for losses caused by the breach, including out-of-pocket expenses incurred by the obligee as well as lost profits (called "income," in order to avoid the "bourgeois" terminology of profits); that liability for breach of contract must be founded on fault unless it is otherwise provided by law or by the contract (a provision compatible with the doctrines of some Western European countries but not with the general Anglo-American doctrine, which imposes liability for breach of contract regardless of fault unless otherwise provided by law or by contract).

At the same time, the Fundamental Principles of Civil Law also introduce certain rules which are connected with the planned nature of the Soviet economy. It is provided that the content of a contract concluded on the basis of a planned task must correspond with that task; that payment of damages (which in Soviet law is generally expressed in the form of a penalty or forfeit) does not release a state enterprise from the duty to perform the contract unless the planned task on which the obligation is based has lost its force; that contracts of delivery between state enterprises must conform to the Statutes on Delivery of Producer and Consumer Goods and to the Special Conditions of Delivery for particular products; that the quality must correspond to state standards, technical conditions or samples.

The requirement that the contract of delivery conform to the planned tasks of the parties has resulted in a considerable amount of litigation in Arbitrazh. In some cases the contract has conformed to the planned task of one party but not of the other. Thus an enterprise will contend that it should be relieved of liability for failing to deliver a large quantity of goods, or for failing to accept a large quantity, on the ground that its planned tasks call for the production or procurement of a smaller amount. In such cases Arbitrazh has held that where the contract violates the plan of only one of the parties it must be enforced.

The tension between plan and contract manifests itself also in the attempt of manufacturing enterprises to avoid contractual responsibilities to their customers when they are unable to acquire materials necessary to produce the goods to be delivered. Despite the general requirement that there is no liability for breach of contract without fault, the failure of the supplier's own sources of supply is not considered to be a valid excuse for his nonperformance; in such cases a fictitious fault is assumed to exist. There are practical justifications for this: the supplier is thereby discouraged from avoiding his contractual obligations by lack of diligence in procuring materials, and at the same time he is encouraged to press his claims for damages against his defaulting suppliers and thus recoup the losses which he suffers by virtue of his own breach of contract.

This solution of the problem was better adapted, however, to the situation which existed prior to 1957, when the operative planning was in the hands of the industrial ministries, than to the post-1957 system under which procurement permits are issued by Gosplan. A concrete example may help to illustrate:

The Bobrovsk Insulation Factory entered into a contract with the Kharkov factory "Elektrotiazhmash" (an abbreviation for "Heavy Electrical Machines") to deliver insulating materials during 1959. Prior to the conclusion of the contract there was a dispute between the parties, which was taken to State Arbitrazh; the Bobrovsk factory argued that it could not agree to provide insulating materials according to the specifications presented by the Kharkov factory, since the procurement permits (*nariady*) which it had received from Gosplan for raw materials were inadequate to enable it to procure the particular raw materials needed to make the particular insulating materials which Kharkov wanted. Gosplan had issued permits sufficient to cover Bobrovsk's needs in terms of quantity, but not sufficiently detailed to enable it to obtain certain specific types. The pre-contract dispute was decided in favor of Kharkov, however, apparently by an extension of the general principle referred to earlier—that an enterprise cannot plead lack of sources of supply as an excuse for nonperformance, and similarly, in this case, as an excuse for not agreeing to perform. The contract was therefore entered into, but Bobrovsk could not perform, and Kharkhov sued for 401,000 (old) rubles for failure to deliver during the fourth quarter of 1959. State Arbitrazh of the Council of Ministers of the U.S.S.R. decided the case, however, in favor of Bobrovsk, on the ground that "under the circumstances . . . the failure to supply the goods occurred through no fault of the Bobrovsk factory." The earlier decision in the pre-contract dispute was criticized by the arbiter, who said that Bobrovsk should have appealed from it to a higher tribunal. It was made clear, however, that Arbitrazh was not abandoning its general rule that a supplier is not relieved of responsibility for not delivering goods merely because it failed to receive raw materials.

The exception to this rule in the instant case was justified on the grounds of "the special features of this case and the character of the mutual relations between the parties." [21]

What were those "special features"? It appeared that the sources of raw materials for one of the items to be delivered were four times less than the quantity required. It also appeared that the Kharkov factory did not do all that it could to go over to the use of insulating materials manufactured from other raw material. The arbiter stated that "the Kharkov and Bobrovsk factories have not regulated their supply relationships in the spirit of collaboration, as a result of which the disputes of these enterprises have been coming systematically for examination." But this was probably not the critical point. In addition, Arbitrazh, it was reported, "asked the planning organs to examine the question of coordinating the production programs of those enterprises using insulating materials with the production program and resources of the supplier enterprises, so as to give attention to the matter of substitution of insulating materials."

The case illustrates one of the principal defects of the system established in 1957 whereby Gosplan issues procurement permits. When these were issued by the ministries it was possible to charge the subordinate enterprise of a ministry with responsibility in cases where the ministry had failed to issue a permit enabling it to procure raw materials. It was possible, that is, without injustice to the supplier ministry, to hold the enterprise responsible for its superior's neglect, especially in view of the fact that delivery contracts were generally entered into on the basis of agreements between distribution offices of the superior ministries themselves. The indication that State Arbitrazh should not have required the Bobrovsk factory to agree to supply insulating materials to Kharkov in the pre-contract case seems to reflect the view that enterprises should not be held accountable for defects in planning. Yet State Arbitrazh has generally refused to permit so-called "conditional" contracts of delivery in which a supplier agrees to perform only on condition that certain materials are allocated to it.[22]

One source of the difficulty lies in the wide variety of types of products: in the Soviet electrotechnical industry there are some 100,000 different types of electrotechnical products and spare parts thereto; in the machine-tool instrument industry there are 70,000 types of metal-cutting instruments, 15,000 types of abrasives, 900 types of machine tools; there are 18,000 types of ferrous metals.[23] Procurement permits cannot possibly be issued in such detail. Another source of the difficulty lies in the tendency of suppliers to attempt to avoid their obligations by reliance upon the excuse of "circumstances beyond their control." If those circumstances are attributable to superior economic agencies which are themselves accountable, it makes sense not to exonerate the supplier. But if they are attributable to administrative agencies like Gosplan, which are not themselves financially responsible, it seems harsh to hold the enterprise liable. Yet if the enterprise is not held liable it will be tempted to relax its pressure on its own suppliers.

The only ultimate solution to these dilemmas is to create conditions of abundance in which the failure of a source of supply can be made up by purchases elsewhere. Under such conditions a rule that such failure does not excuse liability for nonperformance is workable. Under conditions of scarcity, however, the rule can only work if the supplier whose own sources have failed is to some degree in a position to control those sources—a situation which no longer pertains (or at least not to the same extent) with the shift of ultimate responsibility for distribution away from the ministries to Gosplan. The opposite rule, however, leaves too much opportunity for abuse by directors, and State Arbitrazh was therefore careful to qualify its decision in the Kharkov-Bobrovsk case as an exception.

An intermediate solution to the problem faced by Soviet state enterprises, when difficulties arise either in making or performing their contracts, is for them to ask the planning authorities to modify the planned tasks and the procurement permits. This, indeed, is a common practice. In fact, one sometimes gains the impression from reading Soviet legal literature and from talking with Soviet factory directors and economic officials, that the plans are ultimately adapted to the needs, capacities, and desires of the enterprises, despite the overwhelming weight of bureaucratic controls.

Thus a balance is inevitably struck between over-all direction and individual initiative. In the words of an American scholar who worked in the Hungarian State Arbitrazh prior to October 1956, it is a function of contract "to create flexible, civil-law relations between the enterprises. It is not difficult to imagine a planned economy in which the lower agencies slavishly perform their tasks as small gears in a huge machine. The contractual doctrine encourages the economic agencies, the enterprises, to feel that they themselves undertake the tasks, working out and concluding the contracts which alone bind them. The contractual approach seeks to give these economic agencies a certain freedom of decision. An enterprise can refuse to conclude a contract on the ground that it is under no plan obligation, that there is a discrepancy between the planning numbers [that is, the quantities to be delivered], or that its planning obligation [planned task] does not require it to conclude a contract with the enterprise in question. The specific conditions of the contract (quality, assortment, mode of transportation, etc.) are worked out through free bargaining. The enterprises reach agreement through mutual concessions. Even if an enterprise's plan requires that the contract in question be concluded, the enterprise can assert that changes in circumstances have rendered fulfillment of the plan impossible and on this ground refuse to contract. After a contract has been concluded, the enterprise may seek to modify its provisions." [24]

It is recognized by Soviet jurists that the very idea of contract presupposes some freedom on the part of the parties to express their wills. This was formerly challenged as a bourgeois fiction. As stated by a Soviet writer in 1938, "the basic constitutive characteristic of a contract is the agreement of the parties, the coincidence of their wills, directed toward the achievement of a definite legal result. The statements of the wreckers were therefore directed toward showing the absence of the will of the parties, of their agreement, in contracts under Soviet law, primarily in planned contracts of socialist organizations. Plan and Law were placed in contradiction as irreconcilable things. These wrecking tendencies taught a contemptuous attitude toward contract . . . they brought great injury to our national economy." Now upheld as a fundamental principle of Soviet contract law, freedom of will is not considered, however, as a natural right, but rather as a right emerging from social conditions. Its ultimate source is found in the harmony of social and personal interests under socialism, and in the equality of bargaining power of the contracting parties. Actual freedom of contract, it is said, is thus created by socialism itself—by the absence of unemployment, by confidence in the future, by regulation and integration of the national economy. The welfare of the whole economy, in turn, is thought to require the granting of initiative and responsibility to the parties.

Soviet legal literature talks in terms of a polar or dialectical relationship between freedom and authority, between the initiative of the individual enterprise and the undivided will of society. A concrete illustration of this general approach may be found in the manner in which the courts treat invalid contracts. Article 30 of the Civil Code declares invalid any contract made for a purpose contrary to law, made in evasion of the law, or directed to the clear detriment of the state. Article 147 requires that in the event a contract is invalid under Article 30, neither of the parties shall have the right to demand from the other the return of whatever has been performed under the contract; instead it may be treated as unjust enrichment to be forfeit to the state.[25] (Under American law, an illegal contract is often held to create no obligations at all, and the court will leave the parties as they are; in any case, the notion of forfeiture to the state is foreign to us, though it has been urged by some American legal writers.) These articles were originally held applicable to the transactions of private citizens only; with the growth of the economic accountability and juridical personality of state economic enterprises, Arbitrazh began to apply them to contracts between such enterprises, and subsequently, in 1939, the Plenum of the Supreme Court of the U.S.S.R. explicitly overruled the 1927 ruling on which the earlier judicial practice had been based. Particularly, a contract in violation of state-planned tasks may fall within the provisions of Article 30.

The application of Article 147 does not follow automatically from the application of Article 30, however. Under the latter, the intention of the parties is irrelevant. But judicial practice has required for the application of the penalty of Article 147 the presence of a subjective intent. The detriment to the state must have been apparent at the time the contract was made; the parties must have acted in bad faith. Further, the court may or may not apply Article 147 at its discretion; restitution may be granted to an innocent party. In the case of Moscow Central Base of Galantereia versus the Disabled Veterans Cooperative Red October, plaintiff sued for the surrender of 6.5 tons of swans' down purchased by it from defendant. In the course of the proceedings it appeared that an illegal advance payment had been made, covered by a fictitious receipt. Arbitrazh, applying Articles 30 and 147, ordered the defendant to pay over the amount received to the state treasury. In a 1960 case, a railroad purchasing office sued a wood-supply combine for refund of money paid for wood that had been swept away by a flood after purchase, but before the railroad had collected it. The railroad sought to rescind the transaction on the ground that its purchasing agent lacked the power to conclude the contract involved. Arbitrazh found the agent did have power, that title had passed to the railroad, and that therefore the railroad had to bear the loss. However it went on to note that the whole transaction was illegal since the purchaser did not have the allocation certificate required for the purchase of the wood in question. It therefore ordered the purchase money forfeited to the treasury. On the other hand, when a power plant purchased barracks from a construction enterprise and then sued because the barracks were in such a bad state that the city council condemned them, Arbitrazh held that the contract was invalid since it violated the decree on the transfer of the buildings and edifices from one state enterprise to another; however, Arbitrazh merely ordered the defendant to return to the plaintiff the purchase price, and the plaintiff to return to the defendant the barracks.

The variety of the contractual relationships between Soviet state business enterprises makes any general analysis of the cases very difficult. Not only do the strictness and thoroughness of planning depend on the importance and scarcity of the particular commodities involved, but also the methods of distribution vary tremendously with different commodities and in different areas. The types of disputes that come before Arbitrazh are amazingly diverse. Many arise over the quality of the goods supplied under the contract. A large number involve the question of prices, for despite the fact that prices are fixed, many devices exist for avoiding or evading the established prices. The number of cases involving terms of payment are relatively small, for the predominant method of payment is by the payor's acceptance, through his bank, of the payee's demand for payment presented through *his* bank. Since all commercial banks are branches of the State Bank (Gosbank), and since all financial dealings of 100 (new) rubles or more must be handled by the banks, a central clearing house is provided for all commercial transactions, and the entire system operates on the basis of bookkeeping deductions. This gives Gosbank the opportunity to supervise the credit relations of the state economic enterprises. Yet even here disputes arise, and distinctions must be drawn—between refusal by the payor to accept the demand for payment on the ground of the nondelivery of the goods or their defective quality (a refusal which will be rejected by Gosbank, since the transaction calls for cash against documents, and any suit for nondelivery or for defects in the goods must be brought later) and similar refusal on the ground of a defect in the documents presented by the payee (a refusal which will be accepted by Gosbank); between the responsibility of the buyer who refuses acceptance of perishable goods (in which case the buyer must take all necessary measures to prevent their ruin, including the selling of the goods for the account of the seller) and the buyer's responsibility where the goods are nonperishable; and many other such distinctions, most of which are familiar to the entire commercial world.

Soviet contract law is thus a means both of central regulation of the economy and of exercise of initiative by the individual economic units. As a means of exercise of individual initiative, Soviet contract law helps to overcome the rigidities which inhere in any highly centralized system of economic control. Contract law introduces an element of individual responsibility into the economy which otherwise would be lacking. And this element of responsibility is supported by Arbitrazh, whose decisions fix responsibility in terms of the relations of the parties to each other as well as to the economic plan, in terms of the losses suffered by the parties, and in terms of their fault. Although contracts and "contract discipline" play only a secondary role in the allocation of resources in the Soviet economy, in comparison with market economies, nevertheless they play an essential role in helping to overcome the congenital defects of central planning—defects for which the Soviets have developed their own vocabulary: *volokita* ("red tape"), *bezoblichka* (facelessness), *blat* ("pull").

ECONOMIC AND OFFICIAL CRIMES

In analyzing the socialist component of Soviet law we have taken as our starting point the institutional structure of the Soviet planned economy and have attempted to indicate the extent to which Soviet planning relies on the property and contract rights of economic organizations. We have seen that state ownership of the means of production and centralized allocation of resources are not solutions of the problems which confront lawyers and lawgivers, but are only the transposition of these problems onto a new plane. State ownership leaves open the question of possession, use, and disposition. Centralized allocation requires a basis in something more than administrative fiat. Indeed, Soviet experience explodes the myth of the "administrative state" in which all questions are decided in terms of "public policy." The judicial process has been found essential to the life of administration itself. The integrity of the whole has been seen to depend on the integrity of the parts. Stability of laws is itself public policy. And the rights of persons are emphasized as necessary correlatives of that sense of personal responsibility without which the plan ceases to be a living thing. This is the theory. The practice approximates it in varying degrees.

Yet it would be a mistake to think that a planned economy can exist merely on the basis of a synthesis of planning, administrative law, corporation law, and property-contract law. For one thing, there are important extralegal factors which take some of the strain off the legal system. Personal pressures, deals, bribery of one kind or another, and other informal devices, are means of evading the rigid requirements of the official system and may even be essential to its smooth functioning. But even in terms of the legal system as such, there are certain human and social needs which affect the economy and which cannot be met by the neat balancing of Plan against Law. A lawsuit in Arbitrazh may satisfy the enterprise which has suffered a financial loss through the improper acts of another enterprise (for example, the manufacture and sale of goods of poor quality), and the economic equilibrium disrupted by such improper acts may thereby be restored as between the parties. But the planned economy itself, that is, the state ("the whole people") may remain without satisfaction for the violation of a law prohibiting those improper acts. Because of its desire to prevent the recurrence of such prohibited acts and to express its disapproval and condemnation of them, the state must impose, in addition to administrative and civil sanctions, criminal sanctions.

For a state economic enterprise to break a contract is in

itself not a crime under Soviet law. Under the earlier criminal codes an official of a state enterprise who "maliciously" broke a contract was punishable, but that provision has now been eliminated in the 1961 R.S.F.S.R. Criminal Code. Also the 1941 statute making it a punishable offense "equivalent to a counterrevolutionary crime" for a director of a state economic enterprise to sell, exchange or release surplus equipment was repealed in 1955. Nevertheless it remains an economic crime under the 1961 code for a director, chief engineer, or chief of the section of technical control of an industrial enterprise, or one fulfilling the duties of such, to release goods of poor quality in large amounts or repeatedly; the penalties are deprivation of freedom of up to three years or corrective labor tasks (that is, a fine of up to 25 per cent of monthly wages) up to one year, or dismissal.

Also, a Soviet official is subject to a high degree of criminal responsibility in the performance of his official duties; and under Soviet law the term "official" includes not only the holder of political office or of a governmental administrative post, but also managers, engineers, or other officials of a factory, officers of a trade union or a cooperative, or, indeed, anyone exercising responsibility in a state enterprise. Soviet courts have even extended liability for "official crimes" to a waiter in a restaurant and a milkmaid on a collective farm; however, the 1961 R.S.F.S.R. Criminal Code limits the applicability of punishment for official crimes to persons realizing the functions of representatives of authority or occupying offices in state or social institutions, organizations or enterprises connected with the fulfillment of "organizational-regulatory or administrative-economic obligations."

Article 170 of the 1961 R.S.F.S.R. Criminal Code provides:

> Abuse of authority or of a position of service, that is, the intentional exploitation by an official of his position of service against the interests of service, if it is committed from mercenary or other personal interests and causes a substantial harm to state

or other social interests or to legally protected rights and interests of citizens, shall be punished by deprivation of freedom up to three years or by corrective labor tasks up to one year or by dismissal from office. Abuse of authority or of a position of service which has caused serious consequences shall be punished by deprivation of freedom up to eight years.

The crime of "exceeding authority" is defined and made punishable in Article 171, and negligence by an official in the performance of his official duties is defined and made punishable in Article 172. The maximum penalty for these crimes is deprivation of freedom for three years, except that exceeding authority is punishable by up to ten years if accompanied by force or weapons or by acts which torment or offend the personal dignity of the victim.

In 1962 the repeated taking of bribes by officials was made punishable by deprivation of freedom up to 15 years and in some instances by death.

Most cases of official crimes in the Soviet courts concern activities which would be punishable under other rubrics in most legal systems, such as embezzlement of funds, taking or giving of bribes, and the like. Certain official crimes, however, are directly related to the socialist system of planned economy. Thus a law of April 24, 1958, provides that nonfulfillment by directors and other officials of economic organizations of plans and tasks for delivery of products to other economic administrative regions or republics or for all-union needs shall be punishable by disciplinary fines of up to three months' wages, and, if committed repeatedly without satisfactory reasons, by the same penalties as established for official crimes. This law was designed principally to help overcome "localist tendencies" among officials of regional economic councils. If there were prosecutions under it, they were not reported. The law was not included in the 1961 R.S.F.S.R. Criminal Code, but would appear to be embraced within its general definition of abuse of authority or negligence by officials. Procurement of funded goods without a *nariad* also falls within the definition.

The planned economy protects itself further by imposing very severe criminal penalties for the theft of socialist property, as contrasted with the theft of personal property of individuals. By a law of August 7, 1932, social (state, collective-farm or co-operative) property was declared to be "sacred and inviolable," and persons making an attempt on it were "to be considered as enemies of the people." By this law theft of social property was punishable by death by shooting unless committed under mitigating circumstances. At that time, and until 1947, theft of personal property was only punishable by deprivation of liberty for a term of up to three months, and theft by assault (robbery) by deprivation of liberty for a term of up to five years. In 1947, capital punishment was abolished in the Soviet Union, and the sanction for theft of socialist property was changed to internment in a corrective-labor camp for a term of seven to ten years, with or without confiscation, in the case of theft of state property, and five to eight years, with or without confiscation, in the case of collective farm or cooperative property. For a second offense, or for commission of the crime by an organized band or on a large scale, the maximum penalty was twenty-five years with confiscation. (The phrase "enemy of the people" was not used in the 1947 law.) At the same time, the penalty for theft of the personal property of citizens was increased to internment in a corrective-labor camp for a period of from five to six years, and when accompanied by assault, to ten to fifteen years (and in some cases fifteen to twenty years) with confiscation.

A 1955 decree reduced the penalty for "petty" theft of state property to a minimum of corrective labor tasks for six months. Under the 1961 R.S.F.S.R. Criminal Code, the maximum penalty for theft of state or social property varies between three and fifteen years, depending upon the circumstances. However, an all-union statute of May 1961 reimposed the death penalty for such theft "in especially large amounts." The present penalties for theft of personal property include a maximum of ten years, and corrective labor tasks of up to one year for petty offenses.

Other "crimes against socialist property" include "an unconscionable attitude toward the protection of state or social property" by persons entrusted with such protection, resulting in harm to the property, which is punishable by deprivation of freedom up to two years or corrective labor tasks up to one year or by "social censure."

Still more serious is the crime of speculation, which Article 154 defines as the "buying up and resale of goods or other items for the purpose of making a profit." A wide range of punishment is provided, depending upon the seriousness of the offense. "Petty speculation committed more than once" is punishable by corrective labor tasks up to one year or by fine up to twenty rubles with confiscation of the objects of speculation. Speculation as a business or in large amounts is punishable by deprivation of freedom from two to seven years.

The attempt to regulate the planned economic order by means of criminal law perhaps reached its zenith in the edict of June 26, 1940 making it a crime punishable by two to four months' imprisonment to leave one's job without permission of management, and a crime punishable by corrective labor tasks up to six months for absence from work or lateness for more than twenty minutes without urgent reasons. This law, enacted expressly as a wartime measure, was retained after the war. though it largely fell into disuse. In 1951 the criminal sanctions for its violation were removed and Comrades' Courts were given jurisdiction over violations. It was formally repealed in 1956.

The 1940 law penalizing absenteeism and unauthorized quitting well illustrates the limits of effective legal action (to use Dean Roscoe Pound's phrase) in attempting to control economic activity through the criminal courts. The law provided that the manager had to give permission to a worker to quit if the latter was no longer able to perform his regular duties for reasons of health, if he was admitted to a training school to improve his qualifications, or if he was eligible for a retirement pension. The courts expanded these categories, refusing, for example, to convict a mother who quit without permission in order to take care of her children or a wife who quit to join her husband in another city. Also they held that a worker who had served his sentence was not obliged to return to his former job on the theory that the conviction dissolved the labor contract—a decision which no doubt put pressure on managers to accede to requests to leave. Moreover, evasion of the law was extremely widespread. Recruiting officers of plants in need of workers did not ask too many questions, and labor books were easily forged. The press continually complained of the vast amount of "flitting." Apparently use of the criminal courts to maintain labor discipline was more than Soviet law could bear.[26]

Similarly, the blurring of the lines between economic and counterrevolutionary crimes, as in the 1932 law on theft of state property (repealed in 1947) and the 1941 law on the sale, exchange or release of surplus equipment (repealed in 1955), also put a very great strain on the Soviet legal system. For example, in enforcing certain contracts for the lease of surplus equipment in the 1940's, Arbitrazh held that a "lease" could not have been included in the statutory prohibition against "sale, exchange or release," since there was nothing "counterrevolutionary" about such a lease.[27] At the same time, those loyal citizens who were in fact convicted under such laws as "enemies"—though at most they were thieves, and often only hapless managers striving to fulfill their plans—could hardly have incurred the kind of public contempt which the language of laws presupposed that they deserved.

The post-Stalin regime has substantially reduced the political overtones of official and economic crimes. A thief is now a thief, not a "counterrevolutionary." An engineer who negligently designs a munitions plant need not fear that he will be exiled in a secret administrative procedure. Moreover, in the 1950's, many of the crimes themselves were eliminated and the penalty for others was reduced. Nevertheless, negligence in performance of official duties (including those of engineers) remains a crime. Moreover, the resort to the death penalty in 1961 and 1962 as a means of crushing certain offenses of an economic nature as "crimes against the state" once again reflects the temptation of a planned economy to take Draconian measures against private entrepreneurial activity leading to the accumulation of personal wealth.

Such activity is denounced as a "survival of capitalist psychology." Socialism, with its state ownership of the means of production, its prohibition of private commerce, and its system of planning, has its own psychology: the psychology of economic duty, of obedience to higher administrative authority, and of subordination of individual economic ambition to the collective will. Such a psychology inevitably leans heavily for support not only upon administrative law and "contract discipline" but also upon criminal law.

Chapter Four

SOCIALIST AND CAPITALIST LAW

SOCIALISM means many things to many people. In Massachusetts some years ago a Congregationalist minister was asked by two elderly ladies of his church whether it was true he was planning to run for Congress on the socialist ticket. He replied that it was. "Oh, Mr. H——," they said in a horrified whisper, "we didn't know that you believe in bigamy!" More recently the charge has been made by an official of the National Association of Manufacturers that the United States has already adopted the main features of the *Communist Manifesto;* he cites as an example the virtual "abolition of inheritance" through taxation. By such criteria as these, Soviet law is not in the least bit socialist. Its family law is in some ways stricter than ours, and its inheritance law, with regard to taxation, is far more liberal.

In the non-Soviet world there is a tendency to call every limitation of private property and private contract a step towards socialism. A public health program such as has existed in some European countries for more than a generation is today in the United States termed by some "socialized medicine." Legislation protecting labor unions, social security laws, increased public regulation of business, and various other infringements of the laissez-faire economic

individualism of the past, is indiscriminately lumped together under the rubric "socialist."

Soviet theory, on the other hand, categorically denies the
socialist character of such measures. From the Soviet standpoint, the "welfare state" is simply the last stand of monopoly capitalism. Even French socialism is not socialism at
all, according to the Russians, but merely state capitalism.
Only when the last capitalist is gone, and the entire economy is planned, can there be socialism in their sense of
the word.

On both sides there is a tendency to make socialism and
capitalism mutually exclusive. Everything that is not capitalist must be socialist, and everything that is not socialist
must be capitalist.

This is the terminology of Marxism, to which many
non-Marxists have now succumbed. It was Marx who first
identified our entire social order as a capitalist system,
founded on capitalist economics. However justified such an
analysis may have been one hundred years ago in the big
industrial cities of Europe with which Marx was familiar,
it is hardly adequate as an explanation of present-day society. A World War, a world-wide depression and a Second
World War have intervened to create an entirely new social
order not only in Russia but throughout the world. The
Soviets are stuck with Marxist slogans which do not correspond to the underlying economic and legal realities either
of their society or of ours.

Pure capitalism and pure socialism are myths. Nowhere
does either exist. When the Soviets speak of our economic
system as a capitalist system, they do violence to some of
the most important developments of the past forty-five
years. The United States government has purchased and
sold many billion dollars' worth of land alone. Dozens of
administrative agencies and public corporations have been
given vast control over business activities. Taxation has become an important instrument for the redistribution, in
the public interest, of private profits and inherited wealth.
The Atomic Energy Commission—to mention the most
striking example—is a multi-billion dollar government

agency which exercises a very large measure of control over the resources, both human and natural, with which it is concerned. Indeed, atomic energy is a nationalized industry in the strict sense; fissionable materials are a government monopoly, capable of ownership by the state alone. Government expenditures (federal, state and local) in 1961 amounted to 29 per cent of the gross national product. Whatever this is, it isn't pure capitalism.

On the other hand, we have seen that Soviet socialism is dependent for its operation on institutions, both economic and legal, which have been adapted from presocialist eras. The Soviet economy is a money economy; the ruble is not merely a unit of account but also a measure of value, and prices, though fixed by the state, are designed to correspond in some degree to market conditions of supply and demand. Profits are an important incentive for the directors and employees of state business enterprises. The traditional categories and relationships of corporation law, property law, contract law, are restored even in the "socialist sector." In addition, there are important areas of the economy which are relatively free, such as the free market for the produce of individual peasant households and the labor market, which remains at least flexible despite all attempts to stabilize it. Whatever this is, it isn't pure socialism.

This is not to say that socialism, pure or otherwise, necessarily implies a controlled labor market or the absence of money, or that capitalism necessarily excludes an Atomic Energy Commission or a TVA. For one thing, there are many variants of both socialism and capitalism. The point is, however, that to talk in terms of socialism and capitalism makes less and less sense in the second half of the twentieth century. Not only the Soviet and the American economies, but any going modern economy, is a mixture of socialist and capitalist elements. The developments of the past generation in the Soviet Union and the United States show a progressive fusion of these elements. The Soviet system is compelled to restore centers of initiative and responsibility on local, group, and individual levels, for the sake of making the planned economy work. Starting from the opposite pole, the United States is compelled to seek greater integration and "socialization" of its economy in order to preserve local, group, and individual independence.[1]

To socialists, the blunders of the first phase of development of the Soviet system are an obvious object lesson in the dangers of a socialist oversimplification. Planning is in itself no solution to economic and legal problems, but at best only a possible means to a solution. The planners must face the same fundamental economic and legal realities which exist in a nonsocialist society. If anything, the complexities are more overwhelming than before. A good example may be found in the dilemma which has confronted Soviet industry in respect to meeting quantitative and qualitative standards of production. At first the plans called for production in quantitative terms, without much emphasis on the quality of the products. As a result goods were being turned out without essential parts, in order to meet production plans. Automobiles were manufactured, but they wouldn't run. New laws were passed prohibiting this practice, and establishing strict qualitative norms. As a result, manufacturers, lacking necessary parts, turned out nothing. Another problem has arisen from price fixing, which in some instances has resulted in discouraging the production of goods for which the demand is strong and encouraging the production of goods which are already in sufficient supply. It is such bottlenecks as these which have caused Soviet economists and lawyers, both in theory and in practice, to emphasize managerial responsibility and initiative, strong personal incentives both of reward and punishment, "economic accountability," decentralization of operations. With this, the old ghosts return. The parties are now government officials rather than private capitalists, but the questions which confront the courts are similar: Was there a contract? Was there offer and acceptance? Did the director act beyond the scope of his authority? May a railroad contract out of liability for negligence? What is the liability of an enterprise engaged in ultra-hazardous activity? What is the obligation of the recipient of perishable goods not corresponding to his order? There are countless other similar questions arising out of economic relations and demanding legal characterization. A Plan may be a beautiful thing, but it is not self-executing; and in its execution the very problems which socialist theory has sought to eliminate come back to haunt the planners.

To capitalists, on the other hand, the fact that the Soviet planned economy *has* been able to integrate into its pattern the traditional institutions of property and contract is an equally obvious object lesson in the dangers of a capitalist oversimplification. Competition, credit, accountability, are not peculiar to capitalism. The corporation is not a legal form which makes sense only in terms of private property and limited shareholder liability. These and other familiar "capitalist" institutions can be made workable under socialism as well. At the same time, socialism undoubtedly has certain positive values. It is capable of mobilizing huge resources to accomplish specific large-scale objectives, such as the building of hydro-electric power stations or the launching of space satellites. It is capable of solving large-scale problems of public health and public education.

If we avoid both the socialist and the capitalist oversimplifications we shall be on surer ground in facing the implications of Soviet law. We ourselves are moving toward increased public control of economic life. Our ideas of property and contract are changing. In enforcing our new administrative law we too have created new types of economic crimes. In none of these respects have we approached the extreme lengths to which the Soviets have gone. We are moving slowly and cautiously along a path which they have traversed with crude and violent rapidity. Only from a very broad historical perspective may we treat our system and theirs as similar. One might say, for example, that the Council of Economic Advisers, attached to the President, plays a role in our country analogous to that of the State Planning Commission attached to the Soviet Council of Ministers. The point in saying so would be to indicate that in twentieth century industrial society politics can no longer be divorced from economics; some official body is needed to view the economy as a whole and to formulate long-range economic policy. Beyond that, the analogy fails. We both face the same fundamental economic questions; our answers fall along the same line—but at different points.

It makes sense, therefore, to attempt to understand the Soviet answers for the light they may shed on the possibilities and pitfalls of the path we are treading.

Soviet law, in its socialist aspects, furnishes us with an example of the kind of legal system that goes with a planned economy. I have identified as the most important aspects of such a legal system: (1) the interrelation of plan and law, (2) the development of a socialist law of property and contract, and (3) the extension of economic crimes.

1. In a planned economy the state has a double function. It is on the one hand the economic sovereign; it is the supreme banker, the supreme industrialist, the supreme landholder. On the other hand, the state is an economic citizen as well; *its* business enterprises, *its* collective farms, are entities subject to *its* laws. The state is both sovereign and subject; it both plans and operates the economy.

This dualism is made explicit in Soviet law. The plan is elaborated by planning and regulating organs according to certain procedures in which the operative organs participate. Certain criteria, economic and legal, must be followed in composing and articulating it. These procedures and criteria constitute what might be called the *law of the plan,* a field of law nonexistent in our society. On the other hand, the execution of the plan is put in the hands of government corporations, that is, of legal entities with capacity to sue and be sued and with rights of property and contract. The law of government corporations exists outside the Soviet Union; nowhere else, however, has it been extended so far. Every Soviet government agency which carries on economic operations (as distinct from one that merely plans or regulates) has come to be treated as a corporate entity.

The concept of the corporation, taken over by capitalism from the medieval church, today again shows its capacity for survival and new development. Operating without a joint stock and as an agency of the state, the government corporation obtains, through its legal form, autonomy in its dealings with others and unity in its internal structure. Although Soviet law has not adopted the word "corporation," its term "khozraschet"—economic accountability—expresses the essential concept of economic-legal unity and autonomy.

On the other hand, by giving jurisdiction in disputes between state economic organs to a special system of economic courts, the planned economy protects the governmental functions of those organs (the fulfillment of plans), while at the same time providing for the adjudication of their rights and duties. Soviet Arbitrazh has been an important growing-point of the law; its decisions have prepared the way for new administrative and legislative policy as well as for new judicial policy in the regular system of courts.

2. When private ownership is the rule and state ownership the exception, the character of state ownership is assimilated to that of private ownership. The state, in its proprietary functions, appears as another private party. But in a planned economy, where land and means of production are nationalized, state ownership changes its character. It is not ownership in the old sense. The character of private ownership now becomes assimilated to that of state ownership.

This development is apparent in the contrast between the property law of the NEP codes and that of the five-year plans. The NEP law adopted from the continental European legal tradition the conception of ownership as individual and exclusive, with independent and coequal units holding their land or goods in absolute right. This "Roman" idea of absolute private property, with complete and indivisible title, has also made inroads during the past hundred and fifty years upon the traditional English conception, inherited from feudalism, of property relations between dependent and ranked units, of derivative tenure, of "splinters of ownership."

The feudal property regime linked estates in land with status in society. This involved a union of political and proprietary relations, a fusion of public and private law. *Dominium* meant both "ownership" and "lordship." Feudal tenures were intimately bound up with political and military service. With the development of the modern English state, particularly in the seventeenth century, much feudal lore was revived and fashioned into an elaborate structure of property relationships (life estates, future interests) designed once again to link land law with political power and political service, but this time in the interests of the landed gentry, whose political position was buttressed by the system of family settlements which such land law protected.

Against a property law conceived in terms of lasting relationships based on marriage and inheritance, the French Revolution and the Napoleonic codes brought to bear a property law conceived in terms of transitory commercial relationships based on contract. Land and chattels came to be dealt with more and more as a manifestation of the will of the owner; the transfer of property as a meeting of minds. This meant the assimilation of the law of real property to the law of personal property—the abolition of tenurial survivals and of fictitious procedures of transfer, the development of the power of a life tenant to render the land freely alienable even when it is subject to a family settlement, the simplification of title registration. In America, particularly, it meant the divorce of proprietary rights from direct political-social-economic responsibility.

The past generation has seen a general reaction against conceptions of absolute ownership. Both in Europe and America there has been more and more stress on a functional approach to property in terms of the apportionment of use, possession, and disposition. This is most evident in our commercial law, in which the question of title has lost most of its former importance and instead the nature of the goods, the type of transaction, the allocation of risks, and similar factors have become determinative of the rights of the parties.

The planned economy pushes the reaction against absolute ownership to its extreme. Soviet property law has been recreated along functional lines. Legal distinctions are generally made to correspond to economic differences. This is not always successful; for example, generally speaking the means of production fall under socialist ownership and the means of consumption under personal ownership, but in fact most cattle in the Soviet Union are personally owned, and the consumers' goods produced by state economic enterprises are part of state ownership until they are sold. On the other hand, the Soviets have not hesitated to apply different legal norms to different types of property, according to their social-economic functions. Collective-farm land, railroad land, municipal land, forest land, are each subject to special laws. This differentiation is made possible, if not inevitable, by the fact that different administrative bodies are set up to control these various types of land.

At the same time, Soviet law has returned to conceptions of dependent and derivative tenure, and to a fusion of public and private law. One may say of Soviet law what Holdsworth has said of older English law: "There are a large number of interests, recognized and protected by law, which may co-exist in the same piece of land at the same time." This may be seen in Soviet law on all levels of ownership. An individual citizen may own his house, but he holds the land of the state. A collective farm is considered to have "absolute" ownership of its buildings, but this ownership must be defined in terms of the public-law, public-economic role of the collective farm in the national political-economic order. For effective administration of the industrial process it has been found necessary to restore certain proprietary rights in state economic enterprises—rights limited by the purpose for which they have been restored. A peasant household holds its land, in a sense, of the collective farm to which it belongs. The collective farm in turn holds its land, in a sense, of higher economic-administrative agencies culminating in the Republican Council of Ministers (which under certain circumstances may transfer it), and perhaps also of the U.S.S.R. Council of Ministers. Proprietary relations on all levels have an administrative and public, as well as a domestic, personal character. The very word "private" has been replaced by the word "personal" throughout Soviet legal literature, indicating the fusion of social and individual interests. Although Soviet jurists might be shocked by the analogy to feudal tenures, they would at least agree that their system has rejected "bourgeois" concepts of absolute ownership.

What has been said of property is equally true of contract. In regard both to personal contracts and to commercial contracts, the planned economy seeks to give frank expression, in its legal system, fo the actual economic relations which exist in the community as a whole. We have seen that contracts for the transfer of scarce and important commodities are treated differently from contracts for the transfer of more plentiful commodities. Here, too, the rights of economic organs are limited by the powers of their administrative superiors, and the rights of individual citizens are viewed as part of the entire social-economic process. A Soviet citizen may become rich, but he cannot, through his wealth, directly influence economic development; he can invest only in government bonds or in a state bank. He may make contracts, but he may not "speculate."

Behind the relationships of property and contract, constantly replenishing them, is the Plan. Planning gives conscious direction to the whole economy. Property and contract, which in the past have been symbols of rapid economic development, are restored in a planned economy as elements of continuity and stability.[2]

3. There is a tendency to judge an economic system primarily in terms of its efficiency, its "rationality." Here we can maintain a certain objectivity. "Private property," a "free market," and other symbols of economic individualism, no longer evoke the same passions that they once did. Today we tend to ask of an economic system, "Will it work?"

However, in dealing with law, the question "Will it work?" cannot be divorced from the question "Is it just?"

Socialism, we have seen, involves an extension of the domain of criminal law to new areas. New economic crimes are created to protect socialist property, to prevent and punish the negligence or willful misconduct of state economic managers, to deter workers from tardiness and absenteeism. New "official crimes" and "crimes against the administrative order" provide sanctions against willful or negligent breach of planning discipline by officials and administrators. New "counterrevolutionary crimes"—since 1958 renamed "state crimes"—are devised to protect the state against deviation from the fundamental principles of the established order.

Here again we must view Soviet law from the perspective of our own law as it is developing, and not as it was. In recent decades we, too, have extended the domain of criminal law to new spheres. The Securities and Exchange Act, for example, makes it a criminal offense, in certain cases, to market securities without a full and fair disclosure of the condition of the corporation. The anti-trust laws rely not merely on civil suits but also on criminal penalties. To evade the tax laws may subject the taxpayer to a criminal indictment. "As society has grown more complex," writes George Dession, "we have witnessed an ever growing resort to criminal as well as other sanctions to maintain and extend public order in the realms of trade and commerce, of labor-management relations, of ideological conflicts, and of national security."

On the whole, we rely on the "other" sanctions. We dismiss the administrator who has been negligent in his duties. We prefer to invoke economic remedies even in the case of the tax evader. During the war we punished the employer who violated the wage freeze by refusing to allow him to deduct the total wages of his enterprise as a business expense in computing his income tax.

In the last analysis, however, our administrative law depends on criminal sanctions. A crime is by definition a violation of a legal standard set by the state. As the state takes more and more responsibility for setting legal standards for the economy, criminal law inevitably grows. In addition, the very circumstances which compel the creation of public controls may also stimulate new social attitudes which lead to resentment of violations, and this resentment is apt to find expression in criminal sanctions.

Whether or not a planned economy can operate without such an extension of criminal sanctions, whether or not our own movement toward increasing public control of business will be accompanied by an analogous development in the field of economic, official, administrative, and ideological crimes, are questions that cannot be answered with any assurance. The heavy Soviet reliance on criminal law may be explained in part by circumstances not themselves integral to socialism as such; the Soviet regime not only came to power by bloodshed and terror but also carried out the collectivization of agriculture thirteen years later by ruthless and arbitrary methods, thereby alienating large sections of the population; the Soviet regime embarked upon planning as a means of very rapid industrialization, with forced saving and hence enforced poverty, thereby creating conditions conducive to popular resistance and evasion; the Soviet regime has at times been a victim of its own fanatical adherence to the Marxist-Leninist philosophy, with its too great optimism about the future and its too great pessimism about the past, the combination leading to an extreme intolerance of "backwardness"; the Soviet regime has been threatened repeatedly by the hostility of foreign powers and by the antagonism of many of its own people, as well as by intraparty conflicts for positions of power, with the result that it tends to overcompensate for its sense of insecurity.

To the special circumstances under which socialism has been introduced in the Soviet Union must be added special features of Russia's cultural heritage, to be considered in Part II, which contribute to an emphasis upon criminal sanctions. Nevertheless, it seems clear that there are certain elements of Soviet criminal law which arise inevitably from the nature of the Soviet economic system.

The Soviet distinction between theft of personal and theft of state property is probably an essential feature of a socialist system. The socialism of Plato went even farther than that of the Soviets in this respect; his *Laws* in one place provide the death penalty for theft of state property "no matter whether of a small or great amount, whether by guile or force."

The creation of such new economic crimes as "carelessness" on the part of state economic managers, "manufacture of defective products," and the rest, seems also to be intimately connected with the socialist character of the Soviet system. "Soviet law," writes the English criminologist Hermann Mannheim, "is no longer exclusively interested in fighting such comparatively minor derangements in the *distribution* of goods [such as theft]; its primary aim is to help to *extend production* and to *preserve existing* goods." He cites Haldane's statement: " 'Thou shalt not steal' is replaced by 'Thou shalt not waste' as property becomes socialized."

Mannheim attributes this to a new attitude towards public property on the part of the Soviet people, "to the emphasis universally laid on the 'we'-feeling, the sense of common ownership, to be found in particular among the younger generation in present-day Russia." [3] Yet there is no evidence that theft of socialist property is severely frowned on by the population generally, as distinct from the public authorities. On the contrary, stealing in the factories is very widespread and is apparently socially acceptable, while stealing the personal belongings of one's neighbor is infrequent and dishonorable. The reason for the severity of the Soviet laws regarding crimes against socialist property may be just the opposite of what Mannheim supposes.

Here the factor of poverty enters in. The poverty of the economy as a whole and of the individuals within it strongly conditions the nature both of Soviet planning and of Soviet law. It is clear that, generally speaking, as commodities become plentiful a greater contractual freedom is allowed for their disposition and a greater decentralization of administrative control takes place in regard to them. The relation of contract and plan is thus worked out, in part, in terms of the scarcity of the products involved. Similarly, the poverty of the economy—and not merely its planned character—

tends to make waste "criminal." But the poverty of individuals breeds those very crimes which the poverty of the economy makes the state anxious to prevent: crimes against socialist property.

It may be argued, therefore, that Soviet law is the law of a scarcity economy, rather than of a planned economy as such. Certainly the character of Soviet social institutions generally has been very strongly influenced by the decision to sacrifice all other goals to that of rapid industrialization. This has meant forced saving on a large scale, severe restrictions on consumer goods, and the blind elimination of small capitalist producers. It has meant discontent on the part of the people and repression on the part of the rulers. To some observers the frenzied drive for economic development makes Soviet experience seem irrelevant to problems confronted by more advanced countries.

Despite the cogency of this argument, it seems undeniable that Soviet experience reveals some of the difficulties and dangers inherent in all forms of socialism—and at the same time some of the ways in which those difficulties and dangers can, with varying degrees of success, be met. Indeed, it may be that planning, at least in the sense of centralized public direction of all branches of the economy, depends on relative scarcity. In an economy which is not under pressure to increase production there is no necessity for total planning. This is implicit in the provisions of Soviet law itself, which tends to relax controls and to decentralize administration in those areas of the economy where there is relative abundance.

Both partisans and antagonists of the Soviet system tend to view Soviet institutions in terms of the extent to which they embody Marxist theory. This frame of reference has served as a starting point for the present study. Marx said: Economics is basic; law is superstructure, designed to serve the interests of the ruling economic class. The Soviet leaders say: Within the Soviet Union we have eliminated class exploitation and antagonism; our law reflects the classless —or class-conflictless—socialist character of our planned economy. Having analyzed some of the features of Soviet law which stem from socialism, and in particular those aspects of the legal system which implement and protect the planned economy—we may inquire to what extent it is a concrete expression of Marxism.

Affirmatively, three outstanding features of Soviet law may be traced in part to its Marxist heritage. The first is its collectivist character. The Marxist principle of totality, of the basic unity of all social relations, finds expression in the integration of politics and economics and in the conscious treatment of legal problems as social problems. Even a lawsuit between two Soviet citizens has an explicit social character, since the state is interested in fixing responsibility. This is especially important in cases involving state economic enterprises, where Arbitrazh has the duty of "signalizing" gross misconduct on the part of directors to the appropriate administrative organ or to the prosecutor's office.

Second, the dialectical character of Soviet socialist law manifests its Marxist orientation. Despite the struggle for stability, Soviet law changes rapidly to meet changing conditions. It is not static or conceptual. It tolerates logical contradictions and inconsistencies even more readily than our law does. The emphasis on the social-economic purpose of rights is still strong, despite the restoration of the "formal-juridical" element as having equal importance. In particular, the administrative structure of industry undergoes almost continual change. The drive for strict legality is itself conceived in the interests of dynamic social development.

Third, the influence of Marxist theory may be seen in the Soviet emphasis on extralegal and nonlegal means of social control, and the subordination of law to those extra- and nonlegal means. Marxism is a theory of power. Law is created by the social order, which itself, however, is considered to be based ultimately on force. When its existence is threatened, the social order may be compelled, for its own preservation, to abandon law and to revert to its ultimate sanction. Thus Soviet law is always precarious; the secret police may step in at any time. Marxism is also a theory of social harmony. The communist society, in its ideal form, requires only a minimum either of force or of law. In order to reach its goal, the socialist order therefore stresses the development of nonlegal social sanctions, especially those associated with membership in the Communist Party and with Party propaganda and agitation.

Despite these characteristics, the Soviet legal system, even in its socialist aspects, cannot be explained satisfactorily as a Marxist system. The very existence of "socialist law" is an innovation in Marxist theory, and a contradiction of the spirit of Marxism if not its letter. Moreover, many of the features of Soviet law which are considered by the Soviet rulers to be peculiarly socialist bear striking resemblance to the law of those societies which they condemn as capitalist.

In seeking to construct an affirmative theory of law, the Soviet rulers are handicapped by their Marxist heritage. The Marxist features of the Soviet legal system are limiting features. But in spite of Marxism the Soviet rulers have found law necessary—necessary to the planned economy itself—not only because of the rationality and calculability which a legal system provides, but also because of the assurance which it gives to those who operate the economy that their acts will be judged according to some standard of rightness. The rational allocation of resources requires a reasonable adjudication of rights and duties.

-II-
RUSSIAN
LAW

Chapter Five

MARXISM AND THE RUSSIAN HERITAGE

TO ANALYZE Soviet law only in terms of the theory and practice of socialism would be to content ourselves with a one-dimensional picture. A legal system can never be the product of an "ism" alone—no matter how much the rulers of a country may so desire. Despite the will of the Soviet rulers, despite the tightness of their dogma, there are historical forces at work in the shaping of the Soviet legal system. Soviet law is not merely socialist law; it is Russian law. It is the historical Russian background of Soviet law which gives it its second dimension and which allows us to see it in a larger perspective.

That Soviet law is rooted and grounded in the Russian past is now implicitly recognized by Soviet jurists themselves, who, in preparing their new codes, did not merely study the works of Marx and Engels, Lenin and Stalin, but also searched carefully the historical records of prerevolutionary Russian law. Indeed, the Restoration of Law since the mid-1930's is closely associated with the rehabilitation of prerevolutionary Russian traditions; both movements serve the need for continuity and stability. This finds expression in the Soviet law schools, where the history of Russian law is now a required subject and where the

Latin language, previously dispararaged as a symbol of juridical formalism, has been restored to a place of importance as the language of Roman law, in which Russian law has historical roots. The return to older tradition is also evidenced by the revived prestige of law professors who were trained under the *ancien régime*—men who came under a cloud after the NEP was abandoned, but to whom Vyshinsky, in 1937, could refer as "those honest jurists who, being educated in and penetrated by the old legal culture and science, were unable, just because of their weak Marxist-Leninist preparation, effectively to resist the saboteurs"—the "saboteurs" being such erstwhile leaders of the Soviet legal profession as Krylenko and Pashukanis, who (with Vyshinsky himself) had effectively hounded the prerevolutionary jurists from public life. With the aid of the new Vyshinsky, and his strong "Marxist-Leninist preparation," they were restored.

It is not suggested that Soviet Russian law is the same as prerevolutionary Russian law. "We are no longer the Russians we were before 1917, and our Rus is not the same, our character is not the same," stated Andrei Zhdanov in 1946. This statement is undoubtedly true. Yet it must be understood as expressing not only a divergence between Soviet and pre-Soviet Russia, but also, and at the same time, a sense of identification between them. Who are "we Russians"? What is "our Rus"? What did Zhdanov the Marxist mean by these terms?

Marxist theory and Russian history are strange bedfellows. In the cold, systematic, impersonal science of Marx and Engels, every conclusion follows relentlessly from its premises. The only permissible passion is that of bitterness at the injustices of history. Man is stripped of all his clothing, all his "superstructure," and left naked on the rock of economics. In this, classical Marxism is the complete reduction, the *ultima ratio,* of Western rationalism—not rationalism in the specific nineteenth-century sense but rather in the sense characteristic of the Western mind since the eleventh and twelfth centuries; Marx and Engels were rationalists in that they sought to rationalize life, to give order and form to human history, to see society in terms of cause and effect. In their interpretation of the past they fought all nonrational elements—tradition, patriotism, religion, "ideology." They fought Reason, too—that is, nineteenth-century Faith in Reason, Reason with a capital *R,* as the motive force of history. They reduced all the enthusiasms, all the passions, all the "isms" of the past to economic and social laws.

A reverential statement of Lenin regarding his master sheds light on the extent to which classical Marxism derives its method from the whole tradition of Western thought. Lenin says that Marx took the best from German philosophy, English economics, and French socialism. Lenin might have gone further: Marx took something from Western medieval scholasticism as well. Not without accuracy has Marx been called the last of the schoolmen. The Marxian dialectic itself, though usually attributed to Hegel and in fact derived from him by Marx, goes back to Abelard's eleventh-century book *Sic et Non,* and to the method expressed in the title of Gratian's epoch-making legal treatise, published about 1140, "A Concordance of Discordant Canons."

How different are the cast of mind and the way of life usually associated with the Russian tradition! The Orthodox East has repeatedly reproached the West for its excessive emphasis on reason, science, and law. Even the Russian Westernizers, that segment of the Russian intelligentsia which deplored Russia's backwardness and urged a conscious imitation of the West, did so with a passion and a capacity for intense exaggeration that astounded and shocked the West. Russian Marxists of the nineteenth and twentieth centuries transformed the doctrines of Marx and Engels by infusing them with elements of Russian populism (the movement of Russian intelligentsia "back to the people"), anarchism, and apocalyptic fervor. To the West even the Russian Westernizer has often seemed "Eastern."

To view Russia as "East" makes sense, however, only within strict historical limits. Russia is obviously not China, or India, or Persia. Moreover, even if one confines oneself to the proposition that Russia is Russia, one must still note certain important historical affinities with Western Europe. In her foreign policy, Russia has faced East and West, again and again in her history shifting direction from one to the other; and domestically, she has been torn by an internal conflict between those who have sought inspiration in the Western tradition and those who have tried to build on Byzantine and Asiatic foundations. This dualism is manifest again in the Russian Revolution. The reception of Western philosophy, Western economics, and Western political science, in their Marxist form—in the form of a Western theory which no Western country had hitherto found palatable—is characteristically Russian. In the hands of the Bolsheviks, the rejected stone of the West became the head of the corner.

It becomes necessary, therefore, if we are to understand Soviet law, to articulate it into the context of Russian history. Here, too, we cannot avoid comparison; and here, too, we shall find a challenge. For a study of Russian legal history brings into clear focus the polarity that has existed between Russian history and Western history for almost a thousand years. The main events which shaped the development of Western law from the eleventh to the nineteenth century had only distant repercussions in Russian history. Until the middle of the nineteenth century, at least, Russian law remained largely outside the common tradition which has formed the various legal systems of the West —from Poland and Austria-Hungary to England and America. The study of Russian law therefore challenges us to rediscover the unity of Western law. Indeed, the most promising approach to a study of the historical Russian component of Soviet law is to look first at the Western legal tradition and then to compare and contrast it with the main features of Russian legal development.[1]

Chapter Six

THE WESTERN LEGAL TRADITION

LEGALLY, there is no such thing as Western law; there is only English law, French law, German law, and the laws of the other sovereign European and American states. Yet if one looks at legal history from the perspective of a non-Western culture, it becomes apparent that, despite the inroads of nationalism in recent centuries, there is a strong family likeness in the legal systems of the various nations of the West; as Edmund Burke wrote some two hundred years ago, "the law of every country of Europe is derived from the same sources."

Indeed, one of the primary facts distinguishing Western civilization as a whole from the Russian or other non-Western traditions is its concept of law, and in particular its exaltation of law as a fundamental basis of unity in society. Belief in the existence of a "fundamental law" to which governments must adhere or else risk overthrow as despotisms is characteristically Western. It finds expression in the English concept of the Rule of Law as well as in the German idea of the *Rechtsstaat*. This is not to say that there have not been, in the West, significant relapses into illegality, as well as times when the predominant philosophy has been one of a common brotherhood transcending law. We are shocked by the wholesale confiscation of private property by the Bolsheviks in 1917; yet the Republican administration, in freeing the slaves without compensation after the Civil War, carried out one of the most colossal confiscations of all times. Revolution is as much in the Western tradition as Law. In fact the history of Western law must be seen partly in terms of the great total revolutions which, through bloodshed and violence, as well as through apocalyptic visions of a society so perfect as to have no need of law, have laid the basis for new legal categories and concepts.

Looking backward over the centuries we see that each of the great European revolutions ultimately produced new law. Scholars generally agree that the Napoleonic civil, commercial, and criminal codes of 1804-1808, whose influence spread not only throughout the West but into other parts of the world as well, were in part a product of the French Revolution of 1789, with its Reign of Terror and its foreign wars. The Napoleonic codes built on the pre-revolutionary French law but they also added something new. As their influence spread throughout Europe, they revolutionized Western legal systems by the very philosophy of codification implicit in them: through the summation and systematization, in chapters and paragraphs, of the entire mass of existing rules, decisions, statutes, and customs, the codes sought to give certainty and equality in the application of law. A restraint was thereby exercised on judges and legislators—against arbitrariness, against privilege. In their substantive provisions as well, the Napoleonic codes introduced a new epoch in Western legal history, particularly through individualistic and contractualistic conceptions of property relations. In the pre-nineteenth-century legal systems of Europe property rights were defined in terms of the status of various classes, such as the nobility, the clergy, the city-dwellers, the peasantry. In the new French civil code, however, they were given an abstract and universal quality. Ownership was defined in terms of the absolute right of the individual to do with his property as he wills. "Title" was conceived as complete and indivisible. The transfer of property could thus be dealt with as a meeting of minds. This meant the divorce of proprietary rights from direct political privileges and responsibilities.

The connection between the English Revolution of 1640-1689 and the English Common Law is more controversial than that between the French Revolution and the Napoleonic codes, since the seventeenth-century English legal reformers asserted that they were only "restoring" the medieval and Anglo-Saxon tradition which had been abrogated during a hundred and fifty years of Tudor "despotism." Yet it cannot be denied that this so-called "restoration" was a step into the future, that it inaugurated a new era in the development of the English legal system. In the field of public or constitutional law this is clear, for the doctrine of parliamentary supremacy, and the founding of the political power of parliament on the social and economic power of the landed gentry, was new in the seventeenth century. New, too, was the increased power of the judiciary, composed largely of the younger sons of the landed gentry (the older sons going into Parliament). The principle was established that judges were not removable at the will of the monarch but served "on good behavior" (*quamdiu se bene gesserint*). As the repositories of the ancient legal traditions (newly discovered and hardly called ancient before the seventeenth century), the judges had wide powers of discretion; it was against these large discretionary powers of the judiciary that the French Revolution and the Napoleonic codes were, in part, a reaction. (French writers still identify the English judicial system, and especially the doctrine that the courts are bound by their earlier decisions—the doctrine of precedent— with the *ancien régime*.) These principles of English constitutional law had important repercussions in other fields of law as well—in the law of property and contract, in family law, in inheritance, and in other branches. Minus the miltary and ecclesiastical aspects of feudalism, minus also the feudal institution of vassalage, English judges and legislators fashioned a new "feudal" structure of private-law relations, built on a system of family settlements. "Real property" was conceived in terms not of transitory commercial relationships based on contract, as in the later French Civil Code, but in terms of lasting relationships based on marriage and inheritance. Corporation law was freed from restraints by the crown and by monopolies.

The French Revolution reacted against the aristocratic ideas which had spread throughout Europe in the wake of the English Revolution. The English Revolution was, in turn, a reaction against the monarchical ideas which had been given dominance by the German revolution of 1517—the Reformation. The German Reformation, too, is associated with the production of new law. It went hand in hand with the movement known as the Reception of Roman Law, which, from the end of the fifteenth century, swept the continent of Europe and almost engulfed England as well. This was more than a mere reception of ancient law; it was a recreation of the medieval Roman-and-canon legal system out of which it grew and against which it reacted.

When Martin Luther publicly burned the canon law books, he performed both a religious and a political act—symbolizing the revolt against the Roman Catholic conception of a visible, legal Church and the desire to purge the existing political and legal regime of ecclesiastical influence. The success of the Protestant Reformation of the Church meant the transfer of initiative in law and government to new secular classes, with new territorial jurisdictions; and it was these new political states—the principalities—which needed a legal system. The sixteenth-century German princes (and their monarchical counterparts in France, England, and elsewhere) had the task of organizing their territorial jurisdictions without the aid of men whose allegiance was to the pope. In Germany they did so by sponsoring the growth of a new class of secular jurists, and a secular civil service. They also had the task of reorganizing the relations of groups and classes within their territorial jurisdictions, once the power of the Church—and especially the monasteries—was broken. In

Germany they did so by extending Roman Law to spheres into which the Romano-canonical law of the medieval Church had only slightly penetrated.

As the nineteenth-century French system exalted the code (and hence the legislature, which alone can change the code), and as the seventeenth-century English Common Law exalted the judiciary, so the modern Roman Law of sixteenth-century Germany exalted the learned jurist and civil servant, who shapes the law in terms of principles and concepts. German law professors, for example, had actual cases submitted to them, as a body, for decision. This reliance on professors and state councillors and princely advisers had implications not only for the newly emerging bureaucratic "rational" State, but for private law as well. It made possible the development of legal abstractions— such as Contract, Ownership, Inheritance. Both on the Continent and in England, for example, the separation of contract from tort—that is, the distinction between breaking an agreement with another and doing him injury— dates from the sixteenth century. The Reception of Roman Law on the Continent, with its repercussions in England, may be said to have produced our modern conception of freedom of contract. It also produced our modern conception of freedom of wills—freedom, that is, to leave by will both land and personal property.

If we push further into the past, we find that the cornerstone of all the legal systems of the West was laid in the eleventh and twelfth centuries, through a law movement which also went hand in hand with a violent revolution. In the year 1075 Pope Gregory VII declared the secession of the Church from the Empire; in so doing, he proclaimed for the first time the conception of the Roman Catholic Church as a separate legal entity, distinct from secular law, with the pope as its legal head and the papal *curia* as a court of last resort throughout Western Christendom. In his *Dictatus Papae,* the revolutionary document in which this conception was proclaimed, it was stated for the first time that appeals could be taken from the courts of bishops to the court of the bishop of

Rome. Wars were fought before Europe accepted this usurpation of what had previously been the jurisdiction of the Emperor, who up to this point had considered himself the real head of the Church and the appointer of popes. A whole new legal system was established before the interrelations of Church and Empire, and the internal relations within each, could be stabilized on the new basis.

From the so-called renovation of Roman and canon law of the eleventh and twelfth centuries dates the richness of the legal traditions of all the nations of the West. Throughout Western Europe there emerged then, for the first time, lawyers, law schools, law treatises, hierarchies of courts, and a science of law. European jurists, working on the primitive customs of the various Germanic peoples, on the laws of the Frankish empire (and especially the feudal charters of immunity and privilege which had assumed increasing importance with the decentralization of imperial authority in the ninth, tenth, and eleventh centuries), on the liturgy and sacraments of the Church, and on the *Digest* of the Byzantine Emperor Justinian (which after many centuries of oblivion in the West, was then, conveniently, rediscovered)—read into these legal materials certain principles which were new to the history of law. Much of their legal science bore an ideal and abstract character. Yet the secular legal systems of the Western nations, forged in the fires of national revolutions from the sixteenth century on, are founded on these innovations of the eleventh and twelfth centuries; each successive wave of great legal reform in the succeeding centuries is a further development and elaboration of them.

For purposes of analysis, we may classify the changes in law which took place at that time under the headings of three leading principles: the principle of Reason, the principle of Conscience, and the principle of Growth.

Reason, in this context, signifies the principle that conflicting customs, statutes, cases, and doctrines may be reconciled by analysis and synthesis. For the medieval lawyer this meant a dialectical method of investigating texts, a method which had been developed in theology by such men as Abelard and applied to law by canonists such as Gratian. The medieval dialectic—as contrasted with the ancient Greek dialectic, which was essentially a method of classification—enabled European jurists not merely to distinguish and analogize rules of law, as the Greco-Roman jurists had done, but to analyze basic ideas. The Eastern Roman law of Justinian's time and before had attached very great weight to the authority of legal rules stated in semi-sacred texts or by great jurists. Emphasis was on the use of the right words and categories. This gave a certain authoritarian and liturgical character to Eastern Roman law. An illustration of this may be seen in the fifth-century Law of Citations, which named five great jurists whose writings should be authoritative, stating that in case of a difference among the five on a particular point, the opinion of the majority should prevail, unless there was an even split among those of the five who expressed an opinion, in which case the opinion of Papinian was to prevail. Another illustration may be found in the decree of Justinian prohibiting any commentaries on his code.

In the eleventh and twelfth centuries, Western jurists seized on the great law books of the Eastern Roman Empire in a quite new spirit. Now the older Roman legal categories and classes were transmuted into ideas and concepts. Negotiability was a new and characteristic discovery of this period. A claim was for the first time something that could be transferred, and in some cases the transferee who purchased it in good faith could acquire greater rights against the obligor than the person who transferred it. Also a new concept of contract was developed. In the Roman law of Justinian contract had been interpreted in terms of the intention of the parties, but intention was determined by the words uttered or the acts performed; now intention became a concept, not just a category, and the same words could be considered to manifest different intentions when spoken under different circumstances.

The law of evidence and procedure was particularly

affected by the new emphasis upon reconciliation of conflicting authorities ("concordance of discordant canons"). "Legal proof"—proof based on formal procedures, as in the earlier Roman law, or on the sworn testimony of oath-helpers, who had to swear the oath of the accused "without slip or trip," or on ordeals of fire and water, as in the Germanic and Anglo-Saxon law—gave way to "rational proof": the judge's mind had to be convinced, and the judgment based on his convictions.

In fact, the medieval jurists insisted that all law conform to reason; they identified law with reason. Just as the medieval theologian asserted that Reason governs the universe, so the medieval lawyer said that law governs all human relations, including even the relation of the sovereign to his subjects. Everything was susceptible of being either legal or illegal. Thus, from what we have called the principle of Reason there developed the idea that the law is complete, that it covers all situations; and the idea that the law is supreme, that it governs all men.

The principle of *Conscience* means that the judge must find the law not only in books or in reason, but also in his own conscience. This was first stated in an eleventh-century tract which declared that the judge must judge himself before he may judge the accused—that he must, in other words, identify himself with the accused since thereby (it was said) he will know more of the crime than the criminal himself.[1] A new science of pleading and procedure was created "for informing the conscience of the judge" (*ad informandum conscientiam judicis*). A written complaint, written summons by the court, and written records were introduced for the first time. The right to direct legal representation by professional lawyers, interrogation by the judge, exceptions to jurors, special pleas (dilatory and peremptory)—all of which were unknown to earlier Roman law as well as to tribal German law—were now established. From the idea of the importance of the conscience of the judge was elaborated the concept of judicial discretion. The judge was thereby transformed from an umpire to a lawgiver. Moreover, as Reason was associated with the ideas of the supremacy and the completeness of law, so Conscience was associated with the idea of the equality 'of law, since in conscience all litigants are equal; and from the idea of equality, came the systematic protection of the poor and helpless against the rich and powerful, the enforcement of relations of trust and confidence (as in English law, for example, when a man leaves property to another "for the use of" a third person, and the second man is considered a "trustee"; or when two persons exchange mutual promises, with nothing more, and the court treats these promises as legally binding), and the granting of so-called personal remedies such as specific performance of a contract (instead of mere damages for its breach) and injunctions.[2] Here, too, Western law was distinguished both from the older Frankish law and the Eastern Roman law; for although both these latter systems were infused with equitable conceptions—the Byzantine law, in particular, protecting the wife against the husband, the ward against the guardian, the debtor against the creditor—in neither were these equitable conceptions made systematic, and in both procedure remained archaic and intensely formal, lacking a developed concept of judicial discretion.

The principle of *Growth* signifies an emphasis on the organic development of legal institutions, including legal doctrines, over long periods of time. This in turn implies a respect for past decisions in particular cases as a foundation for legal development. Although the doctrine of precedent won for itself a special place in English law from the seventeenth century on, the common belief that the Anglo-American system is unique in relying on past decisions is a mistaken one. Judges may be influenced by previous cases, as cited by the lawyers, without mentioning them in their opinions and without accepting a strict doctrine of "standing by decisions" (*stare decisis*). The judicial *technique* differs in England or America on the one hand and in France or Germany or Russia on the other. Here we cite cases as authority for a decision, though we have developed to a fine art the ability to distinguish one case from another, whereas the continental technique is to rely on cases as illustrations of the law, although in writing its final opinion the court does not generally discuss the cases which were relied upon. This is a technical difference and should not obscure the fact that throughout Europe, wherever the influence of the Roman-and-canon law system was felt, the rule developed that decisions are to be based, at least in part, on precedents, and at the same time are to make precedents for the future. A judicial decision, in the Western tradition, is not an *ad hoc* thing: there is a striving for consistency with the past and for influence upon the future.

Precedents make history. The concept of precedents is thus associated with the idea of the growth of a single body of law. Growth would be impossible if every court could undo the work of every other. Hence the necessity for a hierarchy of courts, with appeals from lower to higher tribunals; hence the development of forms of action—typical complaints which were standardized as similarities appeared in the cases for which writs were demanded; hence the necessity for reports of decisions and collections of statutes; hence the necessity for maintaining a close connection between legislation and judicial decision.

The jurisprudence of the eleventh and twelfth centuries gradually permeated the legal consciousness of the West. It found expression not only in the creation of a new system of canon law, but also in the development of the secular law of the various nations. Under its stimulus the tribal customs of the Western peoples were slowly transformed, in the later Middle Ages, into national legal systems, and feudal economic relations into feudal legal relations. As an example of the common tradition which informs all Western legal systems, one need only mention the decree of the Fourth Lateran Council of 1215 abolishing the ordeal—a legislative act of the Church which forced every country of the West to put its criminal law on a new basis, since without the participation of the priests the ordeals, which had been the principal mode of proof in criminal cases, could not be performed. Moreover, with the end of the Catholic Middle Ages, the medieval legal tradition did not stop but was instead transmuted into various national forms. Each of the great national secular revolutions of modern European history has involved a nationalization and secularization of medieval law. Moreover, each of these national revolutions has had an impact on the other countries of the West. Despite the innumerable changes which have been made over the centuries, the three basic principles of Reason, Conscience, and Growth—and the ideas associated with them of the supremacy and completeness of law, the equality of law, and the continuity of law—remain the foundation of the legal system of every Western people.

It is more than mere coincidence that only now, with the collapse of the European system of national states and the rise to power of Russia, a country which has remained outside the mainstream of Western history, are we able to rediscover the unity and continuity of the Western legal tradition which modern nationalisms have for so long obscured. The Russian Revolution is only superficially a European revolution. The legal system which it is producing is only in part a Western system. To understand it we must study it in the context of the Russian legal tradition which is its heritage.

THE WESTERN LEGAL TRADITION

Year	Revolution	Law Movement	Constitutional Principles	Legal Principles
1075	Papal Revolution	Renovation of Roman-and-Canon Law	Visible, hierarchical, legal church; separation of church and state.	Principles of Reason, Conscience, and Growth.
1517	German Reformation	Reception of Roman Law	Absolute monarchy; secular civil service (Bureaucratic, Rational State).	Freedom of contract; freedom of wills; conceptualist law.

1640	English Revolution	Restoration of Common Law	Parliamentary system; landed aristocracy; independence of the judiciary.	Family property settlements; freedom of corporations; traditionalist law.
1789	French Revolution	Napoleonic Codes	Individualist democracy; separation of powers; government by public opinion.	Absolute private property conceived in contractual terms; contractualist law.

Chapter Seven

THE SPIRIT OF RUSSIAN LAW

A MERE DESCRIPTION of the laws in effect in Russia in
October 1917 will not tell us the nature of the legal system
which the Soviet regime inherited from the prerevolutionary tsardom. A legal system is more than the laws in force
at a given moment. Law is a monument of history, constructed over many centuries, not simply out of words and
documents but out of human actions and human lives.
Law is more than rules; it is the legal profession, the law
schools, the technique and tradition of judging, administer-
ing, and legislating. Law is also the sense of law, the law-
consciousness, of the people. These things exist not only in
space but also in time. How deeply they are imbedded in
the institutions of a society may depend in part on the
length of time they have existed, and even more on the
historical circumstances surrounding their origin and development. This is obvious in the case of our own legal
institutions, such as trial by jury, the writ of habeas corpus,
or the power of judicial review of the constitutionality
of legislation; it is also true of the legal institutions of
other countries, however codified the law of those countries
may be.

Particularly when we are dealing with a legal system

which claims to be entirely new, and which seeks its chief justification not in the past but in the ideology of a Revolution, it is necessary to view it historically. For the past works on us without our knowing it, and by rejecting the past we may in fact bind ourselves to it more closely than by accepting it.

Usually a Revolution revolts not against the whole past but against that part of the past which immediately preceded it: its effect, therefore, may be to restore the still older past. Nicholas II and the tsars of the nineteenth century are anathema to the Soviet regime, but Peter the Great and Ivan the Terrible are once again heroes. The rehabilitation of Russian history since the mid-1930's compels us to ask what parts of the Russian past are being selected and what are being rejected or ignored. We must also try to discover what, in the Russian past, is working on Soviet development subconsciously.

These questions take us as far backward in Russian history as we have had to go in order to find the sources and the main lines of growth of Western legal institutions. Russian legal history, too, goes back a thousand years, and important features of Soviet law date from each epoch of that long development. To make sense out of Soviet law we must therefore try to make sense out of Russian legal history as a whole.*

THE COMMON SOURCES OF RUSSIAN LAW
AND WESTERN LAW

When we are tempted to talk of Russia as "East," we must remember that, historically, Russian social and legal institutions emerged from a background very similar to that of the West. The Slavic peoples who lived in the ninth and tenth centuries in what became Russia seem to have had a social order not essentially different from that of the Germanic peoples who settled down in the West in the fourth and fifth centuries. They produced an essentially similar law. Moreover, the Slavs, like their Western cousins, were converted from paganism to Christianity, and through

Christianity became heirs to the Roman law of the Empire and the canon law of the Church. It is likewise important to remember that the Eastern and Western Church, despite provincial differences, was at this time essentially a unity, and that the Eastern and Western Roman Empire shared common political ideas despite the rivalry of Rome and Constantinople. Thus both Russia and the West, in the year 1000, looked to the canon law of the Church councils and to the Roman law of the Christian emperors.

The diverging streams of Russian and Western legal history must thus be recognized as having a common source in the older (pre-eleventh-century) Eastern Roman law. With all the changes that have taken place over the centuries, this fact remains of primary significance in the comparison of Soviet and American law today.

It is Roman law which, in the first place, has given both Russia and the West a common legal vocabulary and a common system of legal distinctions. We classify law in the Roman fashion—into the law of persons and of things, into obligations arising from contract and obligations arising from personal injury, and so on. Of course the words and categories have changed in meaning over the centuries. Nevertheless it is something to have a basic legal language. Without this common ancestry, Soviet and American lawyers would hardly be able to understand each other.

In the second place, the Roman Empire was the source from which both Russia and the West received the notion that a state may be organized by law; the notion, that is, that on the one hand the state should give expression to its policy and its administration in institutions of public law, and that on the other hand the state has the function of giving expression to the interrelations of its subjects among each other in institutions of private law. The very concept of legislation as a primary source of lasting law was derived, both in Russia and the West, from Roman law. Together with this should be mentioned the Byzantine institutions of summons by the court (instead of by the plaintiff), execution of judgment by the court, judgment by default, appeals to the emperor, and a procedure by which the judge was allowed to conduct the trial in terms of rules laid down by public authority instead of merely supervising a submission to arbitration. Justice, instead of proceeding from a voluntary contract, was now imposed from above.

In the third place, both Russian law and Western law are indebted to the Byzantine emperors for the emphasis on the subjective elements of intent (*animus*), consent, fault— as distinct from the objective facts of a legal relationship. Partly under the influence of Christianity, what a man had in mind became in some instances as important in law as what he said or did. For example, in the earlier Roman law, if two people become co-owners of a piece of property —for instance, by buying it together—they were held to have by that fact entered into a contract of partnership (*societas*), since they had voluntarily joined in a common enterprise. In Byzantine Roman law, however, everything depended not on the existence of a common enterprise but on the intention to enter into a contract of *societas*. The parties had to have it in mind, as indicated by their words or acts. Likewise, in the law of personal injury, the mental element came to have much greater significance, distinguishing negligence from mere accident.

Finally, a significant moral or ethical contribution was made by the Christian emperors of the East to the ancient Roman law. We have mentioned that Byzantine law sought to protect the weak against the strong, the wife against the husband, the ward against the guardian, the debtor against the creditor. Another example is the rule that a man in lawful possession of another's land should be reimbursed for improvements which he made on the land. This was part of the very strong Byzantine conception that no man should be enriched unjustly at the expense of another—a doctrine which entered the Anglo-American common law only in the eighteenth century, when Lord Mansfield resurrected it from the lawbooks of Justinian.

These were some of the features of Eastern Roman law which made it great and which have given it survival value for fifteen hundred years and more, both in Russia and in the West. Yet it has survived in two quite different ways. In the West it was systematized and transformed into a new type of legal system. In Russia it merged with Slavic custom, exercising a civilizing influence but not revolutionizing that custom and not itself undergoing revolutionary change.

RUSSIAN LAW IN THE KIEVAN PERIOD, 862-1240

The most striking difference between early Russian and early Western law is a difference in time. The Russians were five hundred years behind the West. Clovis, the Merovingian king of the Franks, was converted to Christianity in the year 486; Vladimir, the ruler of Kievan Russia, in 988. The development of Russian law from the eleventh to the fifteenth centuries is in many ways a recapitulation of Frankish legal development from the sixth to the tenth centuries.

The first written law of Russian history begins with the rules of the blood feud. "If a man kills a man the following relatives of the murdered man may avenge him: the brother is to avenge his brother; the son, his father; or the father, his son; and the son of the brother of the murdered man or the son of his sister, their respective uncle. If there is no avenger, the murderer pays 40 *grivna* wergeld. . . ." So reads Article 1 of *Russkaia Pravda*, a collection of laws supposed to have been compiled under Yaroslav the Wise (ruled 1015-1054).[1] This whole compilation, comparable to the old *leges barbarorum* of the Germanic peoples of the West, such as *lex Salica, lex Frisionum*, or the laws of Alfred the Great, testifies to a public order which existed, when it did exist, primarily as between families within a clan (or territorial grouping of clans), but which was relatively powerless to reach down into the internal relationships of a household. At best it was interfamily law, analogous to our modern international law. Within the family there was the law of that family, determined by clan custom. The first Russian chronicle, the twelfth-century *Chronicle* of Nestor, depicts the barbaric character of this interfamily custom; wife-capture and general promiscuity were among its characteristic features. The father-husband dominated his family completely: they were his property. Each clan, the chronicler tells us, had its own custom, "not observing the law of God but themselves creating their own law."

Into this primitive social and legal order came the Eastern Orthodox Church, bringing with it, in the eleventh and succeeding centuries, Byzantine art and culture and also Byzantine law, which was an integration of Roman and canon law. It was under the influence of the Church that the tribal customs were at last restated and reformed in *Russkaia Pravda*—just as five hundred years earlier the Church had influenced the restatement and reformation of the Western *leges barbarorum*. Later editions of *Russkaia Pravda* show still more marked traces of Byzantine influence, as, for example, in the provision that the master should be liable for the crime of his slave, as well as in the abolition of the blood feud and in the prohibition against killing a slave for doing injury to a free man.

Russkaia Pravda was a compilation consisting chiefly of lists of penalties to be paid by wrongdoers to those whom they injured. If one cut off another's arm, one must pay him 40 *grivna;* if a finger, 3 *grivna;* if a mustache or a beard, 12 *grivna.* For stealing a horse, 3 *grivna.* And so on. This system of money compensation, or fixed prices for injuries, is a middle stage between crude self-help and a system of public penalties; it is a system familiar to most peoples at a certain stage of their legal development. In later editions of *Russkaia Pravda* fines payable to the prince were imposed in addition to compensation to the injured party.

The judicial procedure in Kievan Russia was exceedingly primitive. Litigation was voluntary; the judge had no power to compel an unwilling defendant to appear. The plaintiff and defendant settled on the issues to be litigated, and the judge simply refereed the contest, which was decided by oath (kissing the cross), or by ordeal of fire or water. Later, witnesses became important, but they too resembled the primitive oath-helpers of Germanic law. Not the state but the injured party prosecuted criminal actions. There was no system of appellate review, no hierarchy of courts. There was no distinction between judicial and political or administrative functions; princes, local officials, land-owners, and church officials judged those groups of people, respectively, who were under their political or economic or spiritual jurisdiction.

The primitiveness of the legal system of Kievan Russia will not shock those who are familiar with Anglo-Saxon and Germanic or Frankish law before the eleventh century. What is shocking is the fact that to a great extent this system continued to exist in Russia down to the fif-teenth and sixteenth centuries and even thereafter. This means that the revolutionary legal development which took place in the West in the eleventh and twelfth centuries found no counterpart in medieval Russia. Indeed, in many respects they were not paralleled until the great law re-forms of the mid-nineteenth century. This is a time-lag of not merely fifty or a hundred years but of 750 or 800 years, and it requires more than a superficial explanation.

THE TARTAR YOKE, 1240-1480

The conquest of Russia and most of the Eurasian con-tinent by the Mongols in the thirteenth century, and their domination for almost 250 years, exercised a deteriorating influence of the first magnitude upon Russian legal develop-ment. At the same time, so long a period of foreign rule could not but shape the course of development of Russian institutions in a positive way as well.

At first the flourishing culture of Kievan Rus, with its many churches and its great art and literature, was com-pletely crushed under the yoke of the cruel, uncouth Tartar nomads. Violence and massacres were followed by systematic exaction of tribute and general disorganization.

One direct result of this upon Russian legal institutions was a general lowering of moral standards and, specifically, an increase in the severity of Russian criminal law.

In time the cultural and legal traditions of the earlier period re-asserted themselves, especially in the great cities of Novgorod and Pskov. Nevertheless the Mongol domination unquestionably exerted a retarding influence on their development.

In a positive sense, Mongol influence on the Russian system of civil law, that is, of interpersonal (noncriminal) legal relations, was negligible. The conquerors were interested almost exclusively in tribute; they took some interest in public administration for the purpose of ensuring the regular flow of tribute. Otherwise they left the law of the subject peoples more or less alone. The Russian civil law as it existed during the period of Mongol domination had almost nothing in common with the civil law by which the Mongols governed their own internal personal and property relations; indeed, the Russian legal materials of this period simply carry further (and not very much further) the provisions of the earlier *Russkaia Pravda*.

In public law, however, in the legal relations of the various branches of government with each other and with the people, the Mongol influence was very great indeed. How far this was a direct influence and how far indirect is a hotly disputed question. Some scholars attribute the emergence of ideas of autocracy and of universal compulsory service in fifteenth- and sixteenth-century Russia to the fact that the Mongols had "laid the basis" for these ideas by their own political and legal system; and in respect to the Russian system of administration, of taxation, and of military organization, these scholars go still further, saying that they were actually received from the Mongols. Others deny all this categorically.[2] It is not necessary, for our purposes, to enter the lists on either side. It is sufficient to note that certain new political-legal institutions emerged during and after the Mongol conquest, if only as a Russian response to Mongol oppression, and that these new institutions took a form remarkably similar in some respects to that which they had had in Mongol law, if only because a conquered people is often forced, in liberating itself, to adopt the ways and methods of the conqueror. Whether Russian law *would have* developed along the same lines *even if* there had been no subjection to the Tartar yoke, is a hypothetical question which need not detain us. If indeed the Mongol influence in certain respects was merely to accelerate certain processes which had begun independently beforehand, then that in itself compels us to take seriously the Mongol impact on the development of Russian law.

That impact made itself felt above all on the position of the Grand Princes of Muscovy, who became, in the course of time, chief tax-gatherers for the Mongol overlord, the Great Khan, and who were thereby able to consolidate the power of Muscovy over the other Russian principalities as well as their own power over their subjects.

By using and enlarging the power of the princes of Muscovy for administrative and taxing purposes, the Tartars in effect selected the instrument for Russian unification and consequently for their own overthrow. At the same time, by their own political organization, and particularly by the absolutism of the khan, the Tartars provided an example of how unity could be achieved. The Mongol social and economic order was predominantly nomadic and tribal, but the power of the khan was imperial in character. He ruled over many clans, and he demanded absolute and unqualified obedience from all his subjects. At the same time he required of them public service. Apparently, those who were not called up to fight were obliged at certain seasons of the year to work for a certain number of days on public structures or in other public works, and in any case to serve one day each week in the employ of the khan.

The *Yasa,* or Code, of Genghis Khan (ruled 1206-1227) assigned to each person in the empire a specific position in service to the State, from which he could not depart without penalty of death. Women were obliged to replace the men of the household if the latter defaulted. All were equal in service. In the words of Vernadsky, "This principle [of universal compulsory service] was later on incorporated into the practice of the Tsardom of Moscow, which, in a sense, might be considered an offspring of the Mongol Empire."

SOURCES AND DEVELOPMENT
OF MUSCOVY LAW, 1480-1689

We have noted the marked similarity between the law of the Russian principalities prior to the Mongol invasion and that of the earlier Anglo-Saxon and Frankish kingdoms of the West. This type of law persisted in Russia throughout the Mongol period. For example, the judicial charter enacted in 1467 by the popular assembly of the city of Pskov is an advanced version of the *Russkaia Pravda*. By the end of this period, however, Russian law began to veer away from the earlier type.

In public law, centralism and autocracy became the dominant features. In 1498 Ivan the Great called himself "Tsar-Autocrat chosen by God." His grandson Ivan the Terrible (tsar, 1547-1584) spelled out the concept of autocracy in clear terms: "The rulers of Russia," he wrote, "have not been accountable to any one, but have been free to reward or chastise their subjects. . . . The Russian autocracy . . . has been ruled in all things by sovereigns, not by notables and magnates." Ivan specifically contrasted the autocratic nature of the Russian tsardom with the contractual basis of the Polish monarchy.

The Muscovy tsardom built its autocracy in part on the ruins of the Mongol despotism. It also developed further the Mongol principle of universal compulsory service. Ivan the Terrible broke the power of the hereditary nobility, the boyars, and created a new nobility bound to the tsar by military and civil service. The boyars as a class had developed from the personal bodyguard of the early princes, which in time became the household staff of the princes and was then gradually dispersed territorially by the gift of lands (often with charters of immunity giving them governmental powers) to the individual household officials. This, too, has its exact parallel in Frankish law. But in the West, in the tenth, eleventh, and twelfth centuries, the landed nobility was transformed from dispersed royal household assistants into political vassals, bound to the king by feudal contract with mutuality of rights and duties; and these vassals, in turn, were served by subvassals and ultimately by the peasants, who were converted into serfs under manorial authority. In Russia no such system of feudal law developed. Prior to the rise of the Muscovy tsardom, men who were in military or economic service to an overlord had the right of departure, and the practice of passing from one allegiance to another was widespread, on all levels, from the lowest to the highest, except for the relatively small class of indentured laborers or slaves. In particular, the boyars could go from prince to prince without losing their independent patrimonial property. But with the unification of Russia under the princes of Moscow, the nobles who attempted to transfer their allegiance to another potentate were not only apt to have their land confiscated but also might find their families annihilated and themselves executed. Thus a great many boyars were either crushed or else transformed in effect into state officials. Alongside the old patrimonial estate (*votchina*) there was created a new type of estate, called *pomestie*. The landholder, or *pomestchik,* was the recipient of a grant of land from the tsar on condition of service, but if the tsar became displeased with the pomestchik he could simply revoke the grant. There was still no feudal contract, no reciprocity of rights and duties. The concept of fealty was only rudimentary. At first the pomestchik's land was not even heritable. This was feudalism, in the economic sense, but without feudal law. As Vernadsky has put it, "The *pomestchik* was not the Tsar's vassal; he was merely the Tsar's servitor."

With the binding of the nobility to the tsar by compulsory service, it followed logically that the peasantry should be bound to the soil. Otherwise the *pomestchiki* were in danger of losing their peasants and being unable to fulfill their economic and military duties to the monarch. The bondage of the peasants came more slowly than the bondage of the nobles. By a decree of 1581 peasants were prevented from leaving their landlords' estates in certain prohibited years. Not until 1649 was this prohibition established for all years and all peasants. The peasants still retained many personal rights and could still own movable property, and they were still full-fledged citizens who exercised such elective rights as existed in judicial and administrative and political institutions.

The position of the Russian peasant in this period was essentially different from that of the serfs under Western feudalism. Not only did Russian serfdom come five hundred years after Western serfdom; it also came in an entirely dissimilar context. The peasants were bound to the land of a bound nobility; hence the peasants, too, were in effect servitors of the tsardom.

If there were no more to be said, the Muscovite tsardom might look for all the world like a later Russian adaptation of the Khanate of Mongolia. But there is another side to the picture. The Muscovy tsardom was built not only on the ruins of the Mongol autocracy but also on the ruins of another quite different autocracy, that of the emperors of Byzantium. Moreover, the Muscovy tsars inherited not only the autocracy of Byzantium but also the religion of Byzantium—Christianity—and this exercised a mitigating and broadening influence that was of the profoundest importance.

The autocracy of Byzantium was founded on the unity of Church and Empire; the Empire was not merely a secular state for the administration of political matters—it had a spiritual function as well, a religious function, and was thus indissolubly bound up with the Church. There was no effective separation of Church and State. The Empire was believed to be sacred, holy, part of God's plan for the salvation of mankind. The emperor was responsible for the religious life of the people; he was Protector of the Church and appointed the chief ecclesiastics. "I am caesar and priest," said the eighth-century Emperor Leo the Isaurian.

With the fall of Constantinople to the Turks in 1453, it came to be widely believed, not only in Russia but throughout Eastern Christendom, that the Orthodox kingdom of Muscovy should succeed to the Byzantine heritage. This found literary expression in the letter of a monk named Philotheus to Tsar Basil III (1505-1533), in which he wrote: "The first Rome fell owing to its heresies, the second Rome fell a victim to the Turks, but a new and third Rome has sprung up illuminating the whole universe like a sun. The first and second Rome have fallen, but the third will stand till the end of history, for it is the last Rome. Moscow has no successor; a fourth Rome is inconceivable."

The conception of Moscow as the successor to the Rome of the West and the Rome of Byzantium gave a spiritual character to the Muscovy tsardom which has no parallel in the Mongol despotism. Tsar Ivan the Terrible, for all his barbarism, taught that a tsar must not only govern the body politic but must also save souls. The tsardom was a missionary state. The Tsar-Autocrat was "chosen by God" to introduce Christian principles into secular life. Unlike the Mongol khanate, which was tolerant of all religions, the Muscovy tsardom introduced into Russia a State Orthodoxy which permitted no dissent.

In the West, the polarization of Church and State has had the effect of limiting the scope of state power, of restricting it to more or less secular functions. In addition, the Church, because of its separate legal existence, has been able to reinforce constitutional restrictions upon secular authority, and has even sponsored the right of tyrannicide. In Russia the fundamental unity of Church-State, or State-Church, has helped to prevent the development of similar restrictions on the scope of state action. On the other hand, at least during the heyday of the conception of Moscow as the Third Rome, the religious character of the empire had a certain limiting effect upon the activities of the tsar. This was manifested in a semi-legal conception of the right of high dignitaries of the Church to intercede in behalf of the victims of the tsar's displeasure or to beg the tsar to reform that which was incompatible with the Christian religion. Such intervention by the Church could be made only in the form of petitions. The decision lay with the tsar and nothing of a legal character could be done to alter that decision. When in 1568 Philip, Metropolitan of Moscow, fearlessly condemned the excesses of Ivan the Terrible's persecution of the old nobility, reproaching him for the absence of law and justice in Russia and petitioning him to change his ways, Philip was arrested and murdered by the tsar's henchmen.[3] Yet this right of petition, which has a special name in Russian (*pechalovanie*), was not meaningless.

Byzantium had an important influence not only on the religious conceptions of Muscovy, but also on its legal system, both ecclesiastical and secular. The ecclesiastical code simply incorporated later Byzantine law. On the secular side, Eastern Roman law served to inspire the establishment of a national system of courts. At the top there was now estabilshed as a permanent body the Boyars' Duma, or king's council, in which a special commission for judicial matters heard cases for which no law was known to exist or in which there was some doubt as to the interpretation of the applicable law. Under this commission were some forty special boards, called *prikazy*, each of which had jurisdiction over a particular problem such as land, serfs, robbery, foreigners, cavalry, infantry, Siberia. There was a great deal of overlapping and no principle of organization except apparent expediency. Financial, administrative, and judicial functions were completely interlocked. Under the prikazy were governors of provinces—appointed and paid by the tsar—and elected judges, who lived by fees received from the litigants. The jurisdiction of the governors and the judges also overlapped.

In spite of the confusion this was a new and more advanced phase of development in Russian law. The powers of the judges were increased. Not the parties but the court now determined the question of whether or not it had jurisdiction over a dispute. The defendant was brought to court not by the plaintiff but by a local official to whom the court issued a writ of summons. The old accusatory procedure, which put the judge in the position of an arbitrator and left the conduct of the trial largely to the parties, was now replaced in certain types of cases, notably the most serious criminal cases, by an inquisitional procedure, in which the judge himself took a large part in questioning the accused and running the trial. Representation of the parties now came to be allowed, though such representation was confined to relatives or friends of the litigants who were not allowed to be paid for their services. Ordeals began to disappear, and by a decree of 1556 trial by combat was abolished and trial by oath, with kissing of the cross, was substituted for it. These and other reforms were embodied in brief codes, the *Sudebniki,* or Court Manuals, of 1497 and 1550, the *Stoglav* (an ecclesiastical code consisting of one hundred articles) of 1551, various manuals on special subjects, and finally, in 1649, a more comprehensive code, the *Sobornoe Ulozhenie.*

Yet the legal system of Muscovy was crude and primitive nonetheless. Procedure remained complicated and formalistic; there was no oral procedure—all pleadings and testimony had to be in writing. In certain types of cases the decision was reached by casting lots. The transition from proof by oath-helpers to proof by witnesses was not complete; the witnesses were still people who swore that what the plaintiff or the defendant said was true. Corruption was very widespread; the system of paying the local judges from the pockets of the litigants was a form of legalized bribery.

THE PETERSBURG EMPIRE TO 1861

The effect of Peter the Great (1689-1725) on Russia has been compared to that of a peasant beating a horse with his fist. A giant of a man both in physique and intellect, Peter exerted a personal influence on Russia to which there is perhaps nothing comparable in the history of the West except the influence of Charlemagne on the Frankish Empire. The comparison with Charlemagne has significance for our understanding of Russian law. Where the legal tradition is weak, the personality of the ruler becomes of crucial importance.

This is not to say that Peter's reforms—or Charlemagne's —did not have their roots in earlier developments. Peter built on broad social and political changes which had been taking place over preceding generations and even centuries. But he placed his own dramatic stamp on these changes and gave them a certain finality.

Peter carried out a secularization of the Russian state and a modernization of Russian life in the Western image. He discarded the priestly robes of the Muscovite tsars and donned a military uniform; from 1721 he was officially called not tsar but emperor (imperator). He cut the beards of the nobility and the civil service. He abolished the patriarchate and set up a Holy Synod, controlled by a lay official, to govern the Church. He brought in scholars and experts from Western Europe to transform Russia. He established an Academy of Sciences on the Western model although it was not until 1755 that the first Russian university, the University of Moscow, was founded. He created a modern "regular" army. He built canals and modernized commerce. He took the first big steps toward the industrialization of Russia, himself establishing factories which he subsequently transferred from state to private ownership.

Peter also reorganized the Russian government on European lines, taking Sweden and Germany as his principal models. In 1708 the country was divided into new administrative units. In 1711 a Senate replaced the long-since defunct Boyars' Duma as the supreme administrative and judicial organ under the tsar, who appointed its members. The old prikazy were replaced in 1718 by a system of "colleges," twelve in number, for the army, the navy, foreign affairs, commerce, finance, justice, industry, mining, and other branches. In 1722 Peter created the Procuracy, headed by a Procurator General with a staff both in the capital and in the provinces; its function was to watch over the legality of the acts of the various governmental organs, including the Senate, and in general to act as the "eye of the tsar."

This was an attempt to incorporate into the Russian social order, at one stroke, a public-law system similar to that which had been developed in Western Europe over centuries. The attempt was bound not to succeed for two reasons. In the first place, the basic principle of autocracy was preserved intact. It was not simply that the monarch remained supreme. There were monarchies, and absolute monarchies, in Western Europe, too. But under the absolute monarchies of the West, the kings ruled—at least most of the time—by law, that is, by means of legal procedures that had roots in the whole structure of society. In Tudor England, for example, the king, for all his absolutism, governed "in his council in his parliament." Further, the public law institutions of the West were not created by these monarchs but were *given;* they were established long before absolutism developed, when kings were weak and only the Church was strong—and they therefore had ultimately an extrapolitical, extralegal sanction. The Russian emperors, on the other hand, ruled by their personal power and authority and merely used legal devices, which *they* created, to assist them, discarding these devices at will.

The second reason for the failure of the attempt of Peter the Great and his successors actually to Westernize the Russian system of public law and administration lay in the absence of a decent system of private law on which to build. For in the West, at least, public law and private law are interdependent. This means two things. It means, first, that the rational organization of governmental functions is bound up with a rational system of settling disputes among subjects; law and justice at the top replenish, and are replenished by, law and justice on the lower levels. It means, second, that the personnel, the cadres, upon whom the rational functioning of government must depend are produced out of the experience of local and private legal or political activity. It is extremely difficult to produce good administrators and legislators and judges when seven-eighths of the population are illiterate slaves without legal rights. But this is exactly what Peter the Great and the eighteenth-century Russian monarchs who followed him, such as Catherine the Great (1762-1796), sought to do.

In fact important law reforms of Peter and Catherine resulted in the enslaving of the Russian peasantry. Under the Muscovy tsardom there had existed both serfs and slaves. The slaves, or indentured laborers, had no legal personality but were considered as chattels. For purposes of taxation of the pomestchiki, who paid on the basis of the number of peasants working on their estates, Peter lumped the serfs and the slaves into one category. This paved the way for the landlords to usurp absolute power over both classes. By the time of Catherine, the landowners had been given the right to punish their serfs, to exile them to Siberia, and to sell them separately from the land. This policy was encouraged by the emperors for reasons of state, since the increased power of pomestchiki over the serfs meant an increased ability to perform their duties not only as taxpayers and general economic agents of the emperor, but also as his military agents with the responsibility of supplying recruits for his army. Gradually, however, the pomestchiki freed themselves from their earlier bondage to the tsar. Their lands had already become heritable in the seventeenth century, and in 1782 the earlier severe restrictions on rights in the subsoil and in timber suitable for shipbuilding were abolished. This meant the establishment of a concept of absolute private property in land, and the word "property" or "ownership" (*sobstvennost'*) appeared in Russian law then, in 1782, for the first time. It was restricted, however, to the nobility. This partial freeing of the nobility from their earlier position of servitude to the tsar made the situation of the subservient peasantry morally intolerable.

The Petersburg emperors wished to establish a Western legal system on Russian soil. They strove to create stable legal forms for governmental and private activity. Peter the Great regularized the procedure for publication and registration of laws with this in mind. Catherine the Great drew up vast plans for legal reform, drawing on the most advanced Western legal thought, including Montesquieu's *Spirit of Laws* and Beccaria's *On Crime and Punishment*. What was actually achieved, however, consisted, for the most part, in minor improvements in administration. How pathetic the imperial efforts proved is strikingly illustrated in the repeated attempts during a period of 115 years to codify the chaotic mass of contradictory statutes, ordinances, and decisions, that was accumulating. Ten successive commissions sat for this purpose, the first beginning in 1700, the last ending in 1815, without success. Not until 1832 did a collection of laws appear, and in 1833 a code—the first since 1649.[4]

The Code (*Ulozhenie*) of 1649 had been written to put in order the laws which existed at that time. However, it was drawn up very hastily, in less than three months, and therefore it was short and contained many gaps. When Peter the Great came to the throne forty years later, over fifteen hundred new legislative acts had been passed, many of them in contradiction with the provisions of the 1649 Code. In 1700 Peter issued a decree ordering that a commission be established to compare the Ulozhenie with the subsequent legislation. This commission sat continuously from 1700 to 1703; the results of its efforts consisted in an incomplete draft of a concordance of the laws covered in the first three chapters of the Ulozhenie.

Peter then decided that it would be better simply to abolish at one stroke all that legislation enacted since 1649 which was not in accord with the provisions of the Ulozhenie. But in order to know which legislation to abolish it was necessary, again, to try to collect the statutes and compare them with the 1649 Code. A second commission was appointed, which sat from 1714 to 1718; it succeeded in composing a draft of ten chapters of what was called a code of concordance (*svodnoe ulozhenie*). This effort also remained without consequence.

In 1720 a new approach was conceived. It was decided to write a new code which would reform the Ulozhenie on the lines of the Swedish and Danish codes. As the first great jurist in Russian history, Michael Speransky, wrote over a hundred years later: "It is easy to form an idea of the obstacles which would be encountered in this new approach—by the diversity of languages, by the radical differences between the two systems of law, and above all by the anomalies and the contradictions of our legislation which, not yet being reduced to a body, offered no possibility of distinguishing with certainty that which should be considered as law in force and that which should be regarded as abolished." The third commission was abandoned in 1727.

The next seven commissions swung back and forth between the idea of a concordance of existing legislation and the idea of an entirely new codification. All that was actually produced, however, were drafts, mostly incomplete, and these remained unrevised and unconfirmed. The members of the commissions, chosen generally by the nobility of the various provinces, were unable even to build on the work of those commissions which had preceded them, since each left only short extracts of the laws which it had collected and the number of new and contradictory decrees kept mounting.

Finally, in 1826, Speransky was charged with the task, and succeeded in publishing in 1830 a Complete Collection (*Polnoe Sobranie*) of the Laws of the Russian Empire. This was simply a forty-two volume reproduction, in chronological order, of the more than 30,000 legislative enactments which had been passed since 1649. Half of the acts were either abolished or modified by subsequent acts, or else were only repetitions of previous acts. This made it necessary for judges and officials to cite ten decrees instead of two, "thus offering," as Speransky said, "a vast field for fraud and chicanery." Moreover, it was impossible for a judge or official to know for sure whether he had the whole law, since—again to quote Speransky—"the constituent parts of one and the same law are often dispersed over a whole century, so that one of its parts appears, for example, in the code of 1649, a second in the regulation of 1741, a third in a supplement of 1830."

Speransky explains as follows the failure of the ten commissions to arrive at a collection of laws or to compile a systematic code:

In respect to the efforts to collect the laws, the difficulties, according to Speransky, were "innumerable." Few of the legislative acts were printed. The chanceries entrusted with the registering of the laws were badly organized, and their archives were in disorder. Most of the decrees were in the form of manuscripts addressed directly to the tribunals and boards concerned with their execution. In respect to the efforts to compose a new code, Speransky states that the commissions were hampered by the fact that their members were also charged with other governmental duties and that consequently there was a high turnover of membership, as well as by the fact that there were no people who combined both the practical and theoretical ability necessary for a task of this kind.

But Speransky's analysis goes still deeper. He recognized that a collection of laws, and even a code, is not the same thing as a legal system. He believed that Russia, lacking a strong tradition of law, would have to create its legal system artificially rather than organically, by starting with a complete collection, moving on to a systematic codification, and then proceeding to commentaries and principles upon which a legal system could finally be based. He wrote:

> In all states where the Roman law predominates cases rarely present themselves . . . which were not foreseen and [whose outcome was not] determined by the laws, since the number of laws is great and their ensemble is definite and extensive. The judicial order can thus proceed and be fulfilled, so to speak, on its own, without having need of recourse

to the legislative power. There the principle can be established that in the absence of a clear and precise law, the judge has the power to decide according to the general principles of the law; since these principles exist already in the body of Roman laws, sanctioned by time and experience.

Among us, however, the number of laws was, in the first place, insufficient, and the judge was continually obliged to have recourse to the legislator. Hence that mass of separate decrees and of decisions of the Boyars' Duma. With legislation in this condition it was not possible to permit the judges to decide according to general principles of law, since the principles were in no wise established. When consequently the number of legislative acts increased, other difficulties then presented themselves: the complication, the dismemberment, the uncertainty of the laws; difficulties perhaps even more serious than the very absence of law. Hence it is here above all that the door is opened to chicanery, to false applications [of laws], to arbitrary decisions, covered with the veil of legality; it is here that one finds the origin and the motive of an ever increasing number of new interpretations and authoritative decisions which leave in their wake new complications. How can one break out of this circle?—The only way is to classify all the legislative enactments, to form a homogeneous ensemble, to make a body of laws.

A fifteen-volume "body of laws" (*Svod Zakonov*) was finally made, largely through the efforts of Speransky himself, in 1832. This was the first codification of Russian laws since 1649 and the first systematic presentation of law as a whole in all Russian history. Basically Russian in content (indeed, Tsar Nicholas had forbidden Speransky to change a particle of the existing Russian law), it nevertheless owed much to Speransky's study of the concepts and systems of classification of the Western European codes. The sections devoted to public law (governmental institutions, military recruitment, taxation, state banking, duties and privileges of various classes, and internal and

external passport regulations, criminal law, and so forth),
which formed over two-thirds of the whole, constituted a
unique achievement, being the first such extensive systematization of public law in legal history. Volume X on
civil law owed much to the French civil code in its general
style and method, though it was adapted to a social-
economic system in which the state played a leading role
and in which property rights still depended on class status.

The first three editions of the *Svod Zakonov,* in 1832,
1842, and 1857, reflect law reforms that had been wrung
from the tsars in the first half of the nineteenth century.
The Napoleonic wars had brought Russia into contact
with the West in a new way. Previously such contact had
been chiefly diplomatic, intellectual, and commercial and
had been undertaken largely on the initiative of the rulers.
Now, by invading Russia, Napoleon brought the French
Revolution, whose ideas he proclaimed, right to the doors
of the Russian people; in repulsing Napoleon's armies, and
in marching to Paris, Russian troops, in their turn, saw and
experienced Western culture on its home grounds. The result was a genuine revolutionary movement, at first among
certain elements of the nobility; then, in the next generation, among sections of the middle class; and finally, by the
end of the nineteenth century, among people who claimed,
at least, to represent the peasants and the emerging proletariat. The demands of the intelligentsia of these three
classes, successively, were more than the reforming, Westernizing emperors had bargained for. They struck at the
roots of autocracy itself. The question which confronted
Russia during the entire nineteenth and the early twentieth
century was whether the law reforms on the surface of the
social order could keep ahead of the revolutionary ferment
underneath. The answer was given in 1917: they could not.

The *Svod Zakonov,* impressive as it was as a piece of
literature, did not—and could not—create for Russia a real
legal system organic to the social structure and meeting the
crying need for justice. In the first place, it was a highly
technical legal document and for its execution it was
necessary to have a class of professional lawyers and

judges and administrators—a class which in 1832 was only barely beginning to emerge in Russia. In the second place it left the masses of people, the peasantry, outside and below the law, and the rulers, the emperors, above and beyond it.

Consider, first, the position of the peasantry. The ninth volume of the *Svod Zakonov,* which was concerned with serfdom, included certain laws in mitigation of the peasant's lot. In 1827 the purchase of serfs without sufficient land for their sustenance had been prohibited. In 1833 it was forbidden to separate families by sale. But the difficulty with such laws was in the enforcement. The nobleman was supreme on his estate; he was the administrator and the policeman for the serfs under his control. A law of 1842 reveals the situation quite clearly: it called for a definition by the landowners of the duties of the peasants subject to them—but it left the matter entirely to their good will. In fact, the landowner could transfer his serfs freely from one job to another, and it was not unusual for him even to arrange their marriages. As late as 1840 there were over a million household serfs in the personal service of their lords, divorced from the soil entirely. The nearest that the law came to protecting the serfs against the nobility was the publication of "tables" in Poland in 1846 and of "inventories" in the southwestern provinces in 1853, consisting of lists and definitions of peasant liabilities. Reform was certainly not outrunning the revolutionary situation.

Consider, next, the position of the emperor. Alexander I (1801-1825) had come to the throne with liberal ideas of establishing a constitutional monarchy, with a representative machine and an independent judiciary. Speransky, who was called "the right hand of Alexander," was chosen to draw up a Plan for implementing these ideas. Speransky's Plan, which was a judicious mixture of Anglo-American, French, Russian, and original political principles, was never adopted. Other constitutional proposals met a similar fate. Alexander did, however, modernize public law by enlarging the judicial functions of the Senate, and by replacing the system of "colleges" with a Committee of Ministers, establishing eight ministries for war, navy, foreign affairs, interior, justice, finance, commerce, and education. He also took Speransky's suggestion of a State Council to advise on legislative matters. The Senate, the Committee of Ministers, and the State Council thus represented a *de facto* distribution of judicial, administrative, and legislative functions. In addition Alexander made some reforms in local administration, setting up special councils to advise the governors in the provinces. His successor, Nicholas I (1825-1855), organized the Imperial Chancery to include a so-called Second Section which was responsible for systematizing the laws, and which supervised the promulgation of the Complete Collection in 1830 and of the Code of Laws in 1832; and also a more famous Third Section which had charge of the police power, with the duty of exiling "suspicious and harmful persons." The Third Section instituted political repression and persecution against those whose views were considered dangerous from the point of view of the imperial authority. The *Svod Zakonov* makes no bones about the nature of that authority. Volume I, Article 1, begins with the words: "The All-Russian Emperor is an autocratic and unlimited monarch. Obedience to his supreme power not only from fear but also from conscience is ordained by God Himself."

The Russian judicial system of the mid-nineteenth century lives up to the worst possible expectations. It was organized on a class basis, with separate courts and different punishments for the nobility, the clergy, the urban population, and the remnants of the free peasantry. The intellectual and moral level of the judges was notoriously low; bribery was almost universal. The courts were in the control of the centrally appointed provincial governors. Procedure was still entirely written, the evidence being presented in the form of documents prepared by the police. Trial was secret, with the judges appearing in public only to pass sentence or to hand down a judgment. There was a confusion of jurisdictions and instances, with unlimited delays. In 1831, for example, in the province of Petersburg there were discovered on investigation to be 120,000 undecided cases in the courts. There was no professional bar. Legal education was poor. The establishment of a Second Section of the Chancery to systematize the law, and the publication of the *Svod Zakonov*, could not significantly alter a situation such as this. As with the legal position of the peasantry and the emperor, as with the whole system of public administration, so with the judicial order, too, reform was far behind the revolutionary demands which had been fermenting among the intelligentsia for two generations.

THE PETERSBURG EMPIRE FROM 1861 TO 1917

It was Speransky's idea that the promulgation of a systematic code would serve as a first step in the construction of a Russian legal system, and that the second step would consist in the publication of interpretations and commentaries. That is in fact what happened. In the 1830's and 40's and 50's the beginnings of a Russian legal literature appeared. A class of Russian jurists emerged, educated abroad in the capitals of Europe. In the 1860's, the decade of the Great Reforms in Russia, this group included men who constituted the most progressive and the most practical section of the intelligentsia. With the support of Alexander II (1855-1881), who was aware that a thoroughgoing reformation of Russian social institutions must come, and that if it did not come peacefully from above it would come violently from below, these jurists took the third step toward the creation of a Russian legal system. At the instance of the emperor, they drew up a plan for the reorganization of the entire court system. This plan was adopted in November 1864. It was the most enthusiastically received of all the reforms, and perhaps the most fruitful. Even the Soviets praise its "positive features" at the same time that they denounce its "bourgeois" character. It is the cornerstone of all subsequent legal development in Russia down to the present day.

Before considering the judiciary reform in detail, however, it is necessary to note two reforms with which it was associated and upon which it was dependent: the abolition of serfdom in 1861 and the creation of organs of local self-government in 1864 and 1870. The emancipation of the serfs gave them legal rights and hence a stake in the legal system. It did not mean, however, that the emancipated serfs in fact acquired private ownership of the land now made available to them. For the most part, the land was transferred to the *mir*, the local communal organization of peasants, which divided it among its members according to the size of their families, with periodic redistributions. The landowners, on the other hand, retained their portion of the land in private ownership. Also, owing to the half-heartedness of the emancipation, the peasants remained economically bound to the nobility. The centuries of legal bondage, however, were ended.

The reform of local government emphasized the fact of the peasantry's newly acquired citizenship. In each county representatives were elected by the private landowners, by the peasant commune, and by the townspeople; these representatives in turn elected an Executive Committee for a three-year period. The new organs of rural government, called collectively the *Zemstvo*, were given control of the schools, medical care, charity, roads, and other problems of local administration. They obtained funds for these purposes from local taxation, particularly of real property. In 1870 a program of municipal self-government was instituted similar to the Zemstvo reform.

With the establishment of the legal rights of the peasants and local self-government, the reform of the judicial system could be undertaken on a new basis, without the worst evils of class privilege and bureaucratic centralism.

The main features of the 1864 judiciary reform were: (1) the establishment of a court system independent of administrative officials, with judges irremovable except for judicial misconduct; (2) the elimination of class courts, with the exception that special district, or *volost'*, courts remained for the peasants; (3) the institution of justices of the peace (on the English model) to be elected by the Zemstvo and town assemblies; (4) the introduction of the principle of the publicity of legal proceedings; (5) the introduction of oral pleadings and oral testimony; (6) the introduction of trial by jury in criminal cases; (7) the creation of a hierarchy of courts, with appeals from the trial court to an appellate court on questions of law and fact, and recourse to a third instance, the so-called court of cassation, on points of law only (two courts of cassation were established in the Senate, one for criminal cases and one for civil); (8) the establishment of the right to be represented in court by a lawyer; (9) the setting up of a professional bar; (10) the placing of pre-trial investigation in criminal cases in the hands of an examining magistrate, on the model of the French *juge d'instruction*, who was under the control of the court rather than of the prosecuting arm as before.

In the 1870's and 1880's, particularly under Alexander III (1881-1894), there was a general reaction and some of the reforms were taken back. The acquittal in 1878 of Vera Zasulich, who shot the governor of St. Petersburg for ordering the flogging of a student revolutionary, was followed by the withdrawal of the right to jury trial in cases of crimes by officials, resistance to official regulations, murder or wounding of officials, crimes of the press against censorship, and especially important crimes against the state. In 1885 restrictions were placed on the independence of the judges; the judges of the lower courts were made more dependent on the president of the appellate court and on the Minister of Justice, and any judge could now be dismissed by a disciplinary board not only for negligence in the performance of his duties but also for offenses against morality or otherwise blameworthy activity committed outside his judicial office. In 1887 the principle of the publicity of trials was violated by the establishment of a procedure behind closed doors whenever, in the opinion of the court or of the Minister of Justice (and, in special cases, of the governor of the province or the Minister of Internal Affairs), public trials could endanger public morality, religion, the state or public order. In 1889 the jurisdiction of most of the justices of the peace was transferred to new officials called "land captains" (*zemskie nachal'niki*), appointed by the Minister of Internal Affairs, on nomination by the governor of the province. The land captains also exercised administrative power over the affairs of the village, so that the principle of separation of judicial and administrative offices was violated. In 1890 the Zemstvo reform was also weakened by the provision that the peasants could only nominate candidates for the Zemstvo assembly, while the selection from among those candidates was to be made by the provincial governors. This measure was repealed after the 1905 Revolution, and in 1912 the judicial functions of the land captains were eliminated and the elective justices of the peace restored.

The reaction of the eighties produced a counter-reaction in the Revolution of 1905, which brought a new wave of drastic law reforms. Now a representative legislature, the Duma, was established, based on a general election (though the system of voting was heavily overweighted in favor of the landed gentry) and, for the first time in Russian history, political parties. The Duma enacted social legislation of a far-reaching character. Shortly before the convocation of the First Duma, payments by the peasants for the land which had been granted to them under the 1861 emancipation had been abruptly terminated. Under the Stolypin reform, the peasant was now given the right to own his land privately, in an attempt to create a new class of small peasant proprietors. This was a serious attempt to reconstruct the very foundations of the Russian social and economic order.

At the same time, in the area of criminal and civil law, substantial reforms were being undertaken. A Criminal Code of 1903, of which only a portion was actually adopted, was a model of legal drafting and a creative adaptation to Russian conditions of the best achievements of Western European criminal legal science. A draft

Civil Code was produced in 1910-1913 which also reflected the highest legal traditions. (Both the 1903 Criminal Code and the draft Civil Code later served as models for the NEP codes.)[5] These achievements were due to the development in the last half of the 19th century of a class of distinguished professional jurists in the universities, the courts and the bar.

The law reform movement of the first years of the century was to some extent frustrated by recurrent waves of reaction and was finally ended by the outbreak of the World War in 1914. At the same time, however, the War exposed the essential weakness of the tsardom, which by 1917 had become a hollow legal shell. When Nicholas II (1894-1917) ordered the dismissal of the Duma in February 1917, its members refused to dissolve; instead they set up a Provisional Executive Committee, and when, three days later, Nicholas abdicated the throne, a Provisional Government was established. Headed later by the mild socialist Kerensky, the new government completed—on paper, at least—the transformation of Russia into a liberal democratic Western state. Now the electoral system was purged of its class character and universal suffrage was instituted for both sexes at the age of eighteen; measures for agrarian reform were undertaken; trade unions, first legalized in 1905, were freed from various restrictions; plans were made for the democratic election of a Constituent Assembly to draw up a constitution and determine the form of government Russia should have in the future. Reform and Revolution had merged. In fifty years the Russian legal system caught up with the eight-hundred-year-old legal development of the West.

The occurrence of the Bolshevik Revolution of October 1917 forces us to consider two hypotheses regarding the development of Russian law from 1864 to 1917. The first is the hypothesis that that legal development, brilliant as it was, took place only on the surface of Russian life, that it was not actually an incorporation of the fundamentals of Western law into the Russian tradition, but largely an adoption of Western forms without the substance, and that it did not penetrate into the consciousness of the Russian people as a whole, particularly the peasants. The second and closely connected hypothesis is that the transformation of Russia into a Western state with a Western constitutional and legal framework did not interest the Russian people as a whole (again, particularly the peasants), and that they were therefore prepared (for the sake of peace and land) to support a revolution which went *against* the liberal democracy of the February Revolution, *against* the constitutional monarchy of the 1905 Revolution, and *against* the individualist, rationalist, and legalist direction of the nineteenth-century reforms altogether.

The first hypothesis takes us to a closer examination of the deficiencies of the law reforms of the 1860's and thereafter. These deficiencies appear not so much in what was done as in what was not done. What was done was to receive Western legal norms and institutions. What was not done was to receive the basic principles underlying Western law—the principles which I have designated as Reason, Conscience, and Growth.

In the West, the principle that law must conform to Reason is associated, as we have seen, with the doctrine that the law is supreme, governing all men, and that it is complete, governing all human relations. Speransky noted that in the West there was an ancient body of law, the Roman law, which served as a basis for the judge to decide by "common sense" in cases for which no applicable statute existed. But this same body of law exists in the Russian tradition, which is even closer than Western history to the Byzantine Emperor Justinian and his *Digest;* and it is not generally thought to exist in the Anglo-American legal tradition, where the common sense of the judges is par excellence a source of law. The belief that the law is supreme and complete, conforming to Reason even as the universe conforms to Reason, is a fiction—or a faith—that dates not from Justinian but from the eleventh-century Papal Revolution and the accompanying renovation of Roman and canon law. Russian legal history provided much less basis for such a belief. In fact there remained in Russian legal history, down to 1906 at least, the unlimited autocratic power of the tsar. Moreover, down to 1917 there were whole spheres of activity, both in public and in private life, for which no legal definition of rights and duties existed. In public life questions of high policy were decided, as B. H. Sumner has put it, "not by any regularized procedure or definite body, but by shifting procedures and by the interplay of various bodies and various favorites or outstanding persons revolving round a formally supreme sovereign, whose sanctions, whether nominal or not, had to be obtained by means that varied with the personal characteristics of this or that sovereign." Moreover, despite the formal declaration of the independence of the judiciary, the administrative-political branch of government, and particularly the Ministry of Internal Affairs, continued to exercise compulsion over it. It is a tribute to the integrity of the Russian judges of the late nineteenth and early twentieth centuries, but not to the Russian legal system, that special steps were taken to reduce their power: extending the grounds for removability, for example, and also making temporary judicial appointments. But apart from pressure on the judiciary there was the extensive authority of the secret police over the population generally, including the right of administrative exile of political suspects. From 1906 to 1917 military courts condemned thousands of revolutionaries and semirevolutionaries to death for various illegal activities. In private law, too, the Western notion that everything is legal or illegal, that all political, economic, and social relations ought to be given legal expression and foundation, did not penetrate. Particularly in regard to land held in common by the peasantry, property rights continued to remain hidden and undefined, in spite of the fact that there were statutes dealing with them.

The Western principle that the judge must find the law also in his conscience—that he must identify himself with the accused or the litigant before him, that he must be not only rational but also "fair"—carries with it the doctrine of the equality of law. In conscience all are equal.

Again it is no reproach to the Russian judges of the late nineteenth and early twentieth centuries that the doctrine of equality before the law, though stated in principle, did not penetrate as deeply as in the West. In general, Russian judges after 1864 were conscientious and fair, but the system under which they operated continued to make sharp distinctions between different estates, different nationalities, and different religious groups. In the first place, the peasants were partly under the jurisdiction of special courts, and from 1889 to 1914 they were under the land captains. In the second place, the peasants and workers were subject to corporal punishment up to 1904. In the third place, even after the judicial functions of the land captains were removed in 1912, they continued to exercise administrative powers over the peasants, and to exercise them often arbitrarily. For the peasants, constituting the vast majority of Russians, the judiciary reform remained to a large extent façade. Likewise in respect to nationality and religious belief certain legal disabilities continued to exist.

Finally, the Western principle that law is a living, growing process, moving into the future with its eye on the past, though it made important strides, was never firmly established in prerevolutionary Russian legal development. Taught law, which has given toughness to the legal tradition of the West, was in Russia too divorced from actual legal practice. The law schools and law writers were often more concerned with the Roman law of Western Europe than with their own law, much less the cases in their courts. It has been suggested that this was perhaps for better rather than for worse, given the Russian past; and perhaps it would have changed had there been given a different future. But it imparted to Russian legal literature and to the teaching of law a quality of abstractness which impeded the development of a legal tradition. This had its effect on the courts. Despite a development toward greater reliance on previous decisions, the Ruling Senate, as the supreme court, often decided cases on the basis of edicts then in force with little reference to past or future, while in the local peasants' courts unlearned magistrates administered justice on the basis of custom and morality. In practice, Russian law, like its Byzantine ancestor, bore the stamp of the moment rather than the stamp of the future. Though similar in its general structure to the Western systems from which it had borrowed, the Russian legal system was not—could not be—so firmly grounded in tradition.[6]

The evidence tends to support our first hypothesis. Expressed more sympathetically to the old Russian regime, it is simply this: despite extraordinary progress in techniques of adjudication, administration and legislation, as well as in the development of a trained and responsible legal profession, half a century was not enough time in which to build a Western legal system, in the full sense, on Russian soil.

POSITIVE VALUES OF RUSSIAN HISTORY

Our second hypothesis is that Russia did not particularly want a Western legal system and that it was prepared for a revolution which in its basic idea went against Western legal and political conceptions, whether of the nineteenth-century monarchy, of the post-1905 aristocracy, or of the Kerensky democracy. This takes us to a consideration of what generally Russia did want. Here we must look to another side of the Russian heritage, a side which has been obscure to Westerners because of their very preoccupation with law and legality.

There are at least four redeeming qualities of Russian life which have given Russia greatness, each originating in a different era of Russian history. The first has to do with the character of human, or interpersonal, relations in society. It originated in Kievan Russia with the development of a special brand of Christianity, Russian Orthodoxy, different from both the Greek Orthodoxy of Byzantium (though it was officially received from Byzantium) and the Roman Catholicism or subsequent Protestantism of the West. It differed from Byzantine Christianity in that it was little concerned with theology, philosophy, or dogma in the strict sense. Until the nineteenth century the Russian Orthodox Church produced no systematic theology or philosophy and, indeed, very few theologians or philosophers. Even today the dogma of Russian Orthodoxy is difficult to identify, with large scope left for individual divergencies. Russian Christianity differed from Western Christianity, on the other side, in that it was not so institutional, not so dominated by the priesthood, not so political in its interest or in its basic structure. Despite the politics of the priesthood at the top, which since Peter the Great was under the thumb of the State, the Church for most Russians was an invisible community of the faithful, a "communion of saints." The Russians did not, however, share the Protestant emphasis on individual faith and conscience. Instead, the Russian Church stressed liturgy; Christianity from the beginning has been for the Russian a profound esthetic and spiritual experience, influencing his personality and the quality of his life and binding him together with others in that common experience. The sense of the community of all men as comprising a single congregation, bound by common ritual, common liturgy, and ultimately by a common sense of brotherhood, was a major unifying factor in saving Russia from being swallowed up by the Mongols, and it persisted through the succeeding centuries. In the nineteenth century a name was found for this quality; it was called *sobornost'*, which means "conciliarity" (*sobor* is, literally, "council"), a spirit of reconciliation, togetherness. It is a sense that life exists only between people, that the individual derives his personality from membership in the community of believers, that, in Maynard's phrase, "truth resides in the congregation."

Maynard, Berdiaev, and others who have stressed this feature of Russian Orthodoxy as central in Russian history, have been severely criticized by some, who assert that this is simply the nineteenth-century Slavophile conception transferred to the whole Russian past and future. By their criticism, these scholars tend to identify themselves with the nineteenth-century Russian Westernizers, who deplored the non-Western elements of Russia's past and believed that her only hope lay in developing closer affinity with the West. Slavophiles and Westernizers opposed each other in a struggle which lasted not only up to the Russian Revolution but which continues, in concealed form, to this day. Stalin, who often reiterated his desire that Russia shall in the shortest possible time "catch up with and surpass the West," and who did not conceal his admiration for Western technology as well as for certain Western ideas, excoriated the modern Soviet Westernizers as victims of "cosmopolitanism."

It is not necessary here to fight out the battle of East and West in Russia, the famous Slavic Soul versus the equally famous Russian dependence on and affinity with Western Europe. Each side tends to exaggerate certain aspects of Russian history. Sir Bernard Pares has rightly said that in every Russian there is both Slavophile and Westernizer.

It *is* necessary, however, to assert that the weakness of legal traditions throughout most of Russian history is not merely a negative thing; that it has also its positive counterpart—a strong tradition of collective social consciousness which relies for its motivation less on reason than on common faith and common worship, and which finds expression less in legal formality and "due process" than in more spontaneous and more impulsive responses.

The two and a half centuries of Mongol domination added a new quality to Russian life, that of universal compulsory service. We have seen how this was embodied in the Mongol legal system, and how it was taken over by the Muscovy tsardom, which bound all classes to the state. At the same time the harshness of the principle as inherited from the Mongols was mitigated by the sense of inner community, the voluntary acceptance of common bondage, which was carried on through the Christian tradition.

A new element was also introduced by the Muscovy tsardom through its inheritance of the Byzantine conception of the empire as sacred, not merely a secular state but a holy Church, and of the emperor as appointed to rule in matters spiritual as well as political. This meant the establishment of a State Orthodoxy, hostile to opposition and dissent in matters of belief. This, too, has remained as an important element of Russian life.

The Petersburg empire made a sharp break with the past—almost as sharp as that which was later made by the Bolshevik Revolution. Yet in spite of this break, the three qualities of which we have spoken remained. Now, however, a new element was added by very reason of this break. "Westernization" is not the same thing as being Western. The result of the conscious imitation of Western Europe by the Russian imperial nobility of the eighteenth century, and by the nobility and the intelligentsia of the nineteenth century, was to create a tension between East and West within Russia itself, and especially a tension between the partially Westernized upper classes and the non-Westernized masses of peasantry. This was a tension of classes and a tension of ideas. It was manifested under Peter the Great in a release of technical energy, a *furor technicus,* which enabled the Russian state to take enormous leaps in the direction of state-controlled economic development. The fourth element of Russian life might be called *the energy of Westernization;* it is most strikingly symbolized in the various economic measures of state intervention which were taken by the emperors of the eighteenth and nineteenth centuries. Industrialization in prerevolutionary Russia was not widespread in terms of the economy as a whole, but it was large-scale in terms of the size of state-owned factories and the dimensions of state-directed commerce. Railroads, banking, and certain aspects of production itself were concentrated largely in the hands of the state; and with the development of capitalism in the nineteenth century, a good deal of private business was from the beginning "big business."

The positive values of Russian history which have been singled out here (undoubtedly others could also be listed) often found reflection in Russian law; indeed, they probably could not have been maintained without law. Yet law served as their implementation rather than as their foundation, and in some ways they were a threat to legality.

Again and again through the centuries Westerners who have been brought in contact with Russia have been shocked and baffled by the relative lawlessness of Russian life. Compared to life in the West it has seemed to them haphazard, inconstant, arbitrary, and aimlessly cruel. At the same time they have been impressed by the extraordinary warmth and spontaneity of the Russians, by their capacity for service and self-sacrifice, by their devotion to and faith in Holy Mother Russia, by their amazing *élan* and energy. Historically weak in lawgivers and jurists, Russia has been from the beginning strong in heroes and in saints. It has been strong in its sense of community, and strong in centrally directed energy, administrative initiative at the top. Many of the greatest Russians have despised the legalism of the West, where, in the scornful words of the nineteenth-century Slavophile I. V. Kireevsky, "brothers make contracts with brothers." They have looked to spontaneous personal and administrative relationships rather than to the formality of law, with its time-consuming emphasis on due process and its rationalism. The peasants looked to the tsar as "little father" rather than as mere monarch. The unity of the Russian empire of 1917 was still, in the eyes of the Russian people as a whole, not essentially political or legal, in the Western sense, but moral and religious.

WESTERN AND RUSSIAN LAW

ROME ⟵————————⟶ CONSTANTINOPLE

Germanic, Slavic tribes
Frankish, Byzantine Church-Empires

1054: SCHISM OF WESTERN AND EASTERN CHURCH

1075: PAPAL REVOLUTION Roman-and-Canon Law; Feudal Law; beginnings of national legal systems	KIEVAN RUS, 862-1240: *Russkaia Pravda* (comparable to Frankish *leges barbarorum*); Influence of Russian Orthodox Christianity (*sobornost'*)

(13th century: Rise of Italian city-states; Development of Law Merchant)

MONGOL YOKE, 1240-1480: *Yasa* of Genghis Khan; Influence of Mongol principle of universal compulsory service; Continuation of *Russkaia Pravda* in judicial charters of Pskov and Novgorod

1517: GERMAN REFORMATION
Reception of Roman Law

MUSCOVY TSARDOM, 1480-1689: Court Manual (*Sudebnik*) of 1497; Code (*Ulozhenie*) of 1649; Influence of messianic conception of Moscow as the Third Rome

1640: ENGLISH REVOLUTION
Restoration of Common Law

PETERSBURG EMPIRE, 1689-1917:

(a) Attempts of successive code commissions to systematize laws and decrees; Westernization of the nobility

1789: FRENCH REVOLUTION
Napoleonic Codes

(b) Code (*Svod Zakonov*) of 1833; Judiciary Reform of 1864; Westernization of the intelligentsia; Reform and Reaction

1914: WORLD WAR

1917: RUSSIAN REVOLUTION

Chapter Eight

THE RUSSIAN CHARACTER OF SOVIET LAW

"JUST AS a contemporary Frenchman who is asked, 'What makes France great?' will at once reply, 'Descartes and Rousseau, Voltaire and Hugo, Baudelaire and Bergson, Louis XIV, Napoleon and the Great Revolution,' our grandsons will answer the question, 'What makes Russia great?' by saying with pride, 'Pushkin and Tolstoy, Dostoevsky and Gogol, Russian music, Russian religious thought, Peter the Great and the great Russian Revolution.' " These words of the Russian *émigré* Ustrialov, written in the first years after the Revolution, may be matched by the statement of another Russian *émigré*, Nicholas Berdiaev, some twenty-five years later: "In 1917 we believed that Communism had swallowed up Russia; today we see that Russia has swallowed up Communism."

Like other major Revolutions, the Russian Revolution is a universal and world-wide event, with implications for all mankind; but it is also a Russian event, a product of Russian experience, "made in Russia." It is as Russian as the Puritan Revolution of 1640 was English. If the Russian Leninists followed the doctrine of the German Karl Marx, so did the English Cromwellians follow the doctrine of the Genevan John Calvin. And the Puritans also had a universal and world-wide vision which they spread not only throughout the British Isles but also across the sea to new continents. Yet finally the Revolution settled down to its English dimensions. As Eugen Rosenstock-Huessy has shown, all the great European revolutions of modern history have had to strike a balance between their universal goals and their national limitations.

Many of the resemblances between the Soviet system and the tsarist system exist because the internal conditions faced by the Soviet rulers are similar to those faced by their predecessors. The vastness of the area to be governed, the existence within that area of a multitude of diverse peoples with different languages and traditions, the very low standards both of material and of cultural life—these are factors which severely limit the choice of political and legal methods. The prerevolutionary Russian Prime Minister, Count Witte, said in 1905, when the government was under attack from all sides: "The world should be surprised that we have any government in Russia, not that we have an imperfect government. With many nationalities, many languages and a nation largely illiterate, the marvel is that the country can be held together even by autocracy." To such internal factors must be added the external problem of military defense. Ever since the expulsion of the Mongols, the Russian state has been a military state; with repeated invasions from north, south, east and west, it has sought to keep its population militarized and mobilized. It is more than symbolic that both in Soviet and in prerevolutionary Russia, certain serious crimes against the state, even when committed by civilians, have been under the jurisdiction of military courts.

The persistence of the same internal and external conditions is not, however, the only explanation for the persistence of similar political and legal institutions. Institutions do not arise spontaneously and automatically from the social environment; they must be created and fostered. The people who create and foster them have received certain ideas and traditions from their parents and their parents' generation, and these transmitted ideas and traditions have a life of their own, in time, and in fact condition the "conditions." There is a social heredity, a heritage, as well as a social environment. A people has a past and a future; it does not merely live in space from moment to moment.

Moreover, there may be breaks in historical continuity and yet conceptions and institutions of an earlier period may survive those breaks and reappear in a later period in new forms. In this way many medieval English conceptions and institutions were revived and reshaped in the seventeenth century, after a hundred and fifty years of "Tudor despotism."

It is in this sense that we may say that the Soviet Union has inherited the old Russian religious conception of the state, and with it the institutions for the repression of all heresies. Conversely it has *not* inherited the legal conception of the state which has had so strong an influence in the West, and which was beginning to develop so rapidly in Russia itself in the late nineteenth and early twentieth centuries.

The Soviet state is not a secular but a religious state, in the sense that it is founded on an idea and a mission. The Soviet rulers stand for an orthodoxy. Like the sixteenth-century princes of Muscovy, they take responsibility for both the political and spiritual life of their subjects and expect from them not only respect but also worship. The embalming of Lenin to preserve him incorruptible forever and the glorification and adulation of Stalin as the "Father of the Soviet Peoples," whose portrait was omnipresent and who in public was spoken of in terms appropriate to a deity, remind one inevitably of the prerevolutionary Russian conception of the tsar as a religious figure. Of course such tendencies are not restricted to Russia. Hitler, too, wanted to be both emperor and pope in Germany. America, also, is founded on an idea and a mission. But that does not alter the fact that it is the Russian tradition upon which the Soviets have built, consciously and unconsciously, and that important elements of that tradition help to explain important features of Soviet law and politics.

We know that Marxism, the idea upon which the Soviet state is founded, was originally a Western theory. Under Lenin and his successors, however, Marxism has been Russified. It has been converted from a science of society into a dogma, and this dogma has in turn become ritualized. Stalinism in Russia was chanted, not merely spoken; it was to be believed *in,* not merely believed. Despite the denunciation of the Stalin "cult of personality" by his successors and the granting of greater freedom of dissent on matters considered politically neutral, Soviet public speech still has a liturgical character. The guardians of this liturgy, the new priesthood, are the members of the Communist Party, the "vanguard" who must show the way and take the responsibility.

If we consider the Soviet Communist Party from the political and legal point of view, its links with the Russian religious heritage become apparent. The Party occupies a position in relation to the Soviet state in some respects similar to that which the Church occupied in relation to the tsarist state in the Muscovy period. As the tsar was the Protector of the Church, and its virtual head, so Khrushchev, like Stalin before him, is not only the head of the state but also the head of the Party. As the Church had no legal or constitutional position in politics, but influenced it indirectly and informally, so the Party is mentioned in the Soviet Constitution only twice, once as the "leading core" of all state and social organizations and once as one of the organizations which has the right to nominate candidates for political office; though in fact it is closely identified with the state indirectly and informally through the Party membership of the political leaders. As the Church stood for the idea upon which the old Russian state was based, Russian Orthodox Christianity, so the Party stands for Marxism, the creed by which all Soviet political action is justified.

In its internal structure the Party resembles nothing so

much as a religious order. In the words of the Party Rules of 1961, "The Communist Party of the Soviet Union is the tried and tested militant vanguard of the Soviet people . . . Ideological and organizational unity, monolithic cohesion of its ranks, and a high degree of conscious discipline on the part of all Communists are an inviolable law of the C.P.S.U. All manifestations of factionalism and group activity are incompatible with Marxist-Leninist Party principles and with Party membership." Its organization is hierarchical, with lower units sending representatives to higher units, the highest body being the Presidium of the Central Committee. The Party Charter proclaims as one of the guiding principles of this organizational structure "the unconditionally binding character of the decisions of higher organs upon lower ones." Before a policy decision on a particular subject is made, there is open discussion and debate; once the Party line is laid down, however, there must be absolute acceptance. Such is the principle of Party Orthodoxy.

Of the relation of the individual member to the Party, the Rules state the following duties and rights:

It is the duty of a Party member: (a) to work for the creation of the material and technical basis of communism; to serve as an example of the communist attitude towards labor; to raise labor productivity; to display the initiative in all that is new and progressive; to support and propagate advanced methods; to master techniques, to improve his skill; to protect and increase public socialist property, the mainstay of the might and prosperity of the Soviet country; (b) to put Party decisions firmly and steadfastly into effect; to explain the policy of the Party to the masses; to help strengthen and multiply the Party's bonds with the people; to be considerate and attentive to people; to respond promptly to the needs and requirements of the working people; (c) to take an active part in the political life of the country, in the administration of state affairs, and in economic and cultural development; to set an example in the fulfilment of his social duty; to assist in developing and strengthening communist social relations; (d) to master Marxist-Leninist theory, to improve his ideological knowledge, and to contribute to the molding and education of the man of communist society. To combat vigorously all manifestations of bourgeois ideology, remnants of a private-property psychology, religious prejudices, and other survivals of the past; to observe the principles of communist morality, and place social interests above his own; (e) to be an active proponent of the ideas of socialist internationalism and Soviet patriotism among the masses of the working people; to combat survivals of nationalism and chauvinism; to contribute by word and by deed to the consolidation of the friendship of the peoples of the U.S.S.R. and the fraternal bonds linking the Soviet people with the peoples of the socialist camp, with the proletarians and other working people in all countries; (f) to strengthen to the utmost the ideological and organizational unity of the Party; to safeguard the Party against the infiltration of people unworthy of the lofty name of Communist; to be truthful and honest with the Party and the people; to display vigilance, to guard Party and state secrets; (g) to develop criticism and self-criticism, boldly lay bare shortcomings and strive for their removal; to combat ostentation, conceit, complacency, and parochial tendencies; to rebuff firmly all attempts at suppressing criticism; to resist all actions injurious to the Party and the state, and to give information of them to Party bodies, up to and including the Central Committee of the Communist Party of the Soviet Union; (h) to implement undeviatingly the Party's policy with regard to the proper selection of personnel according to their political qualifications and personal qualities. To be uncompromising whenever the Leninist principles of the selection and education of personnel are infringed; (i) to observe Party and state discipline, which is equally binding on all Party members. The Party has one discipline, one law, for all Communists, irrespective of their past services or the positions they occupy; (j) to help, in every possible way, to strengthen the defense potential of the U.S.S.R.; to wage an unflagging struggle for peace and friendship among nations;

A Party member has the right: (a) to elect and be elected to Party bodies; (b) to discuss freely questions of the Party's policies and practical activities at Party meetings, conferences and congresses, at the meetings of Party committees and in the Party press; to present motions; openly to express and uphold his opinion as long as the Party organization concerned has not adopted a decision; (c) to criticise any Communist, irrespective of the position he holds, at Party meetings, conferences and congresses, and at the plenary meetings of Party committees. Those who commit the offence of suppressing criticism or victimising anyone for criticism are responsible to and will be penalized by the Party, to the point of expulsion from the C.P.S.U.; (d) to attend in person all Party meetings and all bureau and committee meetings that discuss his activities or conduct; (e) to address any question, statement or proposal to any Party body, up to and including the C.C. C.P.S.U., and to demand an answer on the substance of his address.

Such a body is hardly a political party. It represents no class, no special political interest group. It boasts that its membership is drawn from the "more advanced, politically more conscious section of the working class, collective-farm peasantry and intelligentsia of the U.S.S.R."—that is, from all sections of the population. The Party is the "central core of conscious socialists," the "shock troops" in all phases of social, economic, and political life. It is the new "communion of saints."

The legacy of tsarism may also be seen in the repressive features of the Soviet political system, which go hand in hand with State Orthodoxy. The same right of administrative exile of political enemies existed in Stalin's statute books as in the Tsar's: by a law of November 5, 1934, a Special Board of the People's Commissariat of Internal Affairs was empowered to exile, banish, or intern in corrective labor camps for a period up to five years, persons found to be "socially dangerous." The tsarist Ministry of Internal Affairs used the term "untrustworthy," but the substance of the matter was the same. In tsarist Russia as in the Stalinist Soviet Union, persons who committed no other crime but that of having the wrong friends or the wrong opinions could be banished to Siberia, by a secret administrative hearing, without any right of appeal to the courts. The horror stories that came to us from the Soviet labor camps prior to Stalin's death must be read against the background of the reports of the prerevolutionary Siberian prisons.

There can be no comparison of the prerevolutionary police repression with the Soviet system of terror under Stalin in terms of its extent or its barbarism; the secret agents of the tsarist Ministry of the Interior were amateurs compared to their Soviet successors.[1] Nevertheless it is important to recognize that the seeds of Soviet lawlessness were sown in the prerevolutionary period. This in no way justifies Soviet lawlessness. If anything, it makes it more despicable; Stalin and his cohorts spent enough time in the hands of the tsarist police to have learned the evil, if not the futility, of the method of force and repression. Instead they seem to have been more impressed with its efficiency. This is a partial explanation of their readiness to exploit the weakness of the Russian legal tradition as a means of crushing all opposition.

With the abolition of the Special Board in 1953, the power of administrative exile was absent from the statute books of Russia for the first time in her history as a modern state. This happy condition ended, however, with the introduction of administrative "re-settlement" of "antisocial, parasitic elements" in nine smaller republics from 1957 to 1960 and in the Russian, Ukrainian and other republics in 1961. Thus far there has been no indication that the anti-parasite laws have been used against political opponents of the regime. Yet they remain an example of the government's readiness to exercise extra-judicial powers of punishment, and of the absence of constitutional guarantees against such exercise.[1a]

At the same time, Russia's historic legal backwardness has been a source of embarrassment to the leaders in their efforts to provide stability and order. That they have suffered from this is well illustrated in their attempts to produce an adequate codification. Here we find a surprising recapitulation of the experience of the ten code commissions before Speransky.

Having proclaimed the abolition of all tsarist laws, the Soviet regime—one would have thought—was in a position easily to systematize its own new legislation. A month after the Revolution a division was established within the new People's Commissariat of Justice of the Russian Republic for the express purpose of preparing "a complete collection of the prevailing laws of the Russian Revolution." Apparently this division did nothing. Three years later, in 1920, another resolution provided for the establishment within the Commissariat of Justice of a new division to be charged with codifying existing decrees and directives. (This had nothing to do with the preparation of civil, criminal, or other codes, which are statements of basic rules of law and which may be overridden by legislative and administrative decrees.) Again little or nothing was accomplished. With the formation of the various republics into a federal U.S.S.R. in 1923, a new commission was established for the purpose of "systematizing and unifying the legislative data and directives" of the federal government. This the commission started to do in 1925, noting, however, that such a task "presents, under our conditions, an extremely complicated problem, requiring intensive, careful, and rather prolonged preparation," and stipulating that "the first step in this preparation must be the simple, systematic collection of all the extant all-union laws in force at the present time." The result of the labor of this commission was the publication of a five-volume collection of laws, which the compilers themselves characterized as being merely "material for future consolidation and codification." In 1927 another codifying commission was created, which codified some 4000 acts in force as of January 1, 1929, summarizing them in 746 paragraphs.

This code, however, was not confirmed, since, in the words of a Soviet commentator, "many of the norms [consolidated in the code] had already been revised or were in the process of revision." [2] Since the 1929 attempt, no over-all systematization of Soviet laws has been made; however in recent years a valiant effort has been made to determine which of the hundreds of thousands of laws enacted in the past twenty-five years have lost their force.[3] In addition, unofficial systematic collections of prevailing laws and decrees in particular fields—economic law, labor law, civil law, and others—have been published since 1956.

The state of Soviet legislation is appallingly chaotic. The charge which Speransky leveled against the confusion of Russian laws from the seventeenth to the nineteenth centuries is applicable again today. Obsolete laws remain unrepealed. Decrees and orders may be published in a whole variety of newspapers and journals; the Soviet lawyer or judge can never be sure that he has all the relevant laws before him. Furthermore, laws of 1924 and 1925 expressly provided for the withholding of legislative and administrative acts from publication, upon special order of certain leading governmental bodies. The 1958 and 1959 laws on publication[4] are more liberal: statutes, decrees and other normative acts of the Supreme Soviet of the U.S.S.R. must be published; however, edicts and decrees of the Presidium and decrees of the Council of Ministers need not be published if they do not have general significance or are not of a normative character. Such unpublished laws are merely circulated to appropriate governmental departments and institutions. It is the Presidium and the Council which determine which of their acts are not "general" or "normative." The number of "unpublished" legal acts far exceeds that which is published. There are, therefore, as there were to a far more limited extent in prerevolutionary Russia before 1906, secret laws.[5]

In addition, not all decisions, even of the U.S.S.R. Supreme Court, are reported. Between 1950 and 1956, the reports of its decisions were not "published" at all, but only circulated to authorized officials, libraries, etc. When publication was resumed in 1957, the earlier practice was continued of reporting only those decisions which were considered most important. In 1961 the Supreme Court of the R.S.F.S.R. began to publish its reports on a similar basis.

With respect to the codes of civil law and procedure, criminal law and procedure, labor law, family law, and so forth—codes in the proper sense of the word—it was only after 1958 that the antiquated NEP codes of the 1920's began to be replaced. Throughout the 'thirties, 'forties, and early 'fifties, code commissions sat, and many drafts were produced, but none succeeded in gaining adoption. The reasons for this are still obscure. They appear to have been partly technical and partly political. Technically, it was difficult to harmonize the many conflicting statutes and regulations in force. Politically, there was fear of displeasing Stalin by adopting what he might consider a heretical position. With his death it was possible to repeal the laws which most flagrantly violated basic postulates of legality and, on the basis of wide discussion, to adopt "fundamental principles" in various fields of law upon the basis of which the various republics could enact new codes. Yet legislative policy continues to change rapidly and it remains an open question how long the new codes will last before they will need substantial amendment.

Finally, there is the problem of the gap between the law as written and the law as practiced—a gap which exists in every society, but which, by comparison with Western standards, is extraordinarily large in Russia. A French student of Russian law observed in 1877 that "of all the countries of Europe the Russian Empire is perhaps the one where the written law has the least absolute validity and remains the most often a dead letter." [6] This has a familiar ring. Several times the Soviet Constitution has been changed by decree and only later amended in the proper manner to conform to the changes. The first election of judges took place in 1949, although the constitutional provision requiring such an election dates from 1936. The type of directive most frequently encountered in

Soviet legal literature is one that calls attention to the failure of administrative or judicial organs to follow the provisions of a particular law and directs that henceforth the illegal practices be discontinued.

On the other hand, while the Soviets have inherited the backwardness of the Russian legal tradition—reinforced by the loss through revolution of some of the best legal minds of the *ancien régime*—they have also inherited many of its achievements. Most of the jurists who have written the Soviet codes, the judges who have presided over the Soviet tribunals, the procurators who have conducted prosecutions in the Soviet courts, and, indeed, the people who have brought suit in court or who have been prosecuted—were brought up in prerevolutionary Russia and received certain basic conceptions of law from the past. Many of them studied in prerevolutionary Russian law schools. Especially since the mid-1930's they have been consciously drawing on the resources of their earlier education.

The Soviet procuracy, for instance, is patterned in general after the prerevolutionary Russian system. Soviet criminal law has built on the nineteenth and early twentieth-century reforms, with the Russian criminal code of 1903, in many ways the most advanced in the world at that time, serving as an example. Some Soviet property concepts, particularly those relating to the property relations of the peasant household, derive from the legal experience of the past. The list could be lengthened indefinitely, but these three examples—the procuracy, criminal law, and the law of the peasant household—provide excellent illustrations of the specific Russian component of Soviet law. They have much in common with Western law, and yet they also contain important non-Western elements; they are Russian, and the more they have been "socialized" the more Russian they have remained.

THE PROCURACY

An American lawyer in Moscow would not have great difficulty in acclimating himself to many features of the Soviet system of trials and appeals; the French or German lawyer would have even less. But there is one feature of the law-enforcement process which would be quite unfamiliar to the Western lawyer, and he would soon discover that in many ways it is the most important institution of the whole system. That is the Procuracy.

The Soviet Constitution states that "supreme supervisory power over the strict execution of the laws by all ministries and institutions subordinated to them, as well as by public servants and citizens of the U.S.S.R., is vested in the Procurator General of the U.S.S.R." The Procurator General is appointed by the Supreme Soviet for a term of seven years; he, in turn, appoints procurators of republics, territories and regions, and confirms the appointment by the republican procurator of area, district, and city procurators. "The organs of the Procurator's Office," states the Constitution, "perform their functions independently of any local organs whatsoever, being subordinate solely to the Procurator General of the U.S.S.R." [7]

The "supreme supervisory power" of the Procuracy takes many diverse forms. The procurators keep watch over the entire system of administration, to see that executive and administrative bodies do not overstep their legal authority. They sit in as consultants on sessions of the local city councils and receive copies of orders and regulations issued by regional and republican and federal executive-administrative organs. When the procurator considers that an act is in violation of the Constitution or of laws or decrees of higher bodies, he may "protest" to the executive-administrative organ immediately superior to the body which has issued it. If a ministry has exceeded its authority, the procurator's protest is lodged with the Council of Ministers. The procurator also is supposed to supervise the legality and correctness of actions of the state security organs as well as of the Republican Ministries of Protection of Social Order (the former Ministries of Internal Affairs), the police, the organs of criminal investigation, and the corrective labor institutions. It does not, however, have supervisory power over the U.S.S.R. Council of Ministers.

In respect to the judicial system, the Procuracy's functions are still broader. It has the power to order the arrest of those suspected of crime, and it appoints the examining magistrates ("investigators") who conduct the pre-trial investigations of major criminal cases. It is the prosecuting arm in criminal trials. But beyond that, the procurator watches all civil proceedings and may initiate or enter any lawsuit at any stage on either side. Further, he may "protest" any decision, civil or criminal, of any court to the next higher court. He may move to reopen any case after the decision has been handed down. Before an appellate court renders its opinion in any case, it must hear the opinion of the procurator.

Certain of the functions of the Procuracy are performed by government attorneys (or procurators) in other legal systems. The Scandinavian Ombudsman (who has attracted much attention in the West in recent years[8]) has similar powers of "general supervision" over the legality of administrative acts. United States attorneys and state district attorneys spend more time than is generally realized listening to complaints of citizens against each other or against government officials, and determining ways in which such complaints may be satisfied. In no other system, however, is there a power of public protest on the same scale as that vested in the Soviet Procuracy (and in the procuracies of Eastern European countries which have adopted the Soviet system). The Soviet Procuracy combines in one office functions of the United States Attorney General's Office, Congressional investigating committees, grand jury and public prosecutor. It is the protector of all persons who are the victims of what it, the Procuracy, considers to be an illegal administrative act or unjust or doubtful judicial decision. It cannot annul such act or decision, but can only protest it to a higher administrative or judicial body; it can also, however, indict and prosecute the official responsible for the act if it believes that he has violated a law.

How are we to explain these unusual powers of the Soviet Procuracy? We may explain them as manifestations of a socialist system, in which the proliferation of administrative controls requires the creation of a special agency to watch over the administrators. We shall see later their consonance with a parental legal system, which treats the litigant as a ward of society. But we must also explain them historically, in terms of the ideas and traditions which are part of the Russian cultural heritage. The office of the Procuracy was not invented by the Soviet regime. It was adopted from prerevolutionary Russian law. Here, however, we meet an interesting fact: the Procuracy as it exists under the Soviets resembles not so much the Russian Procuracy of the post-1864 period as that of the period before the Great Reforms.

Peter the Great founded the Procuracy in 1722. From the beginning the two functions of prosecution and supervision were linked. The Procuracy served as an instrument of control over the newly founded Senate, which at that time was both a privy council and a supreme court. Later, when procurators' offices were established in the provinces, they were made subordinate to the Procurator General so that central supervision might be exercised over the provincial governors. In 1802 the Procurator General was transformed into the Minister of Justice, and the Procuracy was subordinated to that body, in a renewed effort to free the provincial procurators from the governors. As in Soviet Russia, so in the early nineteenth century the procurators attended meetings of the various administrative and executive bodies and read their resolutions and decrees to see whether they conformed to law. Again as in Soviet Russia, when a breach of the law was found it was reported to the superior executive-administrative authority —at that time the provincial governor; though in certain cases it was reported to the Ministry of Justice.

The 1864 reform, together with subsequent legislation, tended to confine the activities of the Procuracy chiefly to the prosecution of criminal cases and the presenting of opinions to the appellate courts in civil or criminal matters. To this extent, at least, the Procuracy after 1864 was very much like the corresponding office under French law. The procurators did retain, however, a number of administrative functions, participating as members of various provincial boards. But the procurator was a voting member of these boards and could not protest a decision of the majority—just the reverse of the Soviet practice. In civil cases the right of protest was confined to certain types of cases. In criminal cases the Procuracy was separated from the pre-trial investigation of criminal cases, the pre-trial investigator becoming an independent judicial officer, under the trial court.

In some respects the Soviet Procuracy marks a return to the type of procuracy of the eighteenth century, before the 1802 constitutional reforms of Alexander I. It is not part of the Ministry of Justice, and, theoretically at least, it supervises the legality of the acts of that department as well.

We may learn something of the nature and function of the Soviet Procuracy by studying its eighteenth-century counterpart. Under Peter, judicial administration was so bad that the Senate, acting as the Supreme Court, was unable to control the activities of the various local courts; further, the judicial branch was closely interlocked with the administrative branch, and hence subject to the pressures of local expediency. Peter therefore sought to construct a hierarchy parallel to the judicial and administrative, to be the "eye of the tsar," as he himself called it. The Procuracy which he established bore some resemblance to the old French system of *procureurs,* but its supervisory powers went far beyond those of the French model.

With a similar problem before them, it was natural for the Soviet rulers to reach back into the recesses of their own tradition and to develop the Procuracy along the earlier lines. It was in their heritage; it was Russian; and at the same time it went back beyond the hated "bourgeois liberalism" of the late nineteenth century.

At first, the new Bolshevik regime of 1917 abolished the prerevolutionary Procuracy together with the entire system of prerevolutionary law and government. A People's Commissariat of Justice was soon created, however, which had power to indict and prosecute and also to supervise legality in certain respects—particularly to protest local governmental decrees which conflicted with the decrees of the central government. Also, the People's Commissariat of State Control was given some powers of supervision over the execution of the laws and decrees of the central government, together with the power to indict or propose the dismissal of officials who failed faithfully to execute the laws which they were entrusted to administer. The People's Commissariat of Workers' and Peasants' Inspection later took over these functions of the People's Commissariat of State Control. In 1922, however, after prolonged discussion in which Lenin took an active part, a new body, the Procuracy, was established within the People's Commissariat of Justice with functions of general supervision of legality; the Statute on Procuracy Supervision, which took effect on August 1, 1922, contained two basic principles which have survived until today—first, that the Procuracy was charged with exercising supervision over the legality of acts of all government bodies, economic institutions, social and private organizations and private persons, by means of protesting illegal decrees or decisions and initiating criminal prosecution; and second, that the Procuracy was to be a centralized organization completely independent of local authorities.

The 1922 statute put the Procuracy within the Commissariat of Justice and made the Commissar of Justice the Procurator of the Republic. This was a return to the system established by Alexander I. But in 1933 a separate Procuracy of the U.S.S.R. was established, thereby returning to the eighteenth-century structure established by Peter the Great. It is this structure which has survived. The

Procurator General of the U.S.S.R. is appointed by the Supreme Soviet for a term of seven years, and he appoints the republican, regional and local procurators.

In evaluating the Soviet Procuracy, one must distinguish four principal functions which it exercises, two of which are related to criminal prosecution and two of which are related to supervision of legality. With respect to criminal prosecution, the Procuracy is charged not only with the prosecution in court of persons accused of crime, but also with the investigation and indictment of such persons prior to trial. Although such investigation and indictment is in the hands of professional "investigators," comparable to the French *juge d'instruction* or the German *Untersuchungsrichter,* the Soviet "investigator" (in contradiction to the French or German) is appointed by and responsible to the Procuracy.

In France or Germany, abuses committed against a suspect by an examining magistrate during the investigation of a crime may be appealed by the suspect to the courts; in the Soviet Union, they may be appealed only to the Procuracy. There is an obvious flaw, from the point of view of protection against illegal detention, extortion of confessions, and the like, in a system which commits persons suspected of crime to the charge of an official subordinate to the agency which prosecutes in criminal trials. Under Soviet conditions, however, it is doubtful that much would be gained by placing such protection in the hands of the courts. Under any system it is difficult for the courts to correct abuses of the police or of other bodies which investigate crime; the Soviet courts are probably less capable of maintaining adequate supervision in such cases than are the courts of Western European countries. Indeed, Soviet jurists state that the system in effect in the 1920's, in which the investigators were responsible to the courts rather than to the Procuracy, worked far less satisfactorily than the present system. In this connection it is important to keep in mind that the Procuracy is more than a prosecuting arm of the state; it is supposed to supervise legality generally, and hence higher officials of the Procuracy should be concerned particularly with the legality of the acts of their subordinates.

The 1958 Fundamental Principles of Criminal Procedure and the 1961 R.S.F.S.R. Code of Criminal Procedure attempt to give a certain degree of independence to the investigator as against his superiors in the Procuracy; he may refuse to indict, even though the Procurator would have him do so.

Because of the extensive powers of the impartial officials charged with investigation of crimes in continental European systems, the indictments which they prepare are apt to be treated with great respect by the courts which ultimately hear the criminal cases. The Soviet system, like that of France or Germany, attempts to protect the accused in the criminal trial by providing that no inference of guilt may be drawn from the mere fact of indictment and by providing that the burden of proof of the facts alleged in the indictment is borne by the prosecutor. The Soviet prosecutor thus appears as a party to the case on an equal footing with the accused. Although the phrase "presumption of innocence" has been rejected by the Soviet criminal codes, in fact all that that phrase connotes is contained in specific rules concerning proof. There is nothing, therefore, in the Procuracy's functions of prosecution which distinguishes it sharply from comparable prosecuting agencies of Western countries generally.

With respect to supervision of legality, the Procuracy has the twofold function of protesting judicial and administrative illegality. In exercising its supervisory power over judicial acts, the Procuracy may be found protesting both acquittals and convictions of lower courts in criminal cases and, less frequently, decisions in civil cases as well. Indeed, except for the possibility of a protest by the president of the higher court itself, the protest of the procurator "by way of supervision" is the only means of getting a further judicial review of a case once it has been decided by an appellate court. For instance, after a Soviet civil litigant or accused in a criminal case has lost on trial in the People's Court and has exhausted his right of appeal to the Regional

Court, he asks the Procurator of the Republic (or else the President of the Supreme Court of the Republic) to protest the decision of the Regional Court to the Supreme Court of the Republic. If he loses in the Supreme Court of the Republic, he may ask the Procurator of the U.S.S.R. to protest the decision to the Supreme Court of the U.S.S.R. Indeed, the only way to get to the Supreme Court of the U.S.S.R. on appeal is "by way of supervision" (*v poriadke nadzora*). Whether or not to make the protest is at the discretion of the Procuracy (or of the president of the higher court).

The Procurator need not wait for a petition from the losing party in order to protest a decision. Indeed, if he considers that important public interests are at stake, the Procurator may protest a decision whether or not the losing party wishes to have it reviewed.

The courts are not bound by the wishes of the Procuracy, and one finds cases in which the decision below is affirmed despite the Procuracy's protest. This again illustrates a basic concept of the nature and role of the Procuracy; it has no administrative power of its own (except the power to indict for crimes), but can only set the machinery of other agencies in motion in order to correct errors of their subordinate branches.

The function of the Procuracy in supervising the legality of administrative (as contrasted with judicial) acts is, potentially at least, its most important aspect, for here the work of the Procuracy bears upon the adherence of the Soviet bureaucracy to standards of justice laid down in the Soviet Constitution and Soviet laws. It must be stressed in this connection that even in theory the Procuracy has no supervisory powers over the acts of the Council of Ministers of the U.S.S.R., and whether it has (in theory) such powers over the acts of republican councils of ministers is debated by Soviet jurists. In practice, there are no reported cases of protests by the Procuracy against acts of republican councils of ministers, although there are many cases of protests against illegal acts of city and regional executive committees, as well as of individual ministries, and at least one case of a protest against a regulation of the council of ministers of an autonomous republic. (In that case the regulation had forbidden enterprises to hire nonresidents of the autonomous republic; the Procuracy protested on the grounds of a violation of Article 118 of the Soviet Constitution guaranteeing the right to work; the autonomous republic's council of ministers then revoked the regulation.[8a])

It should also be stressed that in practice the Procuracy was totally ineffective in supervising the multitude of illegal acts of the top Soviet leadership under Stalin. These acts were committed to the jurisdiction of the Ministry of Internal Affairs (or Ministry of State Security), which had its own Procuracy. The post-Stalin regime has emphasized the control of the Procuracy of the U.S.S.R. over the state security agencies, and has reduced the powers of these agencies. Also, through a 1955 statute on Procuracy Supervision in the U.S.S.R., the first comprehensive statute defining the rights and duties of the Procuracy as an agency of supervision of administrative and judicial legality in Soviet history, the duty of Procuracy supervision over places of detention of criminals has been re-emphasized, and procurators have been made "liable" for the observance of legality in those places. It is very doubtful, however, that the Procuracy could exert more than a moral influence against a return to a policy of terror at the highest level.

In an important sense, the Procuracy is a fourth branch of government in the Soviet system, independent of the executive, legislative and judicial branches. For although the Procurator General is appointed by the Supreme Soviet, the very nature of that body makes it impossible for him to have more than the loosest connection with it; and although his supervisory functions extend only to the intermediate and lower levels of the executive and judicial branches, and not to the highest, it is nevertheless misleading to view the Procuracy as a part of either.

What rendered the Procuracy ineffective, however, in protecting the Soviet system against the illegal intervention of its top leaders during the Stalin period was not its lack of independence vis-à-vis the other three branches of government but its lack of independence vis-à-vis the Communist Party leadership, which ruled (and rules) all four branches.

The Procuracy, in short, is, as it was in prerevolutionary Russia (especially before 1864), the "eye of the state," but it is not above the state. It is, essentially, an institution peculiarly characteristic of an autocratic system (though it has some features which recommend themselves to other systems as well), in that it can exercise important governmental functions in controlling other state agencies without threatening in any way the power of the central leadership. The Soviets have adapted the old Russian Procuracy to their own needs, chief of which is the uniform enforcement, by all branches of government and by all citizens, of the policies of the state as enacted into law.

THE SUBJECTIVE SIDE OF CRIME

Founded on prerevolutionary Russian criminal law, Soviet criminal law has, for that very reason, much in common with Western conceptions of crime and punishment. Yet the Soviets have added a great deal that is new. Some of the new features seem to be an inevitable accompaniment of a planned economic order; these have been discussed in the context of Socialist Law. Other features are characteristic of a system which expressly uses law to mold the ideas, the emotions and the character of people; these will be discussed in the context of Parental Law. But much of what the Soviets have added stems from historic Russian conceptions of man and society, conceptions which have developed from early times but which now, in many instances for the first time, are finding expression in law.

Here it is important to avoid a "Russian oversimplification." It is not implied that the new features of Soviet criminal law are unique to the Soviets, nor that they are to be explained solely in terms of the Russian past. Other legal systems may have similar features, stemming from their own history and from their own circumstances. Yet it is a striking fact that despite the similarities between all legal systems, each is peculiarly related to the culture from which it stems. To understand a people's law it is necessary to understand that people and its specific qualities. Indeed, identical rules of law often take on quite different significance in two different legal systems, and the difference in significance may often be explained—or at least illuminated—by the different traditions underlying those systems.

Soviet conceptions of crime and the criminal have deep roots in the Russian Orthodox conception of the corporate character of sin. The Russian peasant has traditionally called the criminal "unfortunate one"—a victim of society or of his own human temptations or perhaps of both. In Maynard's words, "The thief [to the Russian] is a sinner who ought to repent; the person injured by the theft may be expected to retaliate upon him: but other members of the community will naturally pity the sinner and help him to win absolution." Indeed, the community shares in his guilt. Such a conception has nonlegal and even anti-legal implications. If the criminal differs from others only in being more unfortunate, there seems to be no moral justification for prosecuting him. If the community shares in his guilt, why single him out for trial? If it is absolution that he requires, why send him to prison?

This basic antagonism between a religious and a legal conception of crime is well expressed in the novels and stories of Dostoevsky and Tolstoy. In *The Brothers Karamazov*, Dostoevsky visualizes a society in which "everything will become Church"; in such a society, he writes, a thief will not be punished by law but will be regenerated and reformed. Father Zossima declares:

> All these sentences to exile with hard labour, and formerly with flogging also, reform no one, and what's more, deter hardly a single criminal, and the number of crimes does not diminish but is continually on the increase. You must admit that. Consequently the security of society is not preserved, for,

although the obnoxious member is mechanically cut off and sent far away out of sight, another criminal always comes to take his place at once, and often two of them. If anything does preserve society, even in our time, and does regenerate and transform the criminal, it is only the law of Christ speaking in his conscience. It is only by recognizing his wrong-doing as a son of a Christian society—that is, of the Church—that he recognizes his sin against society —that is, against the Church. So that it is only against the Church, and not against the State, that the criminal of today can recognize that he has sinned.

In a society in which there were no State as such, or in which the State were included in the Church (instead of vice versa), "society would know whom to bring back from exclusion and to reunite to itself." [9]

This apocalyptic vision of Dostoevsky corresponded with deep religious and social attitudes of the Russian people— not generally of the Westernized intelligentsia, perhaps, but of the peasants and those who were close to the peasants. Many stories are reported illustrating the leniency of prerevolutionary Russian peasant juries and their tendency to give verdicts of acquittal, leaving punishment to Providence and protecting the family of the accused against loss of support of their breadwinner. "The Russian peasant juryman," Maurice Baring wrote, "is indifferent to legal subtleties, and often quite unaffected by forensic evidence, which he looks on as a thing made to order, bought and sold. He will judge by his conscience, and according to his own code of morals, which, if indulgent, is none the less definite." [10]

The leniency of the Russian jury must be measured in part against the severity of the criminal penalties then in effect. The deep sympathy for the criminal and the sense of the community's share in his guilt, which are reflected in much of prerevolutionary thought, go together in practice with an opposite sympathy for the community and its need to protect itself against those who endanger its unity. Rejecting a concept of crime and punishment based on objective legal procedures and norms of general application, many Russians wavered between a religious sentiment of leniency toward the offender and a political acceptance of the necessity to sacrifice his interests to those of the state.

This wavering back and forth between extremes of indulgence and severity found expression in the prerevolutionary Russian criminal code. Church penance at the discretion of a priest was one of the measures of punishment which a Russian court could apply in certain cases. Sentences for ordinary crimes were, by our standards, light: for murder in the first degree (intentional and premeditated), fifteen to twenty years of penal servitude; for murder in the second degree (intentional but unpremeditated), twelve to fifteen years; for murder committed under the influence of strong emotional excitement, the maximum sentence was eight years of penal servitude. Certain more reprehensible types of murder—for example, the murder of near relatives, or murder by torture—were punishable by penal servitude for life. The death penalty was inflicted only for attempts on the life of the Imperial Family and for treason. On the other hand, deportation to Siberia was the penalty for public blasphemy of Christianity; for conversion, by means of force or threats, of a Christian to a non-Christian faith or of a Russian Orthodox to another Christian belief; as well as for "showing audacious disrespect for the supreme authority, or contempt for the form of government or for the order of succession to the throne, by pronouncement or reading in public of speeches or words, or by spreading of works or pictures by public exhibition."

Further, in many types of crime the Russian judge was given wide leeway in choosing between maximum and minimum sentences; and here the criminal code instructed him to increase the punishment according to the following standards: "(1) the more there was intent and premeditation in the acts of the criminal; (2) the higher his status, calling and degree of education; (3) the more illegal and

unconscionable the inducements to commit the crime . . .
(6) the more there were broken special personal obligations
to the place in which the crime was committed and to the
persons against whom it was committed . . ."

In stating the circumstances to be considered as mitigating guilt and decreasing punishment, the code began
with the voluntary confession of the guilty person before
he was suspected. Other mitigating circumstances included
stupidity (if others had taken advantage of it to involve
the accused in the crime), a voluntary decision based on
sympathy for the victim not to commit as serious a crime
as originally intended, attempt to repay or rectify the
damage caused by the crime, and commission of the crime
because of extreme poverty.

It is not suggested that Russian law was unique in listing
such aggravating and mitigating circumstances. The older
German law did the same. The point is, rather, to identify
the features of Russian law which gave it its character and
which have made it a shaping force in Soviet legal development.

Running throughout these provisions of Russian law,
and manifested in the attitudes of the Russian jury, is a
special concern for the mentality of the criminal, his motivation, his orientation. It was not so much the criminal
act that was to be punished as the criminal himself, the
man; in punishing him, his whole personality was to be
taken into account, including in particular his personal relationship to the whole community. In this sense, a strong
element of subjectivism existed in the Russian law applicable
to the punishment of criminals. To some extent this is a
feature of all modern legal systems; but it seems to have
been carried further in the Russian than in most others.

At the same time prerevolutionary Russian criminal law
(and especially the 1903 criminal code) also laid stress on
the actor's state of mind in determining whether he was
guilty of a crime at all. A person was not to be considered
guilty of a crime unless he intentionally or negligently committed the criminal act—that is, unless he desired the consequences (direct intent) or consciously permitted their

occurrence or only light-mindedly hoped to avert them (indirect intent), or unless he could or should have foreseen them (negligence). The requirement of intent or negligence is familiar to all modern systems of criminal law, though by expanding or narrowing the definitions quite different results are often achieved in different systems (or even within the same system for different crimes). The emphasis of the 1903 code and of the writings of the Russian jurists of the time was upon a subjective standard of guilt.

The Soviets have returned to this subjectivism—both in determining whether to convict or acquit and in determining what punishment to apply—after an initial reaction against it. In the criminal codes of 1923 and 1926 the formulae of the 1903 code concerning intent and negligence were adopted almost verbatim. However, as has already been indicated in Chapter One, the Soviet jurisprudence of the first two decades after 1917 was highly critical of the concept of "guilt" (*vina*) altogether: it stressed the social danger of the act and of the actor, viewing both as the product of class conflict rather than of personal factors. Indeed, the Soviet criminal codes put the words "crime" and "punishment" in parentheses, as subordinate to the principal phrases "socially dangerous acts" and "measures of social defense." Ignoring the code requirement of intent or negligence, the Soviet courts often convicted persons who were in fact innocent of any fault, and in interpreting statutes which seemed to require intent they often convicted on the basis of mere negligence. In the mid-1930's, however, there was a return to the language of crime and punishment and to an approach in terms of the personal, and especially moral, element in the defendant's conduct. Indeed, in many cases stress came to be placed not only on intent or negligence but upon motive.

The most striking example of this shift was a renewed emphasis, from 1938 on, upon the requirement of a specific counterrevolutionary intent in order to be guilty of various counterrevolutionary crimes. A Supreme Court ruling of 1928 which had permitted conviction for certain counterrevolutionary crimes if the defendant "should have foreseen the socially dangerous character of the consequences of his acts" was overruled by the Supreme Court on December 31, 1938. The 1938 ruling, coming after the reaction against the excesses of the great purges, marked a return to a narrower reading of the statute on counterrevolutionary crimes. Similarly, with respect to economic and official crimes, it was said to be a prerequisite of the crime of release of goods of poor quality that the manager foresaw or should have foreseen that his acts would result in squandering state property. With respect to official abuse of authority, the U.S.S.R. Supreme Court has stressed that there must be a mercenary motive or other personal self-interest in order to justify a conviction. Also, the sale of goods by a person at a price higher than that which he paid for them does not constitute the crime of speculation unless the goods were originally purchased for the purpose of resale at a profit. To be guilty of theft of state property the accused must be shown to have known that the property was state property and to have intended to steal it.

The Soviet emphasis on the actor's state of mind, and in many instances his motive, is associated with a parallel emphasis upon his intellectual capabilities in determining whether he was criminally negligent.

It is the general rule of civilized legal systems, including both the prerevolutionary Russian and the Soviet, that a man shall not be liable to criminal punishment unless he was in some way at fault in committing the act with which he is charged. If, for example, he committed it while walking in his sleep, or if his act was for some other reason not his fault, he cannot be said to have committed a crime. But suppose a man makes a mistake which has disastrous consequences—shoots at what he thinks is a bear, for example, only to find that it was actually his hunting companion. In such cases, it is in the tradition of Anglo-American law to inquire whether a "reasonable man" would have foreseen the consequences of the act which was committed, and to hold the accused to the standard of foreseeability or care maintained by society generally. The courts would ask: Was the hunter exercising that degree of care which a prudent man would have exercised under the circumstances? Should he, by ordinary standards of reasonableness, have foreseen that the figure in the distance might actually be a man and not a bear? In the closely related situation of a man who intentionally commits a criminal act which has, however, unforeseeable consequences, the Anglo-American law often assumes that the actor intended such consequences and punishes him for them regardless of his actual intent. If, for example, a man strikes another on the nose intending only to cause him pain, but the victim happens to be a hemophiliac and consequently bleeds to death, the actor may be held for murder or for manslaughter, depending on whether the attack is a serious crime (felony) or a minor crime (misdemeanor).

American courts have placed many limitations upon the "reasonable man" (or "objective") standard of liability for criminal negligence as well as upon the "felony-murder" and "misdemeanor-manslaughter" rules. Criminal negligence is often defined as involving a "gross deviation" from the required standard of care, and criminal negligence, as distinguished from negligence in civil cases, is said to be "culpable" negligence. Also it is sometimes said that a person may not be convicted of a crime unless he had a "guilty mind" (*mens rea*). Nevertheless these limitations are often subordinated to an objective (or external) standard. Thus the New York Penal Law defines negligence as "a want of such attention to the nature or probable consequences of the act or omission as a prudent man ordinarily bestows in acting in his own concerns."

In continental European law, there is less talk of the "reasonable man." Nevertheless most European legal systems, though not all, tend to hold the accused to objective standards of foreseeability and care.[11] Also, in continental European law generally, one may in some cases be punished for a crime which one did not intend to commit but which resulted from another intentional criminal act, though this class of cases has been more strictly limited in continental than in Anglo-American law.

Soviet writers on criminal law take a different approach to this problem. The question of whether the actor ought to have foreseen the consequences of his act is, they say, not to be considered in the light of an objective (or generalized) standard of foreseeability (that of the reasonable man). Soviet criminal law, like other systems (*e.g.,* the Russian Criminal Code of 1903) requires that a person who is careless or negligent, and who ought to have foreseen that defined harmful consequences might result from his carelessness or negligence, should be held criminally liable for causing that harm. But it determines whether or not he should have foreseen the consequences on the basis of a subjective (or personal) standard: it asks "whether under the given circumstances the given personality, with its individual capacities, development and qualifications, could have foreseen the consequences which occurred." [12] This subjective standard has been re-emphasized in the criminal codes of 1960 and 1961, in which the phrase "should have foreseen" was replaced by "could have foreseen," for the purpose, according to Soviet authors, of making clear that the standard of foreseeability is a subjective one.

A Soviet treatise states:

> The objective criterion may serve only for the original orienting of the act which has been committed. Certain requirements of foreseeability are worked out in the exercise of a particular profession; certain requirements of foreseeability in the sphere of everyday customary relations are created by the rules of socialist common life; in a number of instances they are established by the law itself. It is necessary to start from these in order to clarify the real possibility of foresight of the criminal consequences by the given person. But in order to establish the presence of the possibility of the given person's foreseeing the result that happened, it is necessary to clarify the subjective qualities of the given person—his knowledge, qualifications, particular features of his personality, *etc.* . . . For persons who possess special knowledge and high devel-

opment there will be a real possibility of foresight of the criminal consequences in cases where for persons, committing the same act but not possessing such knowledge and such [a high level of] consciousness, it would not be possible to establish the presence of this possibility.[13]

The author of the treatise cites a 1948 case in which B. was accused of criminal negligence in the management of a store. Because of her carelessness, it was claimed, other persons had been able to steal state property from the store. Her defense was that she had been promoted to a position, that of store manager, for which she was not qualified, and had been kept there against her will. (In 1948 it was illegal to quit a job without the employer's permission.) She showed that she was barely literate and did not know how to keep accounts or use an abacus and metric measures, but that she had tried her best. The criminal division of the U.S.S.R. Supreme Court sustained this defense, stating that for conviction it must be shown that the given person in the concrete situation, guided by his own knowledge and abilities, could have avoided the happening of the harmful consequences.[14]

Prerevolutionary Russian criminal law took into account social position, calling, and education in meting out punishment for a criminal act. Soviet law follows the older law in this, and contains in its code a list of aggravating and mitigating circumstances to be taken into account in sentencing. Members of the Communist Party are seldom prosecuted for crimes unless they have first been expelled from the Party for their actions; when a Party member is convicted, however, he is apt to be punished more severely than an ordinary citizen. "You are a member of the Party, one of the vanguard; you should have known better," the judge may say. Khrushchev stated in 1962 that "It is utterly impermissible that individual Party committees take a tolerant attitude toward instances of abuses of office on the part of Communists, and, what is more, sometimes shield and defend them." He quoted an unpublished statement of Lenin that, "the courts are obliged to punish Communists *more strictly* than non-Communists." [15]

But Soviet law goes still further; it sometimes takes personal factors into account not only in sentencing but also in determining whether a crime was committed at all or whether, on the contrary, the act should be considered merely accidental. This means in practice that an educated or more intelligent man is held to a higher standard of care than an ignorant or unintelligent man. Here, too, the Soviets are building on the prerevolutionary criminal code of 1903, which provided that criminal negligence should be based on a subjective standard ("could have foreseen") except that professional people should be held to the standard of their profession ("should have foreseen").

Perhaps the most striking example of the emphasis of Soviet criminal law upon the personality of the accused is the code provision that a person accused of crime may be acquitted, even though he committed the criminal act, if at the time of the trial he personally no longer constituted a social danger.

Thus not merely the act but the "whole man" is tried. At the same time, his crime is considered in the context of the "whole community." This tends to increase the severity of penalties attached to conduct which from the viewpoint of individual morality may not be highly blameworthy, but which it is desired to stamp out in the community as a whole. Thus while Soviet criminal law is merciful in the handling of crimes against persons or personal property, it is also quite ruthless in the handling of crimes which directly affect the society as a whole. The Soviets have carried over and even extended the leniency of prerevolutionary Russian law in the punishment of murder, assault, arson, and the like—and its harshness in the punishment of ideological and political crimes. Murder without aggravating circumstances is punished by ten years' deprivation of liberty—massive theft of state property by death. Also, when the Soviet state is campaigning to eliminate a certain type of crime, the sanctions against it may be suddenly increased. Reference has already been made to the fact that in 1961 and 1962 a series of laws imposed the death penalty for a variety of crimes—many of them economic—which the regime considered incompatible with the new spurt forward toward Communism.[16] This harsh policy followed a period of leniency marked not only by reduction of penalties for many crimes, but also by large-scale amnesties in 1953, 1955 and 1957, which released virtually all the less serious offenders from places of detention.

A mixture of excessive harshness and excessive leniency in penal policy, and a wavering back and forth from one to the other, is characteristic of systems which seek, on the one hand, to convict or acquit the accused solely on the basis of his personal qualities (including his attitudes toward the community) and, on the other hand, to protect the community against all threats to its integrity. Psychologically consistent with each other, the desire to personalize guilt and the desire to integrate society may lead, in practice, in opposite directions. Indeed, Soviet legal history provides at least one example of the complete sacrifice of the first desire to the second. Thus under a law finally repealed in 1958, family members were subject to punishment if one of their number defected from the armed forces even though the others knew nothing of the crime and had no control over it. Such an extreme example of shared guilt is unique in Soviet criminal law, though it has important parallels in Soviet political life and in the extra-legal political punishments which were meted out against whole classes and peoples in the Stalin era. Here the personal and the corporate elements of crime, which Soviet law in general seeks to merge, split asunder and persons were punished solely because of their associations.

Also stemming from the conception of crime as both an individual and a corporate act is the considerable emphasis on the ritual act of confession and repentance as a prerequisite to absolving both the person and the community. Here, perhaps, lies the underlying significance of the famous confessions of Bukharin, Rakovsky, and others who were tried for counterrevolutionary "wrecking" in the late 1930's. To the extent that these confessions were voluntary, they reflected the desire of the accused to identify themselves with their Motherland and with the Revolution, both of which, they said, they had betrayed. To the extent that the confessions were extorted, they reflected the regime's desire to present an external sign of expiation of sins and of purification of the community.

The emphasis on the subjective side of crime thus has implications far beyond the determination of standards of foreseeability in cases of criminal negligence. It is closely connected with the central concern of Soviet politics and law with the state of mind of the Soviet people. This has roots in prerevolutionary conceptions of both the role of the state and the nature of crime and punishment. These prerevolutionary conceptions, however, are now given systematic political and legal expression in a new context.

THE LAW OF THE COLLECTIVE-FARM HOUSEHOLD

The Soviet collective farm is sometimes treated as a historical outgrowth of the prerevolutionary Russian peasant commune, or *mir*. The two are comparable, however, only in a negative sense: in neither is the land privately owned by the individual peasants. Of the direct historical connection between the two it can only be said that in collectivizing agriculture the Soviets could capitalize on the absence in Russian history of a strong tradition of private peasant ownership of the land.

Matters are different, however, regarding the collective-farm household, with its house-and-garden plot, farm implements, livestock, and crops produced on the plot. Here there is a striking similarity between the new and the old, and a direct historical outgrowth of one from the other.

The individual peasant on a Soviet collective farm has a double legal personality. On the one hand he is a member of the collective farm, working the land held by the collective farm, paid by it on the basis of what he produces for it, voting at its meetings. On the other hand he is a member of the household in which he lives, working the small plot of land held by the household, sharing in the proceeds of its joint labors, participating in its management. He is thus doubly collectivized.

Comparable from a legal point of view to the Great Family of the Serbs and Croatians which died out in the last century and perhaps to the customary household of India, the Russian peasant household also echoes primitive Germanic and early Irish family organization.

The household is defined by the Soviet Land Code as "a family-labor association of persons jointly engaged in agriculture." It may consist of any number of persons, related by blood or not, who are linked by a joint or domestic economy as well as by communal ownership of its agricultural property. Gsovski sums up its internal legal relationships as follows:

> For adult membership in the household, relation by blood or marriage must be combined with participation in the conduct of common farming through the contribution of labor or money. Minors and aged persons are members by virtue of their family ties and life under the same roof. Still, a household is not identical with a family, although the family forms its foundation. A household may consist of a single person without family. On the contrary, sons and daughters who carry on separate farming or are engaged in other outside trades, live apart, and do not contribute to the welfare of the "parental" household, are not considered members of such household. Under the Land Code, a six-year period of such separation results in loss of membership. Members who sign a contract for outside jobs with government agencies and register them with the management continue to be members for the duration of the contract. Those leaving for study, military or government service, by appointment or election, continue to be members for the entire period of their absence. Strangers informally taken into the family life and joint work (quasi-adopted members, *priymaki*) are, unless working for definite wages,

members of the household with the standing of relatives. The membership of each household is officially recorded.

Property of the household, which consists of all articles appertaining to the common farming and life, is the common property of all members including minors, the aged, and quasi-adopted strangers. However, in contradistinction to joint property under the Civil Code, no member has a definite share in the common property. It is common property undivided into shares, and no member may in any way convey his or her interest in it. Membership may be increased by marriage, birth, or admittance of strangers; it may also be decreased by death and separation. But the death of a member is not followed by descent and partition. A household is not considered a legal entity; nevertheless, its common property continues to exist undivided, regardless of the change of membership. A member's share is realized only if the household is broken up completely or is partitioned by the separation of one or several members who form a new household. Even in such case, no particular rules define the share, and the whole distribution is a matter of agreement and custom. During the existence of the household, a member has in fact no share in its property but merely an indefinite share in the customary use of the property; he simply enjoys such benefits and comforts as the common life of the household can offer.[17]

The management, use, and disposal of the property of the household are in the members as a whole; in the absence of unanimity, according to the Soviet legal literature, a majority vote of the adult members is decisive. The members select a head of the household to administer it and to represent it in business matters. Such head may be deposed by the members, with the authorization of the public authorities, and another appointed in his place. Property of the household may not be attached in payment of the debts of individual members (including the head of the household) contracted by them for their personal needs.

In a 1946 case involving a contract made in 1940 for the purchase of a building constituting part of a collective-farm household plot, the Moscow Regional Court ordered the contract dissolved and the purchase price of 26,000 rubles refunded, on the ground that the seller, a man named Evmenov, who was apparently the head of the household, "had no right to conclude the above-mentioned contract involving the sale of a part of the house, since he was not the owner of the house." The court added: "The contested building belongs to all the members of the collective-farm household, and Evmenov acted without their consent in selling it." [18]

Centuries of Russian history are embodied in the institution of the Soviet collective-farm household. Originating in ancient times, it has survived many different forms of agricultural organization. Both before and after the emancipation of the serfs, it was closely connected with the peasant commune, which consisted of the heads of the households who assembled in general meeting and elected elders. Before emancipation, the commune regulated the use of common fields, fisheries, forests, and so forth, and distributed and redistributed the three-course open fields among the households. It was also responsible for tax apportionment among the households. It represented the peasantry in their relations with the landlords. After emancipation, the nature and functions of the commune remained essentially the same, only now it dealt directly with the state instead of with the landlord and his bailiffs; and now the periodic redistribution of the newly allotted land among the households gained increased significance.

The great legal and economic difference between the prerevolutionary peasant commune and the Soviet collective farm is that the entire property of the commune was used by the households which comprised it. The commune itself, as a collective entity, did not conduct agricultural operations. However, even in the commune a sharp distinction was made between the "fields" which were subject to redistribution and the house-and-garden plots which belonged to the separate households in perpetuity. Through collectivization the Soviets have withdrawn the fields from the households and have turned them over to the possession and operation of the collective farm, membership in which is not by households but by individuals; the individuals cultivate the collective fields through teams and brigades organized by the collective farm.

In the early 1930's, after collectivization was introduced, leading Soviet authorities on land law considered that "the peasant household will not be united but absorbed by collective agriculture. . . . With the introduction of collective farms, the household as a separate unit is doomed." This approach, which was accompanied by violent and lawless incorporation of peasant households into the new collectives and a general disregard of their property rights, was abandoned in 1935, with the promulgation of a Standard Charter for Artels (collective farms) in which the rights of the household were restored. In an address to the Drafting Committee on the Standard Charter, Stalin stated that so long as the collective farms are not rich enough to satisfy the personal needs of its members, "it is better to admit straightforwardly, openly, and honestly that a household in a collective farm should have its own personal farm plot, a small one, but its own." In fact the households have had increasing economic significance in the total picture of Soviet agriculture. They supply the U.S.S.R. with a large proportion of its meat and dairy produce, vegetables, fruit, honey, and they own almost one third of its cattle.

The reasons for retaining the household plots are by no means solely economic, however. Even on wealthy collective farms, where more than enough is produced collectively to satisfy the needs of the members, the household retains its importance. There is a profound social and psychological reason as well. The peasants have clung to their households, and the Soviet rulers, despite their ideological antagonism to this "petty bourgeois" survival of the prerevolutionary past, have been compelled to yield.

In the post-Stalin period the ideological attack on the

household plot has been renewed. The 1961 Party Program accepts the present necessity of individual farming but argues that, "When collective production on the collective farms is able fully to replace production on the individual plots of the collective-farm members, when the collective farmers see for themselves that their supplementary individual farming is unprofitable, they will give it up of their own accord." Khrushchev stated in 1959: "It is quite clear that in the future the collective-farm-cooperative and state forms of [farm] ownership will completely merge into a single form of communist ownership. . . . In the future, the Party aims to convert the collective-farm villages into urban-type population centers with all the latest communal cultural and service facilities." Nevertheless, the age-old "family collectivism" appears to be strong enough to withstand such attacks. The peasant household, renamed the collective-farm household (*kolkhoznyi dvor*), has been given legal protection. A special category of property, collective-farm household property, has been recognized —different from personal property, different from joint property, and different from collective and state property. The status of the household has been defined and regularized. Serious attention has been given to the difficult problems that arise in regard to the rights of members of the household among each other as well as the rights of the household as against the collective farm.

In prerevolutionary Russian law similar legal problems arose regarding the status of the peasant household. The Emancipation Statutes and other legislation referred to the household but nowhere defined it. It was left to the courts to do so, on the basis of local customs. A series of decisions by the prerevolutionary Supreme Court laid down certain rules which are roughly equivalent to the subsequent Soviet legislation on the subject. However, these rules were not systematized and no general principles were stated which could serve as a basis for such systematization.[19]

The Soviets have built on the prerevolutionary court decisions. They have come forward with a general theory of collective-farm household ownership, based upon principles derived from the unique Russian experience rather than from Western doctrines. They have integrated peasant household law into collective farm law. Yet here as elsewhere in Soviet law, administrative bodies play a very important role, and the unsystematic character of the Soviet administrative process—the absence of established norms and fixed procedures—makes it difficult to judge the effectiveness of the Soviet peasant household in terms of concrete application of the general principles that have been elaborated. Most legal problems arising within a household, or between a household and the collective farm, are resolved administratively, by the district Soviet executive committee or by the organs of the Ministry of Agriculture. The administrative findings of fact are conclusive upon the courts, should there be a resort to the judicial process.

In illustration we may cite a 1944 decision, Dogadin versus the Collective Farm "Red Ploughman," as reported officially in the journal "Court Practice of the Supreme Court of the U.S.S.R.":

> Dogadin brought suit in the People's Court against the collective farm "Red Ploughman" to recover damages caused as the result of illegal withdrawal from him of his garden plot.
>
> The People's Court of the Nogin District of Moscow Province rejected Dogadin's suit in its decision of 6 September 1943. The Court College for Civil Cases of the Moscow Provincial Court affirmed the decision of the People's Court in its opinion of 21 September 1943.
>
> In accordance with the protest of the President of the Supreme Court of the U.S.S.R., the Court College declared that the decision of the People's Court and the opinion of the Provincial Court must be set aside on the following grounds:
>
> The question of the right to use garden plots attached to a collective-farm house is decided by land agencies and not by a court. By its ruling of 7 July 1943, No. 36, which was present in the

record, the Nogin District Executive Committee found that the withdrawal of the garden plot from Dogadin was illegal, and, therefore, the court had no right to concern itself with this question in its decision. In spite of this fact, the court rejected Dogadin's suit solely on the ground that the collective farm-defendant, in withdrawing the garden plot from Dogadin, acted in accordance with law.

Since the withdrawal from Dogadin was found to be illegal by the competent agencies, the court must decide on the rehearing only the question of the value of materials and labor which Dogadin had expended on the plot which was taken from him.

On the basis of what has been set forth, the Court College for Civil Cases of the Supreme Court of the U.S.S.R. at its session of 12 April 1944 ordered:

The decision of the People's Court of the Nogin District of 6 September 1943 and the opinion of the Moscow Provincial Court of 21 September 1943 are set aside and the case remanded for rehearing in the same court with a different bench and with the participation of the Procurator.[20]

Other cases could be cited to show that the collective-farm household has retained its legal identity and its independent rights against encroachments by the collective farm. If the threat to eliminate the household is ever carried out, centuries of Russian history will go with it.

Chapter Nine

RUSSIAN LAW AND WESTERN LAW

WHEN WE TALK of law, we do not think merely of the rules in force at a given moment but rather of a way, or process, of ordering human affairs. There are, of course, other ways. There is the way of terror. "Lynch law" is not law, if only because it is spontaneous and violent. The secret administrative trial of persons accused of being "socially dangerous" is not law, if only for the reason that it is secret and arbitrary. Deliberation (a "fair hearing"), publicity, the consistent application of established norms and standards, are essential features of the law way of ordering human affairs.

Terror may be legalized. A duly enacted law authorizing lynching would be an unjust law, according to civilized standards, but it would be a law. To lynch would then be legal; it would not, however, be a law way of ordering human affairs. A war of self-defense may be legal, under rules of international law; but a legal war between two countries is a settlement of their differences by force, and not by law.

Law differs not only from terror and force, but also from other ways or processes of governing human relations, such as the exercise of economic pressures (through the "forces" of the market, for example), or of family pressures, or of religious sanctions. These other forms of social relations may be subjected to law, may be legalized, but they are distinct from law, which is itself a special and unique form of social relations.

Law in this sense is the product of long historical experience and not merely of the momentary "will" of the sovereign. The modern theory that the supreme lawmaker (parliament) is omnicompetent, and may enact any law it pleases, has obscured the fact that law in a deeper sense, like the institution of the family, or like religious belief, is not an article of manufacture but rather a living, growing tradition. Law is a way of life. It lives only by being passed on from generation to generation, consciously, by people who are dedicated to this task. Law in this sense is intimately bound up with a people's whole historical development.

If we view Russian history as a whole, and compare it with the history of the West, we see at once that perhaps the most striking difference between the two histories is the relative deficiency of the role of law as a special and unique form of Russian social relations. The emergence in the nineteenth century, finally, of a class of lawyers, the separation then for the first time of the judicial from the administrative function, the development in the fifty years before the Bolshevik Revolution of a distinct unified legal system as such, came as part of the Westernization of Russia. The Russian jurists consciously borrowed from Germany, from France, from England; previously, in the seventeenth and eighteenth centuries, Peter the Great and his successors had borrowed from Sweden, from Hungary, from Saxony, from Italy.

Russian law, therefore, challenges us to rediscover the unity and continuity of the Western legal tradition. Russian law proves that the different national legal systems of the West are in reality variations on a single theme. To Speransky, the distinctive features of English law, as compared with continental systems, appeared as differences in technique rather than in fundamental principles. In the face of the Russian challenge it is time for European and American scholars to overcome the nationalistic bias of traditional legal historiography and to rediscover the common sources from which all the legal systems of the West are derived.

At the same time, Russian legal history requires that we view Soviet developments in a larger perspective, seeking to understand them in the light of generations and centuries and not merely in terms of the day-to-day or year-to-year machinations of the regime in power. The Soviet rulers are not the ultimate masters of Russia's fate; on the contrary, Russia is the ultimate master of their fate. It is part of their "realism" that they have again and again yielded to the pressures of tradition—with which, as Marxist Revolutionaries, they presumably have had little sympathy. Stalin himself attempted to integrate Soviet law into the whole movement of Russian legal history.

Above all, the polarity of Russian and Western history over the past thousand years poses the question of the relationship between the law way and other ways of ordering the affairs of society. The West has exalted law, with its principles of Reason, Conscience, and Growth; it has fostered the doctrines of the supremacy and completeness of law, its basis in equality, its organic continuity. It has by the same token tended to forget that law itself is ultimately dependent on the existence of nonlegal realities. Law is not its own justification, nor is it its own sanction. Behind it must lie the "consent of the governed," as manifested in community self-consciousness, common service, a sense of common purpose and destiny. The traditional Russian appreciation of spontaneous, informal social relations, based on an inner intuition of group membership, is a challenge to us to find the link between the political-legal and the moral-spiritual aspects of our own heritage.

By the same token, Western law is a challenge to Russia. In the nineteenth century Russian jurists accepted the challenge of the West and sought to build a Russian legal system in the Western image. The Soviets are now building both on the Westernized Russian legal tradition of the late nineteenth and early twentieth centuries and on the nonlegal social and personal values which have been central in Russian life from early times. They are seeking to reconcile Eastern and Western elements in Russian social relations. They are trying to develop a specifically Soviet legal system, giving legal forms and legal sanctions to the traditional Russian conceptions of the "whole man" and the "whole community." Yet they are unwilling to sacrifice certain traditional habits and beliefs which stand in the way of this goal. Nor are the Soviet leaders willing to risk subjecting their own political power to legal procedures secure against their own intervention.

The Soviet regime has sought to create a system of law which conforms to reason. Soviet jurists have applied their powers of analysis to concepts such as ownership, contracts, the relation of administrative action to judicial decision, the elements of criminal intent, and so forth and so forth. A belief in the completeness of law has been fostered. The supremacy of law has been declared in principle, and judges have been required to base their decisions on established norms and standards rather than on mere considerations of economic expediency. But this movement toward reason, analysis, legality, is seriously impeded by a fundamental belief that life is essentially beyond reason and law, and by a fundamental unwillingness to trust in reason and law absolutely. Hence whole spheres of life still remain outside the law, particularly in the realm of politics and policymaking, where reliance is placed on the nonrational, nonlegal factors of force and violence, on the one hand, and of moral unity and common faith on the other. The personality of the rulers still plays a dominant role; personal influence is a crucial factor in impeding the movement for stability of laws.

Likewise one is struck by the Soviet struggle for the development of a principle of judicial conscience. The Soviet judge is an important means of reconciliation of the abstract "will of the state" with the personal actions of individual citizens. He is a figure in whom the state seeks to have public confidence reposed. He identifies himself with the parties who come before him. He does equity. He has not merely the interests of the state but also the interests of the litigant at heart. Indeed, the People's Courts sometimes show a remarkable leniency, a tendency to acquit, a tendency to mitigate the harshness of the law; on appeal, they are sometimes rebuked for their soft-heartedness. But even here, the conscientious attitude of the Soviet judges are subject to far greater pressure from outside political authorities. They owe their election to the Communist Party, since it is the Party which is responsible for their nomination. Their tenure is relatively short (that of People's Judges was raised from three to five years in 1958), and they may be recalled in the interim by their constituents for misconduct. Their conscience is subject to the demands of Party campaigns to stamp out this or that type of activity among the population. "Social prosecutors" have the right to appear in criminal cases to demand severe punishment of offenders —a practice condemned by the Supreme Court of the U.S.S.R. itself in 1947 "as being irreconcilable with the principle that the court is subject only to the law," but reintroduced in the late 1950's as part of the effort to increase popular participation in the administration of justice. In 1960 an article was published in *Socialist Legality*, the journal of the Procuracy of the U.S.S.R., sharply criticizing a court for deciding a case according to "instructions" of an outside organization; the fact that such an organization would dare to issue "instructions" to a court is itself revealing with regard to the outside pressure which is exerted upon the conscience of the Soviet judge.

Again, the increased stress on past decisions, together with the recognition that Soviet law is a growing historical system, is a significant development of the past twenty-five years; yet here, too, there is a limitation imposed by the weakness of the Russian legal tradition, which still tends to be blown about by every wind of fashionable doctrine. Party directives may tell judges to "intensify the struggle against thefts in the factories," or to make examples of managers who have tampered with the books, or to bear down on some other activity which the Party is seeking to "liquidate." In addition, legislation may be enacted without difficulty or delay. As a result, case law loses something of its importance, and historical growth is swamped under by rapid shifts in policy.

It would be a mistake, however, to concentrate on the weaknesses of the Russian tradition and to underestimate its strength. In demanding absolute obedience from its subjects and, beyond that, in seeking active belief on their part in the institutions of socialism, the Soviet state draws on the resources of a tradition in which the dualism of secular and spiritual never penetrated. The Soviet rulers can speak of the socialist family as a sacred institution, of work as a sacred duty, of socialist property as "sacred and inviolable"—in part because the word "sacred" is meaningful to the Russian people. They could conscript a portion of the youth into the State Labor Reserves, and can list on university bulletin boards the names of "volunteers" required for summer work in cultivating the "virgin lands" of Central Asia—in part because universal compulsory service is not new in Russian history. They can help to justify and make palatable the rapid industrialization of economic life by a reminder of the *furor technicus* of Peter the Great. That they can ultimately consolidate these positive features of Russian life into a stable legal system, in the Westernizing tradition of the late nineteenth and early twentieth centuries, appears more and more likely.

The conflict between law and unlaw still goes on in Russia. One should not conclude that law is the loser simply on the basis that it suffers many defeats. It also scores many victories. In terms of the direction in which events are moving, the "struggle for law" during the past twenty-five years remains one of the most important internal developments in Soviet Russia since 1917. To it Buligin perhaps owes his life, citizeness B. her acquittal, Dogadin his household land and money compensation, and countless other

Soviet citizens the protection of their rights. Especially in the years since Stalin's death the jurists trained in pre-revolutionary Russian law, together with their pupils, have played a prominent part in reforming, systematizing and rationalizing the Soviet system.

-III-
PARENTAL
LAW

Chapter Ten

LAW OF A NEW TYPE

ONE OF the most significant internal developments in the Soviet Union, marking a new phase in the Revolution, has been the elaboration during the past twenty-five years of an affirmative theory of the socialist state and socialist law. All other states, it is now claimed, are instruments of class domination; the Soviet state, not based on class antagonism, is a "new type of state" with a "new type of law," "essentially different from all types of law known to history." [1]

Yet now that Soviet law has been proclaimed to be socialist law, law of a new type, and not merely (as before) an accommodation of the proletarian dictatorship to legal survivals of the bourgeois past, some of the most striking innovations of the first twenty years of the Revolution have been abandoned. In the name of socialism many elements familiar to capitalist systems have been reintroduced, and in the name of Soviet patriotism many institutions of the prerevolutionary Russian past have been restored. From the Left, Trotsky, Koestler, and other former Communists have spoken of these changes since the mid-1930's as "The Great Betrayal"; from another standpoint, Timasheff, Sorokin and other Russian *émigrés* have viewed them as "The Great Retreat." "After long years of destruction and experimentation, feverish efforts were made to restore the situation which existed at the outbreak of the Revolution or even earlier," writes Timasheff.[2]

In fact an American lawyer would not have too great difficulty in accommodating himself to a great many aspects of the Soviet legal system as manifested in the positive law proclaimed by the state. He would find many basic principles, precepts, doctrines, and rules of contract law, tort law, criminal law, family law, procedure, and various other branches of the legal tree essentially the same in the Soviet system as in the German, French, Swiss, Italian, English or American. This similarity is due in part to the fact that the Soviet state, for all its socialism, must meet fundamental social and economic needs similar to those that confront "capitalist" states; it also stems from the common Roman derivation of both Russian and Western law, from the impact of later Western legal developments on prerevolutionary Russia, and from the Soviet reliance on prerevolutionary Russian law as well as on German, Swiss, and French law in the preparation of the NEP codes. The American lawyer would have to reconcile himself to the Marxist emphasis on economic integration and public control of business; and he would have to adjust to the strong Russian spirit of collective consciousness, universal service, and dedication to the mission of Moscow, as well as to the dynamic and energetic quality of Soviet government. But he would have to make similar (though not so radical) reconciliations and adjustments were he to practice law in England, for example, which has its own strong historical tradition of community spirit, service, and mission, and which has incorporated into that tradition stringent public controls of the economy as well.

No doubt our American lawyer in Moscow would be shocked at the extent to which illegal and extralegal activity is still accepted as normal; but that would hardly strike him as manifesting a new type of law, except in the most ironic sense.

Nevertheless, Soviet law is in fact quite different from the law of socialistic countries of Western Europe (or wartime America). The differences are not as apparent in the codes, statutes, decisions, and rules of positive law as in certain basic conceptions which underlie these external normative acts.

Here it is necessary to add a third dimension to our study. We have explained Soviet law, in the first instance, as a Marxian socialist response to the social and economic problems which have confronted the Soviet regime. To this analytical dimension we have added a historical dimension, explaining Soviet law in terms of inherited traditions and experiences as they have imposed themselves on the habits and memories of both the rulers and the people. Yet Soviet law cannot be fully explained either by the logic of socialism or by the experience of Russian history or by both together. Many of its most important features are neither uniquely socialist nor uniquely Russian but are rather a product of a social philosophy which—though entirely congenial to both socialism and the Russian heritage—is to be found in other non-socialist countries as well. We are compelled, therefore, to approach our subject once more, from a quite different angle.

To understand a legal system it is necessary to distinguish between the official law proclaimed by the state and the unofficial law which exists in the minds of men and in the various groups to which they belong. Each of us has his own conceptions of rights, duties, privileges, powers, immunities—his own law-consciousness. And within each of the communities in which we live—the family, school, church, factory, commercial enterprise, profession, neighborhood, city, region, nation—there is likewise an unofficial and largely unwritten pattern of obligations and sanctions. The official law of the state, with its authoritative technical language and its professional practitioners, cannot do violence to the unofficial law-consciousness of the people without creating serious tensions in society. At the same time, official law is more than a reflection of popular law-consciousness; it also shapes it, directly or indirectly.[3]

This distinction between official and unofficial law is essential to a full understanding of the peculiar blending of Marxist theory and Russian history into a "new type" of law. It was the prophecy of classical Marxism that once class domination is eliminated, and once the economy is publicly integrated and rationalized, it will not be necessary to put conflicting claims through the wringer of legal reasoning, judicial conscience, and precedents. Marx and Engels foresaw a classless society in which disputes would be settled by the spontaneous, unofficial social pressure of the whole community, by the group sense of right and wrong or at least of expediency. They saw a precedent for this in the condition of certain primitive peoples who have no positive law, no state, but instead punish aberrational behavior through informal, spontaneous group sanctions. As among primitive societies at the beginning of history, so in classless society at the end of history, they said in effect, control will exist only in the habits and standards of the whole people, in the *mores* of the good society. This moral consciousness implicit in the Marxist utopia is something broader than law-consciousness. Nevertheless the two go together. Both are psychological rather than official. One is the feeling of what one *ought* to do, the feeling of being morally bound; the other is the feeling of what one *has* to do, the *feeling* of being *legally* bound.

The idea of a society without official law goes down hard in a culture such as that of the West, where positive law tends not to be treated as merely one particular means of social control but rather to be identified with social control altogether, so that every social norm, or at least every norm tolerated by the state, is assimilated to positive law. There is no case which does not fall under *some* rule. But in Russia, where both law-consciousness and positive law remained rudimentary through the centuries, where whole spheres of life were left outside the realm of law, the Marxist vision found an echo in the hearts and minds of the people. The Russian revolutionaries were not primarily interested in creating, ultimately, a new legal order, in the external, positive sense; they were interested rather in creating, ultimately, a new sense of justice, as between man and man. They seized on the Marxist promise that, with the elimination of the bourgeoisie and the abolition of all survivals of capitalism, the community would come to be regulated like a family, like a kinship society, by customary standards, by unofficial law, rather than by positive law. This corresponded to the historic Russian ideal of the regeneration of man and to the Russian conception of a society based on love and on service, a society with a mission. Only now such a society was to spring from the materialist conception of history, from class struggle and the end of class struggle, rather than from Christian faith in the Kingdom of God. Dostoevsky's vision of the transformation of the State into the Church was replaced by Lenin's vision of the transformation of the State into the Party.

In the mid-1930's, the Russian Marxist vision of the "withering away" or "dying out" of (official) law under socialism was transformed from a vivid anticipation of an imminent eschaton into a dream of an indefinite far-off end-time. "Law—like the state—will wither away only in the highest phase of communism, with the annihilation of capitalist encirclement," wrote Vyshinsky in 1938. Only then "will all learn to get along without special rules defining the conduct of people under the threat of punishment and with the aid of constraint." Under Khrushchev, the "withering-away" concept has been given new vitality, and there is talk of the gradual replacement, beginning right away, of the coercive machinery of state organizations by the persuasive, voluntary processes of "social" organizations. Thereby, according to the Communist Party Program of 1961, the first stage of Communism will be achieved within two decades. Nevertheless, "the state will be preserved long after the victory of the first phase of communism," Khrushchev stated at the 22nd Party Congress. "The process of withering away of the state will . . . occupy a whole historical epoch and will be completed only when society has matured sufficiently for self-administration." In the meanwhile, "the Party attaches great importance to the strengthening of legality and the legal order, the protection of the rights of citizens." The Party program itself stated: "To ensure that the state dies out completely, it is necessary to provide both internal conditions—the building of a developed communist society—and external conditions—the victory and consolidation of socialism in the world arena." Thus, even with the achievement of Communism in the Socialist bloc alone, state and law will remain. And in the transition periods of the next decades, state and law will continue to play a crucial role in creating the conditions, and above all the mentality, which are necessary for their gradual abolition.

Whether conceived in terms of an immediate or of an ultimate future, the idea that law will die out under Communism has had important repercussions on the Soviet legal system from its initial stages of development until the present. For connected with this mystical concept is a practical distinction between official law and unofficial law-consciousness, and a practical belief that the main purpose of official law is to shape and develop that unofficial law-consciousness, so that people will actually think and feel what the state, through official law, prescribes. When the state has fully educated all people to internalize the legal system, then that legal system will no longer be needed.

LAW AS A TEACHER AND PARENT

Of course every system of law educates the moral and legal conceptions of those who are subject to it. In the *Digest* of Justinian it is explicitly recognized that the task of law is the moral improvement of the people. Thurman Arnold describes the judicial trial as a "series of object lessons and examples." "It is the way in which society is trained in right ways of thought and action, not by compulsion, but by parables which it interprets and follows voluntarily." [4] Justice Brandeis was a leading exponent of the view that the courts should recognize the importance of their educational function.

Nevertheless, the educational role of law has not been traditionally regarded as central. Law has been conceived primarily as a means of delimiting interests, of preventing interference by one person in the domain of another, of enforcing rights and obligations established by the voluntary acts of the parties insofar as that is compatible with the social welfare. It has been assumed that the persons who are the subjects of law, the litigants or potential litigants, know their own interests and are capable of asserting them, that they are independent adults whose law-consciousness has already been formed. In some cases this goes so far, under our adversary procedure, as to enable the judge to sit back as an umpire while the opposing lawyers do battle with each other. The subject of law in our system, "legal man," has been the rugged individualist, who stands or falls by his own claim or defense and is presumed to have intended the natural and probable consequences of his acts. To educate his legal conceptions is no mean task. It requires a very good judge even to attempt it. At best he will succeed in educating only indirectly, secondarily, by seeing that justice is done.

In the Soviet system, on the contrary, the educational role of law has from the beginning been made central to the concept of justice itself.[5] Law still has the functions of delimiting interests, of preventing interference, of enforcing the will and intent of the parties—but the center of gravity has shifted. The subject of law, legal man, is treated less as an independent possessor of rights and duties, who knows what he wants, than as a dependent member of the collective group, a youth, whom the law must not only protect against the consequences of his own ignorance but must also guide and train and discipline. The law now steps in on a lower level, on what in the past has been a prelegal level. It is concerned with the relationships of the parties apart from the voluntary acts by which their alleged rights and duties were established; it is concerned with the whole situation, and above all, with the thoughts and desires and attitudes of the people involved, their moral and legal conceptions, their law-consciousness. Soviet law thus seeks not simply to delimit and segregate and define, but also to unite and organize and educate. The result is the creation of entirely new legal values within a framework of language and doctrine which otherwise appears conventional and orthodox.

It is apparent that the Soviet emphasis on the educational role of law presupposes a new conception of man. The Soviet citizen is considered to be a member of a growing, unfinished, still immature society, which is moving toward a new and higher phase of development. As a subject of law, or a litigant in court, he is like a child or youth to be trained, guided, disciplined, protected. The judge plays the part of a parent or guardian; indeed, the whole legal system is parental.

It should be understood that the words "parental" and "educational" as used in this context are morally inconclusive. The parent or guardian or teacher may be cruel or benevolent, angry or calm, bad or good. He may dislike the child. But he is responsible for the child's upbringing. To speak of "parental law" is therefore not so much to describe the state which proclaims and applies the law as to describe the assumptions which are made regarding the nature of the citizen and his relationship to the state. To say that under Soviet law the state has extended the range of its interests and its powers is not enough. The state has sought in law a means of training people to fulfill the responsibilities now imposed on them—and it has made this function of law central to the whole legal system.

"Parental law" may be implicit in the actual practice of socialism as such. It surely has deep roots in Russian history. Yet it is essential to isolate the parental features of Soviet law from both its socialist and its Russian background, for parental law is not restricted to socialism or to Russia. According to Karl Llewellyn, "our own law moves steadily in a parental direction." [6]

Chapter Eleven

LAW ENFORCEMENT BY SOCIAL ORGANIZATIONS

Discipline and
  self-
      control
Are the backbone of the worker's patrol!
So that if
    you grab by
        the collar
The hooligan shrinks till he's smaller

> —Vladimir Mayakovsky (quoted in a 1959
> Soviet handbook on People's Patrols)

KHRUSHCHEV stated at the 21st Party Congress in 1959:

Many functions performed by government agencies will gradually pass to social organizations . . . Socialist society forms such voluntary organizations for safeguarding social order as the People's Patrol (*narodnaia druzhina*), Comrades' Courts, and the like. They all employ new methods and find new ways of performing social functions. The voluntary detachments of People's Patrols should undertake to keep social order in their respective communities and to see that the rights and interests of all citizens are respected and protected.

The time has come when more attention should be paid to the Comrades' Courts, which should seek chiefly to prevent a different kind of law violation. They should hear not only cases concerning behavior on the job but also cases of everyday deportment and morality, and cases of improper conduct by members of the group who disregard standards of social behavior.

The institutions which Khrushchev mentioned are not innovations; they have existed in one form or another, off and on, ever since the earliest days of the Soviet regime. However, their fullest development has come only in the last few years, for they suit perfectly the current theory that governmental functions should now be transferred gradually to social organizations. These organizations have a dual parental function: they bring the will of the "collective" to bear on miscreants, and at the same time they educate the participants in what Soviet writers call "popular self-government."

THE PEOPLE'S PATROLS

The People's Patrols are a sort of auxiliary police. The Russian term for them, *druzhiny,* is an old Slavic word referring to the band of comrades (*druzhinniki*) who advised the princes of Kievan Rus and at the same time formed the nucleus of their armies. Various organizations performing auxiliary police functions existed during the 1920's. They were often know as "Commissions of Social Order." By 1930, these were reformed into "Voluntary Societies for Aiding the Police." In January 1930 there were 2500 such societies in the Russian Republic alone. In May 1930, through a charter issued by the Council of People's Commissars, the societies were given a legal basis for the police functions they had been exercising. In the later 1930's, the Voluntary Societies were reorganized into Brigades and placed under strict central control. During World War II, "Groups for the Protection of Social Order" were formed to provide protection against spies, saboteurs, and line-crossers. After the war, the Brigades were re-formed and placed under the direction of local detachments of the police, and they devoted themselves largely to the enforcement of traffic regulations and automobile inspection.[1]

Beginning in 1958, People's Patrols, with some millions of members, were formed throughout the country. The 1960 R.S.F.S.R. Statute on Voluntary People's Patrols grants them broader functions than those exercised by the earlier organizations.[2] The statute lists the following tasks:

1. To maintain public order on streets, in stadiums, parks and other public places, at meetings, demonstrations, sports events, etc.;

2. Together with police, court and Procuracy agencies, to combat petty crime ("hooliganism"), drunkenness, theft, violations of trade regulations, speculation, moonshining, and other offenses;

3. To enforce traffic regulations;

4. To combat neglect of children;

5. To make suggestions to state and social organizations for taking measures of influence against persons who violate public order;

6. To send materials concerning offenders to Comrades' Courts or administrative agencies, to send *druzhinniki* as social prosecutors where necessary, and to report offenses in the press, wall newspapers, posters, window displays and bulletins.

7. To participate in educational work among the population concerning the observance of the rules of socialist community life and the prevention of anti-social offenses.

The *druzhinnik* has the right to demand that a citizen stop violating public order and to demand that he produce identification papers or a driver's license; to take an offender to the headquarters of the Patrol, to the police, or to the local soviet; to obtain transportation for the victim of an accident or a crime; freely to enter clubs, stadiums, cinemas and other public places, in order to maintain order.

The Patrols are not subordinate to any ministry or to any government agency, but are independent local (city or district) units. The 1960 statute expressly places them under the direction of Communist Party agencies.

It is evident that in addition to powers normally exercised by regular police in all countries, the Patrols also have specific educational functions. They are concerned with anti-social activities not amounting to crimes—for example, neglect of children. They sometimes ridicule offenders in the press or on public display boards ("Billboards of Shame"). They speak to general meetings of workers and employees in enterprises and institutions. They roam the city in pairs, taking issue with conduct of which they do not approve, such as boisterous parties, drunkenness, wearing of "Western" clothes, or dancing of "Western" dance steps.

Lacking the training of the regular police, they are apt to be rough and discourteous and to exceed their powers. Some have been indicted for brutal crimes. At the same time, disobeying a lawful order of a *druzhinnik,* insulting him, or resisting him, have been made criminal offenses, and an attempt on his life (if accompanied by circumstances which aggravate the offense) has been made punishable by death.

The aim of the People's Patrols is to establish an educational agency for law-enforcement whose members will be an integral part of the society itself, who will, in the words of the 1960 statute, "be an example in work and in everyday life." The aim is a characteristic one. Whether the Soviets can overcome the difficulties inherent in a reliance on amateurs to perform police functions—remains to be seen.

COMRADES' COURTS

Comrades' Courts were first instituted in 1917, in a decree signed by Trotsky, as a means of strengthening military discipline in the Red Army.[3] In 1919 Lenin signed a decree establishing them in industry as a means of improving labor discipline. These were informal, elected bodies, which had the power to try only minor offenses and impose only a reprimand or other minor penalty. In 1921 the industrial Comrades' Courts were given the power to impose up to six months' deprivation of freedom, but their penal powers were again restricted in the late 1920's. In the early 1930's similar courts were established in rural areas and in urban housing precincts. All the Comrades' Courts in the 1930's were supposed to be under the guidance of the regular People's Courts and of the Ministry of Justice, the Procuracy, and the trade unions. By 1938 there were 45,000 Comrades' Courts in the Russian republic alone. However, by the start of the Second World War they had disappeared almost entirely. The most plausible reason for their demise is that the bulk of their jurisdiction was taken away from them by Stalin's legislation providing severe criminal penalties for infractions of labor discipline and other minor offenses. They were revived to some extent by a 1951 statute, but they have regained their former importance only since the 21st Party Congress in 1959.[4]

The 1961 R.S.F.S.R. Statute on Comrades' Courts[5] provides a guide to their present status; Article 1 emphasizes their parental role:

Comrades' Courts are elected social agencies charged with actively contributing to the education of citizens in the spirit of a communist attitude toward work and toward socialist property, the observance of the rules of socialist community life, the development among Soviet people of a feeling of collectivism and of comradely mutual assistance, and respect for the dignity and honor of citizens. The chief task of the Comrades' Courts is to prevent violations of law and misdemeanors detrimental to society, to educate people by persuasion and social influence, and to create an attitude of intolerance toward any antisocial acts. The Comrades' Courts are invested with the trust of the collective, express its will and are responsible to it.

The "social" nature of the Comrades' Courts is reflected in the limitations upon their power to impose sanctions. They may order the offender to apologize; administer a warning or one of various grades of public censure; impose a fine of up to ten rubles in cases not involving violations of labor discipline; propose that the offender be transferred to a lower-paying job or demoted; propose that he be evicted; or require the defendant to pay damages of up to 50 rubles to the victim of his illegal act. A further limitation of their powers is the fact that the accused may obtain review by a higher body on the law and the facts before any penalty other than censure is enforced.

The types of cases which may be tried by Comrades' Courts are limited to less serious offenses. Serious violations of law are beyond their jurisdiction, and indeed they may only try minor violations of law on the recommendation of law-enforcement or judicial officials. With the consent of all the parties, they may try civil cases involving amounts of up to 50 rubles. Probably the most important categories of cases they try in practice are those involving breaches of labor discipline and standards of behavior in communal apartments.

Particularly disturbing to one raised in the tradition of *nulla poena sine lege* is the catch-all provision of the Statute on Comrades' Courts giving them jurisdiction over "other antisocial acts not involving criminal liability." While minor violations of local ordinances and certain minor noncriminal offenses listed in the criminal code would fall under this category, they would not seem to exhaust it. Indeed, to perform fully its parental function, the court would not be able to limit itself to punishing acts which violate only the letter of the law. However, it should be kept in mind that the maximum penalty in such cases is formal censure and a ten-ruble fine.

The standard manual for Comrades' Courts, printed in 1961 in an edition of 75,000 copies, states that the judges of the Comrades' Courts should have ample evidence of the guilt of the offender before a trial is scheduled, and that if it is at all possible, they should arrange to have the offender confess his misdeeds publicly at the trial and ask forgiveness. The manual emphasizes the need for securing attendance at the trial proceedings of the accused's fellow-workers or neighbors in large numbers and the importance

of audience participation. The goal of reforming the offender is emphasized by the suggestion of the manual that
one of the members of the court be appointed to follow the
offender's later conduct and to warn him if he again
starts to stray.[6] Thus the entire procedure is conceived as
a lesson in communist morality.

THE ANTI-PARASITE LAWS

Social organizations also play a role in the enforcement
of the various republican laws concerning "persons avoiding socially useful work and leading an antisocial parasitic
way of life," which were discussed briefly in Chapter 2.
The R.S.F.S.R. edict, enacted in May 1961,[7] is worth
quoting here in full as an example of Soviet "parental"
legislation:

> Our country, under the leadership of the Com-
> munist Party, has entered the period of expanded
> construction of communism. Soviet people are work-
> ing with enthusiasm at enterprises, construction proj-
> ects, collective and state farms and institutions, per-
> forming socially useful work in the family, observing
> the law and respecting the rules of socialist commu-
> nity life.
> However, in cities and in the countryside there
> are still individuals who are stubbornly opposed to
> honest work. Such people frequently hold jobs for
> appearance's sake while in actual fact living on
> unearned income and enriching themselves at the
> expense of the state and the working people or,
> although able-bodied, hold no job at all but engage
> in forbidden businesses, private enterprise, specula-
> tion and begging, derive unearned income from the
> exploitation of personal automobiles, employ hired
> labor and obtain unearned income from dacha and
> land plots, build houses and dachas with funds ob-
> tained by non-labor means, using for this purpose
> illegally acquired building materials, and commit
> other antisocial acts. On the collective farms such
> persons, enjoying the benefits established for col-

lective farmers, avoid honest work, engage in home brewing, lead a parasitic way of life, undermine labor discipline and thereby harm the artel's economy.

The parasitic existence of these persons is as a rule accompanied by drunkenness, moral degradation and violation of the rules of socialist community life, which have an adverse influence on other unstable members of society.

It is necessary to wage a resolute struggle against antisocial, parasitic elements until this disgraceful phenomenon is completely eradicated from our society, creating around such persons an atmosphere of intolerance and general condemnation.

Taking into account the many expressions of desire on the part of the working people that the struggle against antisocial elements be intensified, the Presidium of the Supreme Soviet of the R.S.F.S.R. decrees:

1. To establish that adult able-bodied citizens who do not wish to perform a major Constitutional duty—to work honestly according to their abilities—and who avoid socially useful work, derive unearned income from the exploitation of land plots, automobiles or housing, or commit other antisocial acts which enable them to lead a parasitic way of life shall be subject, upon the order of a district (or city) people's court, to resettlement in specially designated localities for a period of from two to five years, with confiscation of the property acquired by non-labor means, and to obligatory enlistment in work at the place of resettlement.

The same measures of influence, prescribed either by order of a district (city) people's court or by social sentence handed down by the collectives of working people of enterprises, shops, institutions, organizations, collective farms or collective farm brigades, shall be applied to persons who take jobs at enterprises and in state and social institutions or who are members of collective farms only for the sake of appearances and who, while enjoying the benefits and privileges of workers, collective farmers and employees, are in actual fact undermining the discipline of labor, engaging in private enterprise, living on funds obtained by non-labor means or committing other antisocial acts that enable them to lead a parasitic way of life.

An order of a district (city) people's court or a social sentence calling for resettlement shall be handed down if, despite the warning of a social organization or state agency, the person who is leading a parasitic way of life has not taken the path of an honest life of labor within the period of time established in the warning.

2. The order of a district (city) people's court with respect to a person who is avoiding socially useful work and leading an antisocial, parasitic way of life shall be final and shall not be subject to appeal.

A social sentence calling for resettlement shall be subject to approval by the district (city) Soviet executive committee, whose decision shall be final.

3. The exposure of persons leading an antisocial, parasitic way of life and the verification of all the relevant circumstances shall be carried out by agencies of the police and the procuracy on the basis of materials in their possession, at the initiative of state and social organizations, or on the basis of declarations by citizens. Upon completion of the verification, the material shall be sent with the procurator's sanction to a district (city) people's court or to a working people's collective for consideration.

4. If during the verification and examination of materials concerning a person who is leading a parasitic way of life, signs of a criminal offense are established in his actions, his case shall be sent to agencies of the procuracy.

5. Orders of a district (city) people's court and social sentences calling for resettlement shall be executed by police agencies.

Persons who avoid work in the places of resettlement shall be subject, upon representation of the police agencies to the district (city) people's court, to corrective tasks with retention of 10 per cent of their earnings; in cases of evasion of corrective tasks, the court may substitute deprivation of freedom under the procedure provided in Article 28 of the

Criminal Code of the R.S.F.S.R. The term of corrective tasks or deprivation of freedom shall not be considered a part of the term of resettlement.

Escape from the place of settlement or en route to it shall be punished in accordance with Article 186 of the Criminal Code of the R.S.F.S.R.

6. If a person who has been resettled proves by his exemplary conduct and honest attitude toward work that he has reformed, he may, after expiration of not less than half of the term of resettlement, be released in advance upon the petition of social organizations to the district (city) people's court at the place of settlement, with the consent of the district (city) soviet executive committee at the resettled person's former place of residence.

7. To instruct the Council of Ministers of the R.S.F.S.R. to adopt a decree on carrying out the necessary measures stemming from this Edict.

This statute, with all its defects, is a considerable improvement over the earlier anti-parasite laws enacted by the various smaller republics in the years from 1957 to 1960, which were even more vague in their definitions and which provided for no judicial administration whatever, leaving offenders entirely at the mercy of "the public." Indeed, under the earlier laws it was possible for the police to petition the local soviet executive committee directly to "re-settle" an offender, without recourse even to a collective of workers or collective farmers. Such laws had been subject to heated controversy in the popular press as well as in scholarly journals, and there was much criticism of them in letters-to-the-editor, especially by jurists.[8] A few writers contended that some features of the laws violated the Soviet Constitution. After 1958 it was thought by some that they were superseded by the Fundamental Principles of Criminal Procedure and would be repealed.[9] The enactment of the R.S.F.S.R. statute in 1961 (and the subsequent revision of various republican versions to conform to it) represented a defeat for the "strict legality" school. At the same time, the limitations introduced into the statute reflect a certain compromise with that school, and an effort to reconcile the parental features of the law with the more objective standards which have characterized the reform movement since Stalin's death.

The 1961 statute sets up parallel procedures for enforcement. On the one hand, informal "collectives" of workers or peasants in a factory or collective farm—not to be confused with comrades' courts, which operate under a separate statute—may sentence one of their number who is working "only for the sake of appearances" and who is committing "antisocial acts." On the other hand, the people's courts may take jurisdiction over such persons as well as over others who fall under the statute. At the same time, both state and social organizations may warn such persons to desist from their antisocial activities and, if they refuse, may request the police and the procuracy to investigate. A person tried under the law by a people's court has no right of appeal. Indeed, since the statute is considered to establish only "administrative" measures and not criminal penalties, the violator is not entitled to any of the protections of the law of criminal procedure as such; his right to have defense counsel or to summon witnesses, even his right to appear and defend himself, are subject to the discretion of the courts.

Some of these procedural rights, however, though not the right to counsel, have been affirmed by the Supreme Court of the U.S.S.R., which in a decree of September 12, 1961,[10] criticized lower courts for abuses in the enforcement of the various republican anti-parasite statutes. The Supreme Court decree stated that some persons had been sentenced by people's judges sitting singly (that is, without the two people's assessors) and in closed sessions; that some had been sentenced as parasites when in fact they had committed crimes which should have been prosecuted under the codes of criminal procedure; that some had been sentenced to terms lower than the statutory minimum; that some courts had ordered confiscation of property without stating what property was derived from non-labor income; that some persons had not been given sufficient time after warning to find work; that some had been sentenced after they had found work; that some courts decided anti-parasite cases without calling and examining witnesses and even on occasion without hearing the explanations of the persons charged; and that "social accusers" did not participate in the cases often enough.

At the same time, the Supreme Court issued "directive explanations" for the guidance of courts, designed to eliminate the above-mentioned practices. Trials of persons leading a parasitic way of life, the Court ordered, were to be conducted in open sessions by a people's judge and two people's assessors. Sentence should not be imposed on a person who, "having been warned of the necessity of finding work, has not found a job because of the inadequacy of the time allowed therefor or because of other circumstances for which he is not responsible." However, the summoning and questioning of witnesses was left to the discretion of the courts; and no specific instruction was given with respect to the necessity of the presence of the offender himself—perhaps because that was presupposed in the general injunction that the materials of each case should be examined by the court fully and exhaustively. In an article by a senior consultant of the Supreme Court, which appeared in the same issue of the Bulletin of the Supreme Court as the decree, it was stated that the anti-parasite laws are not applicable to wives who spend their time working at home and rearing children, or to persons who are pensioned for reasons of health or age.

Together with these limitations, the Supreme Court also specifically emphasizes the educational purposes of the anti-parasite laws. "It is necesary for the courts to direct their activity [in trying anti-parasite cases] to the widespread attraction of the public to the consideration of the materials concerning such persons," the decree stated. And further: "For the purpose of strengthening the educational significance of judicial trials of persons who lead a parasitic way of life, courts should more often conduct these trials in enterprises and on collective farms, in city and village clubs, attracting the attention of the public."

Thus in the trial of "parasites," the court itself—though

by tradition and by subordination to the Supreme Court inclined to a certain degree of objectivity—tends to assimilate its procedure to that of the collectives of workers or peasants which have a concurrent jurisdiction.

The anti-parasite laws, like the laws establishing People's Patrols and Comrades' Courts, reflect the Soviet conception that it is a primary function of law to help form the character of the people, including their consciousness of their legal and moral obligations to society. The use of para-legal bodies—"collectives" of workers, peasants and neighbors, as well as volunteer "bands"—is a means of taking some of the burden of this task from the official judicial and police agencies. (It is said by Soviet jurists that the number of court cases diminished by 25 per cent in the first year after the adoption of the R.S.F.S.R. Comrades' Court statutes.) By the same token the resort to "popular" tribunals represents a relaxation of criminal sanctions for petty offenses; when those sanctions were more severe, as in the late 'thirties and 'forties, the Comrades' Courts tended to disappear. But the main point of "popular" law-enforcement is to lessen the distance between official law and unofficial law-consciousness. It is an effort to effectuate an internalization of official values in the minds and hearts of the people, by enlisting their direct intervention in proceedings of a legal nature. The use of procedures derived from official law is thought to be an effective means of reintegrating the offender into the collective; and the use of the collective itself to administer those procedures is thought to have educational value for all who participate.

The emphasis on community action to correct the offender and bring him back into harmony with the group has echoes of the strong Russian cultural tradition of collective responsibility for individual misconduct. It also has an important socialist aspect, for in a society which conceives of itself as moving toward a system of distribution according to need it is necessary to create social pressures to maintain the sense of moral and legal obligation which under more individualistic systems is supported also by strong material incentives.

Yet neither Russian culture nor the socialist system totally explains the phenomena of the People's Patrols, Comrades' Courts, anti-parasite laws, and other examples of an organized effort to use popular institutions to instill a new concept of moral and legal obligation. Prerevolutionary Russia had very little that was comparable, and not every socialist society (however defined) would necessarily adopt similar institutions. There is also involved an idea which is by no means uniquely Soviet: that law should be used to mold character, and, conversely, that character can be molded by law. Social courts, and also the administrative procedure for resettling "anti-social elements," reflect a particular conception of the nature of man and of his relationship to law. Man is conceived to be in need of education, guidance and training to make him better-disciplined, more honest and hard-working, more conscious of his social obligations. Law is conceived as having a special role to play in bringing about this result. Soviet "legal man" is not the independent, self-reliant, "rugged" individual of the past two, and possibly four, centuries of Western legal history. He is the more dependent, more helpless "member of the group" who has become increasingly characteristic of the legal traditions which have been developing in Europe and America as well in the decades since 1914.

Chapter Twelve

THE EDUCATIONAL ROLE OF THE SOVIET COURT

THE SOVIET COURT plays a double role in the education of popular law-consciousness. On the one hand it is an instrument for teaching law to the public generally. On the other hand it is a means of educating the parties who come before it with their grievances.

The educational role of the Soviet court must be seen in the context of the state's general interest in instilling a knowledge of law and a respect for law, if not a fear of law, among its subjects. Special pains are taken in the Soviet Union to make law a part of the general education of the average citizen. Lawyers are required to give lectures on law at meetings of trade unions and other organizations. Law is popularized in pamphlets and tracts written for the general public. The lay assessors who sit with the judges in the three-man People's Courts are given short courses in law prior to their undertaking their duties. The elections of People's Judges which take place throughout the Soviet Union every five years (formerly every three years) are accompanied by a tremendous propaganda campaign in the press, on the radio, and in street speeches and interviews. In these campaigns Soviet law is praised as a synthesis of personal and collective interests, and various aspects of labor law, housing law, family law, criminal law, and other fields immediately concerning the general population are discussed.

During the 1949 campaign, for example, one judge reported on seventy cases he had heard having to do with suits against railroads, in sixty-three of which judgment was for the plaintiff, with total recoveries amounting to 146,000 rubles. He went on to describe railroad inefficiency and to urge the creation of a moral atmosphere which would eradicate negligence and theft. The press not only boasted of the achievements of Soviet justice but also criticized deficiencies in judicial administration. *Pravda* reported on the role of the courts in restoring workers to their jobs if they were wrongfully dismissed, citing a case in which a particular People's Court had reinstated a worker who was fired ostensibly because of a general layoff of personnel whereas it appeared on trial that the real reason for his discharge was a critical remark which he had made at a factory meeting.

It may be doubted how effective Soviet legal propaganda is in making drugstore lawyers out of Ivan and Andrei. Much of law is by nature technical, requiring years of special training to understand. However, popular legal literature in the Soviet Union, which formerly was of a low quality, has improved very much in the years since Stalin's death. In any event, it is significant that these efforts are taken to make law comprehensible to the layman, and that the judges themselves are made vehicles of such education, being required to report back to their electors.

With 300,000 agitators active in the judiciary election campaign of 1949, virtually the entire electorate voted.[1] Of the single slate of candidates, 53 per cent were not members of the Communist Party, and 39.2 per cent were women.[2] Apparently at least 30 per cent, and probably more, had no legal education.[3] It may thus be seen that not only did the elections have a "popular" flavor, but the lower courts themselves were "popular" in composition. A serious defect from the point of view of the quality of judicial administration, the lack of legal education of so many People's Judges, nevertheless served to bring official law and popular law-consciousness closer together. The People's Judges chosen in 1957 were far better qualified professionally and politically. Nearly all had either higher or intermediate legal education and 93.9 per cent were members of the Communist Party.[4]

In the conduct of trials, also, Soviet judges both on the higher and lower levels are supposed to be continually aware of the effect of their decisions upon the attitudes of the public. In an address on "The Educational Significance of the Soviet Court," delivered and printed in 1947, I. T. Goliakov, then Chief Justice of the Supreme Court of the U.S.S.R., stated that "the publicity of our court [procedure] means the attraction of the widest public into the courts."[5] For this purpose, he said, "the court arranges its sessions at such time as is most favorable for the toilers to attend." In addition the court may hold "demonstration trials" of important criminal cases in the enterprises and collective farms where the crimes were committed.

"Trying the case in great detail," Goliakov stated, "strictly observing the law, the court step by step discloses the whole picture of the crime or the civil dispute. It raises the explanations of the parties to a higher level, transforming the whole trial not into a spectacle, as the selfish bourgeois court does, but into a serious instructive school for educating those attending the session to observe and respect law and justice."

In a speech given in 1946 President Kalinin also stressed the role of the judge as a teacher. "As a good artist is able wonderfully to paint a landscape, so a skillful, politically developed judge brings to light during the judicial trial, during a particular, concrete case, all those internal processes that go on in our country." Every decision of the judge must therefore be "as convincing as it is sound," said Kalinin, "so that not only he himself and the people's assessors, but also all the persons attending the session should . . . understand [its] correctness."

From the earliest years of the Revolution, Soviet political

leaders as well as Soviet jurists have stressed the educational role of the Soviet court in statements similar to those quoted above. In the years since Stalin's death the number of books, pamphlets and articles devoted to this theme has, if anything, increased.[6]

A still more important test, however, of the significance of the educational role of the Soviet court is in the actual law of procedure as applied in the trial of cases.[7] Here it is necessary to recognize the points of similarity between Soviet procedure and that of other systems, in order to appreciate the points of difference.

Soviet criminal and civil procedure resembles Western procedure generally in providing for a bilateral hearing, in public, with oral testimony and the right of confrontation of witnesses, and with judgment based on rational as contrasted with purely formal proofs. Appeals may be taken. Parties may be represented by lawyers; in fact Soviet law goes so far as to provide that in criminal cases if the prosecution participates in a case the accused must have a lawyer. If he does not choose one, the court will appoint one.

CRIMINAL PROCEDURE

The most obvious difference between Soviet and Anglo-American criminal procedure lies in the emphasis placed by the Soviets upon pre-trial investigation and upon the active participation of the court in the trial itself. Here Soviet law is in the continental European tradition. A preliminary examination is held, in which an examining magistrate (investigator) interrogates the accused and the witnesses and examines evidence prior to preparing the indictment, a document in which the charges and the evidence against the accused are stated in detail.

The 1961 R.S.F.S.R. Code of Criminal Procedure, like that which it replaced, does not provide any punishment for the accused for failing to co-operate at the pre-trial examination. The investigator may not use violence, threats, or similar methods—without violating the law. He "does not have the right to refuse the request of the suspect, of the accused and his attorney [or of others involved in the case] to interrogate witnesses, or to have an expert examination, or to have investigations made for the collection of evidence if the facts or circumstances sought to be established may have significance for the case." The accused must be informed of his rights, including the right to state his side of the case during the pre-trial investigation and to examine any part of the record, including adverse evidence of which he knows nothing. In the trial proper the prosecutor cannot introduce evidence not previously known to the defendant.

The Soviet system of preliminary investigation has three principal defects in comparison with its Western European counterparts. First, appeals from abuses of pre-trial procedure may be taken only to the Procuracy, not to the courts. Second, except for minors and persons with physical or mental defects, a suspect under investigation has no right to counsel until the investigation is completed and the indictment is presented to a preliminary session of the court for approval. Third, the time of detention for investigation, though normally limited to one month, may be extended by permission of higher authorities of the Procuracy up to nine months.

On the other hand, the Soviet system, like its counterparts in Western Europe, has the advantage that the indictment must disclose to the accused all the evidence to be used against him at the trial.

Mr. Justice Jackson, in describing his experiences at the Nürnberg trial of German war criminals, writes: "It was something of a shock to me to hear the Russian delegation object to our Anglo-American practice as not fair to the defendant. The point of the observation was this: we indict merely by charging the crime in general terms and then we produce the evidence at the trial. Their method requires that the defendant be given, as part of the indictment, all evidence to be used against him—both documents and the statements of witnesses . . . [Our] method, it is said, makes a criminal trial something of a game. This criticism is certainly not irrational." [8]

At the trial, the burden of proof of the facts alleged in the indictment is on the prosecutor. However, the judge plays an active part in interrogating the defendant and the witnesses on both sides, and in calling his own impartial experts when necessary. Admissibility of evidence is left to the discretion of the court, though the verdict is supposed to be based on relevant evidence only.

As outlined in the code, Soviet criminal procedure has much in common with general European practice, which places more stress on "inquisitional" features and less on "accusatory" than does Anglo-American law. In a broader perspective, however, both Soviet and American criminal law are a mixture of the so-called inquisitional and accusatory systems. Our judges may and sometimes do interrogate witnesses; they may and sometimes do summon their own impartial experts to testify; they in fact "rule the court" by their decisions about the admission and exclusion of evidence. On the Soviet side, on the other hand, the adversary features of the trial have been increasingly stressed. Both the prosecutor and the defense counsel question the witnesses and argue their respective cases, and the defendant also may put questions personally, at any time during the trial. [9]

What is most significant about Soviet criminal procedure, however, is not its division into pre-trial and trial stages and its emphasis on the leading role of the judge, but rather its educational or parental character, both in its adversary and in its inquisitional aspects. The mere fact that the prosecution and the defense are on an equal basis, each presenting its own side of the case, does not in itself deprive the trial of its educational or parental role. On the contrary, the fact that the parties defend their own rights may itself be a means of teaching them to assume and learn responsibility. On the other hand, the mere fact that the procedure is "inquisitional," with the judge determining the order of witnesses and himself interrogating them, does not in itself guarantee its educational or parental character. The judge may maintain complete formality, and may treat the parties in every way as independent adults.

The clue to the nature of both Soviet criminal and civil procedure lies in Article 3, paragraph 1, of the 1958 Fundamental Principles of Legislation on the Judicial Structure of the U.S.S.R., the Union and Autonomous Republics:

> By all its activities the court shall educate the citizens of the U.S.S.R. in the spirit of devotion to the Motherland and the cause of communism in the spirit of strict and undeviating observance of Soviet laws, of care for socialist property, of labor discipline, of honesty toward public and social duty, of respect for the rights, honor and dignity of citizens, for the rules of socialist common-life.

(A corresponding provision of the 1938 Judiciary Act omitted reference to "respect for the rights, honor and dignity of citizens," and spoke of the "cause of socialism" instead of the "cause of communism," but was otherwise identical.)

In criminal procedure, both the pre-trial investigation and the trial proper, and, in the trial, both the adversary and the inquisitional aspects, are designed to fulfill this educational purpose.

From the educational-parental standpoint, the following features of Soviet criminal procedure, though not necessarily uniquely Soviet, are noteworthy illustrations of a shift of emphasis which Soviet law as a whole has carried further than other modern systems.

1. The preliminary investigation is directed toward clarifying the entire situation in the mind of the accused as well as in the records of the investigator.

2. The "entire situation" sought to be clarified includes not merely the circumstances of the case, in the usual sense of that phrase, but also the whole "case history" of the accused, including any past misconduct, his attitude to-

ward the Revolution, his entire motivation and orientation. In addition, the examiner is required to seek the answer to such questions as: Did the commission of the crime take place under coercion, threat, or by reason of economic strain? Was the alleged offender at that moment in a state of hunger or destitution? Was he influenced by extreme personal or family conditions? Was he in a state of strong excitement?

3. Upon indictment, the trial commences with the court's interrogation of the accused directed, again, to his entire biography. Whether or not he is a Party member, whether or not he has been in trouble before, whether or not he has earned rewards for outstanding achievement of any kind, whether or not he took an honorable part in the Great Fatherland War—these and similar questions make it clear that it is not simply the offensive act that is to be punished or exonerated, but the man himself.

4. It is the duty of the court to protect the accused against the consequences of his ignorance, to clarify to him his rights, to call expert witnesses in his behalf when needed whether or not he so requests.

5. On appeal the higher court not only reviews the entire case, both on the law and on the facts, but may also receive evidence not offered in the original trial.

6. The death of a convicted person does not prevent an appeal or a reopening of the case if newly discovered circumstances may lead to the rehabilitation of his reputation.

7. In imposing a sentence, the court has a large range of penalties from which to choose, including public censure, confiscation of all or part of the criminal's property, a money fine in the form of the monthly deduction of a certain percentage of the criminal's pay (so-called "corrective" labor tasks), prohibition to carry on a particular trade or profession, exile from the city, banishment to remote areas, as well as deprivation of liberty in corrective labor colonies and imprisonment. The punishments prescribed in the Criminal Code often leave to the court a very large leeway between the minimum and maximum. Also worth

mentioning in this connection is the provision that punishment may be omitted altogether if the accused is not socially dangerous at the time of the trial. Before December 1958 the discretionary power of the court was also enhanced by the doctrine of analogy, despite the limitations imposed on that doctrine since the mid-1930's.

Behind these characteristic features of Soviet criminal procedure lies a new conception of the role of law. In the words of former Chief Justice Goliakov, "The most important function of the Socialist state is the fundamental remaking of the conscience of the people." [10] The chief task of Soviet law, according to another prominent writer, is to educate the people to Communist social-consciousness, "ingrafting upon them high, noble feelings." [11]

In 1947 a Soviet writer criticized the one-judge session established in 1940 for cases of absenteeism on the ground that it lacks "the strictness, officiality, and solemnity" of the regular three-judge court, and that "consequently the educational and deterrent significance of these judicial procedures is undoubtedly diminished."

Soviet criminal procedure deals with the "whole man," but it deals with him in a particular way, as a teacher or parent deals with a child. The court is interested in all aspects of his development, and especially in his mental and psychological orientation, because it is its task to try to "remake" him, or at least to make him behave. The Soviet judge may upbraid or counsel the accused, explaining to him what is right and what is wrong in a socialist society. Even if he is acquitted, the court may deliver an official "admonition," that is, a warning of the dangers involved in conduct which is in itself not criminal but which may lead to criminal activity. If he is convicted, the court imposes punishment as a sign of the state's disapproval or condemnation of both him and his criminal act. Punishment is intended, according to Soviet legal theory, to cause the criminal "a definite suffering." [12] Thereby, it is implied, he will be at least purged and perhaps reformed.

It is not our intention to portray the Soviet criminal court as poles apart from the American criminal court.

They have much in common. The difference is a subtle one. The Soviet criminal trial has the atmosphere not so much of our regular criminal courts as of our juvenile courts.

CIVIL PROCEDURE

There is a tendency on the part of Western writers on the Soviet Union to think of the Soviet legal system solely in terms of criminal law. Although criminal law does play a central role in the Soviet system, the importance of claims by one citizen against another (or against a state enterprise) should not be overlooked. Indeed, Soviet legal officials state that 85 per cent of the cases in the courts are civil cases. Most of these concern housing law, labor law and family law, but many also concern personal injuries, personal property, inheritance, copyright, and other matters of civil law.

The implications of the concept of law as parent and teacher run throughout Soviet civil procedure as well. There is, for example, widespread opportunity for use by public agencies of what in American law is called interpleader—an action by a third party to have the conflicting rights of two other parties adjudicated. Thus a Soviet trade union may institute a suit in the name of a member against an employer, without the member's authorization. A local soviet may bring an action on an invalid contract in the name of one of the parties, in order to have determined its (the local soviet's) rights to any unjust enrichment. As we have already seen, the Procuracy may institute a civil suit between two parties if it considers that the "interests of the state or of the toilers" so require, and it may intervene in any case on behalf of either party, and may "protest" any decision to a higher court.

Moreover, once the case is before the court, not merely the issues litigated but any issue arising from the situation may be adjudicated. Also the court is required to certify to the Procuracy evidence of criminal activity revealed in a civil suit. As stated in a Soviet textbook: "In deciding the concrete property disputes of the parties, the court is obliged at the same time to clarify those economic and organizational inadequacies which create the situation out of which disputes arise. On the ground of the defects and inadequacies, established by the court, in the work of state, co-operative, and social organizations, special orders should be handed down (interlocutory orders) and directed to the corresponding organs." [13]

The will of the parties as to the disposition of the case is not decisive, once the court has jurisdiction. Even if they choose to compromise, or if the plaintiff wishes to drop the action, the court may proceed to judgment. It may grant the defendant an unsought remedy against the plaintiff. It may give a remedy beyond the scope of the prayer for relief.

As in criminal procedure, the court in civil cases is concerned not merely with deciding the facts and issues before it, but also in clarifying them to the parties. This is expressed clearly in Article 16 of the Fundamentals of Civil Procedure of the U.S.S.R. and the Union Republics:

> It is the duty of the court, without limiting itself to materials and pleadings submitted, to take all measures provided by law for the detailed, full and objective elucidation of the real circumstances of the case, of the rights and duties of the parties.
>
> The court must explain to the persons taking part in the case their rights and duties, must warn of the consequences of committing or not committing procedural actions, and must render assistance to the persons taking part in the case in realizing their rights.

One is struck by the general informality of the Soviet civil trial. Behind this informality lies the educational and parental role of the court. As the atmosphere of the Soviet criminal trial approximates that of our juvenile courts, so the atmosphere of a Soviet civil suit may perhaps bear an analogy to that of our domestic relations courts.

PROCEDURE IN ARBITRAZH

Although there is no pre-trial investigation in civil suits generally, the procedure of Arbitrazh in intercorporate litigation is marked by a preliminary preparation of the case by the judge-arbiter. He studies in advance the materials and documents presented by the parties as well as supplementary materials received from them at his own request. He may summon officials of the disputing enterprises for preliminary explanation of any circumstances. He may join other parties as participants in the case on his own motion. He may investigate questions not raised by the complaint and answer, if such questions appear to him to be relevant.

Though now considered to be bound by the Code of Civil Procedure, Arbitrazh nevertheless proceeds even more informally and "parentally" than the regular courts. The hearings generally take place with only six participants—the judge-arbiter and his legal counsel, and a representative of each of the litigating enterprises together with the lawyers for each enterprise.

"The active creative role of the arbiter in the Arbitrazh procedure," according to one writer, "does not overshadow, however, the role of the disputing parties, does not diminish their activity in the defense of their interests. On the contrary, the rules of consideration of disputes by Arbitrazh give the parties a broad initiative and independence, require from the parties an active defense of their economic interests, in the struggle for the fulfillment of plan." [14]

Here, too, however, as in criminal and civil procedure generally, the judicial contest is waged against the background of a more intimate relationship among the participants, a relationship more akin to that of a family than to that of an impersonal "civil" society.

If we look for an analogy in American law which will throw light on Arbitrazh procedure, we may find it in our proceedings in bankruptcy and corporate reorganization, where the judge-referee often makes his own "preliminary investigation" of the case, consulting personally in advance with the various parties involved, though the bankruptcy hearing itself is governed by the regular rules of evidence and procedure. Happily, the analogy bears out our thesis: the Soviet litigant is treated not as an independent and self-sufficient "individual" but rather as someone more helpless, more dependent, more to be protected, guided, and if necessary "reorganized."

Chapter Thirteen

LAW AND PSYCHIATRY

SOVIET CRIMINAL PROCEDURE, like that of other countries, provides for a hearing of both prosecution and defense, directed toward ascertaining the facts of the case and the applicable law. Did the accused commit the act with which he is charged? Is the act prohibited by law? Did he commit it intentionally? If not, was he negligent—that is, ought he to have foreseen the consequences of his conduct? These and similar questions are standard and required, both there and here.

We have seen, however, in treating the Russian component of Soviet law, that in cases of criminal negligence the Soviet court applies a subjective standard of foreseeability; its chief inquiry is not what an objective, average, "reasonable" man would have foreseen, but what this particular accused should have foreseen, in the light of his own background and capacities. We have seen a source of this subjectivism in traditional Russian concepts of crime and the criminal, in which attention is centered not on "this act" but on the "whole man," in the context of the "whole community."

To this we may now add that Soviet criminal procedure is peculiarly adapted to an investigation of the state of mind of the accused, by virtue of both the pre-trial investigation and the leading role of the judge, as well as by its general informality and its atmosphere of intimacy.

It would be a mistake, however, to see in Soviet criminal procedure merely a means of bringing to light all aspects of the crime, the criminal, and the situation. To present a romantic picture of Soviet law would be to falsify it completely. The purpose of the Soviet judicial system is not to "do justice" in some abstract sense. The purpose is educational—again, without any romantic connotation, not educational for the sake of being educational, but rather for the purpose of inculcating, in Lenin's phrase, "discipline and self-discipline" in the Soviet people, so that the system may work.

The Soviet criminal court is interested in the state of mind of the accused, his mentality, in order to help shape and influence his thinking, his attitudes, whether by public censure or by severer penalties, and in order to help to develop in the public mind standards of legal responsibility. The court is a conscious instrument for forming the character both of the parties before it and of members of society generally. Its chief function is to inculcate the feeling of legality and of respect for law as such, the love of country and of family, respect for property, a conscientious attitude toward work, fear of punishment, desire for reward and advancement. Because this is not simply an incidental aspect of its activities, but its principal aim and objective, new legal procedures and norms have been developed to meet it, and, indeed, a whole new type of law.

It is to be noted that the psychological premise underlying the educational role of law is that the conscious attitudes of people may be influenced by conscious decisions and actions of legislators, administrators, and judges. Soviet psychology is anti-Freudian in that it plays down the role of the unconscious and exalts the social over the sexual. At the same time, as we have seen in an earlier chapter, the Leninist conception of consciousness as an intellectual process has been transformed by the Stalinist emphasis on its emotional content. It is the impelling factors, rather than the cognitive, that are now stressed. It is conscious loyalty, conscious fears and desires, conscious sense of responsibility, that Soviet law now attempts to instill.

A crucial question for Soviet law, therefore, is how to deal with the offender for whom it is claimed that by reason of mental illness he is incapable of maintaining legal standards of responsibility. On what basis should this claim be accepted or rejected? If it is accepted, what should the court do?

Here the Soviets have taken a long step toward the solution of an age-old conflict between the standards of medical science and the requirements of an effective legal order. The ancient Greeks had differentiated between paranoias, amentias, hypochondrias, and other mental diseases; but the Greeks never succeeded in incarnating their philosophical ideas in a stable legal system as such. The Romans, on the other hand, with their impatience with Greek subtleties and their genius for legal classification, lumped the various mental illnesses together under the legal term *insaniens*. The psychiatrist Jelliffe, in calling attention to this development, adds scornfully: "Hence arose on a complex generality the word insanity. Its stupidities will cling to it and chiefly in that muddy stream of thinking used by lawyers to the present day."

To the psychiatrist who is called on to testify regarding the mental condition of an alleged criminal, the traditional tests of insanity devised by the lawyers seem to have little or no relevance to the medical tests of mental illness. The law has developed criteria based on the intellectual capacity to know the nature of one's acts (and within that, to "know right from wrong") and on the volitional capacity to control one's impulses. For the sake of the legal order, the assumption is made that normal man is a free moral agent. Psychiatry, on the other hand, treats the offender as a patient, and seeks to classify the illness of which he is a victim, without reference to social or moral standards. The psychiatrists are unwilling to sacrifice their patients to the demands of "Roman" legalism, just as the lawyers are unwilling to sacrifice the legal order to the vagaries of "Greek" science.

The Soviets started out in the "Greek" tradition. At first they went so far as to take the question of insanity out of the hands of the courts altogether. Article 14 of the "Leading Principles of Criminal Law" of 1919 stated: "A person shall not be subject to trial and to punishment for a deed which was committed in a condition of mental illness. . . . To such persons shall be applied only medical measures and measures of precaution." The language of this provision was so broad as to have the effect of placing all persons who pleaded mental illness immediately under the jurisdiction of the medical administration.

It should be recalled that at the time it was the official position of Soviet jurisprudence that crime altogether is essentially not a legal but a medical problem and that as such it would ultimately be solved only by rooting out the social-economic evils of capitalism which give rise to it. Combining Marxian sociology with Lombrosian criminology, the Soviet psychiatrists studied the types of crime committed by various types of deviant personalities, attempting to explain the deviant personality, in turn, in terms of social conditions. Free will was denied. In a resolution "On Legislation and the Criminal Question" adopted by the First All-Union Conference on Psychiatry and Neurology in 1925, it was stated: "The idea of imputability [that is, mental capacity to incur criminal responsibility, sanity], as constructed in the studies on free will, must be eliminated from Soviet legislation and replaced with the idea of social dangerousness and socially dangerous conditions, which are stipulated by the neuropsychiatric deviations of the criminal."

The criminal codes of 1923 and 1926 reintroduced "Roman" conceptions of legal insanity. Article 10 of the 1926 Criminal Code provided that punishment (called in the language of the time "measures of social defense of a judicial-correctional character") may be applied to persons who have committed "socially dangerous acts" only in cases in which the persons (1) acted intentionally, that is, foresaw the socially dangerous nature of their acts; or (2) acted negligently, that is, should have foreseen the socially dangerous consequences of their acts. Article 11 then goes on to say that "measures of social defense of a judicial-correctional character may not be applied to persons who have committed a crime while in a condition of chronic mental illness, or of temporary derangement of mental activity, or in other diseased condition, if these persons could not realize the nature of their acts [literally: account to themselves in their acts] or control them, and also to those persons who, although they acted in a condition of mental balance, had become mentally ill at the time of the execution of the sentence. To such persons may be applied only measures of social defense of a medical character." A note to this article states that it "does not apply to persons who have committed a crime in a state of intoxication." These provisions are retained substantially unchanged in Articles 8 and 9 (intentional and negligent commission of crime) and 11 (non-imputability) of the 1961 R.S.F.S.R. Criminal Code.

By these provisions, the traditional tests of intellectual and volitional capacity are restated and jurisdiction is apparently restored to the courts. In fact, however, their effect has been quite different in the two principal phases of Soviet legal development. Until the mid-1930's, the question of criminal insanity was actually decided by the psychiatric expert, who, according to provisions of the Code of Criminal Procedure, is summoned whenever the mental health of the accused is in doubt, whether at the pre-trial examination or at the trial itself. If the psychiatric expert decided that the accused was mentally ill, he was almost invariably committed or released; and if the case proceeded to trial, the court rarely rejected the psychiatrist's conclusions. Thus, although the Criminal Code provided for legal tests of insanity in terms of will and intellect the tests actually applied were the medical-psychiatric tests of mental illness.

Soviet psychiatrists concerned with the examination of

persons suspected or accused of having committed "socially dangerous acts" rejected, in this period, the "juridical scholasticism" of an analysis in terms of will and intellect. The nature of their examination was governed at first by an official circular of the People's Commissariat of Justice, which prescribed that they ask certain questions directed to the discovery of the case history of the alleged offender, but said nothing as to the determination of his intellectual or volitional capacities, in the legal sense. In fact, in those days the psychiatric definition of mental illness amounting to nonresponsibility extended to minor mental disorders which were subsumed under the so-called reactive conditions. In the early years, drug addicts were considered *ipso facto* nonresponsible, and even cases of simple intoxication and strong emotional excitement were similarly classified. Although there was some tightening up in the mid-1920's, a leading jurist wrote in 1929 that excitement produced by a heavy insult might serve as a basis for a finding of nonresponsibility on the ground of "pathological affect." In the early thirties the scorn for legalism reached a new height, and the importance of the medical-psychiatric test seems to have increased still further. At the same time, the question of legal insanity was now decided by the psychiatrists largely in terms of "expediency"—that is, what seemed best for the particular offender and for society in each case.

In 1935 and subsequently, Soviet psychiatrists were under fire for having succumbed to "the influence of Western European science," particularly that of the Lombrosian school of criminology which sees the criminal as a biological type and "explains social forms of behavior by constitutional peculiarities of the personality." In 1936 certain large psychiatric institutions were reprimanded for the "theoretical mistakenness and practical perniciousness of extending the interpretation of schizophrenia." In 1938 the Director of the Serbskii Institute of Forensic Psychiatry, which is the leading agency concerned with the problem of psychiatric examination of persons accused of crime, was attacked for "failing to draw any conclusions for himself from the break in the legal front of wrecking." "The treatment of the problems of imputability and non-imputability by the Institute of Forensic Psychiatry coincided in fact with the wrecking tendencies of Krylenko," it was stated.

The upheaval of the mid-1930's in forensic (court) psychiatry is closely related to the upheaval in law, on the one hand, and the upheaval in psychology on the other. In all three fields there was a new emphasis on moral responsibility and freedom of will. The official textbook on criminal law both in its 1943 and its 1948 editions was distinguished for its sharp rejection of the psychological premises of the earlier criminology. After quoting a long definition of freedom of will by Engels—closing with the sentence: "Freedom of the will is nothing else but the capacity to reach decisions with a knowledge of the facts" —the 1948 textbook added: "This concept of the freedom of the human will, which is fundamentally different from all bourgeois philosophy, Marxism puts at the basis of criminal responsibility."

This was closely related, of course, to the new drive for "stability of laws," which, on the practical side, was directed against the widespread prevalence of recidivism. Too many persons absolved from punishment on the grounds of nonimputability were back in the courts again on fresh charges.

The psychiatrists had run away with the field. Now it was insisted that they, as forensic psychiatrists, concern themselves not solely with the criminal as a personality but also with the requirements of the legal order. Indeed, the discipline of forensic psychiatry was now for the first time clearly identified as involving not merely a doctor-patient relationship but a much more complex relationship in which the psychiatrist and the court share in the application to the accused of both medical and legal norms. Specifically, it was now demanded of the court psychiatrists that they discontinue stating their conclusions, as one criticism put it, "in language incomprehensible to the court and to the organs of investigation," and, affirmatively, that they formulate their opinion as to imputability on the basis not only of medical but also of legal criteria. At the same time, the final decision as to imputability was now placed in the hands of the court.

This certainly does not mean that psychiatry has been thrown overboard, or even that its importance has diminished. It means rather that the psychiatrists have been asked to become more judicious. Whereas in 1922, 46.5 per cent of all psychopaths examined by the Serbskii Institute were declared nonimputable, and 29.3 per cent "partly imputable," the percentage in 1945 was 12 per cent nonimputable, and the category "partly imputable" had long since been abolished altogether. Doctrines of reactive conditions were modified to allow more room for imputability. The label schizophrenia was broken down into more precise differentiations for the same reason.

PRESENT SOVIET TESTS OF RESPONSIBILITY

Under the Soviet law as it has developed since the mid-1930's, whenever any doubt arises as to the mental health of a person accused of crime, the court is obliged to decide the question of his imputability on the basis of both the medical-psychiatric and the juridical criteria. In making its decision, the court relies in part on the conclusions of psychiatric experts, which likewise must be based on both the medical-psychiatric and the juridical criteria. The 1961 R.S.F.S.R. Criminal Code defines nonimputability as the inability of a person "to realize the nature of his acts or to control them as a consequence of chronic mental illness, temporary derangement of mental activity, feeblemindedness or other diseased condition." Prerevolutionary Russian criminal law had virtually the same provision.[2]

This is no solution in itself of the substantive problem of what constitutes legal responsibility, nor is it a reconciliation of the "Greek" and "Roman" *theories*. It is, however, a reconciliation of "Greek" and "Roman" *practice*, in that the decision is made only after carefully weighing both sets of criteria in the balance. The juridical criteria are decisive; the mentally ill offender is exempt from punishment only if he lacks either the capacity to know the nature of his acts or the capacity to control them. On the other hand, the medical-psychiatric criteria, though not decisive, are nevertheless relevant and the court must pass on them. Punishment is not applicable to crimes committed by reason of mental illness—provided that the mental illness results in a sufficient impairment of intellectual or volitional capacity.

Although it has been emphasized since the mid-1930's that in no case is the mere fact of a particular mental illness conclusive, nevertheless Soviet psychiatric and legal literature has tended to associate certain types of medical-psychiatric conditions with nonimputability. This is inevitable, because both the psychiatric and the judicial diagnosis are in those terms. Thus prolonged deprivation of narcotics, malaria in its secondary stages, mental derangements associated with epidemic encephalitis, and other similar specified conditions, are listed as "temporary derangement of mental activity" which *may* give rise to nonimputability. Similarly, "other diseased condition" includes various psychopathies, neuroses, psychogenic reactions.

The result of the conscious juxtaposition of medical-psychiatric and legal criteria is to compel the court to consider in detail the physical, neurological, and psychiatric condition of the accused in determining the question of his nonimputability. If the court fails to relate its conclusion as to imputability specifically to the medical-psychiatric diagnosis, its decision may be reversed on appeal. For example, in 1939 the Railway Division of the Supreme Court of the U.S.S.R. reversed a conviction, on the ground that according to the record of the case the accused committed the crime while in a state of unconsciousness due to intoxication, and that hence he was nonimputable. This decision was in turn reversed by the Plenum of the Supreme Court, on the ground that the assertion of the Railway Collegium that the accused was nonimputable was not based on expert psychiatric testimony. In another, later case one Potapov, charged with anti-Soviet agitation, was subjected to expert psychiatric examination and found imputable. His conviction was nevertheless reversed by the Supreme Court, and the case remanded for retrial, on the ground that the experts did not give a detailed description of the physical, neurological, and psychiatric condition of the examinee, and did not state explicitly whether or not he suffered from any disease. In a 1961 case in which psychiatric experts had found the accused to be imputable although a schizophrene, the U.S.S.R. Supreme Court reversed the conviction and remanded the case for new examination. These cases indicate that the substantive test of criminal insanity includes more than the finding that the accused lacked the capacity to "account to himself in his acts" or to control them; it also includes the finding that he suffered from a certain kind of mental disorder; and the two findings are interdependent.

As a consequence Soviet courts find themselves in the position of having to reach explicit conclusions of a medical-psychiatric character. Thus in a postwar case in the Supreme Court of the U.S.S.R., the accused, charged with embezzlement, offered in defense a report certifying that he suffered from an "amoral syndrome." The Supreme Court asked the Serbskii Institute of Forensic Psychiatry the following question: "Is the assertion correct that the indicated 'amoral syndrome' is 'organically preordained' in the psychopath and leads with fatal inevitability to the commission of this or that crime?" The Serbskii Institute answered: "The formation of the psychopathic personality is to a great extent determined by external influences, by social factors. In particular this concerns complex psychic formulations such as concepts of morality, ethics, social duty, and so forth. Given identical psychopathic attributes, a different social make-up and differing conduct among various psychopaths is possible. The assertion . . . must be considered incorrect from the point of view of Soviet forensic psychiatry . . . as exactly related to Lombrosian and neo-Lombrosian tendencies in forensic psychiatry and the criminal law." We must presume (since we do not have the official report of the case) that the court adopted as a rule of Soviet law the psychiatric principle stated by the Serbskii Institute.[1]

FORENSIC PSYCHIATRIC PROCEDURE

It has long been recognized that the crucial problem in forensic psychiatry is procedural rather than substantive —that is, that the legal tests of insanity, particularly in countries which provide for jury trial, is less important than the methods adopted for ascertaining whether the tests are met. This is inherent in the problem of reconciling in practice two standards of responsibility that are irreconcilable in theory.

The procedural problem arises first in the sorting out of mentally disordered offenders before trial, second in the methods of proof during trial, and third in the disposition of the offender upon conviction or acquittal. In all three aspects, Soviet criminal procedure offers interesting and challenging solutions to the difficulties inherent in the conflict between a legal and a psychiatric approach to criminology.

1. During the pre-trial investigation, if any doubt arises about the psychiatric condition of the accused, or of any witness, it is obligatory for the examining magistrate to call in a qualified psychiatric expert. In addition, the accused (or the witness) may call a psychiatric expert of his own choosing. The experts may examine all the materials in the case, and may request additional materials. In case there are two or more experts, they may consult with each other. If they are unanimous, they submit a joint report, but if there is disagreement they present separate reports.

If the examining magistrate considers the testimony of the psychiatric experts to be insufficiently clear or complete, he may order a new examination by other experts. The accused, who has the right to see the experts' conclusions, may also obtain a new examination if he is dissatisfied. In difficult cases, the examinee may be sent to a psychiatric hospital for prolonged observation before trial.

The report of the expert is embodied in an official report, which is presented to the court, on indictment, as part of the records of the preliminary examination. The form of the report is prescribed by official instructions. It is supposed to be couched in language understandable to the court personnel, and to avoid evaluative terms such as "autistic," "negativistic," "ambivalent," as well as descriptive passages discussing in technical terms the psychopathological peculiarities of the particular examinee. It must contain not only a medical case-history of the examinee and a full description of his physical, neurological and psychological condition during examination, but also an evaluation of his mental condition (both at the time the crime was committed and at the time of examination) in terms of imputability as defined in the criminal code, together with recommendations as to medical measures to be adopted.

2. At trial, the sanity (imputability) of the accused is not presumed but must be proved by the prosecution. The experts who examined the accused in the preliminary examination may be called to testify orally. The accused may again call new experts of his own. If the forensic psychiatric testimony is unclear, or if there is a disagreement among the experts, the court may on its own initiative, or at the request of the accused or the prosecution, order a new examination by new experts, whose procedure is governed by the same rules as those relating to pre-trial expert examination.

The conclusions of the experts are not binding on the courts. However, in case the court disagrees with their conclusions, it must state in detail the reasons for its disagreement.

Like other experts and witnesses generally, forensic psychiatric experts are reimbursed for their expenses, including those resulting from absence from their usual occupation. In addition the psychiatric experts are paid for their services in examining and testifying at both the pre-trial investigation and the trial. The amount of their fees is determined according to a schedule issued by the Ministry of Justice. Such expenses and fees may be assessed to the accused if he is guilty, provided he is not indigent; if he is not guilty, they are assessed to the state treasury. The psychiatrist called in as an expert either by the investigator or by the court or by the accused may not without sufficient reason refuse to appear and to give his conclusions. In addition, heavy penalties may be imposed on experts for giving false testimony.

Only medical doctors who have had psychiatric training may qualify as forensic psychiatric experts.

3. After trial, if the offender is found nonimputable, the court may apply either of two "compulsory measures of a medical character." These are commitment to a regular psychiatric hospital or commitment to a special psychiatric hospital for persons particularly dangerous to society. In either case release is only by court order, following recommendation of the hospital administration.

Prior to 1935 the regulations governing post-trial procedure were obscure. As interpreted, offenders could be committed to psychiatric hospitals at any stage of the criminal proceedings upon recommendation of the forensic psychiatrist. Discharge was entirely in the hands of the hospital administration. A 1935 Instruction of the People's Commissariats of Justice and Health provided that where a criminal act was charged, only a court might commit, and that in serious cases subsequent discharge required a court order; in less serious cases, discharge remained at the discretion of the hospital administration. The present law goes still further than that of 1935 since it requires judicial approval of discharge in all cases of commitment by court order.

If, however, no criminal act is charged against a person, he has no recourse to the courts in combatting commitment to a hospital on grounds of mental illness. According to the Family Code, commitment is imposed on recommendation of a medical commission, which may be appealed only to the local soviet executive committee. A patient who claims he has recovered has only a right to a hearing before a medical commission on the question of his release. (In the United States commitment is by court order and the lawfulness of the detention may be tested in court by the writ of habeas corpus.)

Very few states of the United States have nearly as extensive provisions for expert forensic testimony as is found in Soviet law. The requirement that a qualified psychiatric expert be summoned to testify in any case in which a question arises as to the mental capacity of a person charged with crime; the provision for a joint examination by opposing psychiatrists and, in proper cases, a joint report; the exclusion of testimony concerning the mental state of the accused on the part of persons who are not qualified psychiatrists; the assessment of psychiatrists' expenses and fees to the state treasury if the accused is non-imputable (or if he is indigent); the provision that a psychiatrist, whether called by the investigator, by the court, or by the accused, may not without sufficient reason refuse to appear and give his conclusions—these are features of Soviet law which are either entirely absent in American law or else present in only a small minority of states.

The existence of the Serbskii Institute of Forensic Psychiatry, which is under the Ministry of Health of the U.S.S.R., is an additional factor which greatly strengthens the work of psychiatrists in criminal cases. The nearest approach to such an institute in the United States is the Law-Medicine Research Institute established at Boston University in 1958.

Yet the Soviets have not gone as far as one American jurisdiction, the District of Columbia, which in 1954, in the case of Durham *v.* United States, adopted a rule (theretofore in force only in New Hampshire) that a person is not criminally responsible for an unlawful act which was the product of mental illness or mental defect, without reference to whether he knew the nature of his acts or had the capacity to control his conduct. The so-called Durham rule in effect leaves it to the psychiatrist to say whether the accused should be criminally punished or committed to a mental institution. This is reminiscent of the Soviet law of 1919 and of Soviet practice until 1935.

LESSONS OF THE SOVIET EXPERIENCE

The plea of nonresponsibility ("not guilty by reason of insanity") is troublesome by its very nature. The court is asked to decide whether or not the defendant falls into a category of persons who are, so to speak, outside the law. In making that decision, it must apply criteria appropriate to legal science; if it accepts without question the criteria of medical-psychiatric science, some of the most basic assumptions underlying the whole legal system are threatened. This is particularly true if the psychiatrists deny the validity of such categories as freedom of will and moral responsibility altogether. On the other hand, by entertaining tests of intellectual and volitional capacity the courts necessarily involve themselves in a consideration of the processes of the human psyche. If they base their conclusions on premises which are medically and psychiatrically unsound, the legal order itself must in the long run suffer.

In this country we have done very little, in actual legal practice, to modify traditional modes of resolving the dilemma. The law remains, with some important exceptions, what it was a century ago. The psychiatrists, again with some important exceptions, continue to press their demands on the basis that, ultimately, the criminal responsibility of the mentally ill should be left to them.

Soviet law requires both the psychiatrists and the courts to compromise—the psychiatrists to state the legal implications of their medical-psychiatric conclusions, the courts to state the medical-psychiatric diagnosis upon which their legal conclusions depend. This solution will not satisfy the purists in either camp. On the one hand, it compels the psychiatrist to go beyond his traditional competence and at the same time leaves the final say in the hands of persons without psychiatric training. On the other hand, it compels the court to go beyond its traditional competence as well, and at the same time places heavy reliance on the medical-psychiatric expert. The two tests, psychiatric and legal, remain logically as irreconcilable as ever; both are used, and the court must simply decide whether the mental disorder was of such a character, according to the medical-psychiatric testimony, as to make it desirable to apply more leniently or more strictly the legal test of intellectual and volitional capacity. "Desirable according to what standards?" remains a critical question.

In determining the answer to that question it is necessary to evaluate the role of expert testimony in Soviet pre-trial and trial procedure. The Soviet court expert is not a witness, in the strict sense. In this respect Soviet law follows continental European practice in general. However, the Soviet system does not go so far in eliminating the adversary features of expert testimony as, for example, the Italian system, in which the defense is not allowed to question the court experts. It differs, on the other hand, from certain other continental systems in which the contentious element is retained, in that the Soviet procedure authorizes the court to summon new experts to testify whenever the disagreement of opposing experts leaves the question in doubt.

The Soviet court expert is considered to be independent both of the parties and of the court (or the pre-trial investigator). He is spoken of as a "consultant" of the court. It is noteworthy, however, that the basis for impeaching the court expert is the same as that for impeaching the judges. In the case of experts called by the accused, partiality is minimized by the possibility of joint consultation with court and prosecution experts, as well as by the general informality of Soviet trial procedure.

Both in pre-trial and in trial procedure, the Soviet psychiatric expert is given broad powers. Most of the proposals for broadening the scope of psychiatric examination and testimony which have been made by American criminologists find expression in Soviet law. However, this is not only rendered easier by the fact that Soviet doctors generally are in the employ of state institutions, but also the leeway of the psychiatric expert is thereby limited. The state may more easily subordinate his science to its needs. The Ministries of Justice and Health may direct him to narrow his definition of nonimputability. In the case of political dissidents tried for counterrevolutionary activity in the administrative procedure of the Ministry of Internal Affairs, the forensic psychiatrist may have found his role as an impartial expert reduced to a minimum. Also, the offender committed to a psychiatric hospital, or his relatives, may not apply to the courts for discharge through a writ of habeas corpus, but may only appeal within the administrative order. Again the question arises of the ultimate standard by which the choice is made as to the disposition of the mentally ill offender.

Here some light is shed by the phrase "measures of social defense of a medical character." The Soviet court's focus is not so much on insanity as a defense to the charge of a criminal act, as on how to deal with the social danger of mental illness. To this end the medical profession is introduced to legal tests of social danger and legal procedures of meeting it, and the legal profession is taught something of the psychiatric tests of mental illness. Indeed, the chief lesson of Soviet law in this field perhaps lies in the widespread effort, through courses in both law schools and medical schools, to educate the lawyers and the doctors in their joint responsibilities toward the ill offender. From 1933 to 1945, 6,304 law students and 4,807 medical students took courses in forensic psychiatry, and 2,998 court investigators and 1,289 psychiatrists received some training in this field. The 1961 textbook on forensic psychiatry for law students was published in an edition of 25,000 copies.

Again, to romanticize the picture would be to falsify it. The role of punishment has been enhanced, that of "treatment" reduced. The whole tendency has been away from individualization of disposition on a medical-psychiatric basis and toward an increasing extension of the category of "responsibles." The reason for this is the clue to the Soviet solution of both the substantive and the procedural problems raised by criminal nonresponsibility. Underlying the Soviet definitions and methods is the desire to maintain the mentally ill in the effective performance of their social roles—and to keep them going, if possible, as normal persons. The purpose is not to promote the welfare of the individual, for his own sake, but to maintain his social productivity, in this sense to educate him, for society's sake. It is the task of the courts to make a deliberate choice of the means by which this may be achieved, within the legal standards established for the proper functioning of society as a whole.

In stressing some of the differences between Soviet and American law relating to insanity, we have not intended to suggest that the Soviet law is unique. On the contrary, as already indicated, it is derived in large part from its prerevolutionary Russian antecedents and is by that very token closely related to Western European practice. Yet here, as in other branches of law, doctrines and procedures which are not unfamiliar appear in a new ensemble and are informed by a distinctive purpose. The ensemble and purpose have a socialist dimension—though state ownership of the means of production and national economic planning do not seem to be a decisive factor in shaping this particular branch of the law, nor does Marxist theory have much to contribute to it. It is the emphasis on conditioning, in the Pavlovian sense, which is striking here—coupled with the emphasis on law as a means of such conditioning.

Chapter Fourteen

LAW AND THE FAMILY

"THE FAMILY is ceasing to be a necessity both for its members and for the state," wrote Alexandra Kollontai, *enfant terrible* of the Russian Revolution, in 1919. The chapter headings of her pamphlet on "Communism and the Family" well express the mood of the first years of the Soviet regime: "Workers Learn to Exist without Family Life," "Individual Housekeeping Doomed," "The Dawn of Collective Housekeeping," "The Child [brought up by] the Communist State." Here was ready-made copy for a righteous foreign press.

The more responsible Party leaders fought the tendency toward social and moral anarchy that accompanied the early phase of the Revolution. Lenin, in a famous quotation, attacked the "theory that in a communist society to fulfill sexual desires and love drives is as simple and meaningless as to drink down a glass of water." "From this 'glass of water' theory," he wrote, "our youth has gone mad, gone completely mad. It has become the evil fate of many young men and girls. Its devotees assert that this is Marxist theory. Thank you for such Marxism!"

Nevertheless the belief that the institutions of marriage and the family would eventually disappear under communism was more than an excrescence of war and revolution. It was part of a deeply rooted philosophy, and its exponents found passages in Marx and Engels to justify it. The theory of the "withering away of the family" was in fact officially maintained until the mid-1930's. It must be understood, however, that the attack of the responsible leaders was directed not against the family as such, but against the family as an economic and legal unit. It was not marriage itself that would disappear but the formal institution of marriage; family life would continue, but it would entail no economic or legal responsibilities; the family would be transformed into a free association, bound only by the free will of its members.

This was good classical Marxism. In *The Origin of the Family, Private Property and the State,* Engels had argued that monogamy emerged with private property and the need of the father to pass his estate on to his own children, that it was a means of subjection of one sex by the other, and that it appeared, significantly, at the same time as the first class oppression, that of slaves by their masters. Through the successive stages of civilization, Engels wrote, the institution of the family has served to protect the ruling class in its control of property. In the classless society of the future, the economic basis of monogamous marriage would disappear, and with it the supremacy of men, infidelity, prostitution, the degradation of divorce law. Bound only by love and affection, the family would at last be free to flourish; "monogamy, instead of declining, will finally become a reality—for the men as well."

Classical Marxism thus extended the contractual, or consensual, conception of the family which had already come to play an important role in Western family law in the eighteenth and nineteenth centuries. In Russia, however, up until the Revolution, the family was considered in law to be founded essentially on a religious, or sacramental, conception. A religious marriage ceremony was required. Marriage between members of the Eastern Orthodox or Roman Catholic Church and non-Christians was prohibited entirely, as was marriage between Protestants and pagans.

Persons over eighty were forbidden to wed, on the theory (as stated at a synod of 1744) that "marriage is established by God for the increase of the human race, which is completely hopeless to expect from anyone eighty years old." Grounds for divorce varied according to religious faith, and suits for divorce were heard only in the ecclesiastical courts of the various confessions. The Russian Roman Catholic was bound by Catholic family law, the Russian Protestant by the canon law of his denomination, the Russian Mohammedan by his own religious customs.

The brunt of the Bolshevik attack on family law was therefore directed toward its secularization, toward the liberalization of divorce, and toward the emancipation of women and children, as first steps in the "withering away" process.

In the mid-1930's, the theory that the family would disappear as a legal and economic entity was violently assailed as a "left deviation." The new ideological campaign went hand in hand with legislation imposing liability on parents for the torts and crimes of their children, restricting abortions to cases of medical necessity, introducing bonuses for mothers of large families, charging fees for successive registration of divorces, and finally, in 1944, establishing for the first time a judicial process of divorce. By 1938 it could be said by a prominent Soviet writer on the family that "the people of the U.S.S.R. are convinced that not only in a socialist, but even in a perfect communist society, nobody will be able to replace the parents—the loving father and mother." The family is now considered to be a prime necessity both for its members and for the state, and, more than that, the state attempts through law to form the moral and legal consciousness of the family members in such a way as to promote family stability.

This is not to say that many of the socialist elements of the earlier family law do not remain. At the same time, the sacramental conception of prerevolutionary Russian family life has an echo in the Soviet idea, developed since the mid-1930's, of the sacredness of the "socialist" family. "Soviet marriage reveals the spiritual side of marriage, its moral beauty, inaccessible to capitalist society," *Pravda* declared in 1936, during the debates on the law restricting abortions. In welcoming the 1944 reform of family law, *Pravda* again emphasized the "spiritual side" of marriage and parenthood and the contribution of family life to the development of the "full-valued" personality. "A woman who has not yet known the joy of motherhood," it was stated, "has not yet realized all the greatness of her calling."

The ideals of family life are now linked with the new religion of Soviet socialism, which draws in part on Marxist theory and in part on the Russian heritage. Perhaps more significant than this symbiosis, however, is the attempt—new both to Marxism and to Russia—to use family law as an instrument for maintaining the inner unity of the family, for educating the family members as to their legal responsibilities toward each other, and for inculcating in them an attitude of respect for, and observance of, those legal responsibilities. A new social conception of family law has thus been added to the sacramental and consensual conceptions.[1]

This may be illustrated by developments in the law relating to (1) parents and children, (2) husband and wife, and (3) marriage and divorce.

PARENTS AND CHILDREN

Parents have a moral responsibility to bring up their children to be honest and law-abiding. Is that a legal responsibility as well? It was officially made such in the Soviet Union by the law of May 31, 1935, which authorized the police to fine parents up to 200 rubles for "indecent conduct and street hooliganism" of their children and by the law of July 29, 1935, which imposed civil liability on parents for torts committed by their children.

The relation of parent and child within the family is somewhat altered by these statutes. What had been a purely moral aspect of their relationship now became legal. That this may be an actual and effective psychological change is illustrated by the success reported by two towns in Oregon which adopted similar measures, one in 1947, the other in 1949. By passing an ordinance providing up to $200 fine and 10 days in jail for parents whose children commit misdemeanors, the town of Baker, after all other measures had failed, was able to break up a juvenile gang and to reduce delinquency by an estimated 90 per cent.[2]

The manner in which Soviet law reaches into areas of the parent-child relationship hitherto left to informal social sanctions finds striking illustration in a 1941 case in which bad treatment of a youth by his step-mother, the father acquiescing, led the boy to despondency and finally to suicide. The father, a neuropathologist, and the step-mother, a school teacher, were indicted for the crime of bringing a minor to suicide. The step-mother was sentenced to five years' deprivation of liberty and forbidden to teach for five years thereafter; the father was sentenced to two years' deprivation of liberty.

Another example of the role of the Soviet court in attempting to cultivate a sense of legal responsibility between parents and children is found in a judicial decision exacting support for needy parents from a daughter who did not have an independent wage but was dependent on her husband, by levying on the daughter's share of the community property of her and her husband.

The parental-educational role of the court is emphasized in suits for custody of children. Here, too, the stress since the mid-1930's has been on the predominant right of the parent, and particularly the mother. In the case of Khazhaliia *versus* Shvangiradze, decided in the Supreme Court of the U.S.S.R. in 1944, the plaintiff sued his former wife for the custody of their two-year-old son. The case is reported in the official digest of the U.S.S.R. Supreme Court as follows:

> The People's Court of the Second Precinct of the City of Kutaisi, by its decision of 5 May 1943, ordered the son taken away from the mother and placed in the custody of the father on the grounds

that the father was an Assistant Professor who worked as Deputy Director of the Kutaisi Pedagogical Institute and could provide the child with a responsible communist upbringing. The mother, who was a student of the Institute, was found not to have the means to take care of the child, and did not have enough time to pay attention to the child's upbringing.

The Court College for Civil Cases of the Supreme Court of the Georgian S.S.R. affirmed the decision in its opinion of 31 May 1943.

On the basis of the protest of the President of the Supreme Court of the U.S.S.R., the Court College held that the decision of the People's Court and the opinion of the Supreme Court of Georgia should be set aside for the following reasons:

The conclusions of the Court on the basis of which it found it possible to take the child from its mother, Shvangiradze, and give it to the father for its upbringing cannot be recognized as correct. In deciding the question of taking a child away from its parent in accordance with the requirements of Art. 51 of the Code of Laws for Marriage, the Family and Guardianship of the Georgian SSR, the court must consider solely the interests of the child. In doing so the court must bear in mind that the interests of the child are not secured solely by the material conditions necessary for its upbringing. Better material conditions of a father are not reason for taking a two-and-a-half-year-old child away from its mother. Since the father of the child had better material conditions, he was not deprived of the right to provide the child with supplementary material aid by means of alimony payments. To take a child of such an age away from its mother and give it to its father can be accomplished only under conditions in which the mother deprives the child of necessary material care and does not give it a normal upbringing. No facts of this nature appeared in the case. As was evident from the testimony of the witnesses Machavariani, Gabidzashvili and Lordkipanidze, the child was being reared and was developing under normal conditions. The mother, grandmother and grandfather were taking care of the child. The occupation of the mother at work, studies and elsewhere could not be the basis for taking her child away from her.

On rehearing of the case the court must request the participation of representatives of the agencies of guardianship and trusteeship and conduct an investigation of the living conditions of the parties through these agencies.

On the basis of what has been set forth the Court College for Civil Cases of the Supreme Court of the U.S.S.R. at its sitting of 29 April 1944 declared:

The decision of the People's Court of the Second Precinct of the City of Kutaisi of 5 May 1943 and the opinion of the Supreme Court of the Georgian S.S.R. of 31 May 1943 is set aside and the case remanded for retrial in the same court with a different bench of judges and with the participation of the Procurator and representatives of the agencies of guardianship and trusteeship.

This is a far cry from the attitude expressed in 1920 by Goikhbarg, principal author of the 1918 Family Code, in explaining the abolition of adoption (soon thereafter to be restored): "Our [state institutions of] guardianship . . . must show parents that the social care of children gives far better results than the private, individual, inexpert and irrational care of individual parents who are 'loving' but, in the matter of bringing up children, ignorant."

HUSBANDS AND WIVES

Soviet official law has also sought to foster in the people new moral and legal attitudes toward the rights and duties of women. Here there have been two main emphases. The first, which was part of the original Bolshevik program, is on the deliverance of women from their traditional legal disabilities and their emancipation from all subservience to their husbands. The second, which has accompanied the drive toward stabilization of social relations since the mid-

1930's, is the encouragement of strong bonds of marriage and of motherhood.

The Bolsheviks sought from the beginning to introduce women into all phases of social, economic, and political life. Women went into industry, the learned professions, politics, and even the army, in large numbers and often in positions of leadership. There are about 500,000 women engineers and technicians in the Soviet Union. More than 300,000 women are doctors, comprising over two-thirds the total number of doctors. Over thirty per cent of the judges of People's Courts are women. The proportion of women lawyers is also high—probably about thirty per cent. During World War II some 120,000 Soviet women were awarded combat decorations, and sixty-two received the title of Heroine of the Soviet Union.

Under the Soviet Constitution, women have the right to an equal wage for equal work. Attempts to obstruct the emancipation of women are punished under the criminal codes of the various republics. Parents, relatives, or guardians who prevent a woman from entering into a marriage, or who persecute her after she has married against their will, have been held punishable under the criminal law. Anyone who uses the pressure of a superior position or an economic obligation to induce another to enter into sexual relations is punishable for rape. The wife may recover civil damages from her husband for personal injury or breach of contract. She is free to keep her own name, to choose her occupation or profession, to have an equal share in the conduct of a common household, or to live apart if she prefers. She owns the property which she brought with her into the marriage and has common ownership with her husband of all the property acquired during the marriage.

With the shift of emphasis from woman as wage earner to woman as wife and mother, the principle of her equality with her husband has not been abandoned. In 1939, in her property relations with her husband, the wife was declared to have joint control of property acquired during marriage to the extent that the husband cannot alienate it without her consent. Moreover, the economic position of the mother has been reinforced by the payment of money allowances on the birth of the third and each subsequent child, with the provision that these grants are the personal property of the mother and not part of the community property of the spouses. In addition, maternity leaves for women factory workers and office employees were increased from sixty-three to seventy-seven calendar days in 1944, and again to 112 days in 1956, and annual vacations must be timed to precede or follow maternity leave; women are not to be given overtime work after four months of pregnancy, and women with infants are to be exempted from night work throughout the period of nursing. The network of crèches and nurseries, which in 1940 cared for two million children under school age, in 1961 cared for five million.

As a symbol of the value which the state places upon the bearing of children, the Motherhood Medal, second and first class, the Order of the Glory of Motherhood, third, second, and first class, and the honorary title of Mother Heroine are now conferred (with corresponding money allotments) on mothers of five, six, seven, eight, nine, and ten or more children.

MARRIAGE AND DIVORCE

Early Soviet law reflected a conception of the family as based primarily on descent rather than on marriage. An attempt was made to separate the question of marriage from the question of the family. This found expression in the doctrine of full equality of all children whether born in or out of wedlock. The unmarried mother could demand support during and immediately after pregnancy from the putative father of the child; the father had, moreover, the full paternal obligation of maintenance, support, and supervision of his natural child, who in turn had full rights of inheritance from his father.

The technical problems involved in this solution were

very great. The Procuracy was troubled with the problem of tracking down missing fathers. The courts were troubled with the problem of finding methods of establishing paternity. Even after the establishment of paternity, enforcing payments for support proved difficult. Moreover, it came increasingly to be felt that the marriage of the parents was essential to the welfare of the children.

The law of 1944 eliminated the paternity suit from Soviet jurisprudence. In so doing it emphasized again the importance of the marriage relationship to family life. At the same time, the unmarried mother was given the right to receive from the state an allowance for the support of her child until it reaches the age of twelve, and if she has three or more children she is entitled to the regular allowances for mothers of large families in addition to her special allowance as an unmarried mother. She may, however, put her child in a state institution if she so desires. Thus the child born out of wedlock was no longer to be treated as his father's child; instead the state stepped in to assume a large part of the paternal obligation. In the discussions which have taken place in recent years on the drafting of new legislation in the field of family law, there has been much criticism of the absence of legal responsibility of the natural father for a child born out of wedlock.[3]

Originally Soviet law had treated marriage as a *de facto* relationship arising from mutual consent and cohabitation. Civil registration of marriage, which had been introduced in 1917 as a weapon against the influence of the clergy, was declared optional in the 1926 Code; registration was simply evidence of, and did not itself constitute, marriage. To register a bigamous marriage was a punishable offense, but the second marriage was not necessarily void. As late as 1938 a textbook on family law stated that if a man registered a marriage in Moscow with X, and then moved to another place and entered into a factual marriage with Y, "it is clear that according to the whole spirit of Soviet law all juridical consequences of marriage arise not with X but with Y." This view was based on a circular of the

People's Commissariat of Justice of 1934 stating that "in the decision of the question of the existence of a marriage according to Soviet legislation, it is necessary to proceed from the position that factual marriage is the decisive fact." Indeed, bigamy itself was a sociological rather than a legal concept, punishable only in those areas such as the Central Asiatic republics where it was considered to be a socially dangerous "relic of tribal society, based on the exploitation of woman's toil."

With the reaffirmation of the importance of the family in 1935 and 1936, the courts and law-writers became more emphatic in their disapproval of bigamy. It was stated in 1938 that "there can be only one marriage at a time" and that when disputes arise over inheritance and two people claim to be wives "the court must decide which is the actual marriage"—a sharp contrast to the earlier rule that the property could be divided between the two. Also it was held in a 1938 case that a marriage registered illegally, with a prior registered marriage undissolved, does not create any juridical consequences for the parties, since "the registration of the second marriage was illegal and subject to annulment." Meanwhile the courts became stricter in their requirements for proof of *de facto* marriages. This development culminated in the 1944 legislative provision that "only a registered marriage shall create the rights and duties of spouses prescribed in the present Code."

The new requirement of registration was more than an administrative matter. To emphasize its constitutive nature it was provided that there shall be a "solemn procedure" with "suitable premises properly furnished," and the issuance of "certificates duly drawn up." [4] Recently "marriage palaces" have been opened where marriages may be registered in luxurious and dignified surroundings.

It is in the new divorce procedure, however, that the parental-educational nature of the new Soviet family law is most clearly revealed. A petition for the dissolution of a marriage, including a statement of the reasons therefor, is submitted to the People's Court, and a fee of 10 new rubles is paid. The court summons both parties to ascertain the motives for the divorce, as well as to establish what witnesses are to be summoned. Announcement of the filing of a petition for divorce must be published in the local newspaper at the petitioner's expense. The People's Court is obliged to take steps to reconcile the parties. If no reconciliation is effected, the petitioner has the right to file a petition for divorce with the next higher court. Only in that court may the divorce be granted, in which case the court also determines the custody and support of the children, establishes a procedure for the division of property, restores to the parties their original surnames if they so desire, and fixes the sum to be paid by one or both spouses on issuance of the certificate of divorce. On the basis of the court's decision, the Bureau of Vital Statistics draws up the certificate of divorce, makes a corresponding entry in the internal passports of the parties, and collects from one or both a sum ranging from 50 to 200 new rubles as directed by the court.

In discussing the measures which the People's Court should take to reconcile the parties, Soviet commentators have stated:

> It is impossible to expect any ready-made recipes. Here experience, tact, and the authority of the court are necessary. Far from always do the spouses come into court with a firm decision to separate. Often the suit is the result of a recent quarrel, the product of impetuousness and not a thought-out decision. Some the court may reconcile by means of a quiet explanation of the incorrectness of their behavior; it may convince others of the necessity of explaining to each other in court and forgiving each other; and to others it may give time for reconsideration.

Thus Soviet husbands and wives, in seeking divorces, become, in effect, wards of the court. Soviet divorce law is designed in the first instance to unite the family, to heal its wounds. The emphasis is transposed to the realm of unofficial law.[5]

Soviet legislation has so far refrained from stating on what grounds the higher court should grant the divorce, upon failure of reconciliation. It may be assumed that one reason for this omission is the fact that the lawmakers had no past experience upon which to draw and preferred to leave room for experimentation. After the 1944 law was enacted instructions were sent to the judges by the then People's Commissariat of Justice, however, stating typical conditions under which divorces should be granted, such as adultery, desertion, cruelty, and the like. From the reports appearing in Soviet law journals and other legal literature it is possible to detect the emergence of a judge-made tradition of divorce law, similar to the growth of certain phases of English common law. A general principle is laid down that "divorce should be granted only in those cases where it is actually impossible to reestablish the broken family, where the breach between the spouses is so deep that it is impossible . . . to prolong their married life." By application to various types of cases, this principle is developing into particular rules and doctrines. Mere incompatibility may not serve as a ground for divorce, it is said, when the parties have been married for eight years and have three children, though in the case of a more recent marriage where there are no children a different result might be reached.[6]

In the case of two grandparents, sixty-five and sixty-one years old respectively, who after forty years of married life quarreled over how to bring up their grandchildren, a decision granting the divorce was reversed by the Supreme Court of the RSFSR. One may visualize the reconciliation procedure in the People's Court in such a case, with the judge, perhaps a youngster in comparison, giving fatherly counsel to the old couple on the rights and obligations of marriage in the new socialist society.

Concepts of civil obligation of contract and tort play a very minor role, if any, in Soviet divorce law. Anglo-American doctrines preventing the granting of divorce in cases where the petitioner has "connived" with or "condoned" the misconduct of the respondent, or where there has been "collusion" or "recrimination," would be entirely incomprehensible to the Soviet jurist, while the common American practice of granting uncontested divorces automatically is (since 1944) equally alien.

Divorce is expensive in the Soviet Union and often difficult but by no means impossible to obtain.[7] This in itself manifests a parental conception of the state, which insists on maintaining the legal structure of the family. Still more significant, however, is the procedure established for divorce and the standards evolved for its adjudication. The law enters into family relationships at what has hitherto been a pre-legal level, playing the role of parent and educator, giving guidance to Soviet citizens in the moral and legal responsibilities of marriage, seeking to define those responsibilities in terms of the past and future of the family, its capacity for fruitful growth.

The Soviet rulers have had to recognize certain limitations in such use of the law. The rise in dangerous illegal abortions led to a return to legalized abortions in 1955. In the discussions of recent years on the drafting of new "Fundamental Principles of Legislation Concerning Marriage and the Family," there has been sharp criticism of the present laws relating to illegitimate children. Also some participants in the discussions have suggested that the time-consuming compulsory reconciliation hearings be abolished in those cases where there is obviously no real chance for reconciliation, although it is not proposed that there be a return to the "post-card divorce" of the earlier years.

Here, too, it must not be supposed that the underlying policy is a sentimental or romantic regard for the family for its own sake. The new developments came initially as responses to pressing problems—the alarming spread of juvenile delinquency in the early thirties, the tremendous numbers of abortions (over 12,000 a month in Moscow, according to one report), the rising divorce rate (38.3 divorces per 100 marriages in Moscow in the first half of 1935). The state's interest in an increase of population has been another important factor. In this connection the phrase "parental law" takes on an almost literal connotation. At the same time, the implementation of population policy by an all-out drive to strengthen the inner unity and stability of the family is characteristic.

Not the least of the many considerations which have led to the change in the Soviet approach to the family, however, was the emergence of a new conception of law itself—law not simply as a means of social control but in addition as a means of direct influence upon the moral character, the beliefs and the personalities of the people who are governed by it.

Chapter Fifteen

LAW AND LABOR

THERE IS an inevitable conflict between the specific economic functions of management and of labor, which no amount of socialism can overcome. It is a function of management *as management* to seek efficiency in the form of greater productivity and lower operating costs. It is a function of labor *as labor* to seek adequate compensation, conditions of health and safety, and workers' welfare in general.

Economically, this conflict of functions is governed under pure capitalism by the forces of the market (especially the labor market), under pure socialism by the plan. We know, however, that the market under twentieth-century capitalism is not free from the plans of large corporations, national labor unions, and government, while Soviet planning, on the other hand, is (as we have seen) strongly conditioned by the relation of supply to demand, by the needs of a money economy, by the necessity of stimulating industriousness and initiative through personal incentives, by the requirements of "economic accountability." In both systems, law is a necessity if a balance is to be struck between total centralization and total decentralization.

The conflict between the functions of management and of labor is regulated in the Soviet system directly by the state. This is implicit in socialism, if by socialism is understood the planning and operating of the economy by the state. But the common subordination of management and labor to the state tells us nothing of their interrelationship with each other. *How* does the state regulate their conflict of functions? The answer to this question cannot be deduced from the mere fact of socialism; it may vary considerably from one socialist state to another.

Presumably every socialist state, in the sense in which we have defined socialism, will seek to identify itself with the interests both of management and of labor, and thereby to minimize their mutual conflict. In the Soviet system the managers are state officials; the labor unions are state organs. The director of a state economic enterprise belongs to the union local. Both the director and the union chairman are almost invariably members of the Communist Party. In addition, both management and labor receive government assignments and orders concerning rates of wages, standards of output, funds for social insurance, and hours and conditions of work in general. By such means the Soviet state seeks to merge the conflicting interests, and even the conflicting functions, of management and labor into a larger harmony. In the interests of society, the Party, and the state it is explicitly required that the labor union devote itself to the increase of efficiency and productivity and that management keep in mind the needs and desires of the workers.

Nevertheless beneath this surface harmony they retain their separate and conflicting functions. Management is given most of the power to administer matters concerning production, while labor unions have almost complete control over workers' welfare. Despite strict supervision from the top, considerable leeway is left for local implementation of centrally determined policies. This gives opportunity for clash between the efficiency-oriented functions of the director and the welfare-oriented functions of the union. It is here that labor law comes in.

FUNCTIONS OF UNION AND MANAGEMENT

The factory committee within a Soviet plant is divided, typically, into at least six subcommissions. (1) The Wage Commission represents the union in matters of wage rates and classifications; (2) the Commission on Productive Mass Labor organizes socialist competitions and other group efforts to raise output; (3) the Commission on Workers' Inventions and Rationalizations stimulates suggestions for improvement of efficiency, sees to it that they are utilized, and that the workers are properly remunerated for them; (4) the Commission on Protection of Labor is concerned with matters of hours, working conditions, health and safety; (5) the Commission on Social Insurance administers workmen's compensation, health insurance, old-age pensions, vacation pay, maternity leave and the like; (6) the Housing and Living-Conditions Commission is concerned, as its name implies, with housing priorities of workers and with conditions in housing provided for them.

The Soviets have rejected the concept of workers' control of the factory, which was practiced in the first years after the Revolution. They have also rejected the "triangle" system of joint management by the director, the Party secretary of the factory, and the head of the trade union agency, which prevailed prior to the mid-1930's. In 1958, however, permanent production conferences were established in industrial enterprises which were authorized to "take part in" the discussion of drafts of production plans and of suggestions for improvement of intra-plant planning and to "consider" questions of production, labor, wages, etc. Also higher authorities responsible for planning and organizing production were required to consult with trade union officials. In addition, under a law of 1961 the distribution of bonuses from the Enterprise Fund (before 1955 called Director's Fund) is required to be made by the director "jointly with the factory or plant committee of the trade union" (see Chapter 3).

Despite these examples of increased union control over

production, the organization of labor, wages (bonuses) and other similar matters, there is no sign of a serious breach in the principle of one-man control (*edinonachalie*) of these traditionally managerial functions. The requirement of union consultation and participation still leaves the initiative and ultimate responsibility with the director, who also retains disciplinary power over managerial personnel, the power to hire and (within limits to be discussed below) to fire, the power to promote and demote, control over working capital, control over procurement and deliveries, and, in general, control over all aspects of production and finance.

Union and management within an individual plant exercise their respective functions under the control of superior bodies. We have already seen that management is part of an industrial as well as a territorial hierarchy, being subordinate on the one hand to its regional economic council or ministry and, on the other hand, to the local, district, republican, and federal executive organs. The factory committee of the union is likewise part of a dual hierarchy: it sends delegates to the district council of the particular industry to which it belongs, which in turn is represented on the regional council, from which delegates are sent to the All-Union Central Council of Trade Unions; at the same time, these councils are organized on a territorial basis by district, regional, and republican committees, the republican committee also sending delegates to the All-Union Central Council of Trade Unions. In addition a compromise has been made with the principle of craft unionism, in that trade union sections have been established for certain crafts such as toolmakers, fitters, engineers-technicians, and others.

As management operates under plans enunciated at the top and articulated by the regional economic council or ministry, so the factory committee works on the basis of regulations which descend from the All-Union Central Council of Trade Unions down through the regional and district councils.

THE ROLE OF LAW IN LABOR RELATIONS

If all went smoothly and efficiently in the Soviet industrial system, we could content ourselves with an analysis of the distribution of functions between labor and management, within the over-all administrative framework of the planned economy. It would not be necessary to speak either of rights or of law.

Foreign observers, both friendly and hostile, often assume that such is indeed the case. Sympathizers with Soviet socialism, believing that the Soviet state identifies itself with the proletariat, assume that the administrative machinery works effectively and without serious hitches to protect the worker. Antagonists of Soviet socialism, believing that the Soviet state identifies itself with the managerial function of organizing production, assume that the administrative machinery works equally well to oppress the worker. A benevolent socialist state, says the sympathizer, has no need of labor law as such, since there is no fundamental conflict of interests between labor and management, but only a separation of functions. A despotic socialist state, says the antagonist, has no use for labor law as such, since it recognizes no rights either of labor or of management, but only imposes functions on both, which it enforces not legally but administratively.

We have seen in the first part of our study that such reasoning is based on an outmoded conception of Soviet socialism. In respect to the organization of industry and to the distributive system, it has been found necessary to restore law. Planning is not enough; there must also be contracts, and contractual responsibility. Administration is not enough; there must also be rights of possession, use, and disposition. Fiat and decree are not enough; there must also be adjudication on the basis of established norms. Socialism itself, as a social-economic order based on integral state planning, has required the restoration of orthodox legal principles.

In confronting the problem of Soviet labor relations, it is possible to offer a similar analysis. As "economic accountability" is essential if the enterprise is to play a responsible role in the fulfillment of its planned tasks, so a certain degree of union autonomy is necessary if the workers are to accept their responsibilities. As profits are both an incentive for and a test of sound commerical methods, so piece-rates and bonuses, with the consequent inequalities of remuneration, are an incentive for and a test of effective work methods.

However, Soviet labor law is far less susceptible than property and contract law of an adequate explanation on this basis. Property and contract as legal institutions have been influenced to a very considerable degree by capitalist economic development over the centuries. Socialism started out by rejecting them. The Soviet system now struggles to restore them as institutions of a planned economy. But labor law in the modern sense, as comprising the system of legal relations between union and management, is largely a twentieth-century product. It is not so much a manifestation of capitalism as a compromise forced on capitalism by a society which has grown too complex to permit the unrestricted play of market forces. Moreover, workers' control within each factory, which is perhaps the original definition of "socialist" labor law, is alien to the Soviet system. Therefore it adds little to our understanding of Soviet labor law to interpret it, like Soviet property and contract law, as a mixture of socialist and capitalist ingredients.

In some ways Soviet labor law is as much Russian as it is socialist. Direct employment of industrial workers by the state goes back to Peter the Great and to the use of state serfs in industrial establishments. Serfdom also left its traces in the Soviet attempts to tie the worker to his job through the requirement of managerial permission to quit and through criminal penalties for absenteeism; these criminal-law restrictions on labor mobility were abolished in 1956, although economic pressures remain, including reduced social security benefits for those who have worked in a particular plant for less than a certain amount of time. Other forms of Soviet labor relations correspond to still older Russian traditions. All Soviet citizens are subject to call for work of a temporary nature in connection with floods or fires or other disasters, or with road construction if a labor shortage exists in a particular area. This is strongly reminiscent of Mongol law, with its principle of universal compulsory service. The equal subservience of both management and labor recalls the principle established by the Muscovite tsars that all classes owe official duty to the state. In certain features of the internal life of the Soviet factory, particularly as represented in the institution of the Comrades' Courts, there are survivals of the sense of group identity which stems from the Russian Orthodox religious tradition of Kievan Rus.

Yet Soviet labor law is best explained not only as Socialist Law and as Russian Law, but also and perhaps primarily as Parental Law. By its purpose and its nature it protects, guides, and trains both management and labor, educating them in discipline and self-discipline, inculcating in them a sense of their mutual rights and duties. This may be illustrated by two important aspects of Soviet labor law: the collective contract and the settlement of labor disputes.

THE COLLECTIVE CONTRACT

Collective contracts between union and management were introduced into general practice in Soviet industry immediately after the October Revolution, at first with respect to private industry, later in the nationalized sector as well. However, those were hectic times, and in practice the unions generally ran the enterprises. As War Communism progressed, the government attempted to mobilize labor on the principle of conscription and to regulate labor relations by decree.

With the retreat into the NEP in 1921, government regulation of wages and working conditions was for the most part reduced to the establishment of certain minimum standards. Now for the first time Soviet law encouraged actual collective bargaining, in the sense of free arm's length negotiation without complete subservience to strict state control. During this period trade unionism developed as a movement of both economic and political significance.

The adoption of the First Five-Year Plan in 1928 severely restricted trade unionism and free collective bargaining. The collective contract was retained as a means of expressing the relations between labor and management—chiefly on the level of the individual plant rather than on an industry-wide basis as under the NEP; but those relations were now largely established by economic legislation, rather than by a free or semi-free market. A pattern of wages, hours, standards of output, conditions of work, was created by top planning and administrative organs; within this pattern, union and management agreed upon their respective rights and duties. The All-Union Central Council of Trade Unions became in effect a state organ (although in Soviet terminology it is a "social" organization), replacing the People's Commissariat of Labor.

It is difficult to determine exactly how much leeway has been left to local decision, within the over-all pattern. The picture is confused by the nominal discontinuance of collective contracts in 1935. The reasons for this discontinuance are not clear, although it was probably connected with changes in the status of the All-Union Central Council of Trade Unions. Soviet textbooks on labor law published in 1938 and 1944 did not even mention collective contracts. In 1946 it was explained that "detailed regulation of all aspects of [labor] relations by normative acts of the state has not left room for any kind of contractual agreements concerning various labor conditions. Thus collective contracts have outlived themselves in the period under consideration." In fact, however, agreements between union and management continued to be concluded throughout these years at the level of both plant and industry.[1]

In regard to health and safety, general rules were promulgated by the All-Union Central Committee of Trade Unions, on the basis of which industry-wide agreements were entered into by the union central committee of the industry and the appropriate people's commissariat or other economic organ. However, the factory committee and the plant management were also permitted to conclude "labor-safeguarding agreements," which prescribed the utilization of funds assigned for those purposes. Also supplementary agreements on health and safety for the larger shops within a plant could be concluded by the shop chief and the shop committee.

Similarly in respect to workers' welfare, despite the absence of collective contracts in name, union and management entered into agreements on the disposition of funds assigned for housing, medical care, and similar benefits, and also on the distribution of those portions of the Director's Fund (now called Enterprise Fund) and other special funds which were to be allocated to welfare.

Until 1941 it was the practice to conclude plant agreements on rules of hiring and firing, basic obligations of management and labor, and so forth (the so-called Rules of Internal Order). At that time, however, model rules were issued by the Central Council of Trade Unions and confirmed by the Council of Ministers, to be applied to conditions in each industry by agreement between the union central committee and the appropriate ministry. Here, too, some room was left for supplementary agreements on the plant level, but only when special conditions so warranted.

Control over wage rates and output norms showed a similar trend toward centralization in the period immediately preceding the war. In 1938 individual ministries were forbidden to authorize changes in wage schedules without permission of the Council of Ministers. However, despite this virtual freezing of wages, some leeway for local decision was still left by reason of the frequent definition of wage schedules in terms of minimums and maximums. In 1939 a procedure was established by which orders for the revision of output norms must be agreed upon by the Central Council of Trade Unions and the appropriate ministry, subject to confirmation by the Council of Ministers. But again we find that initiative in revising output norms could be taken on the local level, though after 1939 it was in the hands of the shop chief with the approval of the plant manager, the union local "participating" in the revision but its approval or consent no longer being required.

In 1947 collective contracts were suddenly reintroduced in name. Now the various agreements of the past and the matters previously left to informal coöperation are again formalized in one document.[2]

It is clear from the nature of the collective contracts, as well as from what Soviet writers say of them, that they are designed primarily to play a parental and educational role in the life of the Soviet industrial plant. An intensive campaign of mass indoctrination accompanies the promulgation as well as the fulfillment of the new agreements. Together with this, efforts are made to stimulate the initiative of the rank-and-file workers in the shaping of the agreements and in their enforcement. Above all, by delineating the exact areas of responsibility of management and labor, the contracts serve to bring home to both sides the nature of their rights and duties in the implementation of state plans for production and welfare.

Under the procedure introduced in 1947, the collective contract in each plant was drafted by the union local and the director on the basis of an industry-wide model contract worked out by the union central committee and the ministry, and a letter of instructions containing planned tasks for the plant during the coming year (including planned production, labor productivity, wages, costs, funds for housing, cultural needs, health and safety, and the like). The procedure has been changed slightly as a result of the 1957 economic reforms. Now general agreements are concluded between regional economic councils and trade union councils. Plant contracts are drafted on the basis of these agreements and letters of instructions sent out jointly by the trade union councils and the regional economic councils. The old procedure is apparently retained for plants that have remained under ministry supervision. All contracts must, of course, conform to planned tasks as before.

The parental nature of the Soviet collective contract may

be seen in the preamble to the 1959 Collective Contract of the Moscow machine-tool factory "Red Proletariat":

> The Soviet Union has entered into a new period of its development—the period of large-scale construction of communist society. The basic tasks of this period are defined in the decisions of the historic XXIst Congress of the CPSU, in the directives of the Congress on the seven-year plan of development of the national economy of the U.S.S.R. for 1959-1965. In the next seven-year period a further great advance of all branches of the economy will take place, an advance that will make possible a significant rise in the standard of living of the Soviet people.
>
> The majestic program of construction of communism inspires all the working people of the U.S.S.R. to broad development of competition, to a struggle for further perfection of production.
>
> With the goal of enlisting all workers, engineering-technical workers and employees in active participation in the solution of the politico-economic tasks set by the plan for the national economy for 1959, and of heightening the responsibility of economic and trade union organizations for improving the material-welfare and cultural service to the workers and employees, this collective contract for 1959 is concluded between the director of the Moscow Order of Lenin and Order of the Labor Red Star Machine-tool Factory "Red Proletariat" named after A. I. Efremov, designated hereafter as "the Administration," and the workers, engineering-technical workers and employees in the person of the factory committee of the trade union of machine-building workers.
>
> The collective contract sets as its goal the ensuring of the successful fulfillment and overfulfillment of the plan for 1959, the first year of the seven-year plan, with respect to all quantitative and qualitative indicators, and also further improvement of the conditions of work and living of the workers and employees of the factory.

The basic provisions of the collective contract drafted on the plant level are pre-determined by provisions of labor legislation, the model contract, the specific plan for the factory and current government policies. Thus the contract quoted above contains many required terms: for example, that workers cannot be discharged without the consent of the union factory committee; that the struggle against waste and those responsible for it will be carried on; that gross output shall be increased by 7.8 per cent over that of the preceding year; that the work of Comrades' Courts is to be "activated." The general wage rates in the contract are set by government decree.

However, important details are set in the collective contract on the plant level. Thus the contract under discussion provides: that 225,000 (old) rubles be spent on improving working conditions (dozens of specific improvements, such as installing a new ventilation system in shop no. 29, are listed); that an eight-story apartment house be prepared for occupation by the workers and employees; that 434,000 (old) rubles be spent on culture and sports; that a 100-bed nursery be built: that 875 workers be given courses to improve their skills and that they be promoted upon successful completion of these courses.

The parental-educational role of the Soviet collective contract, both in its general and its specific provisions, is apparent from the means established for its enforcement. So far, no provision has been made for enforcement by third-party adjudication. It is stated by Soviet jurists that "the bilateral obligations [of union and management] acquire [through the collective contract] legal force"; however, the sanctions thus far applied appear to be in the first instance moral, and secondly administrative.

Each of the subcommissions of the union factory committee is assigned the task of exercising "daily supervision" of the specific portion of the contract which falls within its sphere of competence. Superior union agencies check on superior management agencies, as well as on the union local. Every three months the plant management and the union local are required to conduct a survey of contract fulfillment and to report their findings to a meeting of all plant workers as well as to higher management and union organs. The stated purpose of this "mass check" is to stimulate worker participation and interest, and at the same time to create an opportunity for popular pressure by the workers on both management and union.

Conferences of top management and union leaders have resulted in official criticism of union leaders for permitting management violations. According to an editorial of October 16, 1948, in the leading labor newspaper, *Trud,* "incorrect, harmful relations between the factory administration and the union factory committee have arisen in several enterprises . . . Businesslike relations are supplanted by domesticity and mutual backscratching. It is clear that under these conditions criticism and self-criticism are not genuinely developed, insufficiencies and failures are hushed up."

Moral pressure may be supplemented by economic sanctions. The union may refuse to permit a manager who is guilty of violations to share in the production prize won by his plant. Rest-home permits, housing priorities, social insurance benefits, and so forth, are distributed in such a way as to favor workers who overfulfill their norms.

In addition to such pressures, discipline is maintained by administrative penalties imposed on officials by superior organs, ranging from reprimand to dismissal. According to the usual rule of European administrative law, such penalty may be appealed one administrative level above the chief who imposed it. Also union officials may in some cases impose administrative fines on plant managers; thus a fine up to 50 new rubles may be exacted by the chief technical inspector, who is an official of the union central committee, for violation of the safety agreement. Here, too, the director is allowed only an administrative appeal, in this case to the presidium of the union central committee.

Despite some tentative assertions to the contrary by Soviet commentators, it is highly questionable whether the collective contracts create any civil obligations, that is, any claims enforceable in the judicial process. This would seem to follow from the very nature of the Soviet collective contract.

The word "collective" and the word "contract" have a meaning in the context of Soviet labor law quite different from the meaning they have in American labor law. A contract in the American sense (and in the sense applicable to Soviet delivery contracts between state economic enterprises) is a voluntary establishment of mutual rights and duties by persons possessing a certain degree of independence, expressed in the phrase "legal capacity," or "capacity to contract." The negotiation of contracts between labor unions and employers is called "collective" bargaining in our law because union and management are both collective entities. However, the word "collective" in Soviet labor law refers neither to the union nor to management but to the enterprise as a whole. It is the enterprise which is the collective. The union local is not considered a legal entity at all (though the superior union agency is, and may be responsible for acts of the local confirmed by it). The "collective contract" is the plant program. It is indeed negotiated, within fixed limits, by union and management, and it creates mutual rights and duties in both; but the rights and duties which are created are on the borderline between the moral and legal spheres of human behavior. They are "unofficial" rights and duties.

Thus by the very nature of Soviet labor law the area of free bargaining is severely restricted. Also the right to strike is reduced to a formality. Strikes have occasionally occurred in Soviet Russia, but they have no status in law. In some instances the strike leaders have been punished; in other instances the managers and other officials responsible for the workers' grievances have been dismissed and the workers' demands granted. But in any event the problem is dealt with by informal administrative action, for it stands entirely outside the established legal order of labor relations. Soviet jurists put it less frankly and less accurately when they say "Our workers have the right to strike but they never do."

Behind the Soviet collective contract stands the unity of the enterprise, the shop community. The purpose of the collective contract is to guide the collective through the coming year of its life. Such guidance is not achieved, however, simply by an administrative distribution of functions, but also by a bilateral allocation of rights and duties by union and management, designed primarily to prevent disputes by inculcating in workers and officials a sense of responsibility of a moral-legal character.

"Why does the collective contract raise . . . responsibility?" asked a leading Soviet writer on labor law. "Because it is an agreement between concrete persons dealing with the assumption of a series of concrete obligations. Because this agreement embodies the will of the given collective . . . [Because] each obligation is considered and adopted by the whole collective . . . Because these obligations involve weighing every possibility and summarize tremendous lower-echelon experience." [3]

"The Soviet collective contract," states the same writer, "contains not only legal norms, but also norms of socialist morality." It is an instrument for educating "public opinion." It is a "school for communism." Its underlying purpose is to utilize the authority of official law for instilling in popular law-consciousness a sense of mutual rights and duties which, if perfectly developed, would make the official legal system itself superfluous.

SETTLEMENT OF WORKERS' GRIEVANCES

Not all aspects of Soviet labor law operate quite so close to the level of unofficial law-consciousness as does the collective contract. Claims by a worker for wages for work done, for reinstatement with back pay, for reclassification of his job, for overtime pay, for payment for time lost in changing jobs, and similar matters, as well as claims by management for damage to property by a worker, for recovery of a fine for violation of the rules of employment, and the like, are settled by a grievance procedure, with recourse to the People's Courts in certain cases.

The Soviet factory grievance committee, called the Commission on Labor Disputes, is composed of one or more representatives of labor and an equal number of representatives of management. In large factories most disputes go first to Shop Commissions on Labor Disputes whose decision may be appealed by the worker to the factory-wide Commission. Cases also go to the factory-wide Commission when the Shop Commission cannot reach agreement. If the factory-wide Commission cannot reach agreement, the case goes to the Factory Committee of the trade union.

Workers have the right to take disputes to the People's Court in case of an adverse decision of the factory-wide Commission or of the Factory Committee of the trade union. Management also has the right of recourse to the courts against an adverse decision.

Before 1957, appeal to the People's Court was more limited. The decision of the grievance committee (then known as the Rates and Conflicts Commission or RKK) could be disputed in court only if the decision had been disapproved by the labor inspector, a central union official. However, certain types of labor disputes then, as now, could be brought directly to the People's Court without previous submission to the RKK. The dispute could also be taken to the People's Court if the members of the RKK failed to reach an agreement. In a substantial proportion of the cases that come before it, the respective representatives of labor and management did not see eye to eye and hence there was recourse to the courts.

Workers who appear as plaintiffs in labor cases are exempt from the payment of state fees and other court expenses. The court must consider a labor case not later than five days after commencement of the suit. A decision in favor of a worker in an amount not higher than a month's earnings is subject to immediate execution, and a decision in an amount higher than a month's wages is subject to immediate execution to the extent of a month's wages (or in its entirety at the discretion of the court).

The decision of the People's Court may be appealed or protested in the usual order.

There seems to be little doubt that the Soviet courts in general guard jealously the rights of workers in the labor cases which come before them. This appears not only from the case reports but also from the accounts of observers and former participants. It must be understood that Soviet legislation confines the bargaining power of workers within narrow limits. Yet it is interesting that Boris Konstantinovsky, an émigré Soviet lawyer who represented management, expresses an attitude not uncommon among corporation lawyers in other countries in complaining that in labor cases the Soviet courts tended to lean over backwards to decide for the worker. In addition Soviet labor laws impose many substantive restrictions upon the power to discharge a worker or transfer him to a lower-paying job.[4]

Soviet grievance procedure, under the control of the regular courts, is based on the assumption that labor and management live together in a continuing relationship, and that the arbitration and adjudication of their disputes can serve as a means of maintaining the intimate and lasting character of that relationship. The parties to a labor case are not people who have made a deal with each other on the understanding that if one of them breaks it the other will sue for damages. The task of the labor arbitrators is one of preventing new disputes by careful handling of old ones. Hence the need for speedy and informal settlement, without the expense and bitterness of the traditional lawsuit. The parties must be better able to go on living with each other after it is over. They must both receive satisfaction. It is they, their past and future, their growth and development, their feelings and their outlook, that are at issue— not merely the particular act which brought on the grievance. The particular act is only a symptom of an underlying disorder; grievance procedure is concerned with treating the underlying disorder.

This is Parental Law. It exists throughout Europe and

America, wherever industrial peace permits it. It is not peculiarly socialist, nor is it peculiarly Russian. In the Soviet Union it is distinguished by the heavy accent on compulsion, by the fact that the applicable norms are largely legislative in character, by the close supervision of the courts over the grievance procedure within the plant, and by the assumption that a board consisting of an equal number of representatives of management and labor can effectively reach agreement.

Chapter Sixteen

PARENTAL LAW AND PERSONAL FREEDOM

THE AVERAGE CITIZEN of most countries has recourse to the formal processes of law only as a last resort. He knows that law is expensive and time consuming. Its language and its procedures are forbidding. Only when he has a serious claim, and when all other methods of satisfying it have failed, will he ordinarily consult a lawyer and if necessary bring suit.

In considering his suit, the court, too, acts on the assumption that legal adjudication is an extraordinary method of resolving disputes. It will not generally grant him a remedy unless he has been materially damaged, and it will require that the damage result from the acts of the defendant according to certain standards of causation, and that many other considerations be met, including some of a purely formal character.

Underlying the expensiveness of the legal process in time and money, and the severe substantive and procedural requirements which must be met before a legal remedy will be granted, is the belief that society has other, more satisfactory ways of resolving conflicts that arise within it. If a guest spills the soup, the hostess does not bring a lawsuit, even though the *faux pas* may have spoiled her party.

If brothers have a serious quarrel over an inheritance, the decent way of settling it is not in court, and perhaps not even by legal standards. There are informal social processes, undefined practices and standards, by which we are able to adjust ourselves to situations when things go wrong. The pressures of family and friends, the advice of ministers and teachers, the help of social workers, and many other similar forms of social control which are part of our "way of life," enable us to restore disrupted social equilibrium without becoming parties to a legal action. Even in business, it is usually better to find some less drastic way of settling things, regardless of one's legal rights.

What is still largely true of court action used to be true also of legislative and administrative action. Prior to the eighteenth and nineteenth centuries, the method of legislation was also an unusual means of maintaining order in society. Laws were enacted relatively rarely, and to last a very long time. Many spheres of life were entirely unregulated by statute. Before the twentieth century the same was true of administrative law. Far greater leeway was left for the informal, undefined sanctions of social habit and community folkways, on the one hand, and naked exercise of social, economic, and political power on the other.

More and more, we have seen the functions of the family, the school, the church, the factory, the commercial enterprise, and other unofficial associations, subjected to formal legislative, administrative, and judicial control. This has followed upon the increasing complexity of life in an age of huge cities, mass production, concentration of power. Disruptions in social equilibrium are more and more resolved not by general custom and not by arbitrary exercise of political or economic power but by official definition and decision, based on formal process of deliberation and pleading, whether of a legislative, administrative, or judicial character. This is not socialism; it is simply the twentieth century.

The extension of official law, juristic law, to domains once left to the informal processes of family life, the school and church, the local community, work associations, business associations, and the like, has posed a crucial problem for twentieth-century man. Together with the extension of legal controls we are witnessing a withering of the inner strength of these associations. Here are relationships which are so close-knit as to require more spontaneous responses, relationships which are so delicate and so intimate as to demand more mobility and flexibility than law traditionally allows. We are in danger that the life will go out of them, as they become subjected to the formal and time-consuming processes and definitions of law. "The letter killeth, but the spirit giveth life" is a saying which takes on new meaning as our social order becomes more and more legalized.

The significance of Soviet legal development lies in just this conscious extension of law to the most intimate social relations. The Soviet rulers have abandoned the original Marxist theory that the abolition of class struggle will render law unnecessary, that a society without exploitation can live on informal, indefinite, unofficial social practices and standards. They have not officially abandoned their dream of such a time; but classless socialist law itself is now conceived as a means of producing it. In other words, the Soviets take their stand in the future, at the end of time, when life will be regulated by the norms and imperatives of social custom, as written in the conscience of mankind. Looking backward into the present from this end-time, they seek by the use of norms and imperatives of official law to form, in an official sense, the functions of the various social groups and associations to which their citizens belong. They attempt to use law to strengthen those groups and associations by appealing to the conscience of their members in terms of their legal rights and duties, thereby identifying conscience, group consciousness, and loyalty to the state. They thus attempt to preserve the inner strength, the inner mobility and flexibility, of relationships of family, commerce, labor, and so forth—by the formal definitions and processes of law itself. In this way they apparently seek to check the social disintegration, depersonalization, and disenchantment which are produced by a mechanized, industrial, mass-production society. Of course law is not the sole means, or even the primary means, by which they strive to achieve this end. Informal influences, including both political and administrative pressures, play a more important part in shaping day-to-day decisions than does the official legal system. Yet law is one of the major instruments which the Communist Party uses to create the kind of society it wants.

Soviet law cannot be understood unless it is recognized that the whole Soviet society is itself conceived to be a single great family, a gigantic school, a church, a labor union, a business enterprise. The state stands at its head, as the parent, the teacher, the priest, the chairman, the director. As the state, it acts officially through the legal system, but its purpose in so acting is to make its citizens into obedient children, good students, ardent believers, hard workers, successful managers.

This, indeed, is the essential characteristic of the law of a total state.

We have seen that legal consequences follow from this conception of the role of law. Court procedure is informal and speedy; the judge protects the litigants against the consequences of their ignorance, and clarifies to them the nature of their rights and duties; there is elaborate pretrial procedure directed toward uncovering the whole history of the situation. The rule: "Let the punishment fit the crime" is supplemented (though not supplanted) by the rule: "Let the punishment fit the man." The law enters into family relationships at an earlier stage, for the purpose of preventing disruption. Minor offenses of a moral nature are tried by neighbors and fellow-workers. Throughout it is assumed that the parties live in a close and continuing relationship, which it is the purpose of law to foster, with each other and with the whole society.

To preserve and foster this relationship it is sought to give legal sanctions to moral obligations. A murder committed out of jealousy is punished more severely than ordinary murder, rather than less severely as in many other systems, because jealousy is considered an unworthy passion. A man standing on the shore is said to be under a positive legal duty to act to save a drowning man, whereas in most other systems that is simply a moral obligation. Thus the law is used for the purpose of eradicating antisocial, egoistic dispositions. However, this is more than an attempt to inculcate a sense of moral responsibility; it is desired also to instill a sense of legal responsibility. Official sanctions are invoked to make Soviet citizens think and feel not only in terms of what is morally right and wrong but also in terms of their legal rights and duties.

One may discern two distinct elements in this concept of law. On the one hand, parental law is concerned with legal enforcement of basic conditions within which relations between individuals or between groups may be carried on in peace. A good example is the provision of our National Labor Relations Act that labor and management must bargain in "good faith"; we do not care, officially, what kind of collective contract is arrived at, provided that the parties sit around a table together and honestly attempt to reach some sort of agreement. A similar attitude is reflected in the provision of the Securities and Exchange Act for "full and fair disclosure" in the prospectus of a corporation; the law is not expressly concerned with the actual condition of the corporation, so long as it is not concealed from the purchaser of shares. One may think of these as examples of a "maternal" attitude. Figuratively speaking, and according to accepted psychological theory, the mother wants peace and quiet in the household; she is anxious that her children be well adjusted. Soviet law has many "maternal" aspects, but they are overshadowed by the "paternal." The father demands success, achievement, performance. In the handling of criminal insanity, we have seen, every effort is made by the Soviet legal system to maintain the borderline case as a productive member of society. In family law, the traditional grounds for divorce such as intolerable cruelty, desertion, and the like are explicitly related to the underlying aim of maintaining the family as a going concern.

In labor law, the collective agreement must be the right agreement, conforming to the indices established by the state. In economic law, the contracts are governed by overall plans established by superior organs: and if the parties still cannot agree they are besought to let Arbitrazh make the contract for them.

Soviet writers refer to these features of their law as examples of its "educational" role. They do not use the term "parental" law. The term "parental" goes farther than they would wish to go in suggesting a relationship of tutelage between the state and the people, a relationship of guardian and ward, and implicitly a quality of immaturity in the person to whom law is addressed. It is the author's intention to stress these "parental" elements as characteristic not only of Soviet law but also, increasingly in the twentieth century, of other legal systems. It is also the author's intention to use the Soviet example to show both the vices and the virtues of this tendency.

CRIMES AGAINST THE STATE

We return to criminal law, for it is central to the Soviet legal system. It receives more attention in Soviet legal literature than any other branch of law. Its constructs and postulates are basic to every other branch.

The emphasis upon criminal law is a natural tendency of a parental legal system. In all systems criminal law is parental in its very nature, in that the state in prosecuting for crime acts directly to punish the offender and to make an example of him. As the concept of contract, with its principle of reciprocity, was the growing-point of Western law in the eighteenth and nineteenth centuries, and possibly in the sixteenth and seventeenth as well, so the concept of crime, with its principle of punishment and example, has become the growing-point of the twentieth-century law of the "administrative state."

In earlier chapters we have seen that state ownership of the means of production, the elimination of private commerce, and the establishment of a planned economy inevitably result in an expansion of the role of criminal law, especially in the sphere of economic and official crimes. We have also seen that the Russian traditions of autocracy and of community solidarity support the widespread use of criminal penalties against persons guilty of political or "ideological" deviation. We may now add that the concept of law as a parent and teacher, whose "most important task" (to quote once again the former President of the U.S.S.R. Supreme Court, I. T. Goliakov) is "the fundamental remaking of the conscience of the people"—enhances still further the central role of criminal law in the Soviet legal system.

In its parental aspect, Soviet criminal law seeks to foster a socialist morality, a sense of discipline, and a loyalty to Party policy and Party doctrine. Such offenses as speculation, living on unearned income, and the sale of land disguised as the sale of the house or orchard situated on the land, are punished primarily because they reflect a "capitalist mentality" and are demoralizing to those who are striving to subordinate private gain to social service. Abuse of authority by officials, on the other hand, reflects a breakdown in the discipline of the bureaucracy and hence a threat to administrative efficiency in a mobilized economy; it is significant that Soviet officials are subject to a general standard of duty analogous to the standard set for military officers in the United States under the Code of Military Justice. Finally, loyalty to Party policy and doctrine is enforced not only by conventional laws against treason, espionage and sabotage but also by laws against anti-Soviet (formerly called counterrevolutionary) agitation and propaganda. Thus political orthodoxy is reinforced by legal sanctions against making statements or possessing literature defamatory of the Soviet system, stirring up racial animosities, advocating war, or otherwise challenging the political, social or economic principles for which the Soviet state stands.

The trial of ideological offenders puts an even greater strain on the legal process than does its use against persons who commit economic and official crimes. Where the de-

fendants are important political figures passions and in-
trigues inevitably operate behind the scenes and the trial
itself tends to turn into a political demonstration. The purpose of such trials, which is to lend the prestige of the
courts to the policies of the regime, is ultimately frustrated
by the fact that the trials themselves result in a lowering of
the prestige of the courts.

It is significant that for the most part the Soviet regime
has used secret administrative procedures to get rid of those
whom it has considered to be its enemies. The great purge
trials of 1936-1938 were an exception to this policy. There
Stalin sought to seal his condemnation of the "anti-Soviet
bloc of Rights and Trotskyists" with the verdict of the military division of the U.S.S.R. Supreme Court. He apparently
believed that there was sufficient faith in the Soviet judicial
process at home and abroad for their conviction to lend
credence to his charge that the defendants were not merely
opponents but also traitors. The trials almost destroyed that
faith abroad, and seriously damaged it at home. It is interesting that there have been no similar public trials since
1938, unless one includes the post-war trials of persons who
collaborated with the German invaders.

The purge trials were not trials in the ordinary sense, but
great public demonstrations designed to make the Soviet
people and the whole world "understand the correctness"
of the verdicts. They reflect in an exaggerated way the educational role of Soviet criminal law.

Other reported cases of counterrevolutionary or anti-
state crimes reflect the parental quality of Soviet law in a
less distorted way. Thus in a wartime military trial of a
Soviet soldier for anti-Soviet agitation, it appeared that the
defendant had expressed "in rough, unworthy form" certain
negative opinions about the Constitution of the U.S.S.R.,
and other "politically incorrect" views. The U.S.S.R. Supreme Court affirmed an acquittal, stating that "it is necessary to evaluate [the defendant] K.'s personality . . . it is
clear that all these opinions were directed toward the
strengthening of military discipline . . ." It also appeared
that K. had fought against the Whites in the Civil War.

Thus not merely the act, and the intent to commit it, but the personality and the total orientation of the accused are critical factors in determining guilt. In K.'s case the defendant's orientation led to acquittal; in other cases, it has led to conviction.[1]

JUSTICE AND TYRANNY

To many it has seemed that the use of words such as law and justice by Soviet leaders is simply an attempt to disguise the despotic character of their system; that in fact the Soviet state is a tyranny, in which personal rights are entirely swallowed up by a totalitarian regime that demands everything from its subjects and gives little or nothing in return.

Thus one Western scholar raises the question, "Is there really any law in the Soviet Union?" "This question," he states, "does not surprise those who believe that the idea of law is at the same time a concept of justice and as such belongs to the world of ethics." He then continues:

> The legal systems of the Soviet Union and other countries are in fact so different that only a superficial attitude to Soviet law can evoke the idea that they are similar. Soviet law is an expression of might rather than of right. It is not bound by any general principles of morals. It is dictated by Soviet policy and adjusted to the exigencies of the times without any limitations or constraints.[1a]

If, indeed, Soviet regulation lacks any ethical element, if its content consists merely in the arbitrary whims of the Soviet rulers, if its chief function is to restrict and destroy rights—then should we dignify it with the name law? Or, if we do dignify it with that name, should we not recognize that it is law of an entirely different kind from that of civilized countries?

To many, such questions may appear foolish. Adherents of some schools of jurisprudence might say: "Let us analyze Soviet regulations as law and leave it to the theologians to evaluate their relationship to 'justice.' " Adherents of some schools of political science might say: "All systems of law are basically political instruments in the hands of ruling elites; let us evaluate Soviet law not in ethical terms but in terms of its effectiveness in consolidating the political power of the regime."

Yet more and more insistently, historical developments in the twentieth century have compelled both scholars and laymen to distinguish between a system of regulation which is characterized by equality, objectivity, consistency, and other elements of "due process," and a system of regulation which is arbitrary, oppressive, amoral, serving only to protect the power of the state. It may be convenient to retain the word "laws" (*leges, lois, Gesetze, zakony*) to refer to statutes, codes, regulations, and decisions, however tyrannical they may be. Is it not at least equally convenient to retain the word "law" (*jus, droit, Recht, pravo*) to refer to the legal order, the system of right, or legal justice, as something distinct from legalized tyranny?

When the distinction between law and tyranny is applied to a detailed study of particular systems of regulation, however, a question arises which is embarrassing to both believer and skeptic. Cannot the tyrant do justice? Is it not conceivable that he might establish a system of law which will satisfy his subjects' need for justice in their personal, social and economic relations, but which at the same time excludes any possible challenge to his own tyrannical power? Might he not attempt to regulate certain aspects, at least, of family relations, labor relations, property relations, contracts, claims arising from personal injuries, disposition of criminals, and even of administrative acts, through the equal, objective, and consistent definition and allocation of rights and duties? Could he not confine the use of tyranny to persons and acts threatening his own power, while extending the use of justice more and more widely as his power becomes more firmly established? Might he not attempt gradually to establish a legal tradition which could operate in situations where he feels the secret police are not needed?

It is pleasant for foes of tyranny to believe that no tyrant is intelligent enough to attempt this. It is comforting to believe that the devil is stupid, weak, inattentive to the needs of his followers. People who believe this should be reminded that in Christian theology Lucifer is a fallen angel. Before taking it for granted that law and tyranny cannot co-exist in a single society, one should remember that some great legal systems—the Roman, for example—were fashioned under tyrants and autocrats. Before assuming that revolutionaries cannot create a legal order, one should recall Thomas Hobbes' remark that "there is scarce a commonwealth in the world whose beginnings can in conscience be justified."

It would indeed be the height of folly for a tyrant to attempt permanently to deprive his people of all rights, and to make every aspect of their lives forever dependent upon his caprice. The opponents of modern tyranny would be assured an easy victory if confronted with despots who ignored their subjects' need for law and justice in their personal, social and economic relations.

Especially in the Stalin era, the view was widespread in Western scholarly literature that Soviet law lacks any ethical element or concept of justice, that it is only a system of regulation imposed by an omnipotent state to insure its own omnipotence, and that it is not law in any meaningful sense. The Soviet system, according to the author quoted above, is characterized by "the insignificance of the legal order in general. Where the police state reigns, the law is only a stepchild." [2]

Such exaggerated assertions of Soviet lawlessness only obscure the important questions of the nature and quality of Soviet justice. The Soviet system of law and justice is not a peripheral feature of Soviet life, "a stepchild," susceptible of explanation solely as a survival of the past or as a half-hearted concession to popular psychology. Soviet law and justice are an integral part of the Soviet political, economic and social system, and require an explanation compatible with an explanation of the system as a whole.

By describing Soviet law as parental in character we make more vivid and meaningful its relationship both to Soviet tyranny and to Soviet justice.

If the law promulgated and interpreted by the state is designed to play the role of parent and teacher, and the minds and hearts of the people are designed to be educated and formed thereby, there can be no *legal* control of the state by public opinion. In our political-legal system the law-consciousness of individuals and groups stands opposite the power of politically organized society (the state) to make positive law, and acts as a check on that power. The constitutional machinery of government permits our society, in one form or another, to exert legal controls upon state action; indeed, we think of law as one of the primary means whereby society controls the state. In the Soviet Union, on the other hand, law is conceived as one of the primary means whereby the state controls society. There are no legal channels through which society may challenge the state. The Soviet state is not governed by public opinion; it may (and often does) bow to it, but it is not bound by it.

The absence of a system of public control over the political processes of Soviet life is well known and needs little illustration. There is, indeed, a constitutional machinery of government, but that machinery is not intended to be more than a part of the system of political authority. Although the Supreme Soviet of the U.S.S.R., for example, is, according to the Constitution, "the highest organ of state authority," in fact that body consists of some 1,300 representatives (many of them artists, "heroes" of one kind or another, and so forth) who meet for a week at a time twice a year to endorse the measures presented to it. The elections themselves are a ceremonial demonstration of solidarity; there is music and dancing in native costumes and competition to be first at the polls, but there are no programs competing for popular acceptance and only a single slate of candidates. The Supreme Soviet is essentially an honorary society, which, however, like medieval parliaments, may carry the grievances of the people to

the central authority in return for voting the taxes, so
to speak, and going back to the localities to help make
them palatable. Of genuine debate there is almost none, and
all bills which are presented are enacted unanimously. Thus
there is an absence of what might be called due process
of legislation, although once laws are enacted they are
supposed to be applied by due process of adjudication.
The efforts of Soviet jurists today to regularize the procedures of the Supreme Soviet (to get the state budget
presented to it, for example, before that budget has already gone into effect, to have enacted a law on recall of
representatives by their constituents, and so forth) fall
very far short of an attempt to convert that body into a
legislature in the modern Western sense, although the development of the committee system within the Supreme
Soviet is a more hopeful sign, reminiscent of the emergence of the committee system in English parliamentary
history.[3]

The Presidium of the Supreme Soviet (not to be confused with the Presidium of the Central Committee of
the Communist Party, formerly called the Politburo),
consisting of thirty-three members chosen from the Supreme Soviet to conduct its affairs between sessions, would
perhaps qualify in terms of size to be the supreme governing body; and under the Constitution it is authorized to
issue edicts (subject to subsequent confirmation by the
Supreme Soviet) which do in fact form the legal basis
for most of the major activities of the Soviet government.
Also, the Presidium of the Supreme Soviet may review
decisions of the Supreme Court. However, the Presidium's
membership does not include the Chairman of the Council
of Ministers and the First Secretary of the Communist
Party, nor does it include most of the other top Soviet
leaders, so that one may doubt that it exercises the initiative in much, at least, of its legislation. Moreover, many of
the edicts of the Presidium of the Supreme Soviet merely
enact decrees already passed by the Council of Ministers.

Is it, then, the Council of Ministers which really governs
the Soviet Union? Under the Constitution the Council of

Ministers is "the highest executive and administrative organ of state authority," and technically it is called "the Government"—like the British Cabinet. The Soviet Council of Ministers consists of the heads of the various economic, political, military, social and other branches of the Soviet state. It is the Council of Ministers which makes and executes the national economic plan, directs the general organization of the armed forces, and in general runs the day-to-day activities of Soviet officialdom. Its "decrees and regulations" are, in fact, the operative legislation of the Soviet Union.

The importance of the Council of Ministers is precisely indicated by the fact that its chairman and vice-chairmen are drawn from the Presidium of the Central Committee of the Communist Party. Indeed, some of the most important decrees are issued by the Council of Ministers and the Central Committee jointly. While we know nothing of the nature of the deliberations of the Council of Ministers, it seems unquestionable that significant conflicts of interests among the various ministries represented there are *not* resolved by a majority vote of all ministers. Basic policy decisions are undoubtedly made by the chairman and vice-chairmen—that is, by the top Party leaders.

Speaking broadly, it is, of course, the Communist Party which governs the Soviet Union. This is stated in the Constitution itself, which declares that the Communist Party is "the leading core of all organizations, . . . both social and state." The Party is not a political party in the Western sense: it does not represent a class or classes, or a special political-interest group or groups, and it does not campaign against any other party. It is rather "the central core of conscious socialists," the "shock troops" in all phases of social, political and economic life. Long since purged of its revolutionary romantics, the Party is a professional elite of officials, administrators, technicians, and privileged workers; its watchwords are discipline and loyalty.

The Communist Party stands behind the entire complex constitutional and organizational structure of the Soviet

state. Without the Party that structure would be too un-
wieldly to operate. But the Party itself, with its more than
ten million members and candidate members, is itself a
complex and unwieldy mechanism whereby to run a highly
centralized society. Theoretically, the Central Committee
of the Party, elected by local, regional, and republican
Party representatives, designates a Presidium which is responsible to it. In fact, the Presidium controls the Central
Committee which in turn controls the surbordinate Party
organs reaching down through all levels. Only at the very
top—at the Presidium level—is there authority unqualified,
and even there its distribution is precarious.

Speaking more precisely, then, the Soviet Union is
really governed not by any distinct governmental or political body or bodies but by one, two, three, five, or eleven
men, plus whomever else they may bring in to rule with
them—men who have risen to positions of leadership
through any one of a multiplicity of channels: Party organizations as such, economic management, armed forces
—but who are essentially Party leaders rather than leaders
of some organization within or without the Party.

The armed forces, the economic administrative agencies,
even the Party itself, as organizations, do not play independent roles. The top leaders have the initiative and use
the organizations to symbolize and to effectuate their
policies. The authority of the top leaders is essentially
personal rather than organizational. Their relationship to
each other is likewise a personal one and is not determined by the relationship of the organizations to each
other. The last thing that any of the top leaders wants
is to be identified with a particular organizational hierarchy: they want only to be identified with "the Party,"
which is the "central core" of *all* Soviet organizational
hierarchies.

Thus, the principal contribution of the Russian Revolution to the development of constitutional law is the adaptation of autocracy to twentieth-century industrial society.

The Communist principle of leadership seems to have
shown its viability in Soviet Russia, its capacity to survive

the leader's death. Yet the fact that Stalin's successors have maintained their authority in part through their denunciation of the Stalinist system of terror has altered, to some extent, the leadership principle; for the drive to "strengthen socialist legality" has exerted some pressure toward establishing certain controls—still too loose to be called legal—over the men at the top. This pressure, combined with the more powerful political forces which the death of Stalin released, has possibly already resulted in a redistribution of authority within the Communist Party and, more particularly, in the creation of procedures which would give the Central Committee of the Party effective control over the Presidium. There is some evidence to support such a conjecture, for in June 1957, after a majority of the Party Presidium had voted to oust Khrushchev, he refused to resign, stating that only the Central Committee could force him to do so; a meeting of the Central Committee was then called, which supported Khrushchev and ousted Molotov, Malenkov and Kaganovich. If indeed this becomes a precedent for the future, a constitutional machinery may evolve within the Communist Party for an orderly solution to the problem of succession.

Even such a solution, however, cannot eliminate the tyrannical features of the Soviet political system, which are based not only on autocracy but upon the absence of public control over the Communist Party. There is no opportunity in the Soviet Union for any individual or group publicly to challenge the authority of the Party or indeed any particular measure which the Party chooses to exclude from challenge.

Although freedom of speech, press and assembly is proclaimed in Article 125 of the Soviet Constitution, these freedoms are explicitly limited "in conformity with the interests of the working people, and in order to strengthen the socialist system," and their guarantee is stated to be simply the "placing at the disposal of the working people and their organizations printing presses, stocks of paper, public buildings," and so forth. The Constitution thus makes certain minimum concessions to public opinion and civil rights. Its emphasis, however, is on political and economic organization, and on equality (particularly of nationalities and of sexes) and social security. Marx said that "personal freedom is possible only in the collectivity." Russia's cultural heritage stresses collective consciousness, common faith. Soviet paternalism minimizes the freedom of the individual mind or will.

Moreover, the Soviet political system is hierarchically organized. Each executive-administrative organ has large discretionary powers, subject to the control of its superior organs. The jurisdiction of each is limited territorially, but to a large extent it is unlimited as regards the nature of what it may do.[4] This means that corruption and abuse of power are controlled primarily by those higher in the chain of command and not so much, as in this country, by restrictive rules of substantive and procedural law.

Finally, the omnipotence of the state and its hierarchical principle of organization make it possible for the Party to function without public control. The legal system, as the established order, must compete for sovereignty with the Party. The state rests on the pillar of Party as well as on the pillar of Law—and thirdly, it rests on the pillar of Plan. There has been an attempt to legalize Party and Plan; but Law is still a junior member of this trinity. The effect of severe political and economic repression is to impair the collective community spirit which it is the function of law to foster. Fear sets in, and with it, mutual distrust and atomization.

Nevertheless, the parental character of Soviet law sets limits to the arbitrariness of state action. The Soviet state and its officials are bound by the parent-child, teacher-pupil relationship just as the Soviet people are bound. It is true, the state is a total state, in the sense that it takes responsibility for all aspects of social life; the Soviet fetishism of the state is shocking. But the Soviet state is responsible *to* Soviet society, as well as *for* it. Its responsibility *to* society is ultimately a moral and political one, rather than a legal one; it is, nevertheless, a real responsibility which is reflected in many aspects of the legal system—reflected, for example, in legal protection of the citizen against administrative abuses, legal enforcement of tort and contract claims by citizens against state enterprises, legal protection of rights of property, inheritance, and a host of other personal interests, as well as in legal protection of the social and economic order generally.

The absence of legal control by society over the state, or, to put it positively, the conception of law as a means whereby the state directs the social order, changes the character of rights under Soviet law as contrasted with traditional Western legal systems. Under Western systems of law, rights are conceived ultimately as *belonging* to the people who have them, whereas under Soviet law rights are conceived ultimately as *granted* to the people by the state. The difference is not absolute: under Western systems, the state may take away rights which belong to people, and under the Soviet system the state is bound to protect rights which it has granted. Nevertheless, the difference is critical, for rights which are granted by the Soviet state are granted for a purpose—to help make the Soviet people industrious, thrifty, resourceful, respectful of law, loyal to the state and to the Communist social order. Psychologically, the recipient of such rights is in a different position from a person who "has" rights which the state seeks to implement. The moral principles upon which Soviet rights are founded are primarily principles of service to society and to the state, rather than primarily principles of protection of individuals against society or the state. Again, the difference is one of degree, and yet it is critical.

Soviet law treats the individual as a child or youth, as a dependent member who needs to be trained and guided in the interests of the whole as conceived by the state. Nevertheless the Soviet state also identifies itself with the people whom it is training and guiding. Without that identification, the Soviet state loses its reason for being (whether that be defined in Marxist or in Russian terms or in both) and its claim to popular support. To believe

that the Soviet state is not seriously concerned with maintaining its reason for being and its claim to popular support
is to misread the whole history of the Russian Revolution.

Every dictatorship depends in some degree on mass
support. Lacking a strong tradition on which to rely, with
no fifty or one hundred years of established political
authority, the dictator looks to popular acceptance as his
chief bulwark. Absolute monarchies tend to smash aristoc-
racies and seek popularity among the lower classes.

But "the masses" are a precarious foundation on which
to erect a lasting edifice. The Soviet leaders, especially
since the mid-1930's, have been attempting to build traditions, and particularly legal traditions. This is the challenge which Soviet law presents to Marxism, with its basic
contempt for tradition, as well as to the Russian heritage,
which, despite its strong spiritual qualities, has lacked tradition in an organic sense. "There are no sacred traditions
amongst us, especially in the educated classes," says Svi-
drigaïlov in Dostoevsky's *Crime and Punishment.* "At the
best someone will make them up somehow for himself out
of books or from some old chronicle." The Soviet leaders
have fulfilled this prediction, and have created sacred traditions of socialist property, of the right and duty to work,
of loyalty to the Party, and others, out of the books of Marx
and Lenin and from the chronicles of Russian and Western
law.

The Soviet social order is highly dynamic, characterized
by tremendous and rapid change. There is nevertheless considerable evidence that the Soviet leaders have had forced
upon them the task of attempting to bring stability into the
social order. They have been in power for a long time.
Too much power undoubtedly corrupts, but it also imposes
its own limitations. In 1917 and 1918, thinking first that
the regime might collapse in a few weeks, and later that
world revolution was around the corner, Lenin had to
act fast. After twenty years Stalin had more patience; he
seemed to be thinking in terms of *lasting* power. Undoubtedly he was also thinking in terms of the succession
to power on his death. The Revolution was in process of

settling down. His successors have carried this process still further.

But the process is not an easy one. The first and the second phases of the Revolution are in conflict. Because of the absence of political parties in Soviet Russia, or for that matter of any real freedom of public opposition, the conflict is concealed. One may see it somewhat, perhaps, in the informal struggle between the Communist Party and the Russian Orthodox Church. The restoration of real freedom of worship to non-Party members is a signal triumph for stabilization; but the ten million Party members and the twenty million Young Communists are forbidden to go to Church. The very fact that this prohibition must be reiterated in emphatic terms tells us a great deal about the conflict. From time to time the Young Communist *Pravda* has printed a letter from a reader asking if Party principles permit him to be married in a church ceremony, his fiancée being a believer and not a Young Communist. The answer, of course, is no.

The position of the Church has symbolic importance, since the Church explicitly differs from the Party on at least one fundamental question of "ideology," but the underlying conflict goes even deeper. The inner position of the Party is challenged not only by the Church, but also by the family, by one-man management, by property and contract, by the legal system itself. With respect to the Church, however, the challenge is more difficult to conceal; one cannot by any stretch of Marxist terminology talk about the "socialist" Church as one talks about the "socialist" family, "socialist" law, the "socialist" ruble. All these traditional elements of stability are, however, a challenge not to the external political strength of the Party but to its inner position as "leader, guide, and teacher." They foster independent loyalties. The Party therefore tightens its external control over them; but the tension between them, though not overtly manifested, is there. It is a tension within the system, a tension within the Revolution itself. How it will be resolved depends in part on how seriously the Soviet rulers take the development of their own legal system over the past twenty-five years.

THE LESSONS OF SOVIET LAW

From the standpoint of the West, the development of Soviet law requires a revision of some of our conceptions of the Soviet system. The popular view of the Soviet state as a police state run by professional revolutionaries, whose actions are governed solely by the desire to extend their own power, is a dangerous half-truth. Even from a chauvinist standpoint it means that the inner strength of the enemy is seriously underrated. From the standpoint of the establishment of a creative peace it means that possible avenues of reconciliation between conflicting systems are irrevocably cut off. From the standpoint of our own development it means that we learn little from Soviet experience, profiting neither from its blunders nor from its successes.

We may learn from the socialist character of Soviet law that socialism is not an end in itself; nor is capitalism; and that the balance between personal initiative and social-economic integration is one which must be struck again and again in any going legal system. We may learn from the Russian heritage of Soviet law that the cohesive character of community life is an essential foundation of law, which must, however, find legal expression if law is to keep in contact with basic psychological and spiritual drives in society. Above all, we may learn from the parental character of Soviet law the great potentialities and the grave dangers inherent in the development of positive law as a guardian and teacher of the law-consciousness of persons and groups.

. In their focus on the parental and educational role of law, with its conception of the litigant, the subject of law, as a youth to be guided and trained, the Soviets have made a genuine response to the crisis of values which threatens twentieth-century society—a response which has not merely a Marxist and a Russian but a universal sig-

nificance. They have found a basis for law in a new conception of man—a conception which is by no means
uniquely Soviet but which, with variations, is widely shared
in this generation, especially in the totalitarian countries.
We should not allow the violence and injustice which have
accompanied the birth and growth of this conception to
obscure its underlying significance. Indeed, we are in a
sense indebted to the Russians for their excesses, for
thereby the word "revolution" has lost its charm in the
West for all but a lunatic fringe, and we are better able
to seek our own equilibrium between change and continuity. At the same time we must recognize that our evolution is connected with their revolution. That is true whether
we react blindly against the Russian Revolution, or slavishly
imitate it, or creatively make our own response to the
world-wide breakdown out of which it emerged.

Such a response would accept the Soviet challenge by
attempting to integrate our own law around a conception
of man which is fuller and more balanced than the Soviet
conception. Man is not uniformly the dependent and growing youth of Soviet law, nor is he uniformly the reasonable
man of our legal tradition. The varieties of social experience call forth many diverse aspects of his personality. Depending on his situation, he may have the helplessness
of a child, the youth's capacity for dedication and service,
the self-confidence and assertiveness of a young man, the
prudent maturity of middle age, the wisdom of old age.
A healthy legal system must give reflection in procedural
and substantive rights and duties, at appropriate times
and appropriate places, to all the various phases of man's
true nature.[5]

Notes

BIBLIOGRAPHICAL NOTE

Since this book does not attempt to present an exhaustive study of Soviet law, but merely to suggest its broad outlines and its chief implications, footnote references have been kept to a minimum. Scholars who would like to pursue particular points may wish to consult the author's previous articles in various legal periodicals, where citations to Soviet sources may be found. These articles include: "Soviet Family Law in the Light of Russian History and Marxist Theory," *Yale Law Journal,* LVI (1946), 27; "Principles of Soviet Criminal Law," *Yale Law Journal,* LVI (1947), 803; "Commercial Contracts in Soviet Law," *California Law Review,* XXXV (1947), 191; "Soviet Property in Law and in Plan," *Pennsylvania Law Review,* XCVI (1948), 324; "The Spirit of Soviet Law," *Washington Law Review,* XXIII (1948), 152; "The Challenge of Soviet Law," *Harvard Law Review,* LXII (1948-49), 220, 449; with Donald H. Hunt, "Criminal Law and Psychiatry: The Soviet Solution," *Stanford Law Review,* II (1950), 635; "The 'Right to Knowledge' in the Soviet Union," *Columbia Law Review,* LIV (1954), 749; "The Law of the Soviet State," *Soviet Studies,* VI (1955), 225; "Real Property Actions in Soviet Law," *Tulane Law Review,* XXIX (1955), 687; "Soviet

Justice and Soviet Tyranny," *Columbia Law Review*, LV (1955), 795; "The Current Movement for Law Reform in the Soviet Union," *American Slavic and East European Review*, XV (1956), 179; "Soviet Law Reform—Dateline Moscow 1957," *Yale Law Journal*, LXVI (1957), 1191; "Soviet Law and Government," *Modern Law Review*, XXI (1958), 19; "The Comparison of Soviet and American Law," *Indiana Law Journal*, XXXIV (1959), 559; "Law as an Instrument of Mental Health in the United States and Soviet Russia," *Pennsylvania Law Review*, CIX (1961), 361; "Soviet Heirs in American Courts," *Columbia Law Review*, LXII (1962), 257; "The Dilemma of Soviet Law Reform," *Harvard Law Review*, LXXVI (1963), 929. In general, Soviet sources cited in these articles are not repeated in the present book. Grateful acknowledgement is made to the above-mentioned legal periodicals for their permission to use passages from the articles cited.

In addition, the author recommends the following general works on Soviet law: Vladimir Gsovski, *Soviet Civil Law*, 2 vols. (1948-1949); Rudolf Schlesinger, *Soviet Legal Theory: Its Social Background and Development* (1951); John N. Hazard, *Law and Social Change in the U.S.S.R.* (1953); Harold J. Berman and Boris A. Konstantinovsky, *Soviet Law in Action: The Recollected Cases of a Soviet Lawyer* (1953), Harold J. Berman and Miroslav Kerner, *Soviet Military Law and Administration* (1955) and *Documents on Soviet Military Law and Administration* (1955); John N. Hazard, *Settling Disputes in Soviet Society: The Formative Years of Legal Institutions* (1960); Kazimierz Grzybowski, *Soviet Legal Institutions* (1962); and John N. Hazard and Isaac Shapiro, *The Soviet Legal System: Post-Stalin Documentation and Historical Commentary* (1962). The last-named work includes an exhaustive bibliography of Soviet and non-Soviet books and articles on various aspects of Soviet law.

CHAPTER 1: MARXISM—LENINISM—STALINISM

1. G. Plekhanov, *Fundamental Problems of Marxism* (New York: International Publishers, n. d.), p. 72.

2. Karl Marx, *A Contribution to the Critique of Political Economy* (New York, 1904), p. 11. The entire passage, a famous one in the literature of Marxism, is as follows: "The general conclusion at which I arrived and which, once reached, continued to serve as the leading thread in my studies, may be briefly summed up as follows. In the social production which men carry on they enter into definite relations that are indispensable and independent of their will; these relations of production correspond to a definite stage of development of their material powers of production. The sum total of these relations of production constitutes the economic structure of society— the real foundation, on which rise legal and political superstructures and to which correspond definite forms of social consciousness. The mode of production in material life determines the general character of the social, political and spiritual processes of life. It is not the consciousness of men that determines their existence, but, on the contrary, their social existence determines their consciousness. At a certain stage of their development, the material forces of production in society come in conflict with the existing relations of production, or—what is but a legal expression for the same thing—with the property relations within which they had been at work before. From forms of development of the forces of production these relations turn into their fetters. Then comes the period of social revolution. With the change of the economic foundation the entire immense superstructure is more or less rapidly transformed. In considering such transformations the distinction should always be made between the material transformation of the economic conditions of production which can be determined with the precision of natural science, and the legal, political, religious, aesthetic or philosophic—in short ideological forms in which men become conscious of this

conflict and fight it out. Just as our opinion of an individual is not based on what he thinks of himself, so can we not judge of such a period of transformation by its own consciousness; on the contrary, this consciousness must rather be explained from the contradictions of material life, from the existing conflict between the social forces of production and the relations of production. No social order ever disappears before all the productive forces for which there is room in it have been developed; and new higher relations of production never appear before the material conditions of their existence have matured in the womb of the old society. Therefore, mankind always takes up only such problems as it can solve; since, looking at the matter more closely, we will always find that the problem itself arises only when the material conditions necessary for its solution already exist or are at least in the process of formation. In broad outlines we can designate the Asiatic, the ancient, the feudal, and the modern bourgeois methods of production as so many epochs in the progress of the economic formation of society. The bourgeois relations of production are the last antagonistic form of the social process of production—antagonistic not in the sense of individual antagonism, but of one arising from conditions surrounding the life of individuals in society; at the same time the productive forces developing in the womb of bourgeois society create the material conditions for the solution of that antagonism. This social formation constitutes, therefore, the closing chapter of the prehistoric stage of human society."

3. See Friedrich Engels, *Herr Eugen Duehring's Revolution in Science* (*Anti-Duehring*) (Moscow, 1947), p. 417. The chief significance of the phrase "wither away" lies in its implication of a gradual process: it was the answer of Marx and Engels to Bakunin and the Russian anarchists who proposed the immediate "abolition" of the state.

4. Roscoe Pound, "Fifty Years of Jurisprudence," *Journal of the Society of Public Teachers of Law* (1937), p. 20.

5. Friedrich Engels, Introduction to Karl Marx, *The Class Struggles in France, 1848-1850* (New York, 1934), p. 20. This work was published by the German Social Democrat party over Engels' express protest.

6. Lenin expressed these views in instructions he gave to People's Commissar of Justice D. I. Kurskii about the drafting of the Civil Code. Lenin, *Works* (4th Russian edition), vol. 33, pp. 176-177 & vol. 36, p. 518.

7. A. G. Goikhbarg, *Osnovy chastnogo imushchestvennogo prava* (Foundations of Private Property Law; Moscow, 1924), p. 9. He goes on: "The conception of law is wrapped up in such a mystical veil . . . that its replacement by another, a new one, which would embrace those regulative norms, those organizational rules which we are compelled to apply in the transitional period preceding the final and all-embracing spread of the communist structure—such a replacement would be extraordinarily expedient. But there are terms which, so to speak, are sucked in with the mother's milk. To the list of such terms belongs also the term 'law.' "

8. P. I. Stuchka, ed., *Entsiklopediia gosudarstva i prava* (Encyclopedia of State and Law), III (Moscow, 1927), p. 1594.

9. E. B. Pashukanis, *Obshchaia teoriia prava i marksism* (General Theory of Law and Marxism; Foreword to 2nd edition, Moscow, 1926). The third edition of this work has been translated into English by Hugh W. Babb in *Soviet Legal Philosophy* (Harvard, 1951), pp. 111-225. Pashukanis was the Director of the Institute of Soviet Construction and Law, which was attached to the Communist Academy until 1936 and thereafter to the Academy of Sciences of the U.S.S.R.; he was also chief editor of the leading Soviet political-legal journal, *Soviet State and Law*, until his final denunciation early in 1937. In 1930 he made a recantation of certain relatively minor tenets of his theory, only to reaffirm its principal features. The quotations that follow are taken from this speech, entitled *Sovetskoe gosudarstvo i revolutsiia prava* (The Soviet State and the Revolution of Law; Moscow, 1930). This speech

is translated in *Soviet Legal Philosophy, supra,* at pp. 237-280. The theories of Pashukanis are discussed in Vladimir Gsovski, *Soviet Civil Law* (Ann Arbor, 1948), I, 166ff; in Rudolf Schlesinger, *Soviet Legal Theory* (2nd ed., London, 1951); and in numerous articles by John N. Hazard in various legal periodicals. A penetrating analysis may also be found in Lon L. Fuller's article "Pashukanis and Vyshinsky: A Study in the Development of Marxian Legal Theory," *Michigan Law Review,* XLVII (1949), 1157.

10. V. I. Lenin, *State and Revolution,* Ch. V, Part 3.

11. Pashukanis completely recanted in a 1936 article "Gosudarstvo i pravo pri sotsialisme" (State and Law under Socialism), *Sovetskoe Gosudarstvo* (Soviet State), 1936, No. 3, p. 3. His recantation failed to save him from disappearing in 1937. After the public disclosures of Stalin's crimes in 1956 Soviet jurists stated that Pashukanis was shot shortly after he was arrested. His general theory of law remains in disgrace, though he has been "rehabilitated" from charges of treason. See John N. Hazard, "Pashukanis is no Traitor," *American Journal of International Law,* LI, 385 (April 1957).

11a. See John N. Hazard, *Settling Disputes in Soviet Society* (N.Y., 1960), pp. 1-127.

12. *Sobranie uzakonenii i rasporiazhenii RSFSR* (Collection of Laws and Orders of the RSFSR), 1919, No. 66, Item 590.

13. On the similarities between continental European and Anglo-American law, see Chapter 6.

14. To register a divorce it was simply necessary for either spouse to notify the Bureau of Vital Statistics (ZAGS). This was often done by postcard.

15. There is an excellent discussion of the provisions of the civil code relating to tort and contract in Vladimir Gsovski, *Soviet Civil Law,* I (Ann Arbor, 1948), pp. 415ff, 485ff. The civil code itself (as amended to 1947) is translated in Volume II of the same work.

16. As late as 1934 Stalin spoke of socialism as meaning the complete abolition of social classes. See Stalin,

Leninism (11th ed.; New York: International Publishers, 1942), p. 344.

17. Stalin's statements in the early 1930's left no doubt as to the necessity for the state, with all its coerciveness, during the period of transition *to* socialism. As for the state *under* socialism, he carefully avoided saying that it would continue to exist, though at the same time he attacked those who sat back and did nothing in anticipation of its withering away.

18. See Aaron Yugow, *Russia's Economic Front for War and Peace* (1942), pp. 5-6. A penetrating analysis of the economic issues involved in the controversy is Alexander Erlich's, *The Soviet Industrialization Debate, 1924-1928* (Cambridge, Mass., 1960).

19. From Pashukanis' 1930 speech on the Soviet State and the Revolution of Law. See *supra* note 9. It should be noted that the word for "policy" and "politics" is the same in Russian (as it is, for example, also in German).

20. Andrei Ia. Vyshinskii, *Sudoustroistvo v SSSR* (Judiciary of the USSR; 2nd ed., Moscow, 1935), p. 32. Krylenko, People's Commissar of Justice until 1937, was even more outspoken in his statements that law must be subordinated to "expediency."

21. J. N. Hazard, "Correcting Misinterpretations of Soviet Law" (mimeographed; Moscow, 1937), pp. 4-5.

22. The Cheka (Extraordinary Commission for the Struggle against Counterrevolution, Sabotage, and Official Crimes), established in December 1917 as a commission attached to the Council of People's Commissars, was abolished in 1922 and its functions assigned to a new body, the GPU (State Political Administration), a department of the RSFSR Commissariat of the Interior. When the USSR was formed in 1923, the GPU was transformed into the OGPU (federal GPU). In 1934 the OGPU was transformed into a federal People's Commissariat of Internal Affairs (NKVD), which had, however, many functions besides that of "combating counterrevolution." It was also in charge of the investigation of crimes generally, penal institutions,

vital statistics, administration of highways, and much else. Subsequently the security functions of the NKVD were transferred to the People's Commissariat of State Security (NKGB). The two commissariats were renamed ministries in 1946. They were reunited in 1953. For later changes, see below Chapter 2, footnote 40.

23. The Church had to pay a price for its new privileges. Its publication, the Journal of the Moscow Patriarchate, praised Stalin as the divinely appointed leader of the Soviet peoples and professed to see in communism the realization of Christian social principles. Nevertheless, the Journal expressly disputed the atheism of the Soviet state, and thus was the only public voice of dissent on fundamental ideological issues which existed in the Soviet Union. Subsequently some other religious groups were permitted to publish journals.

24. During World War II, peasant households encroached to a large extent on the land of the collective farms. After the war the collective land appropriated by the households was restored to the collective farms. To this extent the statement in the text requires some qualification.

25. The term "dictatorship of the proletariat" was still used, though far less frequently, until 1961, when the new Party Program indicated officially that the dictatorship was over. It had reference primarily to the Soviet state in its foreign relations and to suppression of "survivals of capitalism" in the mentality of people (especially "enemies"). Malenkov, in his 1947 speech to the Cominform, said: "The class struggle in all its acuteness has now shifted from the Soviet Union to the international arena. That is where a contest of two systems is now taking place—capitalist and socialist." Domestically, there were supposed to be no hostile classes to dictate to. The state was considered to represent not merely the "workers" as such but all the "toilers" —a word which includes everyone in the Soviet Union. In this way Marxism could be applied to the explanation of non-Soviet development and in fact disregarded in the explanation of the internal social order.

26. Vyshinsky's 1938 work *Sovetskoe gosudarstvennoe pravo* ("Soviet Constitutional Law" or "Soviet State Law") is available in an American translation misleadingly entitled *The Law of the Soviet State* (New York, 1948). The quotations which follow are taken from this work and from two articles by Vyshinsky, "Osnovnye zadachi nauki sovetskogo sotsialisticheskogo prava" (Basic Tasks of the Science of Soviet Socialist Law) and "Voprosy prava i gosudarstva u K. Marksa" (Questions of Law and of State [as treated] in [the works of] Karl Marx) in *Sovetskoe Gosudarstvo* (Soviet State), 1938, Nos. 4 and 3 respectively.

27. It should be noted that Vyshinsky had written with considerably greater caution than Pashukanis and Krylenko, and that he had stressed the importance of law for the transition period. See A. Ia. Vyshinskii, *Revolutsionnaia zakonnost' na sovremennom etape* (Revolutionary Legality at the Present Stage; Moscow, 1933). At that time, however, he was not so important a figure as he later became.

28. Vyshinsky's 1938 definition of law, which became the official definition, stated: "Law is a combination of rules of conduct which express the will of the ruling class and are established by legislative procedure, and also of customs and rules of community life sanctioned by state authority, whose application is secured by the compulsory force of the state for the purpose of protecting, strengthening and developing relations and procedures advantageous and convenient for the ruling class."

29. Dmitri Buligin, *A Soviet Professor Speaks* (unpublished manuscript, 1949).

30. *Cf.* Alfred G. Meyer, *Leninism* (Cambridge, Mass., 1957).

CHAPTER 2: SOVIET LAW REFORM
AFTER STALIN, 1953-1962

Bibliography: The footnotes to this chapter contain citations to Soviet editions and English translations (where available) of most of the major legislative enactments since the death of Stalin: Fundamental Principles of Civil Law (footnote 28); Fundamental Principles of Criminal Law (footnote 2); Fundamental Principles of Criminal Procedure (footnote 6); Fundamental Principles of the Judicial System (footnote 33); Statute on State Crimes (footnote 8); Statute on Military Crimes (footnote 9); Statute on Military Tribunals (footnote 8); Statute on Procuratorial Supervision in the U.S.S.R. (footnote 6); Statutes of the Bar of the R.S.F.S.R. (footnote 36); Statute on Procedures for Hearing Labor Disputes (footnote 29); Legislation on Publication of Laws, Decrees and Edicts (footnotes 38 and 39); Edict on Petty Hooliganism (footnote 21); Decrees on the Death Penalty (footnote 3). Note also the Fundamental Principles of Civil Procedure of the U.S.S.R. and the Union Republics, *Izvestia,* Dec. 10, 1961, pp. 6-7, translated in the Current Digest of the Soviet Press (hereafter referred to as CDSP), Feb. 28, 1962, pp. 3-9; Draft of the Fundamental Principles of Labor Law, *Sotsialisticheskaia Zakonnost'* (Socialist Legality), 1959, No. 10, p. i, translated in CDSP, Nov. 18, 1959, pp. 5-10. For the Laws on Parasitism, the People's Patrol (*Druzhina*) and Comrades' Courts, see the footnotes to Chapter 11. John N. Hazard and Isaac Shapiro, *The Soviet Legal System, Post-Stalin Documentation and Historical Commentary* (New York, 1962) contains translations of excerpts from many of these enactments and from recent Soviet legal articles and books, as well as reports of recent cases. It also contains brief historical commentaries and an excellent bibliography of books and articles in English on Soviet law.

Hundreds of books and articles have been published in the Soviet Union on problems connected with law reform. Many of these articles have appeared in the leading Soviet legal periodical, *Sovetskoe Gosudarstvo i Pravo* (Soviet State and Law). A number of "Scientific-Practical Commentaries" on the new legislation have appeared: V. A. Boldyrev, ed., on the Fundamental Principles of Criminal Procedure; V. V. Borisoglebskii on the Statute on Military Tribunals; Iu. A. Kalenov on the Fundamental Principles of Legislation on the Judicial System; Iu. A. Kalenov on the Law on the Judicial System of the RSFSR; V. D. Menshagin and B. A. Kurinov on the Law on State Crimes. Other commentaries include: S. A. Golunskii, ed., *Voprosy sudoproizvodstva i sudoustroistva v novom zakonodatel'stve Soiuza SSR* (Questions of Judicial Procedure and the Judicial System in the New Legislation of the U.S.S.R., Moscow, 1959); O. S. Ioffe and Iu. K. Tolstoi, *Osnovy grazhdanskogo zakonodatel'stva* (The Fundamentals of Civil Legislation, Leningrad, 1962); Vsesoiuznii Institut Iuridicheskikh Nauk, *Novoe ugolovnoe zakonodatel'stvo RSFSR* (All-Union Institute of Juridical Sciences, The New Criminal Legislation of the RSFSR, Moscow, 1961).

Several recent books have dealt with problems of codification, including D. A. Kerimov, *Kodifikatsiia i zakonodatel'naia tekhnika* (Codification and Legislative Techniques, Leningrad, 1962); D. A. Kerimov, ed., *Voprosy kodifikatsii sovetskogo prava* (Questions of the Codification of Soviet Law, 3 vols., Leningrad, 1957-1960).

Among the many theoretical works dealing with the question of socialist legality are: N. G. Aleksandrov, *Pravo i zakonnost' v period razvernutogo stroitel'stva kommunizma* (Law and Legality in the Period of Expanded Construction of Communism, Moscow, 1961); L. S. Iavich, *Problemy pravovogo regulirovaniia sovetskikh obshchestvennykh otnoshenii* (Problems of Legal Regulation of Soviet Social Relations, Moscow, 1961); O. S. Ioffe and M. D. Shargorodskii, *Voprosy teorii prava* (Questions of the Theory of Law, Leningrad, 1961); I. S. Samoshchenko, *Okhrana rezhima zakonnosti sovetskim gosudarstvom* (Protection of the Regime of Legality by the Soviet State, Moscow, 1960).

1. See the speech by A. N. Shelepin in *XXII S"ezd Kommunisticheskoi Partii Sovetskogo Soiuza, stenografiicheskii otchet* (Twenty-second Congress of the Communist Party of the Soviet Union, stenographic transcript), Vol. II, p. 399.

2. Compare the 1958 Fundamental Principles of Criminal Law of the U.S.S.R. and of Union Republics, *Izvestia*, Dec. 26, 1958, pp. 2-3, Art. 23, with the R.S.F.S.R. Crimi-

nal Code (1956 ed.), Art. 28. The 1958 Fundamental Principles of Criminal Law are translated in Foreign Languages Publishing House, *Fundamentals of Soviet Criminal Legislation, the Judicial System and Criminal Court Procedure—Official Texts and Commentaries* (Moscow, 1960) (hereafter cited as Official Texts), pp. 5-27; Documentation Office for East European Law, University of Leyden, *Law in Eastern Europe No. 3—The Federal Criminal Law of the Soviet Union* (Leyden, 1959) (hereafter cited as Leyden Texts), pp. 37-71; *Current Digest of the Soviet Press* (hereafter cited as CDSP), March 4, 1959, pp. 3-7. The 1956 edition of the R.S.F.S.R. Criminal Code was translated by Dr. Vladimir Gsovski for the Central Intelligence Agency. Although this translation has not been published formally, it is widely available. An earlier British translation has been published, *The Penal Code of the Russian Socialist Federal Soviet Republic* (Foreign Office, London, 1934); however many changes were made in the code between 1934 and 1956.

3. The decrees extending the death penalty to economic and other crimes appeared in *Izvestia,* May 7, 1961, p. 5 (translated in CDSP, May 24, 1961, p. 8); *Izvestia,* July 2, 1961, p. 2 (translated in CDSP, July 19, 1961, p. 21); *Vedomosti Verkhovnogo Soveta SSSR* (Gazette of the Supreme Soviet of the U.S.S.R., hereafter cited as Vedomosti), No. 8, Feb. 21, 1962, Items 83-84, (translated in CDSP, March 14, 1962, p. 4).

4. Any increase in the crime rate is denied in Soviet texts. However, the author heard the Minister of Justice of the R.S.F.S.R., in a lecture delivered in Moscow on May 3, 1962, refer to a substantial increase in the rate of serious crimes "during the past few years." See also *Kommunist,* 1962, no. 2, p. 117.

5. The Board was created by a Decree of November 5, 1934, *Sobranie Zakonov SSSR* (Collected Laws of the U.S.S.R., hereafter cited as S.Z.), 1935, I, No. 11, Item 84. The abolition, which took place in 1953, was only officially confirmed in January 1956 in a Soviet law journal, *Sovetskoe Gosudarstvo i Pravo* (Soviet State and Law),

Jan. 1956, p. 3. It had been disclosed unofficially in 1955. See Harold J. Berman, "Soviet Law Reform—Dateline Moscow 1957," *Yale Law Journal,* LXVI, 1191, 1192 (1957). *Cf.* below, footnote 40.

6. Statute on Procuratorial Supervision in the U.S.S.R., Decree of the Presidium of the Supreme Soviet of the U.S.S.R. of May 24, 1955, Vedomosti, 1955, No. 9, Item 222, Ch. III (translated in CDSP, July 20, 1955, pp. 3-5; 1958 Fundamental Principles of Criminal Procedure of the U.S.S.R. and the Union Republics; *Izvestia,* Dec. 26, 1958, pp. 5-7, Art. 31. (This law is translated in Official Texts, pp. 61-86; Leyden Texts, pp. 113-151; CDSP, March 4, 1959, pp. 7-11, 25.) Article 28 of the Fundamental Principles limits to certain serious anti-state crimes the power of the organs of state security. The list of such crimes was extended in 1961. However, "the investigative apparatus of the organs of state security are entirely and fully governed by the legislation on [criminal] procedure without any exceptions whatever and supervision by the Procuracy is exercised over it within the same limits as over the investigative apparatus of the Procuracy." See Boldyrev, *supra* (*Bibliography* to Chapter 2), p. 156, footnote 1.

7. Law of December 1, 1934, S.Z., 1934, I, No. 64, Item 459; and Law of September 14, 1937, S.Z., 1937, I, No. 61, Item 266. These laws were later repealed.

8. The older law is discussed in Harold J. Berman and Miroslav Kerner, *Soviet Military Law and Administration* (hereafter referred to as Berman and Kerner Text) (Cambridge, Mass., 1955), pp. 64-75, 106-109. Compare Ch. II of the 1926 Statute on Military Tribunals and the Military Procuracy as Amended through 1940, S.Z., 1926, No. 57, Item 413; *Ibid.,* 1928, No. 19, Item 161; No. 33, Item 291; No. 34, Item 298; *Ibid.,* 1929, No. 13, Item 106; No. 39, Item 336; No. 50, Item 444; No. 70, Item 655; *Ibid.,* 1930, No. 47, Item 485; No. 49, Item 509; *Ibid.,* 1934, No. 12, Item 78; No. 36, Item 284; *Ibid.,* 1935, No. 43, Item 359a; Vedomosti, 1940, No. 51. (This statute is translated in Harold J. Berman and Miroslav Kerner, *Documents on Soviet Military Law and Administration* [hereafter referred

to as Berman and Kerner Documents] [Cambridge, Mass., 1955], pp. 141-156) with Ch. II of the Statute on Military Tribunals, *Izvestia,* Dec. 26, 1958, p. 5 (translated in CDSP, March 11, 1959, pp. 11-12). It should be noted that military courts continue to have jurisdiction over civilians in areas where martial law is declared.

9. Compare Art. 58 (1c) of the R.S.F.S.R. Criminal Code (1956 ed.) (this article is translated in Berman and Kerner Documents 96) with the Statute on State Crimes, *Izvestia,* Dec. 26, 1958, p. 3, Arts. 1 and 2 (translated in Leyden Texts, pp. 73-85) and the Statute on Military Crimes, *Izvestia,* Dec. 26, 1958, p. 4, Art. 11 (translated in Leyden Texts, pp. 87-111 and in CDSP, March 11, 1959, pp. 5-7).

10. *Cf.* Harold J. Berman, Introduction, *The Trial of the U-2,* i, xxii (Chicago, 1960); A. N. Shelepin, *supra* note 1 at 409.

11. "In effect, the burden of proof is on the prosecution, and no inference of guilt may be drawn from the indictment. This is basically what 'presumption of innocence' means. The reason given for the rejection of the phrase —some Soviet jurists argued for its inclusion in the 1958 Fundamental Principles of Criminal Procedure—is that it is not understood properly and is translated into Russian as 'The accused is *considered* innocent until proved guilty.' This is incorrect, it is argued, since the only significance of the 'presumption' is to cast the burden of proof on the prosecution; if the accused were 'considered' innocent, he could not even be kept under arrest.

"The rule that no inference of guilt may be drawn from the indictment is of special importance in a system of preliminary investigation such as the Soviet. It is sometimes charged against that type of system that the trial is in effect an appeal from the indictment. The tendency to attach excessive importance to the findings contained in the indictment is to some extent counteracted, however, by the requirement that the prosecution must prove the charges contained therein.

"The 1958 Fundamental Principles do not expressly state

that the burden of proof is on the prosecution, but instead state that the burden of proof may not be placed upon the accused, and also that a conviction may not be based on 'assumptions,' but can be handed down 'only if in the course of the court trial the person has been proved guilty of having committed a crime.' These formulations presuppose a trial procedure quite different from the Anglo-American. In the first place, although the burden of proof is on the prosecution in the sense that if the accused is not proved guilty the prosecution loses and he is acquitted, the system of trial procedure permits the proof of guilt to be adduced in a variety of ways and not necessarily by the prosecution. As an American lawyer would put it, the prosecution has the burden of persuasion but not the burden of going forward with evidence. In fact, in the usual Soviet criminal trial—as in the usual Continental European criminal trial—the interrogation of witnesses and of the accused is conducted chiefly by the judges. Thus the court takes initiative in eliciting evidence.

"In addition, Soviet law—and Continental European systems generally—do not use the phrase 'proof beyond a reasonable doubt.' In all cases, criminal or civil, the court, it is said, must be 'convinced' of the guilt of the accused or else it must acquit him." Berman, *op. cit., supra* note 10 at p. xxi.

12. Compare Art. 17 of the R.S.F.S.R. Criminal Code (1956 ed.) with Art. 17 of the 1958 Fundamental Principles of Criminal Law which requires an intent to participate in the crime.

13. Compare R.S.F.S.R. Criminal Code (1956 ed.), Art. 588 with 1958 Statute on State Crimes, Art. 3.

14. Compare the "Decree on Responsibility for Disclosure of State Secrets and for Loss of Documents Containing State Secrets, Disclosure of Which Shall be Punished by Law," *Izvestia,* June 10, 1947 (translated in Berman and Kerner Documents 102-103) with the Decree of the Council of Ministers of the U.S.S.R. of April 28, 1956, printed in V. D. Men'shagin and B. A. Kurinov, *Nauchno-Prakticheskii kommentarii k zakonu ob ugolovnoi otvetstven-*

nosti za gosudarstvennye prestupleniia (Scientific-Practical Commentary to the Law on Criminal Responsibility for State Crimes, 2nd rev. ed., Moscow, 1961), pp. 27-28.

15. In 1953 there were about three million prisoners in labor camps, according to a Soviet source, and in 1957 about one million, of whom about one per cent had committed "political" crimes. See Harold J. Berman, "Soviet Law Reform—Dateline Moscow 1957," *Yale Law Journal*, LXVI, 1194-1196 (1957).

16. Statute on State Crimes, Art. 7.

17. Compare 1958 Fundamental Principles of Criminal Procedure, Art. 22, with Art. 239 of the R.S.F.S.R. Code of Criminal Procedure (1957 ed.).

18. Compare Art. 48 of the 1958 Fundamental Principles of Criminal Procedure with the Decree of the Presidium of the Supreme Court of the U.S.S.R. On the Procedure for Consideration of Cases by Presidia of Courts, Vedomosti, 1955, No. 7, Item 166.

19. Compare Art. 35 of the 1958 Fundamental Principles of Criminal Procedure with Arts. 74, 78, 175-188 of the R.S.F.S.R. Code of Criminal Procedure (1957 ed.).

20. Compare R.S.F.S.R. Criminal Code (1956 ed.), Art. 16, with the 1958 Fundamental Principles of Criminal Law, Art. 7. The doctrine had been severely criticized and considerably limited in scope from the mid-1930's. See Chapter 1.

21. Edict of the Presidium of the Supreme Soviet of the R.S.F.S.R. of Dec. 19, 1956, On Responsibility for Petty Hooliganism, *Sovetskaia Rossia* (Soviet Russia), Dec. 20, 1956 (translated in CDSP, Jan. 16, 1957, p. 18) as amended, Vedomosti, 1961, No. 16, p. 248 (translated in CDSP, May 24, 1961, p. 9).

22. Any woman may now have a legal abortion if she requests it. However, the person performing the abortion is subject to punishment if he lacks a medical education or does not follow established procedures. Edict of the Presidium of the Supreme Soviet of Nov. 23, 1955, On Repeal of the Prohibition of Abortions, Vedomosti, 1955, No. 22, Item 425.

23. Edict of the Presidium of the Supreme Soviet of the U.S.S.R. of April 25, 1956. On Repeal of Legal Responsibility of Workers and Employees for Wilfully Quitting an Enterprise or Institution and for Absence Without an Urgent Reason, Vedomosti, 1956, No. 10, Item 203. See Alexandrov, *Soviet Labour Law* (Nayar tr., Delhi, 1961), p. 111. (This is an Indian translation of a Soviet textbook published in 1959.) See also below, Chapter 3, pp. 149-150.

24. These and many other amnesty decrees are collected in P. S. Romashkin, *Amnistiia i pomilovanie v SSSR* (Amnesty and Pardon in the U.S.S.R., Moscow, 1959). The 1953 Amnesty Law is translated in Berman and Kerner Documents 121-122; the 1957 Amnesty Law is translated in CDSP, Dec. 11, 1957, p. 21. Soviet amnesties are also discussed in Berman and Kerner Text, pp. 98-100, 193.

25. New regulations on labor camps were issued in 1957 and 1958. However, they do not seem to have been published, though they are discussed at length in B. S. Utevskii, ed., *Sovetskoe ispravitel'no-trudovoe pravo* (Soviet Corrective-Labor Law), Moscow, 1960. Draft Principles of Corrective-Labor Legislation of the U.S.S.R. and the Union Republics were under consideration by the Legislative Proposals Commissions of the Supreme Soviet of the U.S.S.R. at the end of 1962, *Izvestia*, Dec. 16, 1962, p. 5.

26. See Utevskii, *op. cit. supra* note 25.

27. 1958 Fundamental Principles of Criminal Law, Art. 44.

28. Fundamental Principles of Civil Law of the U.S.S.R. and the Union Republics, *Izvestia*, Dec. 10, 1961, pp. 3-6, Art. 7.

29. Statute on the Procedures for the Hearing of Labor Disputes, Vedomosti, 1957, No. 4, Item 58. See below, Chapter 15.

30. Draft Principles of Legislation on Marriage and the Family were under consideration by the Legislative Proposals Commissions of the Supreme Soviet of the U.S.S.R. at the end of 1962, which would (among other things) ameliorate the position of the child born out of wedlock. *Izvestia*, Dec. 16, 1962, p. 5. See below, Chapter 14.

31. 1936 Constitution, Art. 14u.

32. See below, Chapter 8.

33. See D. S. Karev, ed., *Organizatsiia suda i prokuratury v SSSR* (Organization of Courts and the Procuracy in the U.S.S.R.) Moscow, 1961, pp. 77-78. The governing laws at present are the Fundamental Principles of Court Organization of the U.S.S.R. and the Union Republics, Vedomosti, 1959, No. 1, Item 6, (translated in CDSP, March 11, 1959, pp. 8-10) and the republican laws enacted in accordance therewith. See below, Chapter 12.

34. Vedomosti, 1961, No. 35, pp. 830-834 (translated in CDSP, Oct. 4, 1961, pp. 23-25).

35. *Sovetskaia Iustitsiia*, Sept. 1960, pp. 30-32 (translated in CDSP, Nov. 16, 1960, pp. 15-17). See below, Chapter 3.

36. See, *e.g.,* Statutes of the Bar of the R.S.F.S.R., Vedomosti RSFSR, 1962, No. 29, pp. 457-464 (translated in CDSP, Nov. 7, 1962, pp. 5-7). Note particularly Arts. 33 and 34.

37. A. I. Denisov, Chairman of the Legal Commission of the Council of Ministers of the U.S.S.R. in Vsesoiusnyi Institut Iuridecheskikh Nauk, *Vazhnyi etap v razvitii sovetskogo prava* (All-Union Institute of Juridical Sciences, An Important Stage in the Development of Soviet Law), Moscow, 1960, pp. 124-130.

38. Edict of the Presidium of the Supreme Soviet of the U.S.S.R. of June 19, 1958, On the Procedure for Publication and Entry into Force of Laws of the U.S.S.R., Decrees of the Supreme Soviet of the U.S.S.R., Edicts and Decrees of the Presidium of the Supreme Soviet of the U.S.S.R. See below, pp. 86, 235. Vedomosti, 1958, No. 14, Item 275 (translated in CDSP, Aug. 20, 1958, pp. 13-14).

39. See the Decree of the U.S.S.R. Council of Ministers of March 20, 1959, On the Procedure for Publication and Entry into Force of Decrees and Resolutions of the Government of the U.S.S.R., *Sobranie Postanovlenii SSSR* (Collected Decrees of the Government of the U.S.S.R.), No. 6, Item 37, reprinted in *Sbornik normativnykh materialov po voprosam vneshnei torgovli SSSR,* vypusk 1 (Collection of

normative materials on questions of the foreign trade of the U.S.S.R., issue 1), Moscow, 1961, pp. 50-51.

40. The R.S.F.S.R. Ministry of Internal Affairs was renamed Ministry of Protection of Social Order (*Ministerstvo Okhrany Obshchestvennogo Poriadka*) in 1962. In 1954 the security functions of the earlier all-union Ministry of Internal Affairs had been allocated to the Committee on State Security (KGB) of the U.S.S.R. Council of Ministers.

41. In its draft form, the Statute on Comrades' Courts provided for recommendation of discharge of a worker (Art. 15), but this power was removed from the law as finally passed. See *Izvestia*, Oct. 24, 1959, p. 2, translated in CDSP, Nov. 25, 1959, pp. 15-17. The Comrades' Courts are discussed more fully in Chapter 11.

42. See below, Chapter 11, pp. 291-294 for the text of the law.

43. The trial was widely reported in the Soviet press, but without any mention of the question of retroactivity. See *Pravda*, July 21, 1961, p. 6. In September 1961 the author was shown by a member of the U.S.S.R. Supreme Court a copy of the decree, No. 155/2, dated July 1, 1961, entitled "On the Extension [of the Edict of July 1, 1961] to Ia. T. Rokotov and V. P. Faibishenko." It stated: "As an exception the investigative organ shall be permitted to indict Ia. T. Rokotov and V. P. Faibishenko under part 2 of the Edict . . . of 1 July 1961 . . . and the court, if as a result of consideration of the case it considers it necessary, shall apply to them the sanction established by that edict . . ."

44. See Harold J. Berman, "Soviet Law Reform—Dateline Moscow 1957," *Yale Law Journal*, LXVI, 1191, 1214-1215 (1957).

45. New compilations of, and commentaries on, Lenin's views on law include: V. N. Avilin and A. A. Lipatov, compilers, *V. I. Lenin o gosudarstve i prave, Sbornik proizvedenii i dokumentov v dvukh tomakh* (V. I. Lenin on State and Law, a Collection of Works and Documents in Two Volumes, Moscow, 1958); V. M. Chkhikvadze, *Voprosy sotsialisticheskogo prava i zakonnosti v trudakh V. I. Lenina* (Questions of Socialist Law and Legality in

the Works of V. I. Lenin, Moscow, 1960); A. K. Goncharov, *et al.*, compilers, *V. I. Lenin o sotsialisticheskoi zakonnosti* (V. I. Lenin on Socialist Legality, Moscow, 1961); V. S. Petrov, *et al.*, *V. I. Lenin o gosudarstve i prave* (V. I. Lenin on State and Law), Leningrad, 1961.

46. 1936 Constitution, Art. 126.

47. See *supra* Chapter 1, footnote 28.

48. Shelepin, *supra* note 1.

49. See, *e.g.*, S. A. Golunskii, "Osnovnye napravleniia razvitiia obshchenarodnogo prava" (Basic Directions of Development of an All-People's Law), *Sovetskoe Gosudarstvo i Pravo* (Soviet State and Law), 1962, No. 11, p. 3; A. A. Piontkovskii, "K voprosu ob izuchenii obshchenarodnogo prava" (Toward the Problem of the Study of an All-People's Law), *Sovetskoe Gosudarstvo i Pravo*, 1962, No. 11, p. 15.

CHAPTER 3: SOVIET ECONOMIC LAW

1. Walton Hamilton and Irene Till, "Property," *The Encyclopedia of the Social Sciences* (1934).

2. In addition there were in certain industries *kombinats*, each comprising several plants producing complementary products. Also there still existed examples of an older form of combine, the *ob"edinenie* (union). The structure of Soviet industry was (and remains) in fact very complex; a simplified version is given here for analytical purposes.

2a. *Cf.* H. J. Berman and B. A. Konstantinovsky, *Soviet Law in Action* (Harvard, 1953), p. 38. (Odessa Bread Trust *v.* "The Red Needle-worker." The defendant cooperative was held liable for the cost of cloth materials furnished by the plaintiff for making of workers' uniforms. Apparently the defendant had swindled the plaintiff. Thereafter the plaintiff opened its own workshop for making uniforms.)

3. See O. S. Ioffe, *Pravovoe regulirovanie khoziaistven-*

noi deiatel'nosti v SSSR (Legal Regulation of Economic Activity in the U.S.S.R., Leningrad, 1959).

4. M. I. Bogolepov, "Finansovaia Sistema SSSR" (Financial System of the USSR; mimeographed, undated, approximately 1937, available at American Russian Institute, New York), pp. 55, 74.

5. M. I. Bogolepov, *The Soviet Financial System* (London, 1945), pp. 8-9.

6. *Cf.* Alexander Baykov, *The Development of the Soviet Economic System* (Cambridge, 1948), pp. 294-295. The ending of subsidies in principle did not mean the ending of them for all branches of industry. In 1962 over 20 per cent of Soviet industry was said to require subsidies.

7. See John N. Hazard, "The Public Corporation in the USSR," in *The Public Corporation: A Comparative Symposium* (Friedman ed., Toronto, 1954), pp. 374-409; O. S. Ioffe, "Grazhdanskoe pravo," (Civil law) in *Sorok let sovetskogo prava* (Forty years of Soviet Law, Leningrad, 1957); A. V. Venediktov, *Gosudarstvennaia sotsialisticheskaia sobstvennost'* (State socialist property, Moscow-Leningrad, 1948).

8. Decree (on Bonuses) of the Central Committee of the CPSU and the Council of Ministers of the U.S.S.R. of July 2, 1959, SP SSSR, No. 14, Item 88, reprinted in *Sbornik zakonodatel'nykh aktov o trude* (Collection of Legislative Acts on Labor, 3rd rev. & enl. ed., Moscow, 1960), p. 272; K. V. Sheliutto and E. N. Borovskaia, *Premirovanie inzhenerno-tekhnicheskikh rabotnikov po sovetskomu pravu* (Payment of Engineering and Technical Employees under Soviet Law, Moscow, 1962).

On September 9, 1962, an article in *Pravda* by E. Liberman, Professor at the Kharkov Engineering and Economics Institute, set off a great controversy among Soviet economists on the role of profits in a planned economy. Liberman proposed that *norms* of profit should be set for various industries and enterprises, and that the *rate* of profit of a particular enterprise (measured against the applicable norm) should be the primary success indicator upon which bonuses would be based. The Western press hailed this as a proposal to return to capitalism, and were encouraged in this view by Khrushchev's favorable comments on the Liberman proposals at the November 1962 Plenum of the Communist Party, at which he quoted Lenin's words, "Be able if necessary to learn from the capitalists. Adopt whatever they have that is sensible and advantageous."

The significance of the Liberman proposals was thrown out of focus by the tendency of some Western writers on the Soviet economy unduly to minimize the role which profits have played in the Soviet economy in the past. It is, of course, true that profits do not serve as a *direct* guide to investment in the Soviet Union, as they do in the United States. Nevertheless, the net income which a Soviet enterprise derives from its operations is one of the principal success indicators; even before the 1959 decree a manager who overfulfilled his gross output plan only by excessive expenditures for labor and materials would have fewer bonuses and fewer chances of promotion.

Liberman's proposals would eliminate, at the enterprise level, centrally determined planned tasks for labor productivity, number of workers, wages, production costs, capital savings, capital investment and new technology. These tasks would be set by the enterprise itself. The enterprise's planned tasks for quantitative production, product assortment, and deliveries would remain centrally determined. (Indeed, Liberman seems to impose greater restrictions on managerial leeway in making deliveries than under the existing system.) Thus there would be no restriction from above upon a manager's decision to hire more labor or to build new plant or to introduce new production techniques, but he would still be under orders to produce and deliver to other enterprises a fixed minimum of particular goods. His bonuses, however, would depend solely on the percentage of profit which would be fixed as normal for his industry or enterprise. The latter figure would be calculated partly on the basis of the capital invested in his enterprise. He could use extra profits for his own capital investment.

One principal difficulty of these proposals is the necessity they entail for creating a new structure of prices which would more adequately reflect the actual value of goods. Hitherto the absence of a system of charges on fixed capital has introduced a strong element of artificiality into the Soviet price system.

Liberman's proposals also contain features designed to encourage the manager to seek higher targets of production. At present managers seek to have lower production targets, so that they can overfulfill them more easily and thus earn larger profits while at the same time having a lower *rate* of profits.

Western economists who stress the "command" features of the Soviet economy often underestimate, in the author's opinion, the extent to which the large number of indicators which are required if central "commands" are to be effective, permit industrial managers to juggle the indicators, and thus run their enterprises, in effect, as seems most expedient to them; and secondly, in stressing the "cult of gross output," Western economists often underestimate the role of money values and net money income in determining Soviet managerial bonuses. It is just because profits (without allowance for charges on capital) have in fact played such an important role in determining managerial decisions that Professor Liberman proposed to reform the profit system.

Liberman's original article and subsequent Soviet discussion thereof may be found in translation in the Current Digest of the Soviet Press, October 3, 1962 and thereafter in almost every issue through the end of 1962.

9. See A. K. R. Kiralfy, "Attempts to formulate a Legal Theory of Public Ownership," *Soviet Studies,* VIII (1957), 236; see also the works cited in note 7 supra.

10. See Harold J. Berman, "Commercial Contracts in Soviet Law," *California Law Review* XXXV (1947), 191; Ia. A. Donde, Z. M. Friedman, and G. I. Chirkov, *Khoziastvennyi dogovor i ego rol' v snabzhenii narodnogo khoziaistva SSSR* (The Economic Contract and its Role in the Supply of the National Economy of the U.S.S.R., Moscow, 1960); Kasimierz Grzybowski, *Soviet Legal Institutions, Doctrines and Social Functions* (Ann Arbor,

1962), pp. 41-109; V. N. Mozheiko, *Khoziastvennyi dogovor v SSSR* (The Economic Contract in the U.S.S.R., Moscow, 1962); O. S. Ioffe, *Sovetskoe grazhdanskoe pravo* (Soviet Civil Law, Leningrad, 1958-1961), II; Herbert S. Levine, "The Centralized Planning of Supply in Soviet Industry," in *Comparisons of the United States and Soviet Economies,* printed for the use of the Joint Economic Committee, 86th Congress, 1st Session (Washington, 1959).

11. "The Council of People's Commissars of the U.S.S.R. takes note of the following important deficiencies in the conclusion and fulfillment of contracts in 1935: (a) the substitution, in a series of instances, for low and intermediate business organizations, of centers of economic systems, which have concluded detailed general contracts without regard for the concrete particularities and problems of lower organizations subordinate to them; (b) the unpermissible practice of delivering goods to low organizations on orders of superior organs, without orders of the low organizations; (c) the unsatisfactory performance of contracts, in a series of instances. . . Proceeding from this, the Council of People's Commissars of the U.S.S.R. directs: the basic form of contracts for 1936 shall be Direct Contracts concluded predominantly by low and intermediate links of (the various) economic systems . . ." (Decree of the Council of People's Commissars of the U.S.S.R., "On the Conclusion of Contracts for 1936," January 15, 1936. SZ SSSR, 1936, No. 3, Item 27).

12. Decree of the Council of Ministers, April 21, 1949, in *Sobranie Postanovlenii i Rasporiazhenii Soveta Ministrov SSSR* (Collection of Decrees and Orders of the Council of Ministers of the U.S.S.R.), 1949, No. 9, Item 68. See also I. Baranov, "Khoziaistvennyi dogovor—orudie vypolneniia gosudarstvennykh planov" (The Economic Contract —a Weapon for the Fulfillment of State Plans), *Planovoe Khoziaistvo* (Planned Ecomomy), 1949, No. 5, p. 63.

13. Decree of the Council of Ministers, May 22, 1959, SP SSSR, 1959, No. 11, Item 68, reprinted in *Zakono-*

datel' nye akty po voprosam narodnogo khoziaistva SSSR (Legislative Acts on Questions of the National Economy of the U.S.S.R., Moscow, 1961) (hereafter cited as Legislative Acts), I, 443-459.

14. See the Decree of the Council of Ministers, June 23, 1959, SP SSSR, 1959, No. 15, Item 105 (Legislative Acts, I, pp. 742-744) and the Temporary Rules for Consideration of Economic Cases by Arbitrators, August 31, 1961, in Legislative Acts, I, pp. 750-752.

15. The matters discussed in this paragraph are largely governed by the Decree cited in footnote 14 and by the Statute on State Arbitrazh, August 17, 1960, SP SSSR, 1960, No. 15, Item 127 (Legislative Acts, I, pp. 745-750), translated in *Current Digest of the Soviet Press,* Nov. 16, 1960, pp. 15-17.

16. Similar materials and scholarly articles were contained in the pre-war journal *Arbitrazh,* now discontinued.

17. V. N. Mozheiko and Z. I. Shkundin, *Arbitrazh v sovetskom khoziastve* (Arbitrazh in the Soviet Economy; Moscow, 1938), pp. 10, 21. The same position is taken in A. F. Kleinman ed., *Arbitrazh v SSSR* (Arbitrazh in the U.S.S.R., Moscow, 1960), pp. 16-17.

18. Supra note 15.

19. *Sbornik instruktivnikh ukazanii gosudarstvennogo arbitrazha* (Collection of Instructions of State Arbitrazh), No. 14 (1960), pp. 33-35.

20. See Zoltan M. Mihaly, "The Role of Civil Law Institutions in the Management of Communist Economies: The Hungarian Experience," *American Journal of Comparative Law,* VIII (1959), 310, 321.

21. This case was first reported in *Sotsialisticheskaia Zakonnost'* (Socialist Legality), 1960, No. 10 with a headnote by Gosarbitrazh implying that in case of failure to receive raw materials the supplier is relieved of responsibility. A fuller report appeared in *Sotsialisticheskaia Zakonnost',* 1960, No. 12, p. 77 with an explanation indicating that the first headnote was erroneously phrased in too general terms and did not indicate the special circum-

stances of this case. The latter report is translated in John N. Hazard and Isaac Shapiro, *The Soviet Legal System* (New York, 1962), II, 127-128.

22. See V. N. Mozheiko, *Khoziaistvennyi dogovor v SSSR* (Moscow, 1962), pp. 150-151, citing a letter of Gosarbitrazh of August 6, 1960, No. I-77.

23. See P. V. Smirnov and R. B. Taras'iants, *Organizatsiia i planirovanie sbyta promyshlennoi produktsii v SSSR* (Organization and Planning of the Supply of Industrial Products in the U.S.S.R., Moscow, 1960), pp. 109-110.

24. Zoltan M. Mihaly, "The Role of Civil Law Institutions in the Management of Communist Economies: The Hungarian Experience," *American Journal of Comparative Law*, VIII, 310, 315-316 (1959).

25. The provisions of Articles 30 and 147 of the R.S.F.S.R. Civil Code are incorporated in Article 14 of the Fundamentals of Civil Legislation of the U.S.S.R. and the Union Republics, but are altered somewhat in the interests of protecting innocent, or merely careless, parties.

26. See Harold J. Berman, Book Review, *Harvard Law Review*, LXVI, pp. 950, 954-955 (1953); Harold J. Berman and Boris A. Konstantinovsky, *Soviet Law in Action: The Recollected Cases of a Soviet Lawyer* (Cambridge, Mass., 1953), pp. 46-47.

27. *Cf.* A. V. Venediktov, *Gosudarstvennaia Sotsialisticheskaia Sobstvennost'*, (State Socialist Ownership, Moscow-Leningrad, 1948), p. 438.

CHAPTER 4: SOCIALIST AND CAPITALIST LAW

1. In this connection a remark of President Roosevelt to Sumner Welles appears particularly apt. Welles writes: "[Roosevelt said that] he regarded the American form of democracy as being at the opposite pole from the original form of Soviet Communism. In the years which had elapsed since the Soviet revolution of 1917, the Soviet system had advanced materially toward a modified form of state socialism. In the same way, the American polity since that

time had progressed toward the ideal of true political and social justice. He believed that American democracy and Soviet Communism could never meet. But he told me that he did believe that if one took the figure 100 as representing the difference between American democracy and Soviet Communism in 1917, with the United States at 100 and the Soviet Union at 0, American democracy might eventually reach the figure of 60 and the Soviet system might reach the figure of 40. The gap between these two final figures it seemed to him would never lessen" (*Where Are We Heading* [New York, 1946], p. 37).

2. Gsovski, *Soviet Civil Law* (Ann Arbor, 1948), I, pp. 432ff. draws quite different conclusions from the ones here presented. He considers the Soviet state economic enterprises to be "sham corporations" and their contracts to be "sham contracts." His analysis is based, however, on a rather narrow conception of the nature of a corporation, and it would follow from his premises that the Tennessee Valley Authority, the Port of New York Authority, and other American government corporations, must also be considered "sham." Thus Gsovski finds the essence of a corporation to be the fact that a group of persons join and act together for a common purpose; he also argues that the fact that the Soviet state business enterprises issue no shares of stock and are incapable of holding title deprives them of legal personality. Not only our government corporations but also many private business corporations are formed for purposes other than joint enterprise, however. As to the issuance of stock and the capacity to hold title, stock is merely evidence of ownership and control, which is vested in the government anyway, and United States courts have generally treated the property of our government corporations as property of the United States.

Of course, it would be absurd not to recognize the difference between public and private corporations. However, the words "corporation," "property," "contract," are applicable to both.

Evsey Rashba points out that the legal system elaborated during the NEP has been further and further developed while at the same time the principle of planned economy is also extended to the limit. "Those engaged in economic activities can now be viewed, once again [that is, as under War Communism] as soldiers on a production front, subject to admonition and order. They can, on the other hand, be viewed as persons who continue to buy, to sell, and to transact all kinds of business. An economy having both these aspects cannot be regulated by simply reverting to the traditional law. . . . This novel two-faced system, involving concepts which we have not learned about in law schools, must of necessity give rise to new legal techniques" (Evsey Rashba, Book Review, *Harvard Law Review*, LXIII [1950], 923).

3. Hermann Mannheim, *Criminal Justice and Social Reconstruction* (London, 1946), pp. 109*ff*.

CHAPTER 5: MARXISM AND THE RUSSIAN HERITAGE

1. The first edition of this book was criticized by some reviewers for attempting to present such a broad comparison in a few pages. Yet without such a comparison it is impossible to see Soviet law in proper perspective, and in an interpretive study such as this a fuller historical treatment would be out of place. On the Western legal tradition there is little in English which can be recommended; the reader of German is referred to Paul Koschaker, *Europa und das römische Recht* (3rd ed., Munich and Berlin, 1958). On Russian legal history, see Samuel Kucherov, *Courts, Lawyers and Trials under the Last Three Tsars* (New York, 1953).

CHAPTER 6: THE WESTERN LEGAL TRADITION

The author is greatly indebted in the following pages to the interpretation of the Western Revolutions given by Eugen Rosenstock-Huessy. See especially Rosenstock-Huessy's *The Driving Power of Western Civilization* (Boston, 1949); *Out of Revolution: The Autobiography of Western Man*

(New York, 1938); *Die Europäischen Revolutionen* (Jena, 1932).

1. In context the passage is as follows: For one who judges another . . . condemns himself. Let him therefore know himself and purge himself of what he sees offends others. . . . *Let him who is without sin cast the first stone at her.* (John, viii, 7) . . . For no one was without sin in that it is understood that all have been guilty of crime. For venial sins will always be remitted [only] by holy rites. If therefore the sin was one of these, it was criminal. . . . Let the spiritual judge beware, in order thereby not to commit the crime of injustice, that he not fail to fortify himself with knowledge. It is fitting that he should know how to recognize what he is to judge. For the judicial power is based on the assumption that he discerns what he is to judge. Therefore the diligent inquisitor, the subtle investigator, wisely and almost cunningly interrogates the sinner about that which the sinner perhaps does not know, or because of shame will wish to hide. . . . We write this to you, devotee of truth and lover of certainty, concerning true penitence, separating the truth from the false. . . . ("De Vera et Falsa Poenitentia" c. xx. Migne, *Patrologia Latina,* XL, 1129-30 [pseudo-Augustinian, *circa* 1050].)

Rosenstock-Huessy states that the entire tract was incorporated by Gratian into his *Decretum,* as well as by Peter Lombard into his *Sententiae.* He adds: "It expresses an idea which is quite foreign to antiquity and to classical Roman law, marking the transition from liturgical and sacramental thinking to a science of jurisprudence." *Cf.* Rudolph Sohm, *Das altkatholische Kirchenrecht und das Dekret Gratians* (Leipzig, 1918).

2. In the formative period of English legal history, prior to the fourteenth century, equity was administered in all the English courts, including the King's Bench and Common Pleas. See Harold D. Hazeltine, "The Early History of English Equity," in Paul Vinogradoff, ed., *Essays in Legal History* (Oxford University Press, 1913), p. 261.

English development was unique, in that in the fourteenth and fifteenth centuries the common law courts restricted their jurisdiction largely to land law and ceased to grant equitable remedies. As a result equity came to be administered as such in the Chancellor's court. Only if law is treated as something distinct from equity can English law be treated in isolation from the rest of European law.

CHAPTER 7: THE SPIRIT OF RUSSIAN LAW

* The following pages represent an attempt to describe and interpret in a relatively few pages the whole of Russian legal history. Undoubtedly the lines are drawn too sharply, in the sense that many qualifying facts are omitted. As in the other parts of the book, the present purpose is to give a suggestive interpretation rather than an exhaustive description. Here, in particular, attention is directed to those aspects of Russian legal history which seem most meaningful for our understanding of Soviet law today. For this reason the author has felt justified in not dealing with the unsuccessful efforts to establish representative governments in the formative stages of Russian development. Students of Russian history will also miss reference to the fact that serfdom was never universal, the fact that the peasant commune did not exist in certain large areas, and many other similar facts important in themselves but not important enough to alter the essential outlines of the picture here presented.

The influence of Professor George Vernadsky of Yale University will be noticed in many parts of the chapter. See especially George Vernadsky, *A History of Russia* (rev. ed.; New Haven, 1944); *Medieval Russian Laws* (New York, 1947); *Ocherk istorii prava Rossiiskogo gosudarstva XVIII i XIX vv.* (Outline of the History of the Law of the Russian State in the XVIII and XIX Centuries; Prague, 1924); "The Scope and Content of Chingis Khan's *Yasa*," *Harvard Journal of Asiatic Studies,* III (1938), 337; "Feudalism in Russia," *Speculum,* XIV (1939), 300.

1. *The Russkaia Pravda* of Yaroslav, and the revision of his sons, are translated, together with other medieval legal documents, by Vernadsky in *Medieval Russian Laws.*

2. See especially V. A. Riasanovsky, *Fundamental Principles of Mongol Law* (Tientsin, 1937).

3. Philip condemned Ivan to his face at a Church service. According to the report of Elert Kruse in 1572 (as given in F. von Adelung, *Reisende in Russland,* I, 266-267), Philip said: "Most merciful Tsar and Grand Duke, how long wilt thou shed the innocent blood of thy faithful people and Christians? How long shall unrighteousness last in this Russian empire? The Tartars and the heathen and the whole world knows that all other peoples have law and justice, only in Russia is there none; in the whole world evildoers who seek mercy from the authorities find it, and here in Russia there is no pity for the innocent and the righteous. Remember, however, although God lifts thee up in the world, thou art nevertheless a mortal man, and He will demand the innocent blood of thy hands. The stones under thy feet, if not the living souls, will complain, cry and judge over thee; and I must tell it to thee at God's command, even though I accept and receive death for it" (quoted in Valentin Gitterman, *Geschichte Russlands* [Zurich, 1944] I, 431).

4. The following description of the efforts at codification is taken largely from M. M. Speranski, *Precis des notions historiques sur la formation du corps des lois russes, traduit de russe* (Saint-Petersbourg, 1833).

5. See N. S. Timasheff, "The Impact of the Penal Law of Imperial Russia on Soviet Penal Law," *The American Slavic and East European Review,* Vol. XII, No. 4 (Dec. 1953), p. 441; and Timasheff, "Das Strafprozessrecht der Sowjetunion in seinem Verhältnis zum kaiserlich-russischen Recht," *Osteuropa-recht,* Vol. 2, No. 1 (May 1956), p. 194.

6. It is doubtless true that the "case method" is an Anglo-American and not a Continental European institution, strictly speaking. This fact is particularly important in

comparing legal education on the Continent with that of the United States (though not so much of England). In the operation of the legal system itself, however, many scholars are coming to feel that the differences between the two systems have been greatly exaggerated. Although the Anglo-American tradition was developed largely without codes, it has always had a body of principles to perform many of the functions of the European codes; at the same time, continental European legal systems have not minimized the importance of cases, at least in practice. In any event the distinction between "case law" and "code law" is not relevant to the argument made here concerning the unhistorical character—as compared with Western law—of the Russian legal system.

CHAPTER 8: THE RUSSIAN CHARACTER OF SOVIET LAW

1. Michael Karpovich, in reading the manuscript of the first edition of this book, noted: "The case of Stalin is particularly illuminating. He was sent into administrative exile several times. The police knew that he was an important revolutionary, but they could not send him to hard labor or to prison *because they had no evidence against him.* Personally, I find in this rather a touching concern for legality."

1a. See below Chapter 11.

2. A. N. Iodkovskii, "O kodifikatsii zakonodatel'stva Soiuza SSR" (On the Codification of the Legislation of the U.S.S.R.) *Sovetskoe Gosudarstvo i Pravo* (Soviet State and Law), 1949, No. 4, p. 18.

3. See *supra* p. 76.

4. See *supra* pp. 76-77.

5. For the situation prior to 1948 see Vladimir Gsovski, *Soviet Civil Law* (Ann Arbor, 1948), I, 224-229.

6. Ernest Lehr, *Eléments de droit civil russe* (Paris, 1877), p. xi.

7. See generally Glenn G. Morgan, *Soviet Administrative*

Legality: The Role of the Attorney General's Office (Stanford, 1962) and citations therein to Soviet and Western literature on the Procuracy.

8. *Cf.* S. Jägerskiöld, "Swedish Ombudsman," *University of Pennsylvania Law Review,* CIX (1961), 1077; B. Cristensen, "Danish Ombudsman," *Id.,* 1100; *The Citizen and the Administration: The Redress of Grievances (A Report by "Justice")* (London, 1961).

8a. "Procurator's Protest on Violation of Art. 118 of the Constitution of the U.S.S.R.," *Sotsialisticheskaia Zakonnost'* (Socialist Legality), 1960, No. 5, p. 87. This and other cases of protests by the Procuracy against administrative regulations are translated in John N. Hazard and Isaac Shapiro, *The Soviet Legal System* (N.Y., 1962), Chapter XV.

9. *The Brothers Karamazov* (Modern Library ed.), pp. 72-74.

10. Maurice Baring, *The Mainsprings of Russia* (Edinburgh, 1914), pp. 282*ff.*

11. The German Supreme Court has declared the subjective standard to apply, but Mannheim has stated that nevertheless it "has really never treated the subjective standard seriously." (Hermann Mannheim, *"Mens Rea* in German and English Criminal Law," *Journal of Comparative Legislation and International Law,* XVII (1935), 100).

12. Vsesoiuznyi Institut Iuridicheskikh Nauk, *Ugolovnoe pravo—obshchaia chast'* (All-Union Institute of Juridical Science, "Criminal Law—General Part") Moscow, 1948, pp. 346ff. The "reasonable man" standard is explicitly rejected.

13. A. A. Piontkovskii, *Uchenie o prestuplenii po sovetskomu ugolovnomu pravu* (The Theory of Crime in Soviet Criminal Law, Moscow, 1961), p. 379. The same passage appears almost word for word in the treatise cited in note 12 *supra.*

14. Piontkovskii, above, footnote 12 at p. 381. Grzybowski reaches an opposite conclusion from the one here presented, but relies on lower court decisions criticized by Soviet writers and inconsistent with Supreme Court de-

cisions. See Kasimierz Grzybowski, *Soviet Legal Institutions* (Ann Arbor, 1962), pp. 137-140.

15. *Pravda,* Nov. 20, 1962, pp. 1-8, translated in *Current Digest of the Soviet Press,* XIV, No. 48 (Dec. 26, 1962), 3-9.

16. See Chap. 2. The history of capital punishment in Russia illustrates a tendency to fluctuate between the aspiration of humanitarian leniency and the demands of political firmness. According to the fourteenth-century manuscript of the Lavrentian chronicle, Vladimir Monomach in the year 1095 ordained: "Do not kill either the just or the unjust, nor command that he be killed; though he might deserve death, do not destroy a Christian soul." This may express what Maynard calls the Russian's "special horror of the legal enforcement, with all its paraphernalia and solemnity, of the capital sentence." (This theme recurs particularly in the writings of Dostoevsky, as, for example, in *The Idiot.*) With the development of a modern criminal law in the fifteenth and sixteenth centuries, nevertheless, capital punishment was introduced, and the *Ulozhenie* of 1649 expanded the application of the death penalty to nearly all types of crimes. However, Russia seems to have been the first country in Europe actually to abolish capital punishment when the institution was under fire from the philosophers of the eighteenth-century Enlightenment. The absolute prohibition against execution, enacted by Empress Elizabeth in 1754, only remained in force for a brief period. From then on it was applied, but for political crimes only, down to February 1917. Both the Provisional Government and the Bolsheviks experimented with abolition, the Bolsheviks abolishing capital punishment first in June 1918 and again in 1919, each time restoring it after a few months when the political situation worsened. Its application was confined to political offenses and, after 1932, theft of state property. Always against it in theory, the Soviet government again abolished the death penalty in May 1947. The decree explicitly stated (and the commentators emphasized) that the reasons for the new law were: first, "the historic victory of the Soviet

people" in the recent war and "their exceptional devotion
. . . to the Soviet Motherland and government"; and
second, that "the cause of peace can be considered secure
despite attempts being made by aggressive elements to
provoke war." The decree then stated: "Considering these
circumstances and in response to the wishes of the trade
unions of workers and employees and other authoritative
organizations expressing the opinion of large circles of people, the Presidium of the Supreme Soviet of the U.S.S.R.
feels that the application of death sentences is no longer
necessary under peacetime conditions." In January 1950,
the death penalty was restored for treason, espionage,
wrecking, terrorist acts and banditism and in 1954 for
murder committed under aggravating circumstances. Application of the death penalty was considerably expanded
by 1961 and 1962 decrees discussed in Chapter 2. However the 1961 Party Program still promises the eventual
elimination of capital punishment.

17. Gsovski, above, footnote 5, 776-777. Acknowledgment is made to Michigan University and to Dr. Gsovski for
permission to use this passage. Gsovski's chapters on agrarian
law are probably the best in his book. See also William T.
Shinn, Jr., "The Law of the Russian Peasant Household,"
Slavic Review, XX (1961), 601-621. A recent Soviet book
on the subject is M. P. Voloshin, *Pravo lichnoi sobstven-
nosti kolkhoznogo dvora* (The Law of Personal Ownership
of the Collective Farm Household, Moscow, 1961).

18. *Sudebnaia Praktika Verkhovnogo Suda SSSR* (Judicial Practice of the Supreme Court of the U.S.S.R.), 1946,
IX (XXXIII), 13.

19. See Gsovski, above, footnote 5, 703.

20. *Sudebnaia Praktika Verkhovnogo Suda SSSR,* 1944,
VI (XII), 28.

CHAPTER 10: LAW OF A NEW TYPE

1. See M. Kareva, *Rol' sovetskogo prava v vospitanii
kommunisticheskogo soznaniia* (The Role of Soviet Law in

the Education of Communist Consciousness), *Bol'shevik*, 1947, No. 4, p. 47.

2. Nicholas S. Timasheff, *The Great Retreat: The Growth and Decline of Communism in Russia* (New York, 1946), p. 225. The quotation refers specifically to the school and the family, but it also expresses the general theme of the book.

3. See L. I. Petrazhitskii, *Teoriia prava i gosudarstva v sviazi s teoriei nravstvennosti* (The Theory of Law and State in Connection with the Theory of Character; Saint Petersburg, 1909). Petrazhitskii gave the name "intuitive" law to the "law in the minds of men." See H. W. Babb, "Petrazhitskii: Science of Legal Policy and Theory of Law," *Boston University Law Review*, XVII (1937), 793.

4. Thurman Arnold, *The Symbols of Government* (New Haven, 1935), p. 129.

5. Lenin stated as the most important task of the new Soviet courts that of *"securing the strictest carrying out of the discipline and self-discipline of the toilers.* We would be ridiculous utopians if we imagined that such a task could be realized on the next day after the fall of the power of the bourgeoisie, that is, in the first stage of transition from capitalism to socialism, or (that it could be realized) without compulsion. *Without compulsion* such a task is completely unrealizable. The Soviet courts must be an organ of the proletarian state, realizing such compulsion. *And on them is imposed the huge task of educating the population to labor discipline."* (*Works* (4th Russian ed.), XXVII, 191.) The educational role of the courts continued to be emphasized. The changes in the mid-1930's only affected this idea insofar as they gave new dignity to the concept of law, which was now to survive into socialism and even communism. Of course law has never been considered the only or even the most important Soviet instrument of education, but since the mid-1930's its prestige has been considerably enhanced. At the same time there has developed a much greater respect for the educational value of traditional legal institutions—of criminal sanctions, for example. Law now educates by its very dignity and authority.

This is a shift in emphasis which reflects the new goals of such "legal education." See the discussion in Chapter I.

6. Karl N. Llewellyn, "Lectures on Jurisprudence" (mimeographed; 1948). Llewellyn contrasts the "adversary" with the "parental" system, drawing for his definition of "parental" on the law of the New Mexican Pueblo Indians, the medieval Inquisition, and the Soviet trials of major political offenders. He lists the following characteristics of the parental system: (1) the court may dig up evidence for the defendant. (2) The court may make a prior investigation of facts. (3) The objective of the trial is reintegration of the offender with the Entirety; confession and repentance are normal preliminaries to a treatment viewed primarily as reeducational ("making an example," elimination of the offender, are out of key with the procedure, an extreme measure of panic; love for the Entirety and for the erring member is the proper emotional and intellectual keynote). (4) Criminal and civil offenses tend to merge, though reparation and restitution aspects are readily seen as involving private rights which need to be respected. (5) It is natural and right to draw into the case any past misconduct, even though previously punished, and defendant's attitude as well as his actions; prior good conduct can weigh in mitigation (the wrong was a mere lapse) or in severity (knowledge and experience entail extra responsibility); not the offense alone but the whole man is in question.

Llewellyn here focuses on the parental role of the court, particularly in its procedural aspects. Roscoe Pound uses the word "socialization" to describe the dominant tendency of American legal development in the twentieth century, focusing on the changes in substantive law. There is a close connection between Pound's "socialization" (which is not necessarily connected with socialism in the Soviet sense of a planned economy) and Llewellyn's "parentalism." Pound lists the following changes: (1) growing limitations on an owner's use of his own property, and notably on the antisocial exercise of rights; (2) growing limitations on freedom of contract; (3) growing limitations on an owner's freedom of disposition of his own property; (4) growing limitations on the power of a creditor or an injured party to exact satisfaction; (5) liability without fault merging into the insurance principle of liability, making enterprises and ultimately the community as a whole responsible for agencies employed for their benefit; (6) increased assertion of public rights in basic natural resources ("the change of *res communes* and *res nullius* into *res publicae*"); (7) growing intervention of society through law to protect dependent persons, whether physically or economically dependent; (8) tendency to hold that public funds should respond for injuries to individuals by public agencies; (9) replacement of a purely contentious conception of litigation by one of adjustment of interests; (10) reading of the obligation of contract as subject to the overriding requirement of reasonableness, of which, despite current confusion of grounds, the doctrine of frustration seems to be an example; (11) increased legal recognition of groups and persons in stable relations to each other as legal units instead of exclusive recognition of individuals and juristic persons as their analogues (the collective labor contract, and the "common rule" of an industry, and the labor union itself are examples); (12) the tendency to relax the rule as to trespassers (Roscoe Pound, *Outlines of Lectures on Jurisprudence* [5th ed.; Cambridge: Harvard University Press, 1943], pp. 43-48).

The idea of parental law and the idea of socialized law (in Pound's sense) are brought together in Petrazhitskii's phrase, "the socialization of the psyche."

Obviously many of the features of parental law exist in all legal systems. The reason that a new term such as parental law is needed is to indicate a shift in the center of gravity of the legal system. Any particular rule or institution of the Soviet legal system may be found in some other system; the ensemble, however, is different.

One difficulty with the word "parental" is that it may connote the idea of kinship in a literal sense. Of course the state does not literally reproduce the litigants in a parental system of law. "Parental" is used here in a broader and more figurative sense. The state, through law, plays the role of guardian, and the individual before the law is like a ward.

Any absolutism tends toward parentalism. Parental law should not, however, be identified with the absolute state as such. In many ways a more appropriate analogy may be made to the Church in its Roman Catholic, Anglican, or Eastern Orthodox forms. The priest is called father; the very word pope (*papa*) means father.

The Soviet writers do not use the phrase "parental law." However, there is great stress in Soviet legal literature on the educational role of Soviet law, and here the word "educational" (*vospitatel'naia*) has a very wide connotation, implying rearing or upbringing. Whatever the particular word used, the crux of the matter is the focus on the role of law in the upbringing of people.

CHAPTER 11: LAW ENFORCEMENT
BY SOCIAL ORGANIZATIONS

1. The history of the forerunners of the People's Patrols is given in Dement'ev, *Trudiashchiesia na strazhe obshchestvennogo poriadka* (Working People on Guard for Social Order, Moscow, 1959), pp. 7-27.

2. Statute on Voluntary People's Patrols of the R.S.F.S.R. for the Protection of Social Order, *Sovetskaia Iustitsiia* (Soviet Justice), 1960, No. 5; *Spravochnik Druzhinnika* (Patrolman's Handbook, Moscow, 1961), pp. 16-24.

3. Statute on Company Comrades' Courts, *Sobranie uzakonenii i rasporiazhenii RSFSR* (Collection of Legislation and Decrees of the RSFSR), 1918, No. 55, Item 613.

4. This account is based upon V. M. Savitskii and N. M. Keizerov, "Razvitie pravovykh form organizatsii i deiatel'nosti tovarishcheskikh sudov" (Development of Legal Forms of Organization and Activity of Comrades' Courts), *Sovetskoe Gosudarstvo i Pravo* (Soviet State and Law), 1961, No. 4, p. 41, which contains full citations to the statutes involved.

The revival of Comrades' Courts in 1951 was probably connected with the removal of criminal sanctions for lateness, absenteeism and quitting, for their jurisdiction was limited to those offenses. See above pp. 149-150.

5. *Vedomosti Verkhovnogo Soveta RSFSR,* 1961, No. 6, p. 401, translated in the *Current Digest of the Soviet Press,* Sept. 13, 1961, pp. 8-9.

6. K. S. Iudel'son, ed., *Prakticheskoe posobie dlia tovaricheskikh sudov* (Practical Manual for Comrades' Courts, Moscow, 1961), pp. 35-38, 40, 46, 55-56, 75.

7. On Strengthening the Struggle Against Persons Who Avoid Socially Useful Work and Lead an Anti-social Parasitic Way of Life, *Vedomosti Verkhovnogo Soveta RSFSR,* 1961, No. 6, p. 401, translated in *Current Digest of the Soviet Press,* Sept. 13, 1961, pp. 8-9. Similar laws were enacted in May and June, 1961, in the Ukrainian, Byelorussian, Lithuanian, Estonian and Moldavian republics. The earlier laws of the other republics were amended to conform to the R.S.F.S.R. version. See A. S. Shliapochnikov, "Sovetskoe zakonodatel'stvo i obshchestvennost' v borbe c parasiticheskimi elementami" (Soviet Legislation and Society in the Struggle with Parasitic Elements," *Sovetskoe Gosudarstvo i Pravo* (Soviet State and Law), 1961, No. 8, pp. 61-70.

8. See the translations of such comments in *Current Digest of the Soviet Press,* Vol. 9, Nos. 17, 21, 27, 31, 34, 40, and 42.

9. The principal draftsman of the 1958 Fundamental Principles of Criminal Procedure told the author in 1959 that in his opinion the anti-parasite laws contradict the provision of the Fundamental Principles that "no person may be subjected to a criminal penalty except by sentence of a court." He said that he expected the anti-parasite laws to be repealed.

10. *Biulleten' Verkhovnogo Suda SSSR* (Bulletin of the Supreme Court of the U.S.S.R.), 1961, No. 5, p. 8.

CHAPTER 12: THE EDUCATIONAL ROLE OF THE SOVIET COURT

1. *Pravda,* Feb. 21, 1949, p. 3.
2. *Izvestia,* Mar. 18, 1949, p. 1.
3. *Pravda,* Jan. 16, 1949, p. 3.
4. Boldyrev, *Sovetskii sud* (The Soviet Court; Moscow, 1960), p. 38. See D. S. Karev, "Dal'neishee sovershenstvovanie sovetskoi sudebnoi sistemy" (Further Improvement of the Soviet Judicial System), *Sovetskoe Gosudarstvo i Pravo* (Soviet State and Law), 1959, No. 2, pp. 61, 67, where it is stated that 55.4% of the lower court judges have higher legal education and an additional 37.1% have intermediate legal education.
5. I. T. Goliakov, *Vospitatel'noe znachenie sovetskogo suda* (The Educational Significance of the Soviet Court; Moscow, 1947). For English translation see I. T. Golyakov, *The Role of the Soviet Court* (Washington, 1948). The quotation is on page 17 of the translation.
6. See, *e.g.,* P. El'kind, *Vospitatel'naia rol' sovetskogo suda* (The Educational Role of the Soviet Court, Leningrad, 1953); I. T. Goliakov, *Sovetskii sud* (The Soviet Court, Moscow, 1958); pp. 94-128; M. Iu. Raginskii, *Vospitatel'naia rol' sovetskogo suda* (Moscow, 1959); A. A. Volin, *Vospitatel'naia rol' sovetskogo suda* (Moscow, 1955).
7. Verbatim records of Soviet trials (other than the great "purge trials" of 1936-1938) are not available in this country. In the present chapter the author has relied not only on Soviet descriptions and discussions, but also on his own and others' recollections of trials observed in the Soviet Union.
8. Robert H. Jackson, *The Nürnberg Case* (New York, 1947), pp. vi-vii.
9. Suggestions to expand the adversary aspect of trial procedure were not adopted in the 1958 Fundamental Principles of Criminal Procedure of the U.S.S.R. and the Union Republics.
10. Golyakov, *The Role of the Soviet Court,* p. 16.

11. Kareva, *Bol'shevik*, 1947, No. 4, p. 47.

12. "The mark of punishment which distinguishes it from other measures of political compulsion is that it inevitably causes the criminal a definite suffering which is painful to him." "Punishment is the measure of state compulsion applied publicly by the court to the criminal, causing him suffering and expressing in the name of the state a condemnation of the crime and of the criminal." Vsesoiuznyi Institut Iuridicheskikh Nauk, *Ugolovnoe pravo —obshchaia chast'* (All-Union Institute of Juridical Science, "Criminal Law—General Part," Moscow, 1943), p. 218.

13. Institut Prava Akademii Nauk SSSR, *Osnovy sovetskogo gosudarstva i prava* (Institute of Law of the Academy of Sciences, "Foundations of Soviet State and Law," Moscow, 1947), p. 633.

14. V. N. Mozheiko and Z. I. Shkundin, *Arbitrazh v sovetskom khoziaistve* (Arbitrazh in the Soviet Economy, Moscow, 1948), p. 52.

CHAPTER 13: LAW AND PSYCHIATRY

The present chapter appeared in expanded form, with footnote references to sources and extensive quotation of code provisions, statutes and cases, in Harold J. Berman and Donald H. Hunt, "Criminal Law and Psychiatry: the Soviet Solution," *Stanford Law Review*, II (1950), 635. It has been revised in the light of developments since 1950. See Harold J. Berman, "Law as an Instrument of Mental Health in the United States and Soviet Russia," *University of Pennsylvania Law Review*, CIX (1961), 361.

1. In ruling that there is no such thing as an "organically preordained amoral syndrome," the Supreme Court and the Serbskii Institute were following the post-1935 trend in Soviet psychology. In a 1936 decree of the Central Committee of the Communist Party, psychological testing in the

schools was abolished on the ground that such testing was based "on the fatalistic theory that the child's fate is determined by his heredity and his environment." Henceforth a third factor, "training," was to be emphasized. By training (and "self-training") it is considered possible to overcome the deleterious effect of both heredity and environment. As Raymond Bauer has put it, the Soviets are attempting not only to dangle the carrot and crack the whip, but also to remake the horse. See Bauer, *The New Man in Soviet Psychology* (Cambridge, Mass., 1952).

2. See Nicholas Timasheff, "The Impact of the Penal Law of Imperial Russia on Soviet Penal Law," *The American Slavic and East European Review,* XII, 441, 450-451 (1953). Timasheff states that the formula of the Russian Criminal Code of 1903 concerning imputability "was highly praised by Russian and other European criminologists" and was reproduced with slight changes in the Swiss Criminal Code of 1937.

CHAPTER 14: LAW AND THE FAMILY

1. The three conceptions—sacramental, consensual, and social (parental)—are not necessarily incompatible with each other. The sacramental view emphasizes the life-long unity of marriage, based on divine ordinance. The consensual view emphasizes the element of voluntary partnership. The social (parental) conception stresses the community's need for family stability and the organized maintenance of it by legal and other means. The sacramental conception has been reduced to legal doctrine in canon law and has to a large extent passed over into secular law wherever Christianity has been the dominant religion. More and more, however, secular law has stressed consensual elements, and in many Western countries divorce by mutual consent is now tolerated in practice though not in official doctrine. The social conception is still for the most part unformulated, except for more or less vague judicial references to "public policy." All three conceptions find reflection in Soviet law.

2. Reported in an Associated Press dispatch in the *Boston Sunday Globe*, December 18, 1949, p. 50, col. 2.

The Soviet legislation of 1935 included a law of April 7 which abolished juvenile courts and subjected youths over 12 years of age to "all measures of criminal punishment." However, capital punishment continued to be prohibited, under Article 22 of the Criminal Code, for minors under 18. The harshness of the law of April 7, 1935, was considerably mitigated in practice. Special sessions for juvenile cases functioned at times and milder treatment was authorized. See Harold J. Berman, "Principles of Soviet Criminal Law," *Yale Law Journal*, LVI (1947), 803, 817-818. The new 1961 criminal codes marked a return to a system much like that in effect before 1935. The juvenile courts (called now, as earlier, "Commissions on Minors' Cases") were reestablished and given jurisdiction over all crimes committed by youths from fourteen to sixteen years of age, and over all but a few serious crimes committed by youths from sixteen to eighteen years of age. Cf. G. M. Minkovskii, *Osobennosti rassledovaniia i sudebnogo razbiratel'stva del o nesovershennoletnikh* (Particular Features of the Investigation and Judicial Consideration of Cases Involving Minors), Moscow, 1959.

3. *Cf.* Rudolf A. Schlesinger, "Proposed Changes in Family Law," *Soviet Studies,* viii, p. 453 (1957).

4. The formalities of marriage had come to be stressed even before the new legislation. This was undoubtedly connected with the new attitude toward religion. During the war wedding rings became available in the stores. Many couples who had had a registered marriage or else simply a *de facto* marriage were remarried by a church ceremony.

5. Although this is not the place for a detailed comparison of Soviet law with the law of other countries, it perhaps should be noted that Soviet Russia is by no means unique in having a reconciliation procedure in divorce. The ecclesiastical courts of the Russian Orthodox Church had such a procedure before the Revolution, and it is a feature of the secular law of many European countries and of at least two states of the United States. Other features

of Soviet family law may likewise be found elsewhere. The emancipation of women, though perhaps carried further in the Soviet Union than anywhere else, is hardly a Soviet invention. Massachusetts law, for example, provides that women shall receive equal pay for equal work.

6. For example, in a 1948 case the Supreme Court of the U.S.S.R. reversed a decision of the Supreme Court of the Azerbaijan Soviet Socialist Republic, which had granted a divorce on the ground of mutual incompatibility, and remanded the case for retrial. The court said: "The decree of the Supreme Soviet of the USSR of July 8, 1944 . . . is directed to the strengthening in every way of the family and of the marital life of the spouses. The dissolution of marriage can consequently take place only if such facts were established by the court which provide a basis for considering that the family has disintegrated and there is no possibility of its restoration." And further: "The reference to 'incompatibility,'" without explanation of how it manifested itself, is obviously insufficient and cannot provide a basis for the decision pronouncing the dissolution of the marriage. The court also ought not to have overlooked the fact that the spouses have been married since 1945 and that they have a little boy" (*Sotsialisticheskaia Zakonnost'* [Socialist Legality], 1948, No. 5, p. 60).

7. In 1961, 1.3 divorces were granted per thousand persons in the U.S.S.R. In the U.S.A. the rate was 2.2 per thousand persons in 1959. *Narodnoe Khoziaistvo SSSR v 1961 godu* (National Economy of the U.S.S.R. in 1961, Moscow, 1962), p. 165.

CHAPTER 15: LAW AND LABOR

1. *Cf.* "Collective Bargaining in the Soviet Union," *Harvard Law Review,* LXII (1949), 1191, 1196.

2. The collective contract is discussed in N. G. Alexandrov, *Soviet Labour Law* (Nayar tr., Delhi, 1961), pp. 185-240. See also John N. Hazard, *Law and Social Change in the U.S.S.R.* (London, 1953), pp. 166*ff.;* M. L. Weisberg, "The Transformation of the Collective Agreement in Soviet

Law," *University of Chicago Law Review,* XVI (1949), 444, 473.

3. A. E. Pasherstnik, "Voprosy kollektivnogo dogovora v SSSR" (Questions concerning the Collective Contract in the U.S.S.R.), *Sovetskoe Gosudarstvo i Pravo* (Soviet State and Law), 1948, No. 4, p. 45. Cf. F. M. Leviant and A. S. Pashkov, "Trudovoe Pravo" (Labor Law) in *Sorok let sovetskogo Prava* (Forty Years of Soviet Law, Leningrad, 1957), I, 306-360.

4. See Harold J. Berman and Boris A. Konstantinovsky, *Soviet Law in Action: The Recollected Cases of a Soviet Lawyer* (Cambridge, Mass., 1953), Chapter 4.

CHAPTER 16: PARENTAL LAW AND PERSONAL FREEDOM

1. The case is discussed at some length in Harold J. Berman and Miroslav Kerner, *Soviet Military Law and Administration* (Cambridge, Mass., 1955), pp. 156-158, and the decision is translated in *id., Documents on Soviet Military Law and Administration* (Cambridge, Mass., 1955), pp. 108-110.

1a. George C. Guins, *Soviet Law and Soviet Society* (The Hague, 1954), p. 362.

2. *Id.* at p. 24.

3. See Chapter 2, *supra.* Each chamber of the Supreme Soviet of the U.S.S.R. has the following permanent committees: Committee on Legislative Proposals, Budget Committee, Foreign Affairs Committee, Credentials Committee. The Soviet of Nationalities also has an Economic Committee. These committees have established many subcommittees. See S. G. Novikov, *Postoiannye komissii verkhovnogo soveta SSSR* (Permanent Committees of the Supreme Soviet of the U.S.S.R., Moscow, 1962). The Supreme Soviets of the various republics also have permanent committees. Besides committees of the types mentioned above, they also have committees on such matters as industry, agriculture, trade, education, and health. See S. G. Drobiazko, *Komissii verkhovnogo soveta soiuznoi res-*

publiki (Committees of the Supreme Soviet of a Union Republic, Moscow, 1961).

4. In the post-Stalin period greater efforts have been made to control *ultra vires* acts of local governing bodies, such as the imposition of unauthorized taxes or restrictions upon the lawful economic activities of enterprises. *Cf.* above, pp. 238, 245-246.

5. Support for these conclusions may be found in Kazimierz Grzybowski, *Soviet Legal Institutions* (Ann Arbor, 1962), Chapter 4, entitled "Homo Sovieticus." Dr. Grzybowski's treatment of the subject differs in important respects from the present author's. See Harold J. Berman, Book Review, *New York University Law Review*, XXXVIII, 425, 426-428. Dr. Grzybowski contrasts the "disciplined man" which the Soviet legal order under Stalin took as its model with the individualistic type of hypothetical Frenchman predicated in the French Civil Code. He states (p. 112): "One may say that the progress of modern societies is characterized by the emergence of an ever-growing number of social types to whom various legal rules address their commands, without prejudice to their universality."

INDEX

Page numbers in *italics* indicate principal discussions of a topic.

Russian Research Center Studies

* Out of print.
† Publications of the Harvard Project on the Soviet Social System.
‡ Published jointly with the Center for International Affairs, Harvard University.